The Economy

The Economy

An Interpretative Introduction

C.T. KURIEN

Sage Publications
New Delhi/Newbury Park/London

First published in 1992 by

Sage Publications India Pvt Ltd
M-32 Greater Kailash Market I
New Delhi 110 048

Sage Publications Inc
2455 Teller Road
Newbury Park, California 91320

Sage Publications Ltd
6 Bonhill Street
London EC2A 4PU

Published by Tejeshwar Singh for Sage Publications India Pvt Ltd, phototypeset by Jayigee Enterprises, Madras, and printed at Chaman Enterprises, Delhi.

Library of Congress Cataloging-in-Publication Data

Kurien, C.T.
   The economy: an interpretative introduction/C.T. Kurien.
     p.   cm.
  Includes bibliographical references and index.
   1. Economics. 2. India—Economic conditions—1947– I.Title.
HB72. K83   1992   330.954—dc20   92–11992

ISBN 0–8039–9428–1 (US-hbk.) 81–7036–284–9 (India-hbk.)
     0–8039–9429–x (US-pbk.) 81–7036–285–7 (India-pbk.)

Economic life is not economy in the abstract; it is the realisation of the idea of economy in a concrete, historical form. To understand economic life is to understand this historical objectification of the elements of the idea of economy.

ZAKIR HUSSAIN

Capitalism: Essays in Understanding

Contents

List of Tables   8

Preface   9

Part I: Understanding the Economy   13

1 : The Economy   15
2 : Rudimentary Economy   28
3 : Village Economy   45
4 : Exchange   74
5 : Capitalist Economy   111
6 : Post-Capitalist Economy   158

Part II: The Indian Economy   209

7 : The Indian Economy: An Analytical Description   211
8 : The Evolution of the Indian Economy   246
9 : Indian Economy since Independence   277
10 : Growth and Change: A Macro View   323
11 : Poverty and Affluence   350
12 : Shaping the Economy   389

Bibliography   418

Index   426

List of Tables

7.1 Unit Structure in the 'Other Workers' Sector of the Indian Economy 241
7.2 Units (other than own-account units) by Size of Employment 242
8.1 Distribution of Produce to Village Functionaries in a Deccan Village 253
8.2 Price of a Pound of Cotton Yarn in England and India, 1832 262
8.3 All-India Estimates of Food Crop, Commercial Crop and Total Crop Production, 1893–94 to 1945–46 266
9.1 Vadamalaipuram—Occupational Profile, 1958 & 1983 282
9.2 Changes in Inputs in Indian Agriculture since Independence 307
9.3 A Profile of Asset Distribution in the Indian Economy 317
9.4 Percentage Distribution of Assets by Type of Households and Type of Assets 319
9.5 Distribution of Households and Area Owned over Size Class of Household Ownership Holdings, (Rural) 1982 320
9.6 Distribution of Land by Major Size Classes, 1982 321
10.1 Death and Birth Rates (per 1000 population) 325
10.2 Worker Population Ratios, 1961, 1971 & 1981 329
10.3 Occupational Classification of Workers: 1951 to 1981 329
10.4 Workers in Organised and Unorganised Sectors, 1981 334
10.5 Increase in Production (Selected Items) 335
10.6 Analysis of the Growth of the Indian Economy: 1950–51 to 1988–89 341
10.7 Changes in the Sectoral Composition of National Income 343
10.8 Share of the State in the Value of Output in Different Sectors, 1984–85 344
11.1 Growth Rate of Employment by Major Sectors, 1973–88 382

Preface

'Never lose sight of the role your subject has within the great performance of the tragi-comedy of human life; keep in touch with life... and keep life in touch with you'. These are not the words of an economist or a social scientist, but of the physicist Erwin Schrodinger in his *Science and Humanism: Physics in Our Times*. One would think that they would be applicable with greater relevance to economics and economists. But, sadly, this has not been the case. In the excessive eagerness to make it a precise and quantitative science, most votaries of economics have tended to take it further and further away from the texture of life and the complexities of the world of reality to a world of their own creation, where the accent appears to have been on elegance and internal consistency. Not long ago, the late Joan Robinson who had a firm commitment to keep economics linked to life and society, bemoaned the fact that economic theory seemed to be moving in a direction that left it with nothing to say about those very questions which—to everyone except economists—appeared most in need of answers.

While this has been so in most parts of the world, (perhaps with some reversal of the trend during the past decade) it has been particularly acute in India. Many of us in the profession have expressed great dissatisfaction with the teaching and learning of economics in the country, and especially with the gulf that seems to exist between economic theory, or theories, on the one hand and the treatment of the problems of the Indian economy on the other. My own involvement with economics and the Indian economy over the past four decades and more—as student, teacher, researcher and commentator on economic problems and policies—have brought home this gap very poignantly. In my earlier writings, particularly, *Indian Economic Crisis, A Theoretical Approach to the Indian Economy* and *Poverty, Planning and Social Transformation*, I have wrestled with this problem and made an attempt to make economic theories shed some light on real-life problems of the Indian economy.

Over the years I have become convinced that the real issue is one of methodology and concerns the manner in which economic theories are constructed. This is most clearly seen in the case of neo-classical economics which (along with some elements of Keynesian macro-economics thrown in) has become economic theory *per se* in our classrooms. Starting out from the classical attempts to theorise about real-life situations, neo-classical theory has become a logical system meant to explicate certain theoretical propositions like 'a decentralized economy motivated by self-interest and guided by price signals would be compatible with a coherent disposition of economic resources that would be regarded, in a well-defined sense, as superior to a large class of possible dispositions', as Kenneth Arrow and Frank Hahn have stated. How such a theoretical system can elucidate the working of any actual economy then becomes a matter of debate, where one answer has been that it sets up an *a priori* theoretical norm from which all actual economies will fall short to some extent and that if this distance can be identified and explained, a theoretical understanding about them becomes possible.

This is not the place to enter into a discussion on the validity of that proposition. My reflections have led me to think that an alternative approach is necessary and possible. A direct attempt should be made to provide an analytical description of the actual functioning of the economy, for instance, the Indian economy. This work is an exercise of that kind. The building blocks are introduced in Part I through an exposition of some 'ideal type' versions of economies that have been the historical experience of humanity in the past as well as the present. With the help of these building blocks the Indian economy itself is dealt with in Part II, with the first chapter in that section (Chapter 7) providing an analytical description of it. If any novelty can be claimed for this work it is this expository device. Towards the end of my teaching career, I concentrated on introducing under-graduates to the Indian economy. I used to tell them that to get to know an economy three related questions have to be examined: 'Who owns what?'; 'Who does what?'; and 'Who gets what?' I have accepted these three questions as the basis for probing into economies in general and the Indian economy in particular. Working on this book I have learned that concentrating on the economy—rather than economics—can yield many new insights. In particular, this approach addresses some basic questions which have a bearing on the economy and which are not settled within economics and, in any case, it is more helpful to keep close to life. While my approach has been different, I have not attempted any theoretical re-formulation as such; I am also not entering directly into a critique of existing theoretical systems. My task has been to indicate what needs to be theorised, if the role of theory is seen essentially to illuminate the world of reality, instead of providing a substitute for it. Even in that respect this work can only claim to be an introduction.

As my attempt has been to demonstrate how crucial to daily life are matters relating to the economy, I have tried to keep the exposition as simple as possible using technical expressions only where they are absolutely necessary. But I would not claim that the book makes easy reading. This is basically because the economy is a very complex phenomenon, and to understand the economy is to grapple with that complexity. I was surprised that exchange, that everyday activity through which all of us become directly involved in the economy, is one of the most difficult to unravel, and readers may find Chapter 4 which deals with it (and Chapter 5 on the capitalist economy which is closely related) somewhat difficult to follow. However, I can give the assurance that anyone who is genuinely interested in getting to know how economies, including our own, function and has the patience to read through the material (this is important!) should have no difficulty in making sense of it.

Since the expository device I have chosen had few precedents to go by and since the available literature, in most instances, is of a highly technical nature, not easily rendered into everyday language, it is possible that the style is rather uneven. I would not be surprised also if some errors of interpretation have crept in, though I hope they are not of a fundamental nature. If the procedure I have adopted is valid and helpful, perhaps some-one else, perhaps someone younger, will be able to provide a more satis-factory and elegant exposition in the future.

I would like to acknowledge the help I have received from different people in the preparation and production of this book. P.S. Syamala did the typing and V. Mohan and M. Suvakkin the processing. Millie Nihila arranged the bibliography in alphabetical order. The members of the library staff and the administrative personnel of the Madras Institute of Develop-ment Studies were particularly helpful to me throughout. But for the skill and devotion of all of them it would have been impossible for me to con-centrate on my part of the work, and I am most grateful to them.

I owe a special debt of gratitude to the Madras Institute of Develop-ment Studies. I was entrusted the responsibility of shaping its evolution in the early stages, but when I expressed the desire to devote my time to the writing of this book, the Institute granted me the freedom and the facilities to do so. It is through constant interaction with colleagues in the Institute for over a decade that my approach to the economy became clarified. Chapter 9 shows how much I have drawn on the studies of these colleagues in analysing the nature of change in the Indian economy since Independence. The programmes of the Institute also brought me in constant contact with disciplines in the social sciences other than economics and an important aspect of my learning process has been to recognise how much one has to go beyond economics to understand the economy. Specialists in anthro-pology, history, law, politics and sociology may find my dabblings in their fields rather amateurish—and so they are—while purists within econ-omics are likely to find fault with me for diluting the rigour of the discipline. But these are risks I have had to take in my quest to understand the economy and to make it comprehensible. It is for readers to decide whether my efforts have been worthwhile.

My thanks are due to those who have gone through the drafts—Malcolm S. Adiseshiah, S. Ambirajan, Abdul Aziz, P. Balakrishnan, D.N. Dhanagare, John M. Itty, Prema Kurien, Primila Lewis, S. Neelakantan, M.A. Oommen, M.S.S. Pandian, George Rosen, Nirmal Sengupta, E.S. Srinivasan, K. Srinivasan, Padmini Swaminathan and Nasir Tyabji. Their comments have been extremely useful in preparing the final version. I am deeply indebted to them. But I accept full responsibility for what this book contains.

In writing a book of this kind after a long period of professional work, one is also indebted to a larger network of people—those whose writings one has imbibed, teachers, students and colleagues with whom one has directly interacted and the many whose struggles and adventures one has watched. My decision to take up the study of economics was prompted by a desire to understand the economic factors in the ordinary business of life and I have learned as much by observing life as by conventional methods of learning. I would like to record my gratitude to all who in diverse ways have contributed to my learning process.

Among them special mention should be made of the one person who has shared her life with me. She is the one who has helped me most to devote time to learn, reflect and write. In the writing of this book, too, her contribution has been immense. As a token of my gratitude, I dedicate this book to her.

C.T. Kurien

Part I

Understanding the Economy

1

The Economy

This introductory chapter deals with the question of what is an economy. Though there are many and diverse definitions of economics, it has not been easy to come across a satisfactory account of what it is. This is surprising, partly because the term is widely used in day-to-day language and partly also because if economics is a scientific enquiry, its field of study is the economy. What is attempted in this chapter is to start from the intuitive understanding of the term and to move on to a more adequate description. The economy is seen as society's organisation to provision the material needs of its members, consisting of ways in which resources are owned and controlled, resources and labour are put to use in production and how claims on the produce are settled.

This chapter also spells-out the procedure of enquiry involving abstraction as the main tool, indicating how abstract representations capturing the essence are to be used to enlighten concrete and specific issues.

The term economy is one of the frequently used expressions in everyday life. Newspapers are full of comments about the economy, the Indian economy, other national economies and the international economy. References to household economy, village economy, urban economy and so on are also common. At a somewhat different level one talks about the feudal economy, capitalist economy, socialist economy and the like.

The wide use of the term in everyday language means that most of us have an intuitive understanding of what the economy is. This is not surprising, because like family, nation and society, the economy is part of our experiential reality. When we buy and sell, when we earn and spend, we are participating in the economy as well as creating it. But precisely because we are so intimately involved with it we may not have given much thought to what it is and how it works. An intuitive understanding of the economy is certainly very useful. But we know from experience that an intuitive understanding alone is not quite accurate, and often not adequate. And, from time to time, there are questions which are not easy to explain. Why is it that in a country like ours, rich in natural resources and with an abundance of people, many essential tasks remain unattended? Why is it that mass poverty still continues in spite of determined efforts to eradicate it? Or again, how do we reconcile the claim that the country is now self-sufficient in food along with the fact that millions of people still live in semi-starvation?

Instances of this kind show that in order to understand the economy intuitive knowledge may not be enough; it may be necessary to search for something more systematic. The purpose of this book is to provide such a systematic view of the economy, particularly the Indian economy.

TOWARDS UNDERSTANDING THE ECONOMY

A moment of reflection will show that we use different procedures to understand things, events and persons around us. There are things—such as tables and chairs, mangoes and oranges, rain and sunshine—that we come to know and understand through our sense organs; that is, by seeing, hearing, feeling, tasting. But even about things, this kind of knowledge may not be enough. We may see, hear and feel the rain, but much more than that is required if we desire to understand what it is or how it happens. When we move from things to events, understanding becomes more demanding. We may have seen and heard a fight in the street. But that is not enough to make sense of it. Understanding a person is even more diffi-cult. We can understand a person by seeing him and hearing him. We may understand him more by interacting with him, but even then our under-standing may be far from adequate.

In all these instances, however, our sense organs are of immense help to us in the process of understanding. But our everyday life does not consist solely of things, events and persons. For most of us one of the greatest realities of day-to-day life is the family. We cannot actually see the dynamics of family life with our eyes, but that does not mean that it is an illusion. We know the phenomenon exists and that without it (whatever it may be), we will not be what we are. Though somewhat more remote, nation and society are also like the family, part of our living reality. The economy too is such an entity—difficult to identify and analyse, but there, all the same.

The economy as relationships
What family, nation, society and economy have in common is that they are all basically relationships. The family, for instance, consists of the parents-children, husband-wife, brother-sister relationships. These relation-ships are usually intimate and informal. The nation, too, is a network of relationships, mediated through laws and regulations and hence tending to be more formal. One of the first tasks in understanding the economy is to specify the kinds of relationships it represents. But the fact that we frequently refer to the household economy and the national economy shows that the relationships that constitute the economy are somewhat different; they are embedded in both the household and the nation, but

different from them. If so, the economy cosists of a set of relationships which may be abstracted from other forms of social relationships. What makes it somewhat difficult to understand the economy is its special nature; that of being derived from other forms of social relationships and thus not as easily identifiable as other kinds of relationships.

On the other hand, if the economy is embedded in different forms of social relationships or organisations, it should be possible to pick out its essential features by examining those factors that come to be identified as *economic* relationships in different situations. For that identification we can rely to a large extent on our intuitive and commonsense knowledge of the economy or of economic activities. Whether at the household level or at the national level, we know that a major part of economic activity is concerned with the use of resources even when it is clear that what is considered a resource may be different in the two instances. Similarly, it is evident that resources are meant to produce or procure goods and services that are considered necessary and useful. There must also be some procedure to enable distribution among the members of the household or nation, as the case may be, of what is produced or procured. Once again, it is clear that the principles and procedures of distribution need not be, and usually will not be, the same in a household and a nation, and yet it is possible to say that whichever social organisation we are dealing with, production and distribution are basic features of its economy.

Labour process as the basis of the economy

There is something in common that underlies all these economic activities—the use of labour-power both physical and mental. For each one of these activities is based on decisions made by human beings. To a large extent resources made use of by human beings in the process of production are provided by nature; and yet identifying and shaping them are all human activities as are arrangements necessary for exercising control over them. And, of course, the settling of the claims of different members over the product is very much a human activity. Central to the study of the economy, therefore, is what may be termed the labour process, decision-making and action.

The labour process, however, is not exercised in isolation: it is invariably a group or social activity. This is the reason why the economy is always related to and embedded in a social organisation—a household, a tribe, a village community, a nation–state etc., each representing a set of social relationships larger than the relationships that constitute the economy. It also explains why the economy always has to be intellectually separated from a wider set of relationships within which human beings exist and function. This sorting-out process is referred to as abstraction. Abstraction is an aid to the understanding of phenomena that cannot be comprehended through the senses alone. It has a role in any systematised knowledge and is, therefore, inherent in any body of knowledge that claims to be a science. Any science dealing with social relationships will have to accept it as an important part of its procedure. In the study of the economy it is even more crucial because of the need to be selective about the kinds of relationships that constitute the economy.

Consider for a moment a household and its economy. A household may be thought of as a set of social relationships within, or through, which its members satisfy a wide variety of their needs. Members of a household need food, clothing and shelter. They also need affection, appreciation, and correction. There is a difference between these two kinds of needs, and to draw that distinction let us refer to the former as material needs and the latter as emotional needs. The satisfaction of material needs directly or indirectly calls for the use of physical resources. Food, for instance, has to be produced on land with the help of ploughs or other forms of tools. If clothing is required, cotton may have to be grown on land, yarn woven on looms, stitching done on machines etc. The reliance on physical resources to satisfy material needs must be self-evident for those in rural areas where most people are involved in direct interaction with the land and other forms of physical resources. On the other hand, it may not appear so obvious to people in urban areas who purchase their food, clothing and similar requirements by paying money. The use of money facilitates a great deal of economic activity but it also makes the economy a very complex entity. However, it is not difficult to see that money is essentially a claim on physical resources. That is why we are able to buy 'things' using money.

The economy as provisioning material needs

If what we have designated as material needs require physical resources for their satisfaction, the distinction between material needs and emotional needs is that the latter are not primarily based on physical resources. A mother loves her child and gives him a hug. That is a way of expressing and meeting an emotional need and there is no physical resource involved in the process. True, a sharp distinction between material and emotional needs cannot be drawn. For instance, it is because a mother has a sense of affection for her child that she provides him with food and takes the trouble to prepare it. And it is by providing food (among other things) that she expresses her affection. Even so, a distinction can be made between material needs and emotional needs. In its Greek origin the term 'economy' was first used to refer to the management of physical resources by a household to provide for the material needs of its members. Generalising from that, economy is now used frequently to refer to the management of resources by any one of the many social groups that one recognises—the household itself, a tribe, a village community, a nation–state and so forth.

For instance, what is usually referred to as the national economy is the arrangement that a nation–state has for providing for the material needs of its members. A nation has other needs which cannot be described as material needs such as defending its national honour, and that cannot be done without relying on some material factors. But, again, we shall retain the distinction between material needs and other needs (social, cultural, etc.) and concentrate on the former so that a national economy may be thought of as the way in which a nation–state manages its resources to meet the material needs of its members. While a household economy and a national economy have this aspect in common, it may be noted that they are not exactly the same: they may differ in what they consider to be resources and few national economies have the option that many households may have of purchasing all the goods that will be required to meet the needs of its members. We shall note these differences now and deal with them in subsequent chapters; but here we shall concentrate on what different economies have in common. In order to do that, let us also note that material needs can be met in different ways, producing and purchasing being the most common and which may be brought together under the common expression 'provisioning'. If so, as a first step, we may say that an economy is the arrangement that a group (a household, a tribe, a village community, a nation–state etc.) makes to provision the material needs of its members. But recalling that each one of these groups is basically a community, or a set of human relationships, the economy may also be designated as a set of human relationships associated with the provisioning of material needs. It is important to grasp this because otherwise, consciously or unconsciously, in the discussion of the economy the emphasis may shift away from human relationships to the management of material things or resources. Of course, as noted already, resources play an important role in any economy, and this is most clearly seen in production. In the process of production things are used and things are produced; but production is basically a form of human relationship. Similarly, property or ownership which plays an important part in most economies may appear to be a relationship between human beings and things. But a moment of reflection will show that it is primarily a relationship between people mediated through things.

This also implies that in dealing with an economy we are dealing with both material things and human beings. Consider production again. Even in the simplest of production processes—that of raising grain on a piece of land, for instance—we are dealing with land itself, a plough at least and seeds as material things. We are also dealing with the farmer and possibly members of the family who together do the production activities. If he purchases fertilisers and sells the grain there are other material things and human beings to be considered. There will, then, also be new relationships between buyer and seller. And if he has leased-in the land from somebody else, that again brings in another dimension of relationships. As we move to more complicated production processes the relationships, too, may become more complex. Similarly, once things are produced, they must be distributed among the members of the group, and as economic activity becomes more complex, there will be different kinds of claims on what is produced and the arrangements to define and settle these claims will give rise to new forms of relationships.

The economy described
Taking all these factors into account, we can now move on to a more detailed statement about what an economy is:

> An economy is a structure of relationships among a group of people in terms of the manner in which they exercise control over resources, use resources and labour in the production of goods and services, and define and settle the claims of the members over what is produced.[1]

This is not a formal definition of the economy, but simply a more detailed account about it to try and understand what it is. This description states that the economy (of any group) addresses itself to three basic questions: that of ownership and/or control over resources; that of production, and that of the distribution of produce among the members. This statement can also be used to elaborate some of the issues we have briefly noted. First that the economy is concerned with a *group* of people. This is worth pointing out because some traditions in the study of the economy imply that while the economy is about people, it is primarily about individuals in terms of their innate individual characteristics. Such an approach is referred to as the Robinson Crusoe economy, the economy of the isolated individual.[2] It is, no doubt, possible to interpret social relationships as though they are different functions performed by a single individual. Thus, Robinson Crusoe can be thought of both as producer and consumer; employer and employee etc. performing assigned tasks in each different role. To say the least, such attempts are rather far-fetched. Useful perhaps in fiction, but inadequate and misleading if they are meant to communicate the basic features of social interaction. The economy is essentially about human interactions and relations and hence can be properly studied only with reference to a group, not an isolated individual who is made to perform different roles.

Secondly, the economy is concerned with only certain aspects of human relationships; namely, the relationships within which the three broad activities take place and the relationships that arise from those activities. Human beings develop other kinds of relationships and it is not easy to enumerate them all. To say that the economy is concerned with only three types of relationships may appear to suggest that it is only an insignificant aspect of the totality of human relationships that the economy encompasses. But that seems to be contrary to our intuitive understanding of what the economy is, because even from casual observations of everyday life it would appear that most human relationships have at least some economic component.

But then the three activities we have identified as constituting the economy have some special attributes; they are basic activities of human existence. We can accept the truth of the saying, 'Man does not live by bread alone.' But then we must also accept the truth of the fact that human beings cannot live at all without bread and, in a sense, the economy is the set of relationships that human beings enter into in order to sustain life. As human societies rise above the limits of the basic necessities of life, there may be a tendency to overlook the crucial significance of the processes that are necessary to just sustain life. But we know that in our country (and indeed in many other parts of the globe as well) for millions of people it is a struggle day after day to get the basic necessities of life. Many of our languages have a saying which cannot be adequately translated into English, but when translated will be something like, 'After all *everything* that one does is to fill the little belly.' We may not literally agree with this, but to many of our fellow human beings it is the one truth of their existence. It is, therefore, right to think of the economy as consisting of activities which make life possible and sustain it.

Thirdly, it may be noted that the statement about the economy refers not only to relationships, but the *structure* of relationships. The expression is used to suggest that the relationships within which the three activities take place and which arise from and through them are not just casual ones. They manifest certain principles or logic and are mediated through a variety of institutions. In that sense the relationships come to have structure or form, and that is why it becomes possible to analyse them systematically. In other words, the structure of relationships that constitute the economy can be analysed, studied and understood because there are principles underlying them and because they are expressed through institutions. A study of the economy, therefore, is at once logical (relating to the basic principles) and empirical (relating to their institutional manifestations).

Fourthly, therefore, understanding economies is to get to know their different structures. All economies have some structure, but economies also differ from one another in terms of their structures. It should not be difficult to see that although a household economy and a national economy must exercise control over resources, use resources and labour in production and settle claims of members over the produce, the *manner* in which these are done cannot be the same in both instances. At another level, the structure of relationships in an economy where most people produce all their material needs will be different from one in which people specialise in production and exchange their produce with one another. Or, to give another example, the structure of relationships in a capitalist economy and a socialist economy cannot be the same. In general then, if economies differ, it is because they have different structures. Tracing the structure of relationships among different kinds of economies as a prelude to exploring the structure of relationships underlying the Indian economy, and the attempt to understand the working of the Indian economy in terms of its structure, are the main objectives of this book.

Procedure of Analysis

Having obtained some insights into what constitutes an economy and its main characteristics we may now turn to a discussion of how to go about examining it. As has already been indicated, we shall have to rely a great deal on what has been referred to as *abstraction*. Abstraction is a sort of mental exercise, or a sorting-out and categorisation. A little more detailed treatment of the method of abstraction will be useful at this stage.

The role of abstraction

One of the crucial aspects of abstraction is to decide on what is essential and what is not.[3] In spelling out the essential features of what we mean by the economy we have done some preliminary sorting-out. Obviously, any actual economy will have many more features than those already dealt with, and others, like exchange, will have to be introduced as we go along. But the three features we have indicated are the minimum conditions in identifying what may be designated as the economy.

A second procedure in abstraction is to find out whether there is any interrelationship among the essentials identified. This aspect has not been explicitly taken up so far. But it should not be difficult to see that the manner of exercising control over resources will have a bearing on how resources and labour are combined in production. Similarly, how resources and labour are combined and how claims on the product are settled will also be related. They can be related in both directions: what is available for distribution will depend on what is produced; so also the manner in which claims are settled may determine the amount produced.

If the chief features or elements of an entity can be identified and their interrelationships traced, it will be possible to construct a stylised version of this entity which can be thought of as its representation, or model. Now, a representation or model of something can be produced in at least two different ways. A representation of the Taj Mahal can either be a miniature version which looks exactly like it save for size, or a sketch on a two-dimensional surface which consists only of lines. Which of these will be the more adequate representation will depend on what the representation is meant for. If its purpose is to convey something of the beauty and majesty of the building then the miniature version may be more suitable. On the other hand, if the intention is to understand the structure of the building, a line drawing is likely to be more useful even if it does not look like the real thing at all. Perhaps a combination of the two will enable someone who has never seen the building to have a better understanding and appreciation of what it is like. This is the reason why when a new building is to be constructed the architect provides both a line-sketch (known as a blueprint) as well as a miniature.

Through abstraction it also is possible to produce a stylised version of the economy—a representation of it or a model.[4] But there is a big difference between a representation of an economy and a representation of the Taj Mahal. In the case of the Taj Mahal the representation can be verified with the real thing whereas in the case of the economy the real thing cannot be seen! This imposes a serious limitation on abstraction as a procedure of analysis as far as the economy is concerned. A representation of the economy can turn out to be a distortion of it rather than a true representation. Abstraction, in other words, can be used to inform and thus aid in understanding, but it can also be used to *misinform* and distort understanding. This limitation, however, is not peculiar to the study of the economy alone. Even in a hard science like physics it has been recognised in recent years as a problem. For instance, how does one go about understanding the universe except by producing mental representations and setting up models of it, knowing full well that the real thing cannot be seen and there is no easy way of verifying the accuracy and adequacy of the representation?

This is not to suggest that there are no ways at all of verification of representations as far as entities like the economy are concerned. Let us look at the two forms of representation once again, the line-sketch and the miniature. The emphasis in the former is on what may be described as the logic of the structure and in the latter on the substance, appearance, elegance and so forth. It was stated earlier that a combination of the two may provide a better understanding of the real thing. The same procedure can be adopted to some extent in the case of the economy. A representation of the economy can be generated to emphasise the logic of its structure and this is what most economic models are. The focus in such a model will be on the logic of interrelationships. An exercise of this kind can be very useful indeed. But because the exercise is essentially in the realm of logic, there may be a tendency to take flights into the imagination and thus lose touch with reality. Hence the line-sketch version of the economy with its accent on logic must be supplemented and underpinned by what one knows about the reality. In the study of the economy this is achieved by resorting to history—of the past and of the present.[5] History here must be understood not as mere chronology, but an account of the real, or concrete. Any true sketch representation of the Indian economy, where the emphasis has to be on logic, must be pitted against what one knows to be the facts about the Indian economy, both of the past and of the present. The proper procedure for understanding the economy is to rely simultaneously on logic and history, or analysis and description. This should ensure that analysis does not become a mere flight of fancy, and description does not become an ill-digested assortment of statistics. Unfortunately, most treatments of the economy—especially introductory accounts—specialise either in logic (theory), thus becoming books on 'economics', or on factual accounts, claiming to be primarily empirical studies. While both are necessary in order to understand the economy, that understanding will remain very inadequate if the two are not brought together. Bringing analysis and description together in order to understand different kinds of economies and the Indian economy in particular, is what this book is about.

The specific procedure that will be followed may also be indicated. Attention, throughout, will be paid to the three essential features of the economy already identified. But these features are invariably embedded in some form of organisation which we shall refer to as the *social organisation* of the economy. The social organisation of an economy is reflected through its institutions and one way in which economies differ is in terms of the institutions that give expression to the essential features. For instance, as we shall see in subsequent chapters, the institutions through which control is exercised over resources are different in different kinds of economies. The institutions that organise production also vary among economies, and so forth. We shall, therefore, constantly search for what may be designated as the *institutional mould* of economies.

Social framework

But it is a well known fact that any organisation has some basic principle that governs and guides it—that is, its *organising principle*. For each of the economies that we deal with we shall, therefore, try to identify the organising principle as well. We may say that the organising principle of the economy finds expression through its institutions or that the institutions are moulded together by the organising principle. The organising principle and the social organisation of the economy together constitute what may be described as its *social framework*. The discerning reader will have noticed that the attempt is to combine logical analysis and empirical enquiry; the organising principle being the focus of the former and social organisation or the institutional features providing the basis for the latter. In the text the emphasis will be on logical analysis, especially in Part I, with references being given to empirical material from other sources. It follows that in Part II both aspects will be woven together as carefully as possible.

In order to complete the account of our procedure of enquiry, let us look a little more closely into the organising principles of economies. What makes logical abstraction easy in the study of economies is that while economies differ from one another a great deal in terms of their social organisations, there is not much diversity as far as organising principles are concerned. In fact, there are only *two* organising principles that we shall be identifying, despite the wide range of economies that can be recognised. This may appear somewhat surprising and hence it will be useful to consider its rationale.

Use value and exchange value

Let us go back to our first statement about the economy that it is society's arrangement to provision the material needs of its members. These needs are met through a wide range of goods and services which are produced through the combination of resources and labour. If the goods and services produced by an economy are enumerated, it will be a very long list. But the rationale can be stated simply. Goods are produced because they satisfy some needs, or more simply, because they are useful. We shall rely on convention and say that goods are produced because they have *use value*. This being the case, we should recognize *generation of use value* as an organising principle of the economy in terms of which all its activities and institutions can be understood.

While this is important, we know also that goods are not *always* produced to satisfy needs directly, but for sale or exchange. Ultimately, of course, no good will be produced unless it satisfies some need somewhere, however indirect the processes are. But production for exchange or sale comes to have certain characteristics arising from that very fact and the organisation of an economy where production is for exchange will be very different from one where production is meant to meet needs directly. Once production is geared to exchange (or *where* production is geared to exchange) *exchange value* becomes a consideration in addition to, or even in place of, use value.[6] Exchange value usually finds expression as a sum of money. Unlike other goods and services money by itself does not satisfy any need (except perhaps the needs of those who derive use value by looking at money, or holding on to money) but only provides command over other goods and services that do satisfy needs. And the more money one accumulates the greater will be one's control over (other) goods. Once production gets oriented towards exchange, there is a tendency to orient everything towards the accumulation of exchange value and so the organising principle in such an economy will be *the accumulation of exchange value*.

Subsequent chapters in Part I will show that we need to have only these two organising principles to deal with all the major types of economies. This is not to imply that there are only two types of economies. Economies are identified not solely in terms of their organising principles, but effectively in terms of their social framework. This is a manifestation of organising principles in and through social organisations which are space and time specific and are, therefore, of great diversity. So we do have many kinds of economies which we shall identify and try to and deal with a few 'basic' types.

OUTLINE OF THE BOOK

As a social entity the economy is perpetually in motion and is undergoing change, unlike a machine which, once manufactured and set in operation, goes on doing the same thing over and over again. In understanding an economy, therefore, a major aspect is to gain insight into its transformation over time. Over time it also tends to become more complex. Any modern economy, including the Indian economy, is a very complex entity. That complexity, however, cannot be comprehended all at once. The procedure adopted in this book is, therefore, to move gradually from very simple economies to more complex ones. The emphasis is on detailing the working of economies at different levels of complexity. The progression we trace is both chronological and logical, moving from the earliest forms of economies to the most recent forms in one sense and from very rudimentary to more complex ones in another sense. Chapter 2 examines the working of a tribal economy which has unlimited resources and has no interaction with any other group. The analysis is that of an economy with generation of use value as the organising principle. In Chapter 3 we move to an economy which consists of several units which are substantially self-sufficient but which have to interact with other units. Inter-unit transfers are, therefore, brought into analysis along with a more defined concept of ownership than is the case in a tribal economy. Towards the end of that chapter exchange is considered as a specific form of interunit transfer. Chapter 4 concentrates on exchange itself, understandng its analytical and institutional aspects and paving the way for the treatment of an economy with accumulation of exchange value as its organising principle. In Chapter 5 capitalism is described not only as an economy dominated by exchange, but one where utilisation of labour power is geared towards the accumulation of exchange value and where the ownership of resources and the organisation of production are all brought into line with that organising principle. After dealing with both the achievements and the inherent weakness of capitalism as an economic system we move on in Chapter 6 to outline the basic features of a post-capitalist economy, only approximations to which have been seen in what is there designated as historical socialism. The central systemic weakness of historical socialism and its many manifestations are examined in an attempt to explain the recent failure of many of the socialist regimes.

With this background we move in Part II to the treatment of the Indian economy. Chapter 7 provides an analytical description of the structure of the Indian economy. This is followed in Chapter 8 by an evolution of the Indian economy up to Independence, concentrating on the changes that the economy experienced during the colonial period. Chapter 9 examines the working of the Indian economy since Independence, relying on what is described as a microglobal approach. In Chapter 10 the post-Independence transformation of the economy is examined at the aggregate or macro level. Chapter 11 deals with one of the striking features of the economy, the poverty of the masses and the affluence of a few. In the concluding chapter the problem addressed is whether the Indian economy can be shaped to meet the needs of all the people.

NOTES

1. In formulating this description of the economy one of the most helpful works has been Godelier, 1986. However, the book is not simple reading.
2. Robinson Crusoe is the character created by the English novelist Daniel Defoe in his story (1719) of a castaway on a desert island, and has, therefore, become the symbol of an isolated individual.
3. On the role of abstraction in the study of economic problems reference may be made to Marshall, 1890, Appendix D.
4. Models play an important role in economic analysis. A model may refer to a verbal representation; it could also be a mathematical representation. Earlier economists like Adam Smith, David Ricardo and Karl Marx relied on the former kind of representation. Mathematical representations have become very popular in the second half of the twentieth century.
5. A reading of E.H. Carr's *What is History?* (Carr, 1964) is strongly recommended.
6. The distinction between use value and exchange value (or value in use and value in exchange) goes back to the writings of Aristotle.

2

Rudimentary Economy

One of the simplest possible economies is dealt with in this chapter—that of an isolated tribe set in the midst of a forest. It is described as a work-sharing and goods-sharing economy which does not confront issues of ownership and exchange. The decision-making processes in such an economy and their implications are examined. A sense of community and the recognition of authority are shown to be significant ingredients of the economy. The empirical significance of this essentially logical construct is brought out.

The first economy that we shall deal with is one of the simplest possible, that of an isolated tribe. It deserves the adjective 'simple' for more reasons than one. If the tribe is assumed to be living in a forest area and living off forest produce, its production activity must be largely the simple one of gathering what nature provides—fruits, nuts, roots, etc. Since it is described as isolated, it has no interaction with other communities which means that it does not enter into exchange transactions. If there are no others around, the tribe will not also be concerned with ownership issues because owner-ship too is basically a question of relationship with others in regard to right over things. We may describe such an economy as a *primitive economy* recalling that the dictionary meaning of 'primitive' is 'of an early, un-developed, simple unsophisticated', or as a 'rudimentary economy' because 'rudiment' means an early form on which a later development usually takes place. From our point of view an economy of this kind also represents one where the organising principle is the generation of use value.

RUDIMENTARY ECONOMY—ITS COMPOSITION

The group of people who are members of such an economy are likely to be a fairly small and closely-knit community bound together by conside-rations of flesh and blood, of language and customs. A rudimentary economy, in fact, *presupposes* such a community—because the structure of relationships that constitute the economy will be deeply embedded in the structure of relationships that underlie the community; so much so that separating the boundaries of the economy from the larger community is a very difficult task. This means, for instance, that if the intention is to study a specific tribal economy, it cannot be done apart from an understanding of its wider community set-up.

As a living community, its members will consist of men and women, adults and children. Analytically, the most significant classification of the members of the community and economy is into those who are actively involved in work (we shall see soon that 'work' in rudimentary economy has a special meaning) and those who are not. The latter category consists of infants, those who are infirm and those too old to be engaged in work. We shall not try to specify at what age a person ceases to be an infant or becomes old, or what conditions designate infirmity. But the basic distinction between those who are actively engaged in work and those who are not is important, because *all* members will be consumers, but only *some* of them will be actively engaged in work. We shall designate the total population of the tribe by P and the workers by W so that $P > W$ or $P/W > 1$.[1] The numerical values of P and W, naturally, will not remain the same for ever. We shall soon see that the P/W ratio or the relationship that it represents is an important factor in understanding a rudimentary economy.

We have already stated that 'work' has a specific meaning in a rudimentary economy. We are culturally conditioned into thinking of work as what is done outside the home, during certain specified hours in office, factory or institution and in return for wages and salaries. (For instance, if the man of the house sits behind his desk in the office from 10 a.m. to 5 p.m. it is considered work even if no work is done, but the labour that the woman of the house puts in without any specification of time, day or night is not work!) A rudimentary economy has none of these distinctions. Members of the community make use of their labour—they are active in the home and outside. They participate in economic activity and cultural activity, sometimes day and night without much break, and sometimes with plenty of break during both day and night. Hence a more appropriate term to describe work may be 'activity' and we should divide the group into 'activists' and 'non-activists'. But, again, our cultural conditioning will give very different interpretations to these terms! There is no easy way out and it is worth considering whether the problem is with the culture of a rudimentary economy or that of our own.

Be that as it may, some division of labour may naturally develop within the group, some elementary specialisation of activities. One such possibility is a sexual division of labour whose basis is the fact that adult women in the community have the capacity and responsibility that men do not have, that is to bear children. In other words the perpetuation of the community (which from its point of view is likely to be a matter of the highest concern and priority) is primarily the responsibility of women. In this sense it is possible that mother-children groups constitute the nucleus of the community with men added to it as necessary adjuncts. It is possible, too, that men are not fully integrated into the community where the mother-children group tends to stay put and the men are moving about, let us say, hunting and gathering. Or perhaps, the mother-children group does the gathering also for daily living and the men bring in from time to time little luxuries for special meals.

The point to note is that even if there was a sexual division of labour it would not be along what many modern societies have come to institu-tionalise as (unpaid) domestic work in which women specialise and (paid) work elsewhere, which men do. Consequently, it is also necessary that the work of women (even if quite a bit of it were domestic) would not be considered less important or less dignified. In fact it could be just the opposite. The crux of the matter is that work (or, more accurately, activity as seen above) in a rudimentary economy is anything and everything that is necessary for the survival and sustenance of the community; and members of the community share in it according to the specific situations and requirements of the community concerned. As a general principle we may say that a rudimentary economy is an activity sharing group. We shall see subsequently that it is also a goods-sharing group. Thus a distinctive feature of a rudimentary economy is that it is an activity-sharing and goods-sharing entity: sharing is its underlying principle. But here we anticipate much that is to follow.

To probe further into the rudimentary economy we shall follow the three key issues we have already identified in our description of the economy, viz., how the group of people exercise control over resources, how they combine resources and labour to produce goods and how they define and settle claims of members on what is produced.

CONTROL OVER RESOURCES AND PRODUCTIVE ACTIVITY

In a rudimentary economy of the kind we are considering, there is a close relationship between the manner in which control is exercised over re-sources and the way productive activity is organised and so we shall take the two together.

The first thing to note is that resources for the economy are provided by nature, in our case, the forest. It is the source of the livelihood of the members of the economy. It provides them the material required for housing and for whatever tools they may wish to make. Consequently, productive activity consists of human interaction with nature, and it is through such interaction that control over resources is exercised. Conse-quently, control over resources in this case does not necessitate what is normally taken to be ownership of resources. As has been noted already, in a rudimentary economy which is totally isolated from 'others', there is no ownership issue as we have come to understand it. Another way of putting it is that members of a rudimentary economy are 'monarchs of all that they survey.' They can use all that is within their reach with no one else to hinder or challenge them. Hence the extent of resources that they will make use of is something that they must decide. For instance, the entire forest is there at their disposal, but they must decide how much of it they will utilise. What are the factors on which such decisions will be based?

Limits to activity or use of resources

It is obvious that one such factor is the numerical strength of the community; the more people there are in the community (the W members, that is) the greater can be their 'coverage' of the forest. But their interest in the forest cannot be merely to exercise dominion over it (which they already have) but because of what it yields them for their sustenance. Hence a second factor which will decide on the extent to which they will exercise control over resources is their assessment of what they need—the fruits, nuts and roots, to serve as food; the barks and leaves to serve as clothing; branches and leaves to provide shelter; twigs to light a fire and so on. But although nature provides them with everything, these resources do not fall into their laps. They have to exert themselves to get what they need. And so a third factor that will decide the extent of resources they will control is their willingness to exert themselves. We have now identified three factors which will decide the extent of control the community will exercise over resources, the size of the community, their perception of their needs and their willingness to exert themselves. Now, the last two are not quite independent. The dependence between the two can be expressed in different ways. We may say, for instance, that the more they exert themselves the more fruits, nuts and berries they can have. On the other hand, if they first decide what their needs are, that decision determines the extent of effort they should put in.

No outsider can say exactly how these decisions will be arrived at and even the members of the community may not be able to throw much light on it. But just as we identified the factors involved in the decision, we can also set some limits within which the actual decisions will take place. The first of these is what we shall call the 'survival limit' or *constraint*. There is a minimum amount of food that human beings must have for sheer survival. Although it is a physiological requirement, it is not easy to specify its content and quantum. But food is not the only requirement for survival. The human body requires protection against the weather and hence clothing and shelter may also have to be included within the requirements for survival. Once these are also introduced it will become even more difficult to specify the contents of what may be called the 'survival kit,' for it will invariably come to be influenced by social and cultural considerations as well as by physiological requirements. Even so, we can assert with absolute certainty that any community of human beings requires a certain quantum of goods (and the resources required to provide them) for their physical survival. That quantum of goods, therefore, will set the lower limit of needs and the human effort and re-soures required to provide them.

Similarly, we may also designate an upper limit of the goods that a community can have. In the specific instance that we are discussing, the upper limit is set by the maximum of exertion that can be expected from the members of the community. That maximum also cannot be unambi-guously identified for a variety of reasons. For one thing we have already divided the members of the community into workers (W) and non-workers. But that division is not rigid. Those who are not ordinarily working, whether they are retired workers or future workers, can be pressed into service if some situation necessitates more work to be done. Even the exertion that the W members are capable of is somewhat elastic. We must also recognise that exertion is not only a physical activity. Part of it is the way in which the mind functions and human beings have shown many ingenious ways of coping with pressure and meeting challenges. A common manifestation is the use of tools. More fruit can be gathered if human effort is supplemented by even the simplest of tools like that of a pole, and more roots can be obtained by using simple tools for digging and so on. But, once again, we may say that under any given condition there is an upper boundary for what can be achieved through human exertion. What may be described as the normal level of activity will, obviously, take place somewhere in the range between the two limits. It is likely that this normal level is determined by the traditional practices of the community and so there is no conscious decision about it.

On the other hand, it is possible to argue that the traditional practices themselves are based on certain clear principles. One of these could be the awareness of the community about the role that nature plays in its survival and the consequent need to be restrained about the extent to which nature's bounty is consumed. It is reasonable to imagine that a community that maintains such intimate contacts with nature is more aware of the role of the natural environment in human lives than those who view everything, including nature, in terms of the profitability calculus. If this is true, a tribal economy may decide not to move up to the upper limit even if its members could if they so decided. Secondly, we must note that the upper limit is defined with reference to the effort that the community is willing to exert. As noted already, it is not easy to identify what is the 'maximum effort' of the community, but it is not difficult to see that under normal circumstances the community may not want to exert that kind of effort. There can be a third consideration. The community may set a limit to the goods it requires. Since most of the goods available to it are items of food, it is reasonable to assume that the members will become satiated with them.

To the extent that the third consideration is a major factor in determining the community's normal level of activity, it is correct to say that the effort that the community must exert depends on the norms it accepts about its requirements or needs. Needs determine effort, and these in turn determine the extent to which resources will be put to use.

Scarcity or abundance?

This sequence is different from (and in a sense the opposite of) the usual way of posing the economic problem where resources are taken as given and the question posed is the extent of goods that can be obtained from them, with the assumption that there is no limit to what are considered as needs. Where needs are considered to be limitless, resources will turn out to be inadequate in meeting all needs, with scarcity as the central or basic economic problem.

Let us consider these two ways of presenting the economic problem. We shall first examine the problem as experienced by the rudimentary economy. One of the common observations about such economies is that they operate at a rather low-level of productive activity, let us say just a little above what we have designated as the survival limit. In fact this means that the goods they produce are food, some other basic necessities of life and hardly anything else. The quantum and range of their production are generally seen to be very limited. Consequently they have earned the name *subsistence economies*. The expression subsistence economy may be interpreted in two distinctly different ways. The first is to imply an economy where production is meant for the consumption of its members and *not* for exchange. Obviously, a rudimentary economy is a subsistence economy in that sense, because that is the way we have set it up. The second sense in which the expression subsistence economy is used, is to denote an economy where production *cannot* rise above the level required to keep its members at the minimum level of survival. Is the rudimentary economy a subsistence economy in that sense? It may appear to be so if we judge it solely in terms of the quantum and range of its production. But the crucial question is whether it *can* produce more, and whether the actual low level of production observed is one of deliberate choice. If such indeed is the case, then the description of a rudimentary economy as a 'subsistence economy' is not correct. Is there some way of resolving the issue?

A possible test is to enquire whether the members of the economy have adequate basic necessities of life. However, 'adequate' is a relative term. In the case of food some calorific measure could be designed (as is being done now in relation to the specification of 'poverty lines'), but even there it is not easy to determine how many calories the members require or the calorific content of the items that constitute the diet of the community. Anyway, beyond that it is even more difficult to apply norms taken from another context to see whether the members of the community are adequately provided for in terms of the necessities of life. For instance, the standards of clothing and shelter that its members have may appear to be inadequate in terms of some external norm; but such an approach is not valid, and will not help to decide the question as to whether the observed low-level of production and consumption is a matter of choice.

However, it is possible to verify empirically whether the economy *can* produce more than what it usually does if and when the need arises. This question has received the attention of those who are specialists in the study of tribal economies; and the evidence indicates a significant variation in the level of production and production activity over a period of time, showing that such economies can indeed go beyond what they themselves consider to be 'usual'.[2] That finding, certainly, stands to reason. In conditions of the kind we have been examining, it should not be difficult for members of the community to gather on some days and occasions more fruits and nuts and other things than they normally do because one of the premises we are working with is that the forest, with all that it yields, is there and it is for the community to decide how much of it they should make use of. We come across similar situations among other groups for whom resources are supplied directly by nature. Fisherfolk who catch fish from the ocean are an example, although in many other respects tribal and fisherfolk economies differ considerably.[3]

In all such instances there is a deliberate decision to keep the economy's productive potential less than fully utilised normally, and to press it more into use when it is found necessary. The economy is said to show *slack* and it could be said that this is because the demand for goods is low, for if the demand for goods goes up, production can indeed increase. We, therefore, arrive at another conclusion. The level of productive activity and production in a rudimentary economy is decided by the demand for goods. Or, slack (unused but readily usable productive potential) exists because of 'demand constraint', so that when demand increases the supply of goods also increases.

When such is the case, the pattern of production will show some identifiable features. One of these is that productive activity will be discontinuous; members decide when they will engage in it and when they will withdraw from it. Sometimes they will work very hard and exert themselves considerably; at other times they will take it easy. The slack can also be thought of as an insurance against unexpected contingencies. This enables the members of the community not to worry too much about the future and not to carry too much stock. Why should they, when they know that any time they want more goods, they can just go out and gather them?

Many of these characteristics have also been observed by those who have been studying tribal economies. In particular, it is noticed that their members devote a great deal of their time in folk music and celebrations of various sorts, or simply lazing around. And a question often posed is whether they are rational in what they are doing. Specifically, it is asked whether they should not work harder and more regularly so as to raise their levels of living. It is not difficult to see that the question hides certain assumptions about what rational behaviour should be. It is assumed that where it is possible to have more goods, one should certainly go for them. We shall not, at this stage, consider whether remaining at a low-level of production and consumption is a virtue in itself—although we shall insist that in every economy (whether rudimentary or not) questions about the level and composition of production must be seriously examined. For the moment we shall only say that if the members of an economy make a deliberate choice to keep the level of their production and consumption low, there is nothing irrational about it. After all, it is a way of saying that they have a high preference for leisure-time activities, and they are entitled to act accordingly.

Some of those who have studied tribal economies and taken into account their peculiarities have argued that such economies are not subsistence economies, but the 'original affluent societies'.[4] Just as we examined whether they may be characterised as subsistence economies, we must also consider whether they can be thought of as affluent societies. In recent years the expression affluent society has referred to the United States of America (and other rich nations of the world) and hence affluence has come to be identified with the abundance of material goods.[5] Obviously, the kind of economies that we have been dealing with do not answer that description. But if we use the term 'abundance' instead of 'affluence', we can see that like scarcity it too is a relative term. Both abundance and scarcity can be understood only in relation to needs and the resources available to meet them. Members of a tribal economy set the level of their needs low and find that they have more than adequate resources to satisfy that level of need. Hence it can be argued that they have a sense of abundance, or affluence. Normally, economic analysis starts with a given level of resources and treats needs or wants as unlimited. Where limited resources must try to satisfy unlimited wants, the resulting situation can be said to be one of scarcity. When we interpret abundance and scarcity in this manner we can see that neither of them can be said to be the innate nature of any economy. In other words, abundance and scarcity are not objective conditions that can be said to become the basic feature of any economy and of economic analysis, although it is frequently claimed that scarcity is the basis of all economic analysis. We must insist that neither scarcity nor abundance is the initial condition for economic analysis. On the other hand, they are both derived concepts and depend very much on the assumptions made about the nature of needs (are they limitless or can they be limited?) and of resources (are they adequate in terms of their ability to satisfy needs?).

In the case of a tribal economy it seems eminently reasonable to say that though its level of production may be low, its condition is one of abundance, that is, the specified needs can be met without fully utilising accessible resources. As we move to other types of economies we shall see the profile getting reversed; even where the level of production may be high, economies experience scarcity, the inability of available resources to satisfy growing wants.

Three constraints

Let us now review what we know about the characteristics of a rudimentary economy in terms of the manner in which it exercises control over resources and uses resources and labour in productive activity. We shall do that with reference to the limits (constraints) we have noted. Since an economy for us is primarily a group of people, we shall use as our reference point the size of the group. Given the size of the rudimentary economy, there is an *upper limit* to the extent of resources it can control and use. This is reached where the members of the group are exerting themselves to the maximum. Hence we shall refer to it as the *labour constraint*. There is also a *lower limit* to the level of productive activity. That is the minimum level of goods required to ensure the survival of its members. We have already referred to it as the survival constraint. It can also be referred to as the *resource constraint*, because that level of productive activity indicates the minimum of resources required to ensure the survival of the members even when the members are exerting themselves to the maximum. The limits can also be expressed in terms of resources. The upper limit is the maximum extent of resources the economy can use given its size in terms of labour. The lower limit is the minimum extent of resources that the economy requires to function.

Granted that the members have free access to resources, the actual level of production activity of the economy will be between these two boundaries (usually closer to the lower limit than to the upper one, but moving up as and when required). The actual level, therefore, is determined by the community's requirement of goods, and hence may be said to be subject to the *demand constraint*. Stated somewhat differently, the actual level is determined by the community's preference between material goods and leisure-time activities.

While we have referred to the option that the economy has to move towards the upper limit (the labour constraint) we have not yet examined what will happen if it gets pushed towards the lower limit (the resource constraint). On the resource side this may result from some calamity like a sudden flood, or severe drought in the vicinity, a volcanic eruption or whatever denies the members the resources they were counting on. If this is a neighbourhood phenomenon, the members of the community have the option to migrate (either all of them or some of them) and to replicate their economy in some other location. Indeed, one reason why many tribal communities are seen to be migrants may be because of such situations. A second possibility is for the W members in the economy to put in more effort than they have been doing. This will be the case especially if the impact of the calamity is to raise the P/W ratio, let us say, because some W members die or become invalids. As a general rule, therefore, as the economy is pushed to its lower limit the W members will have to exert themselves more and more if replication through migration is not a possibility. From this we can infer also that the higher the P/W ratio, the greater will be the effort that the W members have to put in as the economy approaches the lower limit. And at the lower limit the choice that the members exercised between effort to produce material goods and leisure-time activities completely disappears. It is a realm of all work and no play! If the downward pressure still continues, the only way out is what is sometimes referred to as the *hardboiled solution*—some members, (the non-W members, that is) will have to die.

There is a concluding remark we must make about productive activity and production in a rudimentary economy. We have seen that its productive activity must be geared to the production of goods of use value. The members of the community will have to specify these goods in great detail—not just 'food', but fruits, roots, honey, leaves, etc. In fact even that may not be specific enough. For instance, leaves meant for eating and roofing may not be the same. In other words, the rudimentary economy is a good specific economy where there is no possibility of aggregation into 'products', 'output' etc. The same can be said about 'resources' and 'productive activity' which must also be specified in detail. This implies that on the organisation of production, sufficient attention will have to be paid to the physical complementarities of production. Precisely how this is to be done can be decided only by taking into account all specific aspects of the situation. It is likely, too, that these considerations will get institutionalised through practice and may, therefore, appear to be the most natural thing to do.

SETTLEMENT OF CLAIMS

We shall now turn to the last major issue pertaining to the rudimentary economy—how claims are defined and settled. We have already had occasion to refer to two aspects of it. First, that a rudimentary economy has a group of persons who do not 'work', but who have to be 'fed'. And, second, that a rudimentary economy is a product-sharing system. The second is the more general principle of which the first is a more specific instance.

Principles and problems of sharing

What does this mean? In a technical sense we would refer to it as a redistributory system. It is as though the products of the economy are 'centrally' pooled after which they are distributed among all members. It is difficult to suggest what the specific guidelines are of such sharing. One could be that the W members will receive more than the others for which the justification is fairly obvious. It is possible also that among the P, growing children may receive more than 'retired' old people. It will be recognised that these reflect the general principle: 'To each according to his/her need; from each according to his/her capacity.'

While this is a possibility, it should not lead us to romanticise a rudimentary economy as an ideal set-up of sharing and caring. For, there is nothing to prevent the principle of 'sharing' from taking other, and not such noble, forms. One such is what has come to be known as the 'life boat' principle—that of considering the needs of the infirm and the aged as less important in relation to the needs of those who are likely to survive and continue to assist in the survival of others. After all, what prevents the basic principle of the generation of use value being applied to this realm as well to get rid of 'useless' people? It is easy to see that this principle is most likely to be invoked when a rudimentary economy is pushed towards the lower limit whereas the former can be (but need not be) implemented when the going is good.

But there are more subtle problems too. If the former principle is in vogue, can a member of the community pretend to be infirm and thus escape his obligations to the community while continuing to be taken care of by it? Can he not, in other words, get a free ride at the expense of the community? Even if this is not happening, won't the W members protest because of feeling that they are made to slog for the sake of others who are not putting in any effort? To take the opposite case, if the community is against a certain member, can he not be declared invalid or insane and be abandoned according to the latter principle? These are the kind of dilemmas that a rudimentary economy may have to confront.

Who makes the decisions?

There is a basic question arising from these considerations. Who makes the decisions? In effect the answer is that in most such communities these decisions are not arrived at through conscious deliberative processes, but are taken as ordained by customs and traditions. But that is hardly a satisfactory answer. For, it is necessary to know how traditions get established and who becomes the custodian of customs. The former is rather difficult to answer, and in any case, customs themselves depend on how they are interpreted. Who performs that crucial function of interpreting customs and principles? Even in the benevolent case of 'to each according to his needs, from each according to his ability', how are individual needs defined? How are individual abilities assessed? Can it be done solely according to individual preferences? Is there a procedure by which through the expression of individual preferences, society's preferences can be determined? These may appear to be philosophical questions, and so they are up to a point. But they have arisen from matters relating to everyday living—very earthy matters indeed of food and clothing. Truly has a writer claimed that economists are 'worldly philosophers'.[6] The point to note is that the problems we have touched upon do not arise only when a society is satiated with material goods. They arise even in situations of low levels of material production; it is difficult to be assured that they will disappear when a society reaches very high levels of material production. To the extent that they arise from matters related to the economy, they will be present in any society which has to provide answers to the basic issues of the economy, which we dealt with in the previous chapter.

We shall get back to what appears to be the most likely case in a rudimentary economy. It is usually said 'custom is king' in such contexts. That statement needs to be amended to 'the *custodian* is king'. For it will be the person or persons who have the right to *interpret* customs who become supreme. In the case of the tribal community, it is the chief. In other instances it could be the patriarch or a priest. Whoever it may be, the underlying issue is one of authority. Thus the custom-oriented economy is intrinsically a command economy.

We have already stated that our enquiry is not into the details of how authority gets established in any specific situation or at any specific time and how it is passed on over time. We shall concentrate on general principles. What we can say is that in a rudimentary economy a subset of its members will emerge as custodians or persons exercising authority. They will have a predominant voice on how claims are defined and settled. Not only that. To the extent that utilisation of labour is the main aspect in production, they will also have a decisive say in productive activity as well. Obviously, then, they will also exercise control over other resources. It will be an instance of domination over human beings becoming instrumental in effective control over resources.

If this is so, we must infer that the structure of relationships that constitute a rudimentary economy is likely to be the domination of a subset of the group, a small minority (in the most limited case, just one person) over the rest. While we must recognise this strand of domination in that structure, we must also note that it arises from, or exists within, the context of a strand of co-operation, harmony and communality of traditions, involvements of the present and hopes for the future. This means that it is not necessary that domination must invariably express itself as violence. In fact the more likely case is that the basis of the domination of the minority is the *consent* of the dominated because of their conviction that they are receiving benefits from it. One writer has said: 'In the deepest sense, coercion and consent combine and collude, albeit in different ways, to the same end' (Godelier, 1986:13). This can be illustrated in terms of how men come to dominate over women and the older generation over the younger, even in modern societies. A look at any modern dictatorship will convince us that the nature of domination which we have noted has a more general validity.

We have not said anything explicitly so far about the social institutions of a rudimentary economy. This is partly because, as we have frequently stated, the institutions are temporally and spatially specific. But the main reason for being silent so far about the institution of a rudimentary economy is that it does not have institutions that are *specifically economic* such as firms, markets and banks as can be seen in some other kinds of economies. The economic aspects of a rudimentary economy are embedded in its major general institutions such as kinship, religion etc. What it means is that rudimentary economy can have only the vaguest identity within an overall institutional milieu. It is also likely that non-economic factors will dominate over economic factors. There is nothing abnormal about this, for instance, as it finds expression in the slogan of some modern societies: 'Put politics in command'. In other words, in a rudimentary economy economic activities are part of, and instrumental to, the overall efforts of a community to establish and maintain, according to their perception, 'a good society'. If so, is that in any sense peculiar?

RUDIMENTARY ECONOMY: A ROUND UP

This provides the opportunity to raise the question as to why a rudimentary economy of the kind that we have dealt with is important in our
fundamental quest towards understanding the economy. To understand
the economy is to figure out how it functions and what holds it together
or, more accurately, what orchestrates it. Our analysis of a rudimentary
economy has been an attempt to demonstrate one pattern of that orchestration. Sometimes it is argued (or, frankly speaking, simply asserted) that
every economy has, or must have, a single principle holding it together,
integrating principle, as it is referred to. That is not the way a rudimentary
economy is constituted. What we have tried to show is that a rudimentary
economy is held together by an organising principle, *and* a variety of
social institutions—those that ensure a sense of community, those that
exercise authority, and those that govern the economic activities. It is an
ensemble of these various entities that needs to be orchestrated. As we go
along we will see that these ingredients are (have to be) present in *all*
economies, but not necessarily in the manner in which they are in a
rudimentary economy. But the rudimentary economy has the rudiments
of everything that is to be designated as an 'economy'. That is the significance
of the analysis of this chapter. That statement can be misunderstood if
immediately we do not also point out how a rudimentary economy differs
from all other economies. The difference is this. In a rudimentary economy
the diverse aspects that we have listed above tend to coalesce into one
grand entity—whatever is designated as kinship, tribe etc—which ensures
its integration. This is a rudiment too. But as societies and economies
change over time orchestration through natural coalescence becomes
impossible because of a wide variety of factors. The orchestration aspect,
then, becomes more complex even when, in some instances as we shall
see, it appears to have become simpler.

THE EMPIRICAL RELEVANCE OF THE RUDIMENTARY ECONOMY CONSTRUCT

It must now be evident that our treatment of the rudimentary economy is
not meant merely to analyse tribal economies although tribal economies
that function more or less as shown here exist in many parts of our country
and in other parts of the world as well. Rudimentary economies similar to
tribal economies can be seen in other instances. A reference has already
been made to the economy of traditional fishing communities. Just as
forests are the natural resources of tribal communities, the ocean is the
natural resource of fishing communities along the coasts. The extent to
which they will utilise this resource to gather the produce is determined as

already discussed in the case of tribal economies. The practical arrangements for the utilisation of labour in productive activity are dictated to a large extent by the physical features of the sea, weather, currents etc., and the patterns of reproduction and movements of the fish. Taking these into account the organisation of production and the settlement of claims over production are arranged by the community and over time get accepted as 'rules' of the community. In all these respects traditional fishing communities may also be said to be rudimentary economies. There is a major difference, though. Most fishing communities interact with one another in order to exchange activities of one kind or another much more naturally than tribal communities, and hence may not be the 'pure types' that we have described. It may be noted, too, that more often than not fishing communities have other fishing communities in their neighbourhood and hence though nobody owns the ocean, no one community can claim to be 'the monarchs of all they survey'. Access to the waters gets fairly well regulated through mutual understandings.

In fact, some of the basic features of a rudimentary economy can prevail even where ownership is fairly well established and where productive activity has to be much more complex than the 'gathering processes' common to tribes in forests and fishing communities along the sea coasts. Consider an isolated farming household with a large but limited extent of land, owned by it and entirely at its disposal. The analysis of the economy of such a community can be almost exactly along the lines of the economy of tribals. Given the number of members of the household (with the distinction between P and W retained) assume that the land owned by it is more than what is required to meet the survival constraint and also more than can be put to use by the 'maximum effort' of its members. Under such conditions the household will have to decide how much land and labour it will put to use to produce its requirements. The decision will depend very much on how much produce it considers necessary for its needs. The 'normal' level of productive activity of the household is likely to be less than the maximum it can achieve and 'normally' both land and labour are likely to be less than fully utilised, indicating the presence of slack in the economy. Land and labour remaining idle in such a situation is not irrational; and one may quite correctly say that the farm household is in a state of abundance even if its level of production (and consequently consumption) is low.

Hence, wherever there are groups of people who have resources available to them (whether they own these or not) which enable them to utilise the labour at their disposal to produce goods they require, and where they make all decisions regarding production and settlement of claims among the members without reference to any external social factors, a rudimentary economy may be said to exist with features such as we have noted in the preceding sections. If so, the empirical relevance of the rudimentary economy construct must be quite wide-ranging, at least in countries like ours, because even today a vast proportion of the people in our country are engaged in productive activities largely dependent on resources (especially land) available to them and where their economic decisions are substantially (though not entirely) internal. Such economies are usually referred to as *household production units* and in Part II we shall be dealing with them in detail. Their economic decisions are not entirely internal to them because many of them, particularly those that are not producing food crops, are and have to be dependent on exchange and thus come under external influences, at least to some extent. That, however, does not lead them to lose their internal autonomy. We do not want to create the impression that their autonomy is always a matter of deliberate choice. On the contrary, in most instances it is a matter of sheer necessity for survival.

If household production units function within a larger economic system and in relation to it, it is not quite correct to treat them as 'economies'; rather, they must be considered as *sub-economies* within a larger economy. To put it differently, what is usually considered a national economy may consist of sub-economies many of which may show features of the rudimentary economy that we have examined in this chapter. That is the analytical and empirical significance of the rudimentary economy construct.

With that understanding we can go a step further. All national economies that we know have households within them, even if not all of them are recognised as household production units. But, if production is the use of resources and labour in the generation of useful things (or of use values) then practically all households everywhere must be thought of as production units and thus as household economies or more accurately as household sub-economies. Households put resources and labour to use in generating use values (most important of these being food cooked in the kitchen) and also settle the claims of the members in what is thus produced, with the decisions in both these regards being substantially, but not entirely, internal. We must, therefore, conclude that all national economies have as one of their components sub-economies which are of the rudimentary economy type. Hence the empirical and analytical aspects of the rudimentary economy concept is indeed very significant.

NOTES

1. One of the clearest treatments of the internal arrangements of an essentially self-sufficient and self-contained economic unit is that of a peasant economy by the Russian economist A.V. Chayanov, who carried out his studies prior to the Russian Revolution of 1917. His work (Chayanov, 1966) became available to a wider audience only after it was (translated into English and) edited by Daniel Thorner and his associates. Chayanov uses C to represent total population converted into consumer units (eg. children are less than full consumer units) and shows the importance of P/W ratio for understanding the working of a peasant economy at any given time and of its transformation over time. Whether total population is represented by P or C, the crucial point is that those who work have to support themselves and some others also.
2. See Sahlins, 1974.
3. The main difference is that fisherfolk usually have to sell most of the catch they make and hence are quite dependent on exchange for their livelihood.
4. Sahlins, 1974, especially ch. 1.
5. *The Affluent Society* is the title of a widely discussed book by the American economist, John Kenneth Galbraith (Galbraith, 1958).
6. *The Worldly Philosophers* is a well known book by Robert L. Heilborner (Heilborner, 1953). The subtitle of the book, 'the lives, times and ideas of the great economic thinkers' indicates the content of the book. For those who are interested in the development of economic thought, this book (particularly its fifth revised edition) is highly recommended.

   Aspects of what has been described as 'rudimentary economy' can also be found in the following works: Heilborner, 1962; Hicks, 1969; Marx, 1972; 1973; Marx and Engels, 1976; Stinchcombe, 1983; Seddon, 1978; especially the essay by Claude Meillassoux, *The Economy in Agricultural Self-sustaining Societies*.

3

Village Economy

In this chapter a collection of interacting rudimentary economies are examined for which land is the principal means of production and which constitute a village community. Variants of the village economy have been the historical legacy of practically the whole of humankind. In some parts of the world, as in Europe, the village economy, known widely as feudalism, is a thing of the past; but in other parts of the world, including India and many other Asian countries, it continues to be a reality. It will be useful to get acquainted with descriptive accounts of what is designated here as village economy through such standard works as Bloch (1965), Baden-Powell (1977), and Postan (1972).

Analytically the significance of the village economy is that it gives rise to inter-unit transactions (including exchange) and the concept of ownership, as also claims on the produce on the basis of ownership. There is also greater diversification of economic activities in a village economy in comparison with a rudimentary economy.

The essential feature of the rudimentary economy as we have seen, is that all its decisions are 'internal' without reference to any external social factors, i.e., the absence of the 'other'. Starting out with an isolated tribal economy where this condition was assumed to be strictly satisfied we examined a few other instances where decision-making, regarding the use of resources and labour in production, and the settlement of claims is substantially internal. One of the consequences of the absence of the 'other' is that two major societal features are alien to such an economy. These two are ownership and exchange which are key features in most modern economies. Examining an economy where these two are absent reminds us that they are indeed societal features that emerge under specified social conditions, and not in any sense natural features which all economies are inevitably subject to. But since they are crucial features of modern economies we must examine how they have emerged. This is one of the themes of this chapter.

The 'village economy' which we shall consider in this chapter is a group of rudimentary economies that interact with one another. The introduction of the 'other' changes the analysis in many quite significant ways.

The first thing to notice is that if these rudimentary economies interact among themselves within a larger entity, the village economy, they become its constituent units and in that sense cease to be autonomous economies. They become sub-economies in the sense in which we used the expression towards the end of the last chapter. If the village economy, in its turn, is incorporated into a larger entity—let us say a national economy—then it too will only be a sub-economy. But we will not enter into that question just yet. However, the village economy itself has to be viewed at two levels—as a single entity and as a collection of units, a possibility which we did not have when we were dealing with a single, isolated rudimentary economy. The view of an economy as a totality is referred to as *the macro* view; an approach to it in terms of its constituent units as *the micro* view. Our treatment of the rudimentary economy in the last chapter may be described as either a macro view or as a micro view in as much as it is an entity with a single unit in it. But since it is an analysis of an economy in terms of its totality, it is more accurate to describe it as a macro view. A micro view is primarily about the units that constitute a larger entity. Since our attention, in this chapter, will be on a village economy in terms of its constituent units, it is primarily a micro analysis. We shall see that though we must recognise a macro approach also in such a context, the macro view cannot be fully formed under the conditions we are dealing with.

Emergence of Ownership and Exchange

In order to understand what happens when there is a collection of rudimentary economies, we shall, in the first instance, deal with just two rudimentary units A and B both of which have generation of use values as their organising principle. What may be the nature of their interaction?

Ownership and exchange emerge
In the first place, if they are within reach of each other, both will have to have a different way of exercising control over resources. The members of neither of these two units can any longer claim that they are the monarchs of all that they survey. They have the 'other' to take into account. The 'other' may also reach out exactly where they do, and hence it may become necessary to designate 'what is ours' and 'what is yours'. This is not only because there is the 'other' to take into account but also because the extent of resources is such that it has to become an 'either/or' issue; if there are enough resources for both A and B to reach out as much as they wish to, then there will not be any problem to resolve. Hence we can see that there is a relationship between the ownership issue and scarcity: ownership is one of the ways in which a community determines how scarce resources will be utilised. But the relationship between ownership and scarcity is not a one-way process. It can be shown that under certain conditions it is

ownership that gives rise to scarcity. To examine this proposition, consider that the extent of resources in the village economy is such that both A and B can reach the upper limit indicated in the last chapter with more resources still available. However, imagine that A is the first to reach the village, and claims ownership over all resources when B shows up. It would then appear that there is a situation of scarcity of resources in the village in the sense that B has no access to resources because A has, by ownership, decided to exclude B from exercising any kind of control over resources. Where private ownership of resources becomes a regular feature, it will, therefore be difficult to say whether ownership reflects scarcity or *gives rise to* scarcity. In either case, it is seen that the crucial aspect of ownership in relation to scarcity is the power to *exclude* the 'other'. Hence instead of thinking of a cause-and-effect relationship, it may be more appropriate to consider that ownership and scarcity are correlates within a social set-up.

Now, the two rudimentary units A and B will have to settle the question of 'who owns what' one way or the other: through peaceful negotiation or through confrontation. There is nothing to say that a settlement arrived at will be lasting, since there is no third party to guarantee the settlement. Hence it is possible that the ownership question will come up over and over again till ways are found to institutionalise the negotiation of settlements and to guarantee their observance. One of the possible settlements is for one or both of the units to move away spatially so that both can become isolated entities and thus cease to be sub-economies within a village economy, in which case the analysis will return to what we examined in the previous chapter. Hence we shall not treat it as one of the options. There are, however, other possibilities—some of which we examine later in the chapter.

Closely related to ownership and scarcity is exchange. One exchanges only what one owns in return for what the 'other' owns. And in view of the connection between ownership and scarcity noted already exchange, too, gets related to scarcity; only scarce things enter into exchange. But for A and B to enter into exchange other conditions are also necessary. Thus if A and B are both peasants producing paddy and using land and labour, no exchange is likely. On the other hand if A produces paddy and B produces pulses and if paddy and pulses are *both* use values to A and B, they will be able to enter into an economic transaction for transferring grain from community A to community B in exchange for pulses from community B to community A.

Thus, the introduction of the 'other' gives rise to both ownership and exchange as possibilities. But ownership and exchange take many forms and the forms change over time. For an understanding of contemporary economies, especially ones like ours, it is important to appreciate the metamorphosis of ownership and exchange as economic categories. In this chapter we shall look into some aspects of ownership in its bearing on production and the settlement of claims. In the next chapter we shall study the phenomenon of exchange in greater depth.

VILLAGE ECONOMY AS A HISTORICAL ENTITY

Our attempt so far has been to take note of some formal differences between a rudimentary economy and a village economy which we have postulated as a collection of rudimentary economies. In our treatment of the rudimentary economy we concentrated largely on its logical structure and only in the final stages did we address ourselves to the empirical relevance of that logical structure. But the treatment of the village economy has to be different because it is much closer to the reality of our own experience. In fact the village economy, whose essential features we shall be examining in this chapter, is the historical legacy of practically the whole of humankind: for some it is a legacy of the past; for many it is their own, contemporary reality.

Let us, therefore, identify its main features. In the first place, a village economy is primarily a food-producing economy, just like a rudimentary economy. The reason for this is that in a village economy productive forces are still at a rather low level, and technology is rather primitive. Hence a great proportion of labour time *has* to be devoted to the production of food for survival. In the past some village economies came to be noted for their non-food production—certain kinds of luxury goods like fine cloth and certain kinds of durable goods like temples and pyramids; but even in such instances resources and labour were being utilised basically for the production of food. Recalling that a village economy is but a collection of rudimentary economies (and in that sense not different from them in terms of the organising principle) we may say that its social organisation makes it possible to convert the slack or production potential into certain forms of material goods. How this is achieved is something that we shall enquire into.

Secondly, a village economy while being a food-providing economy like a rudimentary economy, represents a more settled stage, that of agriculture. This fact has a bearing on its techniques of production as well as its social organisation. In terms of techniques of production, a village economy has greater reliance on tools—ploughs, for example—and domesticated animals than a rudimentary economy. The fact that there are tools also means that there is production of tools also, apart from the production of food, and consequently greater possibilities of specialisation in production. Similarly, a village economy may also have to be concerned with the creation of facilities for irrigation, grain storage etc. Each one of these, in turn, is likely to influence the social organisations in a village economy.

Thirdly, and arising from the first two, land becomes the crucial resource in a village economy and the control over land emerges as the main economic issue. It is the combination of these three that justifies the economy being described as a 'village economy'. In addition, the village economy brings in for discussion a spatial dimension. Control over land is control over a spatial territory and thus adds a further dimension to the issues of authority, touched upon in the treatment of the rudimentary economy.

The central issue in the study of a village economy has been posed thus by a writer: 'since a village is a group of persons as well as a system of land-holdings, what kind of connection is there between the persons and the land?' (Baden-Powell, 1977; 398). We may add further, how does this connection shape production activity and the settlement of claims?

In the history of human civilisations these have been the perennial economic questions. Whether consciously recognised or not, these questions have been asked all over the world from a very early stage in history until about two centuries ago. Even today these are the major economic issues for millions of people all over the world, including the vast majority in our country.

The characterisation of the village economy as the longest historical experience of humankind in terms of economic activity should not be interpreted to mean that the organisation of the village economy has been the same all over the world and all through the ages. Far from it. There were enormous differences in economic organisations in different parts of the world and across the ages. But all of them had one common feature: in essence they were all concerned with the generation of use values—even when exchange became an established economic activity. In terms of our terminology all of them have had the same organising principle. However, their social organisations did differ substantially, and thus they have had different social frameworks. We shall try to capture both these aspects: a single organising principle and a plurality of social organisations in the variety of economies for which we have given the common title 'village economy.'

BASIC ASPECTS OF A VILLAGE ECONOMY

Like a rudimentary economy, a village economy is also a group of people—a community—and the relationships that they enter into, in the three spheres we have designated. What can we indicate as the nature of such a community, and what implication does it have on their economic activity? One thing is quite clear. All members of the community have, directly, or at least indirectly, a deep interest in land. For some, land is the source of their sustenance; for others, it is the base of their opulence. Many of them work on the land; some live off the land. Hence even if they are not united by bonds of flesh and blood they have much in common. This sense of commonality is further strengthened by dwelling together in one place, usually separated physically and socially from other communities. A village community, however, is likely to be larger in size than the communities constituting a rudimentary economy. The larger size of the village economy in terms of numbers and resources implies not only that the volume of economic activities will be larger, but that they can be more differentiated; thus resulting from and providing scope for a greater degree of specialisation and division of labour. As already noted, while the main economic activity in a village economy will be production of food, it can also accommodate some production of tools, some production of other necessities of life, some kinds of non-essentials and some durable goods as well. A village economy, therefore, will have a more differentiated group of producers—cultivators, blacksmiths, carpenters, spinners, weavers and construction workers. It will provide not only for these producers (or workers) but also for non-producers as in a rudimentary economy. The non-producers in a village economy will also tend to be more differentiated, some playing supportive roles such as defending the village territory and its economic activities, but some far removed from production.

These considerations show that members of a village economy may not be as closely knit together as members of a rudimentary economy. In the latter, in a sense, the economy is a derivative of the sense of community that the members have as belonging to a single tribe, or group, and the economy is very deeply embedded within such a community. In a village economy on the other hand, the sense of community goes beyond the considerations of flesh and blood with some forms of relationships arising from the production process itself and starting to be visible. The distinction between social relationships of a broad kind and social relationships of production does not emerge clearly and sharply in the village economy, but the hazy outlines between the two are beginning to be seen.

To look into this aspect further we may consider how a village economy gets formed. We may recognise different strands in its formation. One of these could be kinship or tribal relationship itself, as may happen when a whole tribe moves out from its earlier habitat into a new settlement with better opportunities. On its way it may come across another tribe in a similar situation and the two may decide to merge to take advantage of a larger number—either to clear new territory or to fight against potential rivals. The larger group may now move into a location which it considers desirable, but may have to take it forcibly from those who already claim to be in possession of it. Once the territory is conquered, and the right over it is established through might, those original settlers who are willing to accept the lordship of the conquerors might be permitted to stay on. Subsequently, more settlers may be brought from outside either to attend to special functions (such as manufacture of tools) or simply to increase the numerical strength of the community. After these different strands have dwelt together for a while and shared in the common activities of production and other tasks, there may emerge some kind of a loosely-knit village community of reciprocal relationships. Such relationships, however, are very unlikely to be on a footing of equality. Indeed, for reasons that we shall soon discover, what characterises a village economy is 'reciprocity in unequal obligations' (Bloch, 1965, II: 228).

OWNERSHIP RIGHTS AND CLAIMS

What we have seen as the nature of the community in a village economy provides some clues to understanding its special features of ownership. We have already noted that since a village economy is not a single entity unlike the rudimentary economy, but consists of different units, the question of ownership emerges as an important aspect. But is it private ownership of the kind we are familiar with, or is it collective ownership that some socialist economies have experimented with, or is it something distinctly different?

Nature of ownership

The ownership issue relates primarily to land. There are two distinct ways in which ownership over land gets established which we shall refer to as colonisation and conquest. In the past, any group of people who could move to land that was not yet occupied by anybody else, clear it and occupy it would claim it as their land. This is what we have indicated as colonisation. The territory as a whole would be owned by the group, but units within the group could claim as theirs whatever they were able to clear and cultivate by using their own labour. Through conquest also a group could claim ownership over a territory and within that territory each unit might claim some portion as its own. The ownership by the group as a whole over the entire territory could be just notional, or a leader or chief (whether the operation is colonisation or conquest) could exercise control over the group and hence over what the group claims to be its territory. When there is a chief, he would have the right to assign land under his jurisdiction to anyone in return for services already rendered, or expected to be rendered. In the past, a common form was for the chief or lord to promise protection to a subordinate, who in turn was obliged to fight under the leadership of the chief in case of aggression by an outsider. The assigning of the land to a subordinate was considered to be as a token of the agreement of mutual obligation.

Similarly, a unit that claimed its land through expending labour for clearing, ploughing and cultivation, could give part of its land to a tenant who would cultivate it and give a part of the produce to the owner. In all these instances 'ownership meant possession made venerable by lapse of time' (Bloch, 1965, I: 116). Those who were not cultivators, but still part of the village community (a carpenter or barber or astrologer) could also claim some land in order to raise food for their sustenance; although, as we shall subsequently see, such people also had a claim over other people's produce. Over time all these would come to have customary sanctions and there would emerge what would distinctly be some sort of 'participatory ownership' or 'shared ownership'—neither purely private nor clearly collective. A writer has described it thus:

The tenant who—from father to son as a rule—ploughs the land and gathers the crop; his immediate lord to whom he pays dues and who, in certain circumstances, can resume possession of the land; the lord of the lord and so on, right up the... scale—how many persons there were who can say, each with as much justification as the other, 'That is my field!' Even this is an understatement. For the ramifications extended horizontally as well as vertically an account should be taken of the village community, which normally recovered that use of the whole of its agricultural land as soon as it was cleared of crops; of the tenant's family without whose consent the property could not be alienated; and the families of successive lords (Bloch, 1965, I: 116).

There is one other factor also to be taken into account in describing the nature of ownership under such circumstances. This is the fact that usually a village settlement would have two kinds of common property—the forests and the wasteland—to which individual units would have free access, but according to norms prescribed by the group. Thus every household in the village would have access to forests to gather fruits and roots and nuts for food, twigs for firewood, reeds to provide roofs and branches to make ploughs. Similarly all households could send their livestock to the wasteland for grazing. In these ways private ownership is supplemented by collective ownership both being very intimately related to the day-to-day activities of the members of the group.

Multiple rights and claims

But perhaps the preoccupation with ownership as such reflects more of our thinking than that of the members of a village economy. We must recall that ownership is a way of exercising control over resources, and control over resources serves different purposes. Control over resources is necessary to engage in production, for production is achieved by combining resources and labour. Control over resources also enables one to put forward claims on the produce. And thirdly, control over resources is a way of enhancing one's power which may serve either as an end in itself (something of a use value to some people) or as a means to exercise further control over resources and people. Ownership may achieve all these simultaneously as when a cultivator who owns land is able to produce grain, claim all of the grain as his possession and comes to have a sense of self-esteem as an independent producer and owner. But these three aspects of ownership may also disintegrate. In particular, depending on specific social conditions, the first two aspects of ownership may come to vest in different groups of people enabling those who have no direct role in production to have a claim on the produce. If that happens, the role of ownership will be more to support a claim on the produce, than to press for any legal claims on resources as such. For reasons that are fairly obvious, in a village economy claim on produce is likely to be more important than claim on resources, because the former yields use value directly and the latter only indirectly. To put it in different words, in a predominantly agricultural economy, where land as a resource is used only to produce grain (and other kinds of goods for consumption) claim on the produce is more important than claim on the resource; but ownership of resource can become a convenient means to stake claims on the produce. If, therefore, there are many people who can claim that a plot of land belongs to them (ownership) it is because there are many who make a claim on the produce of that plot. 'Participatory ownership', therefore, is more an expression of multiple rights and a way of settling claims on the produce than one of ownership. A village economy, thus, is one where claims on produce are legitimised as rights via the concept of ownership. Hence to understand a village economy we must pay more attention to the patterns of rights and claims (a network of mutual but unequal obligations) than to the institutions of ownership. However, an important implication of ownership in such a context must be noted. A village economy marks the beginning of the separation of the first two aspects of ownership mentioned above, viz., ownership as control over resources to facilitate production and ownership as the basis of claim on the produce. The former is a producer's view of ownership and the latter is a rentier's view of ownership; a rentier being one who, though not involved in production, comes to have a claim on the produce. The distinction between producer and rentier is crucial

X may find itself in a situation where it does not have enough grain for the survival of its members during the period of waiting. If household Y has enough grain reserves, X can borrow from Y and agree to repay either in grain at the time of the harvest, or more likely in terms of labour services over a period of time. The latter is the most likely procedure if X is a chronically deficit household which cannot therefore afford to repay in terms of grain. Hence X and Y may strike a deal between them; X to provide labour service to Y and Y to provide grain to X. It is not difficult to see that Y will have the upper hand in the deal because X requires the deal for sheer survival; for Y the deal is not a necessity, but a matter of convenience. This kind of deal is typical of what has come to be known as a *patron-client relationship* with one of the parties in the deal having a dominant role (patron Y in our example) and the other a subordinate role (X in the example).

Production relations

This is but a special form of the 'reciprocity in unequal obligations', which we have already noted as one of the basic features of a village economy. It has two underlying causes which we may identify as social and economic which, however, we will not be able to distinguish clearly in a village economy context. Since we are dealing with productive activity we shall first locate the economic factor which is fairly obvious. It is the *differential effective control* that different households (sub-economies) in the village economy have over resources, in this case land. We shall not try to figure out why such differential control over resources comes about; we can only say that that is a more realistic situation than all households having equal effective control over resources. We can presume that in a village economy some households will be near the labour constraint limit, some close to the resource constraint limit and some in between. Concentrating on the ones near the limit we may say that some households are *resources-rich* and *labour-scarce* (household Y in the example) and others *labour-abundant* and *resource-scarce* (household X). We have seen why the former type of households will come to have an upper hand in any deal they may enter into with the latter type of household.

The social cause of domination and subordination differs in different contexts. In feudal Europe, society consisted of a pyramidal structure with, frequently, a monarch at the apex who would claim to be the owner of all land (because of 'the divine right of kings') with his chosen vassals coming immediately below him who, in turn, would become 'lords' to those below and so on with the serfs, the actual cultivators, situated at the bottom. Society was, thus, considered to consist of the 'high' and the 'low' and although it was one of reciprocal obligations it was clearly also one of unequal obligations. In traditional Indian village economy the social factor responsible for a hierarchical structure was the caste system which in terms of the hierarchical principle was much more rigid than the feudal European set-up.

In both these cases, however, the social and economic hierarchies tended to coincide because of the close link that social hierarchy had with land. Thus, in our situation, land was very much under the effective control of the high castes with the lower castes being at the mercy of the 'superior' castes. We also had a group of people (a substantial number in most villages) who were prevented from owning any land at all. For these reasons, in practically all village economy contexts, the social and economic factors reinforce one another in generating a set-up of 'reciprocity in unequal obligations'.

This can manifest itself in different ways in production relations. The patron-client relationship which we have already seen is one of them. A second standard practice is for a household of the Y type (which would claim to be a *landlord* household because it lords over a lot of land) to provide some land to another household (of the X type) which the latter may use to cultivate for its own needs, but in return for which it must provide labour services (for farming, herding and household chores) to the landlord. In such instances practically all members of the X type household get 'attached' to a Y type household (men to work on the farm, women to attend to household chores and children to take care of the cattle, for instance). Obviously, not the entire labour time of the members of the X household will be spent on 'its' Y household, and it may be that the labour services thus spent may get compensated—a meal once a day, left-overs, clothing, gifts at the time of marriages and festivals, funeral expenses being typical forms of compensations (apart from the use of a portion of the lord's land already mentioned).

Different kinds of tenancies may also arise whereby a landlord lets out part of his land to a tenant who will cultivate the land and pay a rent, usually in kind (a part of the produce) to the landlord. The terms of tenancy can vary considerably. It could be a fixed rent, irrespective of what the output turns out to be; it could be a share of the crop (hence the term 'share-cropping tenancy') with the shares themselves varying in favour of the landlord or the tenant as the case may be, but frequently turning out to be a fifty-fifty deal. Other conditions may also be included. Thus the landlord may meet certain kinds of the cost of cultivation (usually expenses pertaining to improvements to the land) and so on.

We can now move to another area of the interaction between the physical and social aspects of production. From a technical angle neither land by itself nor labour by itself can become productive; a combination of the two is needed for production to take place. In the context of a village economy, land does not have much other use except as a means of production in agriculture. Hence, if it is not used in farming it remains unused. In this sense, for use in farming there is no 'opportunity cost' in as much as it is not withdrawn from any other use to make farming possible. This is largely true about labour in a village economy as well, which we consider to be primarily concerned with agriculture and the production of food. However, there is an asymmetry between land and labour. Land has no 'real cost' as it will not cost anything if it remains unutilised. On the other hand a human being needs food whether or not his/her labour time is utilised in productive activity. The quantity of food (and other basic necessities of life to be more accurate) required to keep a human being alive and fit to engage in productive activity is the 'real cost' of labour. The asymmetry between land and labour in this regard has important consequences under certain social conditions, especially where the two are not owned by the same set of people.

To examine this aspect let us go back to the two types of households we have dealt with earlier, the X–type households which we shall refer to as *labour-households* (which own very little land) and the Y–type households which we shall designate *landlord-households* because their primary ownership is land. Since the landlord households can by using its own labour produce enough grain for the survival of its members (and more) and since land has no real or opportunity cost, they can afford to let part of this resource, land, remain idle. On the other hand, since the labour-households have to provide for the survival of its members, and since they may not be able to do so based solely on the land they have, they will be eager to lease in land from the landlord households. The landlord-households, of course, have the option of employing labour from the labour-households to put more of their land to use, and thus increase the produce. But for this they will incur as cost whatever is to be paid to the labourers they employ. Only if the *increase* in the produce is more than sufficient to pay for the cost will it be worthwhile for the landlord-households to employ the labour of the labour-households. This is the reason why on the whole the landlord-households will be more ready to lease out land because any *positive rent* at all will be a net addition to the produce they will come to have.

Labour-households on the other hand, would be eager to find employment in the landlord's farms because any wages earned will be a net addition to the total grain available to them. But in view of the positive real cost of labour and the zero real and opportunity cost of land, the landlord-households are likely to have their way, since the labour-households must lease in land if there is no other way for them to acquire the grain they require for survival. They are, of course, taking the risk that the increase in output resulting from cultivating the leased-in land will leave some surplus after paying the rent. But they have very little choice in the matter and will normally be willing to take the risk. Thus, landlord-households will be eager to lease out land and the labour-households may have no choice but to lease-in land. This accounts for the widespread prevalence of tenancy in village economies.

There is a further aspect of the land-labour asymmetry that we must take note of. Labour-households have to use their labour intensively on any land they have and lease-in, and hence productivity per unit of land under the control of such households is likely to be higher than on land under the control of landlord-households. On the other hand, as we have noted already, it does not cost anything for the landlord-households to allow land to remain unutilised, especially if they figure that employing labour to utilise their land is not worthwhile because payment to labour is a cost to them. If this is the case, a village economy may also have slack as we noticed in the rudimentary economy, both land and labour not adequately utilised in productive activity, and thus the productive potential of the village economy remaining not fully utilised. The manifestation of the slack will be somewhat different in this case. Land will remain inadequately utilised in landlord-households because according to their calculation using land fully is not worthwhile; labour will remain inadequately utilised in labour-households because they do not have enough land to work on. This is a clear case where the village economy as a macro entity does not have its production potential fully realised because of differences in the economic calculations of its micro units. The micro units can be said to be quite rational in their calculations and yet in the macro or social sense the outcome is not rational. The asymmetry between private and social rationalities arises, it can be seen, because of the nature of ownership and other conditions in the economy. Under the circumstances described, the village economy can come to have an increase in the output of grain if land (that remains idle) can be transferred from the landlord-households to labour-households where it will be put to more intensive and effective use.

DISTRIBUTION OF THE PRODUCE

In a village economy production is achieved by labour working on land. But claims on the produce are not settled on the basis of effort put in, or in terms of the recognition of needs. The basis of the distribution of the produce, instead, is the property rights on land. In other words, in a village economy the 'Who gets what?' question depends very much on 'Who owns what?' rather than on 'Who does what?' This is the specific feature a village economy which affects the link between control over resources, the combination of resources and labour in production and the definition and settlement of claims on the produce. These are interrelated aspects whose implications can be seen only in terms of that totality. But if we were to look at the process sequentially, it will be as follows: There is initially a definition of the claims to the produce on the basis of the multiplicity of proprietory rights on land, spelt out fairly meticulously as a series of mutual obligations of an unequal nature and made venerable and almost irrevocable by the lapse of time. The combination of land and labour in the technical process of production takes place within such a social milieu. Once production is completed, the claims are settled as already established. If a single principle of distribution is to be discerned it is this: 'To each according to his status as ordained by custom.'

But we must note immediately that the *a priori* definition of claims, and the final settlement of claims are both usually in terms of shares—*pangu* as is expressed in many of our languages—of the total output. The total output itself is determined in the actual process of production. Hence the larger the quantum of output, the larger will be the absolute quantity that any share holder will get, including the persons who put in their labour in productive activity. This is the 'incentive clause' in the agreement: the harder you work, the more will become available to you. That is some consolation. But it is accompanied by the knowledge that the harder you work, more will become available to those who do not work, and that, in the final analysis, everything depends on the initial distribution of land which ensures that those who work hard are those who have received less.

Horizontal and vertical transfers

The distribution of the produce in a village economy is institutionalised through a network of transfer of goods within a larger framework of mutual (but unequal) transactions of goods and services, some though not all of which are bilateral although most are general. These transactions and flows may be divided into two kinds which we shall refer to as *horizontal* and *vertical*.[2]

The basis of the horizontal transfers is the mutual interdependence of the units within a village economy. Underlying that mutual interdependence is the fact that all of them have one thing in common, viz., that they are all dependent on farming whether or not all of them are farmers. Here there is a consideration that *reduces* mutual interdependence and points in the direction of the independence of individual units. This is the fact that they are all producers of the same basic food, let us say grain. Practically all units in a village economy have to be self-sufficient in terms of grain. To this extent, therefore, mutual interdependence is premissed on basic self-sufficiency. But this is not to say that there can be no variety in a village economy. Some units in a village economy may produce other agricultural goods like pulses, vegetables etc. in addition to grain. A few units may even come to concentrate on non-basic agricultural goods. A village economy may also produce (usually will) non-agricultural goods, cloth being the most important. Since clothing is almost as basic as food, it may be that most units will have spinning and weaving as part of their production activity. Frequently there is a sexual division of labour within units that accommodate the two, with the men concentrating on cultivation and the women on spinning and weaving. But if there comes about an *inter-unit* division of labour, between the production of food and of clothing, mutual transfer of these will become necessary in as much as both are necessities of life.

A second area where inter-unit transactions become necessary is where some units come to specialise in services that are necessary for others. These may include the services of blacksmiths and carpenters whose role in farming is quite evident. They may include the services of a goldsmith and an astrologer who may have nothing to do with productive activity, but may be recognised as socially necessary. In instances like these, a village economy must have provision for the transfer of goods, especially grain, to those who perform services recognised as necessary. Such provision is usually in the form of a fixed periodic contribution such as, for instance, some sheaves of grain immediately after harvest, either from each farming unit or from the farming units as a whole.

A third type of transaction is collective in form. We have already seen that the nature of productive activity itself may necessitate inter-unit co-operation which may call for inter-unit transfer of labour from time to time. Another area where inter-unit transfer of labour is frequently practised is in the periodic renewal of the roofs (especially thatched roofs) of dwellings. Practically all units donate labour to get this job done for every dwelling in the village, and the work is done as a collective work, usually ending up with a meal in which everybody has a share.

Two observations may be made about these horizontal inter-unit trans-actions. The first is that all of them are based on, and sanctioned by, custom and the same pattern may continue for generations. That is not surprising. But there is a complementary aspect: the acceptance of what is customary by *everyone*, for whatever reason. It is possible that there are occasional voices of dissent and refusal to fall in line. But while the system prevails intact, those who cannot conform to its norms have no choice except to drop out, and this option will remain limited. Thus the inter-unit transactions in a village economy are built on common consent, whether given willingly or not. Secondly, though these transactions have some of the semblances of exchange, they cannot be, strictly speaking, considered as exchange because they do not have (as we shall see in the next chapter) some of the essential characteristics of exchange, such as the element of *quid pro quo* based on quantitative specifications and considerations of transactions meant to move towards rate determination. The horizontal inter-unit transfers in a village economy are rather like the intra-unit transfers in a rudimentary economy, transfers based almost exclusively on considerations of use values. But at the beginning of this chapter we saw that a village economy provides one of the basic requirements of exchange, viz., the presence of the 'other' indicating that exchange as an economic activity evolves over time, depending on a variety of factors. We may here add one more of those conditions, although a fuller treatment of all these aspects must be postponed until the next chapter. That factor is that the less self-sufficient the units within a village economy are (or become) the easier it will be for exchange to develop. The exchange-like inter-unit transfers and transactions are indications that the units are not strictly self-sufficient and so we may say that a village economy provides some of the crucial conditions of exchange even when it does not become a full-fledged exchange economy.

A major inhibiting factor that prevents the full development of exchange is that, for reasons which are easy to understand, while the exchange of some good for another may become common in a village economy, the sale of land and the use of labour on wage payment does not come about easily. Both these *can* happen, but only rarely. In the case of land, transactions do not become common because ownership may still remain ill-defined and because control over land is control over a bundle of claims of some complexity which cannot easily be reduced to a single item, which is a condition required for easy transactions. The same applies to labour also, in so far as what is commonly described as 'labour' is not just one factor but a bundle of skills. But in the case of labour there is another consideration. Only where there is a fairly well-established system of exchange of goods, and in particular exchange of the necessities of life (sometimes also referred to as 'wage-goods') will a worker find it worthwhile—or even possible—to work for wages. What would he do with wages if he cannot procure the wage-goods that he requires? Hence where some units in a village economy have to provide their labour to other units, they will want to get a share in the produce, or some rights on land which, as we have already seen, are basically means to lay claims on the produce.

With that comment we can turn to the second kind of transfer in a village economy which we have described as the 'vertical' transfer. We have seen that a village economy is something of a hierarchical system. There is a social component to this hierarchy. This may be lord-and-vassal arrangement of European feudalism or the caste system of the traditional Indian village economy. We have seen also that these social arrangements have their bearings on the economy to the extent that 'economy' and 'society' can be separated in a village economy. In our treatment of the vertical transfer in a village economy we shall concentrate on the economic dimension of the hierarchy.

The vertical transfer is the transfer from the actual producers to the rentier class, that we have already come across, for which the basis is the claims to the produce proposed by the latter based on their property rights. Let us note that, as in the case of horizontal transfers, the vertical transfer is sanctioned by custom and has the common consent of all. Otherwise it is difficult to see how such a transfer which appears to be patently unjust comes to have legitimacy.

Generation, appropriation and utilisation of surplus

However, the nature of the vertical transfer is very different from that of the horizontal transfer which can be given a kind of 'mutual aid' interpretation. If the vertical transfer is to take place, the actual producers should be producing a surplus over what they themselves require for survival. It is this surplus (all or part of it) that gets transferred to 'the lord above.' The rationale that is put forward may be that the lord has provided his land to the cultivator, or that the lord offers him protection, and that therefore is entitled to a share in the produce. Whatever may be the case, the fact remains that it is the difference between what the cultivator actually produces and what is necessary for his subsistence that gets transferred and that the 'share' of the non-producers is palpably the surplus that the producers generate.

Those who appropriate the surplus and also those who lend intellectual support to them will certainly argue that, after all, the cultivator is not able to produce anything by himself and that he needs land as a 'factor of production' for him to produce anything at all; and that therefore a share of the produce must go to land as its share as rent. Two comments need to be made about this view. The claim that the cultivator by himself cannot produce anything is, no doubt, true. And certainly he is dependent on land. But he is also dependent on other provisions of nature such as sunshine and rain. But no part of the produce is claimed as the share of these contributions of nature. Only land makes a claim and hence that claim cannot be for the part that land contributes towards production. The difference between land on the one hand, and sunshine and rain on the other is that certain social arrangements make it possible for land to be owned by some and to be excluded from others. Hence the share that is claimed for land as rent is not for its contribution to production, but arises through the fact of ownership. In other words, land offers an opportunity for a cultivator to exercise his labour in productive activity and the ownership of land offers to a non-producer the possibility to make a claim on what is produced. Secondly, even granting this aspect of ownership, the legitimacy of the claim of a non-producer to ownership of land which is a means of production does not get established because ownership can belong to the producer himself.

There is, therefore, no claim that a non-producer can make to a share in the produce except through the institution over property rights. Thus we see again that the basis of the vertical transfer of the surplus generated by the producer to the 'lord' is the claim made by the latter based on property rights. Which shows also that property rights are not the rights of people over things as they are sometimes interpreted, but the right of some people over other people via certain kinds of social arrangements to exercise control over resources. The crucial role of land, the property rights in land, in a village economy once again becomes manifest.

We must note also that the generation of surplus (by the producers) and its appropriation (by non-producers who take the appellation of *land-lords*) can take place in a less obvious manner also. Where a landlord gives part of his land for a farmer to cultivate for his subsistence, in return for which the latter must provide labour to cultivate the 'lord's' land, there is again surplus generation and its appropriation, though it does not appear as a transfer of the produce. What happens in this case is that it is the cultivator's surplus generating capacity (a part of his labour time) that is appropriated by the 'lord,' but in essence the phenomenon is a variant of surplus appropriation. So are the different forms of tenancies we have seen.

In the light of this understanding of the nature of surplus generation and appropriation we can reinterpret the differences in the economic calculus of the X–type households (resource-poor worker households) and the Y–type households (resource-rich non-working households). The main interest of the former will be to get as much *output* as it can; the latter's concern will be to get as much *surplus* as it can. It will not be surprising if as a result of this difference Y–type households come to think of production itself as the creating of opportunities to appropriate the surplus. Under the circumstances, production which we saw earlier as the interaction of human beings with nature may appear to get meta-morphosed as the domination of one set of human being over others.

Now that we have seen how surplus is generated and appropriated in a village economy, we must see how it gets utilised. Obviously, part of the surplus that the 'lords' appropriate will be used for their consumption which certainly will be of a higher order than that of those below. Since one form of surplus appropriation is indirectly through the appropriation of labour-power, what usually happens is that the land of the 'lords' will have considerable variety in production. They will have more than grain produced in their fields—pulses, vegetables and fruits for instance—so that a more varied consumption pattern becomes possible for them.

Another part of the appropriated surplus will be spent on supporting a large retinue of people. These may be of different kinds. One group of people will be rendering personal services to the 'lords', military services when necessary. A second group of people will be permitted to concentrate their attention on the arts and literary works. A third group will be engaged in the production of goods that are not produced down below, especially luxury goods which the 'lords' can enjoy directly or trade with others. And, of course, another part of the surplus gets converted into the construction of monuments, buildings for worship, buildings for public purposes etc.

In all these ways the surplus generated in a village economy gets transformed into goods and services that are not part of the production processes down below. In this sense many village economies of the past have become noted for their literary and artistic works, their exquisite luxury goods and their many buildings of beauty and strength. But these take place in a very different circle altogether, far above the normal run of things. Indeed, one of the distinguishing features of a village economy (in contrast to a capitalist economy which we shall examine in later chapters) is that the surplus generated in it does not at all, or does very little to, alter the pattern of production below, but sets up production processes of a different kind (in particular non-agricultural production) in another sphere of the economy. A village economy, therefore, is a kind of dual economy in a technical sense functioning at two levels—large numbers struggling for survival at the bottom level and small minority revelling in luxury and adventures at the top—linked together through peculiar social organisations. Truly has an author said that systems of this kind meant, 'the rigorous economic subjection of a host of humble folk to a few powerful men' (Bloch, 1965, II: 443).

Urban economy

We may note that it is not necessary for the lords to be physically present within the village. Indeed, since productive activity in the upper level is not land-related unlike in the lower level and since the social life of the 'lords' and their retinue is distinctly different from that of the working people in the village, there is a natural propensity for the settlement of the higher sector to be located somewhat away from the village. These settlements constitute the beginnings of urban development and of what may be designated the *city economy* or the *urban economy*. It is interesting to note that a village economy, thus, gives rise to an urban economy which is, in a way, its anti-thesis. As can be seen, an urban economy will have a functioning which is very different from that of the rural component of the village economy. For one thing, it is not concerned with agriculture and the production of food which makes a world of difference between it and the village or rural economy on which, however, it has to depend. The urban economy also has many of the conditions necessary to emerge as essentially an exchange economy. With all of these the dualism mentioned above begins to also become more clearly pronounced. The rural economy is characterised by physical labour on land: it is agricultural, with a kind of reciprocity arising from that kind of a set-up and the main concern of its members being that of survival: the urban economy, by contrast, is non-agricultural with less of an accent on physical labour; it also has a sense of affluence distinctly different from the ethos of the rural economy. And the fact that the ease and the indulgence of the urban economy is based substantially on the appropriation of the surplus from the rural economy makes the urban settlements the epitome of exploitation. For this reason, the town and country divide has been one of the major themes in economic analysis from very early times. But it can be seen that the problem really is not one of habitations and that what appears as the rural-urban divide is a reflection of deeper economic issues.

Authority from above

There is one more aspect of the distribution of the produce of a village economy that we must touch upon. The fact that the village economy is not spatially confined to the geographical territory of the village, but also encompasses, though not fully, the urban economy that it gives rise to is of further analytical significance. It shows that a village economy is not necessarily an isolated entity. Just as the households in a village economy are its sub-economies, the village economy, in turn, can be viewed as a sub-economy within a larger entity. Historically, more often than not, this has been the case even where that larger entity has been a rather nebulous one. If, for instance, we set aside the temporal question for a moment, that larger entity would naturally be the national economy of which the village economy can be considered to be a constituent unit. But historically national economies emerged only after the village economies, as we have characterised them in this chapter, practically disintegrated. However, it is right to say that village economies have practically always been under the suzerainty of some higher and external authority. In medieval Europe it was alternatively the monarch, the emperor and the pope. This shows that while the authority was from above, it was also rather remote. The same was true in the Indian context also.

Whatever may have been the pattern, the economic significance of this remote, but not invisible, authority from above is that it too became a claimant on the produce of the village economy. The claim could simply be that, as in the case of a conqueror, he was the owner of all land as long as there was no one to challenge him. And on the basis of that ownership, he could put forward a claim to the produce which in the final analysis, had to come from the actual producer, though it could and usually would pass through several hands. This would be the tax component in the vertical transfer in the village economy set-up. But a remote authority would not go round collecting the tax from all the producers. Tax collection would be subcontracted through a welter of intermediaries some of whom at least would also have claims of rent on the producer. In fact in most instances it would be difficult to draw a distinction between rent and tax under these circumstances. Even if it could be drawn it would not make much of a difference. For, as noted already, both would have to come from the surplus of the producer extracted from him under different pretexts by different agents.

The term 'extracted' is used advisedly. For the taking away of surplus from the actual producer by those above him was not only appropriation in a technical sense, but frequently involved coercion and physical threats of various kinds. This would be particularly true where, for whatever reason, the requirements of those placed above (especially of that remote authority) would go up. Under some conditions it would be the need to provide for public works such as major irrigation systems which would be considered to be beneficial to the producers themselves. It could be to fight a war, or to make a payment to buy peace from a threatening outsider. And, of course, it could be for more riotous living. While custom would normally regulate the labourers of a village economy and the horizontal transfers associated with it, the aboveness and the vertical transfer could easily become capricious especially because of the undefined and undefinable element of the tax component in it. Harassment of the actual producer in various forms and by numerous intermediaries for additional collections, in the form of the produce or compulsory labour contributions, would be a fairly regular feature of a village economy and of its transfer mechanism.

The fact that taxes are, or have to be, frequently paid in kind has a somewhat unexpected but easily understandable consequence. Although in a political sense a village economy is subject to a remote central authority, a (national) economy of which village economies are the constituent units or sub-economies have to be substantially decentralised in an economic sense. This is because while the tax is ultimately supposed to reach that distant central authority, goods and labour in terms of which the tax is paid cannot easily be carried too far in a spatial sense. They tend to get congregated in different parts of the empire, especially in or around the urban economy (wherein also dwell the soldiers, retinue and the retainers of the monarch or emperor) thus reinforcing the potential of the urban economy to grow and diversify. A political consequence of this kind of formation is that whatever may be the nature of the centralised authority, it has a built-in bias in favour of different shades of anarchy. Consequently the society in which a village economy is situated is one that is in a state of flux. That is the characteristic feature of its social framework.

THE TRANSFORMATION OF A VILLAGE ECONOMY

We have seen that a village economy, whose essential features we have tried to capture in this chapter, is the economic formation that has historically dominated human civilisation. Its concrete manifestations have been time-and-space-specific; but in essential features—a land and agricultural economy of reciprocal but unequal obligations and a social world of over-lapping claims and powers with the subjugation of the majority of humble producers by a minority of non-producers or rentiers—it had continued from the very early days of settled civilisation till it was replaced by the capitalist economy. That process of replacement has been fairly completed in some parts of the world, but is still the socio-economic reality in many parts of the globe, including our country.

In the analysis in the earlier sections, we have concentrated on its elements of stability or resilience. But we have also touched upon, especially in the immediately preceding section, some of the components that led to its transformation. Now, the transformation of an economy or social formation is more of a time-and-space-specific phenomenon than what may be described as its structure. Hence one ought not to generalise on how a transformation *takes* place. The best one can do is to indicate how a particular transformation *took* place, although there are possibilities of differences of interpretation and opinion. For instance, the question of how feudalism in Western Europe gave place to capitalism has been and continues to be one of the most heatedly debated controversies in economics.[3]

So, in turning to a treatment of the transformation of a village economy we are entering risky territory. But here, there is an advantage in confining ourselves to analysis (rather than to history) for our task is to identify some possible or even plausible factors and combination of factors that account for the transformation of a village economy. We shall initiate such a limited treatment here, which we shall pick up again in our discussion of how a capitalist economy emerges.

Limited opportunities
A village economy is very much embedded within a social mould, but it emerges as a fairly distinct entity within that mould unlike in the case of the rudimentary economy. And yet a village economy is still something of

a constricted economy which is what gives it the kind of stability we have noted. Why is it so constrained? If we can find an answer to this question, we may also get some clues regarding its metamorphosis. Consider the following observation of a scholar who has studied the manifestations of feudalism in different parts of the world. About a feudal land-holder he says:

His land was held as a family trust, or it was entailed, or it was subject to a feudal superior... The feudal lord could not change his occupation. If he was free to transfer his resources from one activity to another, whether in pursuit of gain or to maximise any of his wants, his rationality had to be applied to a different and more restricted set of variables. The choice was between animals or arable, between one crop or one beast and another... For most medieval lords massive transport costs meant that the only markets were local, and in consequence the only prices, wildly fluctuating. Figures were not available to make calculations of comparative profit. The economics of production and marketing in agriculture were much more difficult... (Critchley, 1978: 168).

These observations are about landlords; they would be more valid in the case of ordinary peasants. They point to one crucial factor. A village economy is one of limited opportunities. It is land-based economy with the use of land almost completely confined to cultivation. Within cultivation too the options are limited. This situation arises because of two complementary factors. On the one hand the technology in production (and in a wider sense the productive forces) remain at a low level restricting the level of output. On the other the demand for goods also remains low and limited partly because custom regulates consumption and partly because total population remains stable. The limited role of markets and exchange is another constricting factor. And the separation between the lower and the upper levels substantially determines the options for the use of the surplus, making it particularly difficult for production at the lower level to experience any major change.

Factors in the transformation

And yet we have also seen that a village economy carries within it the seeds of its transformation. The unavoidable growth of the urban economy and the juxtaposition of the antithetical features of the rural economy and the urban economy are some of these seeds. The 'dynamic opposition' of the two, as Anderson (1978: 150) says, with the urban economy of increasing production and exchange, the greater freedom of operation within it and the role of a group of producers and traders not constricted by customs brings about changes in the village economy as a whole. For instance, if the demand for certain kinds of non-agricultural goods increases as a result of trade with other economies (let us say the demand for woollen textiles as was the case in England) then, for the first time land will come to have non-agricultural uses and hence its use in agriculture will have an *opportunity cost*. If the use of land for sheep-rearing (for the production of woollen clothing) becomes a more attractive proposition than its use in cultivation, then other changes will follow. Those in the village community who have the power to do so will take advantage of the ill-defined property rights and begin to stake their exclusive claims to what until then have been considered as commons. They will enforce their exclusive rights by 'enclosing' their land and throwing out those who were cultivating the commons or the animals that were grazing on them. Overall there will be a tendency to redefine the nature of relationships that constituted the village economy in which increasing monetisation that comes about as a consequence of increasing exchange will also play a part. Thus, changes in the patterns of ownership, of production and of transfers and the patterns of relationships may all come about in the village economy, thereby also changing what we have indicated as its essential features.

Another possibility of the transformation of a village economy is through changes in demographic features—either a major increase or a substantial decrease in the size of population. In either case, there will be a change in the relative resource-labour ratio. If that ratio turns out to be adverse as a result of an increase in population, either more land has to be brought under cultivation—which may result in the reduction in the commons or of forests—which in turn may lead to changes in the patterns of claims; or it may alter the production-transfer circuits, especially the vertical transfers, with the attendant social consequences including more intensified pressures from above. If the resource-labour ratio changes in the opposite direction because of a decrease in population, methods of production may have to undergo changes to respond to labour scarcity. This again will have a bearing on ownership patterns and the structure of claims.

Such changes, whatever may be their sources and nature, should not, however, be dealt with at the macro level of the village economy alone. It is in the nature of the transformation of the village economy that it must be analysed in terms of its constituent units, the households, because these are already differentiated from the point of effective control over resources as well as of social standing. Consequently few changes are likely to be neutral in their impact because the units will have different perceptions of the changes and different abilities to respond to them. We shall, once again, go back to the X–type and Y–type households, the former (to recall) experiencing resource constraint and the latter labour constraint.

If the P/W ratio within some of the X–type households is increasing over time, they will be pushed more and more to the lower limit, making it extremely difficult for them to discharge their vertical transfer obligations initially and then forcing them down to the barest survival level. On the other hand, the Y–type households already have the resource potential to increase production and they may, therefore, be more responsive to external stimuli to increase and diversify production. Both types may benefit by certain kinds of opportunities, but changes that repudiate the customary claims of the peasants (such as closures of the commons) will adversely affect the X–type and may favour the Y–type. Thus, if claims on land get privatised leading to the acceptance of the exclusive concept of owner-ship, peasants who were cultivating land under tenurial conditions may be left with no choice except to become wage-labourers in Y–type house-holds with hardly any bargaining power with regard to wage determination. Not that they will yield without resistance. The period of the transition from feudalism to capitalism, for instance, witnessed many peasant agitations and uprisings when the peasants found their customary rights eroded through the machinations of the larger farmers, landlords and members of the urban economy. The point to emphasise is that the transformation of a village economy is not in its entirety: the process takes place in and through its sub-economies. The micro and macro aspects of the trans-formation may be quite different. A grasp of both is needed to gain an understanding of what is going on.

VILLAGE ECONOMY: A ROUND UP

A detailed comparison between the rudimentary economy of the previous chapter and the village economy of this chapter is not necessary, but a few points need to be noted.

The first is that our treatment of the village economy in this chapter is not complete. It has concentrated on the *inter*-unit interactions (a micro analysis) in the general setting of the village economy as a whole (a macro perspective). For the analysis to be complete we must take into account the *intra* unit aspects also. Let us recall that the main economic activity, viz., production takes place *within* the household economies which are the sub-economies or constituent units of the village economy. We have not entered into it because we have set up the village economy as a collec-tion of rudimentary economies. Each household in the village economy will have to decide how it will combine its labour with the resources over which it exercises control; each household also will have to decide how the produce it makes will be shared among its members. We have not entered into these questions because the analysis will proceed more or less along the lines in the previous chapter. But there is a major difference too. Each household unit in a village economy is also subject to influences—opportunities and constraints—that come from outside, or from other units. The internal decision-making will get altered to some extent because of it. But we have seen also that the households are not all alike. We have seen also that the options and constraints that they come to have are also not alike. Hence, there is not anything of a general nature that we can say about the patterns of interaction between the internal organisation of the units and the external factors operating on them. We shall only say that it is very unlikely that the distinction between the internal and external considerations will get completely wiped out. For the rest we will have to make a case-by-case analysis of the patterns of that interaction.

Secondly, we note that in the context of the village economy, the 'economy' emerges much more distinctly than in the case of the rudimentary economy although it still remains heavily circumscribed by or deeply embedded in, its overall societal framework. The 'orchestration' aspect that we touched upon at the end of the last chapter, therefore, becomes more difficult to deal with. Custom still plays a crucial role in that respect. But we have seen that 'command'—and command through remote control—frequently overrides custom, not in all respects, but in terms of the economic aspects, especially the claims on the produce which, in the long run, will influence both patterns of control over resources and production processes.

Thirdly, the element of domination and subordination that we saw in the context of the rudimentary economy becomes more pronounced in the village economy taking an *inter*-unit manifestation (in addition to the *intra*-unit manifestation which may continue). In particular, we have seen that the environment, interests and calculations of the rentier class are likely to be very different from those of the ordinary cultivators or peasants as a class. This class distinction does not yet become stark in the village economy because of the common considerations that the two groups continue to have and because of the social affinities they may share and the fact that they are all huddled together in the same limited geographical area. However, we have also seen that conflicts of interest do become pronounced especially when the command elements or external factors interfere with the superficial stability and 'harmony' that custom provides.

There is a final issue we wish to touch upon. Are village economies self-sufficient? The question is significant because there is a powerful body of opinion in our country that village economies in this country, at least, have been self-sufficient in the past and that the future economic organisation of the country must be a revival of that past. It will be noticed that the question has both an empirical and a logical dimension and we can address ourselves only to the latter which, of course, will have a bearing on the former.

In a logical sense there are some factors that lend support to a positive answer to the question posed. The first is that the village economy is one that concentrates on the production of the basic necessities of life–in particular food. Second, usually a village economy is a geographically isolated and identified entity in a situation where means of transport and communication are extremely limited. A combination of these two factors will suggest that village economies will have some advantage if they can produce all that they require and that normally the conditions under which they operate will tend to make them self-sufficient. However, there are factors that operate in the opposite direction as well, among them the most important being the emergence of the urban economy from the actual functioning of the village economy. And the urban economy makes sense only to the extent that it is different from the (bottom level) rural economy. It has to produce a variety of goods including luxury goods; it has to be an *open* economy. In a macro sense, therefore, trade with other economies is part of a village economy; some exchange within it is also possible. But exchange and trade have only a limited role within a village economy and its openness is also likely to be limited and confined substantially to its upper circuit. Bloch's comment in this regard about the feudal society of the past may apply to all village economies that 'the society of this age was certainly not unacquainted with either buying or selling. But it did not, like our own, live by buying and selling.' (Bloch, 1965, I:67).

NOTES

1. A good account of the physical aspects of production can be seen in Hayami and Kikuchi, 1981. This book also has an extensive bibliography on issues relating to village economy.
2. For a discussion of these transactions in the Indian context in the past refer to Ch. 8.
3. On the transition from feudalism to capitalism see Sweezy, 1978; Holton, 1985; Dobb, 1947, especially Ch. 2.

   The following works also may be useful in understanding different aspects of village economies: Scot, 1976; Rosen, 1975.

4

Exchange

Exchange arises out of productive activity and is based on the surplus that is generated through it. Exchange itself does not generate surplus, but often becomes a method for the appropriation of surplus. Starting out as barter between two production units in the quest for use values, exchange soon leads to the recognition of an appropriate medium which becomes money and which leads to a substantial expansion of exchange as an activity. It also gives rise to traders who are specialists in exchange whose motivation becomes the accumulation of exchange value.

If exchange arises from productive activity, its spread–the process of commoditisation–tremendously influences productive activity as well; it makes it possible to have more extensive division of labour, activating the slack in the economy and by making production responsive to prices and costs. Exchange also leads to a sharper identification of ownership and comes to be directed by the distribution of resource power in the economy. It also affects the definition and settlements of claims. Thus the spread of exchange brings about a major transformation in the economy.

While exchange has a tendency to spread and thereby to commoditise more and more goods and services, it never reaches out to take over the economic system fully. Every society sets limits to exchange and its institutional manifestation, the market. In this sense there is no such thing as a *free market economy* although it is frequently paraded as a highly canvassed ideology.

In Chapter 3 we saw how exchange emerges in a village economy, especially in its urban component, and how it contributes to its transformation. The rudimentary economy was depicted as one with no exchange at all and the village economy as one with limited exchange. But in most modern economies exchange is one of the most important economic activities and, perhaps, the most obvious one. And it is their participation in exchange–buying and selling, earning and spending - that makes people conscious of their involvement in the economy. In the next chapter which deals with the capitalist economy, we shall see that the working of an economy in which exchange plays a major part is fundamentally different from one where its role is limited. It is, therefore, necessary to understand the nature of exchange itself and its impact on other economic activities. That is the theme of this chapter.

Exchange as an activity, especially when it is mediated through money, has a deceptively simple appearance about it. For most of us, and for most of the time, exchange means getting from a shop or trader an article for which we pay money. But the discussions in the preceding two chapters will have shown that that was not always so. The use of money is a relatively recent phenomenon (a few thousand years, possibly) in the long history of humankind. Also, exchange itself is something that has evolved over-time from economies where it did not take place at all, or in which it took place but seldom. Similarly, even in economies which can claim to be based substantially on exchange principles, and where the use of money is quite common, it is not difficult to come across instances of exchange which are not mediated through any form of money. These considerations indicate two things. They show, first, that however ubiquitous exchange may be in some economies, exchange is certainly not the central economic activity. This needs to be emphasised because some economists and economic theories insist that all economic activities are basically exchange categories. Secondly, exchange itself is not the same kind of activity under all circumstances: it has changed over time, and even in a contemporary situation exchange takes different forms under different circumstances. In this chapter we shall try to see what some of these forms are and under what conditions they manifest themselves.

RUDIMENTARY FORM OF EXCHANGE

In order to understand the nature of exchange at its most elementary level, consider two economic units that do not have exchange *within* them, but go in for exchange *between* them. Both parties are, therefore, rudimentary economies of the kind analysed in Chapter 2 which are concerned with the generation of use values. Karl Marx, who among all leading economists has made one of the most incisive analyses of exchange and its transformation, indicates how this happens. 'Different communities find different means of production, and different means of subsistence in their natural environment. Hence their modes of production and of living, and their products are different. It is this spontaneously developed difference which, when different communities come into contact, calls forth the mutual exchange of products...' (Marx, 1971, I: 332). These may be thought of as the objective factors of exchange under those conditions. But for exchange to take place, a subjective aspect must also be present. The two communities must have different assessments of the use values of the goods that they exchange.

Nature of barter

Let us try to be more specific regarding these matters and consider two rudimentary economies A and B as the parties to the exchange. Let us assume that both parties produce enough grain for their needs, but A produces some pulses in addition and B produces some bananas. These are produced mainly for use, but A finds that it has more pulses than it needs and B also finds that it has some bananas to spare. Under these circumstances a banana-pulse exchange *can* take place. But whether it will take place or not will depend on some more conditions being satisfied. The first is that A must be aware of the use value of bananas and similarly B must be aware of the use value of pulses. Secondly, A who has pulses to offer must be willing to take bananas in exchange *and* B who has bananas to offer must be willing to accept pulses in return. This condition is sometimes referred to as the *double coincidence of needs*. The third is that the quantity of pulses that A is willing to offer for bananas must be the same as the quantity of pulses that B is willing to accept for bananas and *vice-versa*. It can be seen that condition two is a rather difficult one, but it is the crucial one among the three on which the possibility of exchange decisively depends. It can be seen also that the condition is unavoidable where goods have to be directly exchanged for other goods, without a commonly accepted medium of exchange. But that is what rudimentary exchange is—it is barter. Barter exchange is not between a buyer and a seller. Each party to the exchange has to be simultaneously a buyer *and* a seller. A is the seller of pulses and the buyer of bananas; B, correspondingly, is the seller of bananas and the buyer of pulses.

If conditions one and two mentioned above are not satisfied, A and B will not engage themselves in exchange and so to proceed further we shall assume that the two have been satisfied and take up the third for further consideration. The third condition is not likely to be satisfied straightaway, but if the parties are interested in the exchange they will enter into negotiations. The negotiations will be in the form of biddings. A must bid for bananas in terms of pulses, and B must bid for pulses in terms of bananas. To begin with A is likely to offer a small quantity of pulses for a large quantity of bananas, but B will want to get as large a quantity of pulses as possible for the quantity of bananas it offers. The biddings, therefore, are more like bargaining as we normally understand the expression, but still with a difference. The parties concerned are not bargaining about prices— at least not directly. They are bargaining about quantities of the two commodities. But every time a bid for a certain quantity of bananas is made in terms of a certain quantity of pulses, and *vice-versa*, the bids reflect or have implicit in them some price ratios. In fact the quantity of pulses: quantity of banana ratio is a price, the price of pulses in terms of bananas (rather than in terms of rupees). The pulse:banana ratios offered by A and B are likely to diverge initially (that is, the third condition is unlikely to be satisfied in the first bid) and so no transaction actually takes place. The bids are then repeated, each side making adjustments to reduce the gap. If the gap is completely eliminated, that is, if the ratios of quantities offered by the two sides turn out to be the same, then the transaction takes place with the agreed quantities of pulses and bananas changing hands.

The agreed quantities also 'reveal' the agreed prices–of pulses in terms of bananas and bananas in terms of pulses. (A numerical example is given in the notes to this chapter.)[1] This means that the quantity determination (of the two goods) for exchange also results in a price determination because every bid in terms of quantities also carries an implicit price with it. Thus exchange can be thought of as an activity simultaneously determining the quantities (of the two goods) that will change hands and the price at which the transaction will take place. In the case of barter this is achieved through biddings or bargaining. Bargaining is an unavoidable part of barter. We shall later see whether bargaining plays a part in other forms of exchange also.

Some other aspects of barter are also worth noting. Barter as a form of exchange is the relationship between two sets of owners: the relationship between the owner of pulses and the owner of bananas in the case above. This will be seen to be an important aspect of all forms of exchange. Exchange, therefore, is a way of expressing ownership, the right to alienate that which is one's own. As a form of social relationship exchange is, thus, one between two parties who are both 'at the same level', as both are owners and enter into the transaction in their capacity as owners. In this sense exchange is a distinct form of social relationship as can be seen if it is compared with other forms of relationships we have already noted. In a village economy a typical form of social or economic relationship is that between a landlord and a tenant where the landlord is certainly at a 'higher' level. More obvious is the relationship between a slave owner and his slaves. All forms of patron–client relationships too are between parties at two different levels. In the exchange relationship there are clear distinctions that can be noticed and which form the basis of exchange. Thus, A and B *must differ* in their assessment of pulses and bananas if they are to enter into exchange, but they enter into the exchange relationship as owner of pulses and of bananas respectively. This formal equality in 'status' is important because pre-exchange relationships tend to be hierarchical. On the other hand, it must be noted also that in many instances the equality of relationship in exchange tends to be a mere formality, because parties to the exchange may differ considerably in their bargaining power and that will have much impact on how the terms of the exchange are settled.

In as much as exchange is a relationship entered into freely by two parties, both of them must also be considered to benefit by the transactions. It is possible that at least one party may feel that he did not get as good a deal as he deserved or desired from an exchange, but he had the freedom not to enter into the transaction at all; and hence if he did, he should be considered to have benefited by it. Here, again, it is important to examine whether the freedom that a party has to refuse to enter into an act of exchange is real or not. We shall consider this aspect again in Chapter 5 and in Part II, particularly Chapter 9.

TRANSFORMATION OF EXCHANGE[2]

Barter as the rudimentary form of exchange is not a thing of the past. It tends to appear in many ways, usually of an informal nature as when two friends exchange a shirt which is the wrong size for one of them for a cassette which the other finds uninteresting. As a one-time transaction between friends there may not be any bargaining or price determination here. Barter may also appear on a more calculated basis as when a doctor who needs legal advice and a lawyer who requires medical help may enter into an arrangement to exchange their services on a *quid pro quo* basis, the motivation in both cases being to avoid payment of taxes. Such arrangements are not uncommon even in highly monetised economies. Barter is also practised between trading countries at the international level.

However, no one will argue that barter is a common form of exchange these days. This is because exchange as an activity has a tendency to move out of its rudimentary form and to metamorphose itself. We need to look into this aspect of exchange too. In order to do so it is necessary to introduce a concept that will be frequently referred to from now on, the concept of *commodity*. A commodity is an item (service) that enters into an exchange transaction or is produced to be exchanged. An item that enters into exchange must obviously have some use value. It is very unlikely that anyone will purchase or procure it unless it has some use. But an item that is exchanged comes to have another kind of value in addition, viz., exchange value. Now, use value is essentially the *qualitative* aspect of goods which is why it is not easy to assess and why there will be a difference of opinion about it. On the other hand, exchange value is always a ratio (the quantity of one item exchanged for the quantity of another item) and is, therefore, a pure quantity. A commodity or an item that is exchanged, thus has two attributes: it has a use value which is qualitative and does not lend itself to easy assessment or comparison and an exchange value which is a quantity, but can be expressed only in comparison with some other commodity.

Barter as C–C form of exchange
Barter is a commodity to commodity transaction which we shall refer to as the *C–C form of exchange*. Both pulses and bananas get commoditised

as they enter into exchange and come to have a new value apart from the use values they already have. However, the C–C form of exchange is not meant to establish exchange value between pulses and bananas. Because of the condition of the double coincidence of needs that governs all C–C forms of exchange, each act of exchange is independent and separate and gets 'extinguished' as soon as it is over. But there is nothing to prevent the two parties from' entering into exchange of the same goods or some other goods at some other time. Or each of the parties may take on another party for a different transaction. Thus a series of bilateral transactions can take place thereby increasing the frequency of exchange. Even so, unlike some other forms of exchange which we shall come across, the C–C form of exchange is intrinsically limited in scope.

Related to it is the fact that in the C–C form of exchange the two parties involved are very closely drawn into the transaction, and hence it becomes a highly personalised activity. For better or for worse, barter as a form of exchange comes to be centred more on the parties than on the commodities. In a way this is not surprising because exchange is not a transfer of commodities or a physical activity, but a social activity of transactions between two parties (individuals, groups, countries etc.). The rudimentary form of exchange reminds us of this important aspect.

The more extensive C–C transactions become, the greater will be the tendency to look for a generally accepted medium of exchange. The choice of such a medium is not an easy one. The requirements of the object to become the medium of exchange are fairly evident. It must be durable so that exchange today and sometime in the future can be mediated through it. But its carrying cost must be low so that keeping it over time does not turn out to be difficult and expensive. It must be easily divisible to enable exchange of different commodities in different quantities. It must be in common use so that anyone wishing to enter into exchange will have access to it. And it must be generally acceptable. These conditions show why the choice of an appropriate object to become the medium of exchange is not easy and different kinds of goods have been tried out— cattle, shells, precious metal etc. Among the qualities that the medium of exchange must possess, the crucial one is acceptability, and in fact, whatever is generally accepted for this purpose becomes 'money'. Whatever it is that gets recognised as money not only facilitates exchange as an activity, but also becomes the common denominator in terms of which all exchange ratios can be expressed (one unit of this good exchanging for x,y,z units of other goods) and which will, therefore, establish the exchange ratios between any two goods that enter into exchange. It, thus, becomes the *universal equivalent*. When this happens the C–C exchange gets transformed into C–M–C *exchange* (commodity–money–commodity). Exchange of two commodities which was a simultaneous activity in the C–C form now gets split up into two: the exchange of the first commodity for money and then the exchange of the money for the second commodity. Exchange still remains an attempt to get use values from goods, but through the mediation of money.

From C–C to C–M–C

But the transformation is not merely technical. It has very significant social consequences, much more than making exchange widespread which it does. No longer is it necessary that someone who has pulses, but is looking for bananas should find another who has bananas and is searching for pulses for exchange to take place. Pulses can now be 'sold' for money, and with money bananas can be 'bought'. The distinction between buyer and seller gets established: the party that enters into exchange with money becomes buyer and the party that comes into exchange with the commodity becomes the seller. The same party, consequently, can be a buyer in one instance and a seller in another, but not simultaneously in one transaction. Even more significant is the fact that the direct personal dealings between two parties which was the requirement of the C–C form of exchange disappears. The seller of pulses need not and may not spend the entire proceeds of it on bananas, but may buy—apart from bananas—salt, chillies, oil, pots and pans and many other things. This means that more and more goods and more and more parties are drawn into exchange and a kind of chain reaction is set in motion. Thus, with the mediation of money, exchange tends to 'burst' its local bonds and the limited nature of bilateralism and turns into a widespread and multilateral activity involving many parties and commodities. Exchange of the C–M–C type, therefore, 'breaks through all local and personal bonds inseparable from direct barter...and develops a whole network of social relations spontaneous in their growth and entirely beyond the control of the actors' (Marx, 1971, I: 114).

Exchange itself marked a major step in social development. Exchange mediated through money is another significant social and economic transformation.

The introduction of money into the exchange process and the generalisation of exchange resulting from it has certain other consequences too. Money which emerged as a facilitator of exchange itself undergoes change. The basis of exchange, we may recall, is the alienation of goods. Money that comes to occupy the centre of exchange soon becomes the most alienable good, especially where the item chosen for money does not have any intrinsic use value of its own (shells, rather than cattle, for instance). Indeed, the less use value that it has, the more suited it will be to play its role as the mediator of exchange, because it can become a pure quantity without any qualitative attribute and hence concentrate on the quantitative specification of exchange values.

Traders as specialists in exchange

While money specialises in this function, the C–M–C exchange also generates specialists in exchange. The C–C type of exchange is basically a transaction between two producers without a medium or mediator between them. When exchange comes to be mediated through money, it gives rise to mediators as well. Exchange does not have to be between producers any more: it can be between a producer and a non-producer; it can be between two non-producers. All these are possible as long as those who specialise in exchange–buying goods in order to sell them using money—are available to facilitate the transactions. Exchange of the C–M–C type, therefore, gives rise to a new group of people in the economy, the facilitators of exchange—traders or merchants. These specialists in, or facilitators of, exchange perform some very distinct functions. If they buy goods to sell, they will store them too and that is one of their functions. The C–M–C exchange, we have seen, enables the seller of pulses to buy many goods (and not just bananas as in the C–C case). It will be advantageous to this party if, instead of having to hunt for the producers of each one of these goods, he could obtain them from just one party, the trader. So, the trader is the one who knows where the goods are available. Equally, he would know also who are likely to need them. The trader, therefore, becomes a convenient mediator both for sellers and buyers. He is a 'contact person' and hence stores not only goods, but information as well. As a matter of fact, storing of and sorting-out information is one of the major functions of the trader because if he has the information, he can put many sellers and buyers into contact without having to store the goods. It is not surprising that as a specialist go-between he comes to have a lot of information about parties and wares that he deals with.

One of the welcome consequences of this is that a great deal of the informational inadequacies of the C–C form of exchange can be reduced in the C–M–C form. There is someone who knows, perhaps not everything, but a good deal, and he can make the information available to the parties, and the parties are no longer just two, but manifold in number. Thus, as exchange itself expands when it changes into the C–M–C form, information too can spread, further facilitating exchange. At the same time we must note too that the trader is under no obligation to disseminate information, and he certainly has no commitment to reduce informational asymmetries among parties to the exchange, those who sell to him and those who buy from him. After all, he now becomes a (third) party to every exchange and thus can derive benefits by distorting information, withholding information and so on. He would, for instance, want to make use of information (or misinformation) to buy cheap and sell dear.

To understand the role of trader further we must consider what he is after. When exchange is of the C–C form, the two parties turn to exchange in their quest for use values. But the trader as a specialist in exchange has no special concern for use values as such. Rather, his interest is in exchange values. When he mediates between selling and buying he does not come to share the use values of the goods he deals with. But he can come to have a share in the exchange values by selling at a higher exchange value what he buys. Thus the specialists in exchange also emerge as those whose primary concern is with exchange values. Traders, or merchants therefore, are a new kind of economic agent, distinctly different from those whom we have seen so far. The transformation of exchange from C–C to C–M–C, consequently brings in major changes in the economy.

It seems reasonable to say that the expansion of exchange resulting from the use of money as medium may give rise to merchants as specialists in trade. It also seems reasonable to suggest that as specialists in trade, merchants have no direct concern with use values, and that they concentrate on generating and expanding exchange values. But we have seen that exchange value is a qualityless, pure quantity. Why would anyone want to go after a mere quantity represented by that medium, money? The answer to this apparent puzzle is that money, though it is only a mere quantity is not totally worthless. It is a condensed command over commodities, goods and thus use values. Thus, paradoxical as it may appear, what a useless thing does in fact is to confer command over useful things. In other words, though money may appear to be nothing, in another sense it can also appear to be everything, the only thing worth going after because it places everything else at one's disposal.

M–C–M form of exchange

Merchants who specialise in exchange become the first group to recognise, that money is not only a medium of exchange, but also a store of value and hence to turn to money-making as their primary concern. This would mean that their wealth and resources also turn out to be in the form of money. We may recall that in economies prior to the emergence of merchants, wealth was (had to be) in the form of specific things–land, grain, cattle, or even slaves for that matter. This is one of the major changes that takes place in the economy as money emerges as a store of value and merchants come to be in pursuit of money.

If so, exchange itself will undergo a further change. Merchants do not enter into exchange with commodities; neither do they want to end up with commodities. They start with money and wish to conclude with money. Hence apart from the C–M–C form, another form of exchange emerges which is of the M–C–M form (Money–Commodity–Money).

At first sight it may appear that the difference between C–M–C and M–C–M types of exchange is only one of ordering. But a closer examination shows that such is not the case. In the C–M–C type, although exchange begins and ends in commodities, the second C cannot be obviously the same as the first one. In the example with which we started, the first C is pulses and the second C bananas for one party and the other way around for the other party. Strictly speaking, therefore, that form of exchange should be expressed as C–C' or C–M–C', to convey that the two Cs are different goods, representing different use values. Whether it is the C–C' form or C–M–C' form, both parties in the transaction are interested in acquiring further use values. It is because they differ in their assessment of use values of C and C' that they enter into exchange. This is quite clear in the C–C' case. In the C–M–C' case too for both parties exchange is a means to achieve use values and money is just a means to facilitate exchange. But the purpose behind exchange changes completely in the M–C–M case. There exchange is no longer an aid to the acquisition of use values because money as such has no use value (except, perhaps, for a miser who gets use value by looking at money, or handling it!). Indeed, the M–C–M form of exchange is a quest for money using commodities as a means to achieve it.

That may look strange. But let us recall that while money does not have use value of its own, it gives to its owners command over (all) commodities and consequently over use values also. And hence the quest for money through exchange may not be as foolish as it may first appear. We must note too that as in the case of the C–M–C exchange, where the first and second Cs cannot be the same, in the M–C–M exchange the M at the beginning and M at the end cannot be the same. Thus, we must denote it by M–C–M'. But the two Cs (in the earlier cases) can be different in terms of their qualities because they are two different goods. This cannot be said about money because it is totally homogeneous and thus incapable of *qualitative* differences. Therefore, the difference between M and M' can only be in terms of *quantity*, and M' must be presumed to be larger than M. We may show this as $M' = M + \Delta M$ where ΔM shows the *addition* to M that comes through the process.

In ordinary parlance this amounts to saying that those who engage in the M–C–M' exchange (traders or merchants) go into exchange to make money, and ΔM, or surplus value as it can be termed is what they are after in each transaction. That helps us to see more clearly the difference between the C–M–C' and the M–C–M' kinds of exchange. The former begins with a sale (C sold for M) and ends with a purchase (C' bought with M) while the latter begins with a purchase (C bought with M) and ends in a sale (C sold for M'). The use of money itself is, therefore, different in the two cases. In the first it is acquired and spent for a purpose other than itself; in the second it initiates and sustains a process augmenting itself. The ΔM that a trader gets in each transaction is soon put into a second transaction generating further ΔM, and then into a third and so on and on generating a circulation. In this process money 'comes out of circulation, enters into it again, preserves and multiplies itself within its circuit, comes back out of it with expanded bulk and begins the same round afresh.' (Marx, 1971, I: 153).

But the difference between the two is not merely a formal one. It is a crucial difference of purpose. The C–M–C' exchange is a method of acquiring more (strictly speaking different kinds of) use value than one has. The M–C–M' exchange is a method to accumulate exchange value. Here we begin to see the distinction between the two basic organising principles that we referred to in Chapter 1 emerging, viz., generation of use value and accumulation of exchange value. The difference between the two is not primarily in the realm of exchange although it gets reflected in the nature of exchange. The difference between the two, as we have already noted, is in the manner in which different economies are organised and orchestrated. The rudimentary economy is organised without any exchange. In the village economy exchange emerges, but is either of the C–C' type or the C–M–C' type where exchange does not play a prominent role in organising the economy. In the capitalist economy which we shall examine in the next chapter the M–C–M' type of exchange finds its home ground and the accumulation of exchange value becomes the organising principle. One reason for this is that when exchange emerges as the M–C–M' type, it tends to become increasingly generalised drawing in more and more goods and services into its domain. This process, is referred to as *commoditisation* and in the next chapter we shall see that in this aggressive commoditisation process exchange is ably assisted by capitalist production. In fact the distinctive feature of the capitalist economy is the synchronisation of exchange and production in the pursuit of money, successive ΔM_s, that is. But, for the moment, let us continue with exchange as such.

How are the varieties of forms of exchange to be interpreted? Do they represent only the historical evolution of exchange or something else? Obviously, there is a chronological aspect in the metamorphosis of exchange from barter into transactions through the medium of money, and then transactions to make money. And yet, as we have already noted, barter as a form of exchange has not completely disappeared even with the extensive use of money. Sometimes it is a matter of convenience; at other times (as in the case of the doctor and the lawyer) one of shrewd calculation. This means that different forms of exchange must be viewed contextually, rather than chronologically, and in order to understand them we must examine the conditions under which they manifest themselves.

Let us look at the most standardised form of exchange, exchange done through the medium of money. Can that at least be thought of as 'exchange, pure and simple'? We know that the answer has to be in the negative, for both C–M–C' and M–C–M' are forms of exchange using money and yet they have different characteristics and implications. A farmer who sells grain to buy fertilisers is engaging in exchange of the C–M–C' form; a merchant who buys grain and sells fertilisers is conducting an exchange transaction of the M–C–M' form. Hence the same transaction (between a farmer and a merchant as parties and grain and fertilisers as commodities) may represent two different forms of exchange. On the other hand, sometimes the same form may have different meanings in different contexts. The M–C–M' form, it has been noted already, can be split into a purchase (represented by M–C) and a sale (represented by C–M). Does that mean that the motivations of a person who buys newspapers for a month (M–C) and then sells them later (C–M) in exchange are the same as those of a merchant who specialises in the M–C–M' form? Once again, it is seen that to understand and interpret exchange it is necessary not only to grasp its logical features, but to set it in the context and conditions under which it takes place.

GENERALISED EXCHANGES

When the frequency of exchange of the C–C form increases, there is a tendency to search for an appropriate medium to facilitate exchange, and when such a medium comes to be accepted it tends to generalise exchange, converting more and more goods and services into commodities. Along with it the generalisation of exchange also has a tendency to increase the number of people selling the same item and the number of people buying the same item. In this sense the transformation of exchange is also from the bilateralism inherent in barter to multilateralism that the mediation of money makes possible. We shall now turn to an examination of the characteristics of generalised exchange.

Generalised exchange and bargaining
One of the questions to consider is whether the generalisation of exchange will eliminate bargaining, which was seen to be an intrinsic aspect of barter, the rudimentary form of exchange. How is bargaining affected when the number of participants in exchange increases? In order to answer this question it is necessary to understand why there is bargaining in the barter form of exchange. Let us go back to the pulses–banana exchange between A and B. In that situation bargaining is based principally on the difficulty in assessing the 'quality' or worth of the goods under consideration. A is

uncertain about the worth of bananas, and B has a similar problem. Indeed, the situation is more complex. A cannot know what B considers the worth of bananas or pulses to be and B too is in the same position. Bargaining is a shot in the dark to make an appraisal of the other party's assessments of the item or items in question. It is not surprising that this happens when transactions are infrequent. But frequency of transactions is not the main issue. Bargaining is related to inadequacy of information or inability to acquire information and is likely to arise when either party to a potential exchange has doubts about (that is, does not have full information regarding) the other party's assessment of the situation. Thus local traders quote very high prices for their wares when they deal with foreign tourists partly because they think that the tourists do not know the worth of the ware and partly because they assume that the tourists are rich and are likely to have a low assessment of their ware, money.

To take another example, a real-estate agent is likely to quote a higher price to a party who, in his assessment, is ignorant or rich or both, than to a party who is well-informed about the worth of properties. Such being the case, we must infer that most instances of exchange are likely to materialise through the process of bargaining. 'Bargaining' may appear to be a bad word, and *negotiations* may be more acceptable. If so, we may conclude that negotiations preceding transactions are quite common and most natural.

Let us pursue this aspect further. We have noted that the basis of bargaining or negotiations is that the two parties have different views about the worth of the goods under consideration which, in turn, is related to the use value or qualitative attribute of the goods. Now, a good may have more than one use value. Pulses may be used for human consumption or to feed animals. Bananas too are usually meant for human consumption, but banana peels may be used for very different purposes. In other words, goods may have a variety of qualitative attributes. This can be seen more clearly in the case of property that we have referred to—let us say a building. A building may be put to a variety of uses, for residential purposes, as an office, as a shop, etc. When the owner of such a building is trying to sell it, the bids will come from different potential buyers who view it from these different purposes. Hence the qualitative attributes of goods may depend not only on intrinsic qualities, but also on associated aspects. In the case of the building, the potential buyer who wants to use it as a shop will come to have a higher assessment of its worth if it is situated along a busy street; this may lead to a lower assessment of its worth by someone who is considering it for residential purposes. Thus location (*site value*) may become a major part of the qualitative attributes of the building. More complex examples can easily be thought of such as modern weapons where there are many more 'qualitative attributes' to be taken into account and hence there are likely to be very divergent assessments of worth. The multiplicity of the qualitative attributes of goods is the reason for bargaining in most instances. The inadequacy of information referred to in the previous paragraph can be seen to arise from this fact. We shall see subsequently the bearing of different perceptions about the qualitative attribute of goods in the exchange process. To give just a hint at this stage, advertisement and differentiation of products are ways to add to the diversity of the qualitative attributes of goods.

Bargaining power

We may make a further comment about bargaining. Bargaining is not an attempt to somehow clinch a deal. It is part of the effort to take the best advantage of a given situation. More often than not bargaining involves the use of pressure—subtle where possible, crude where necessary—to get the other party to yield; hence the frequent reference to 'bargaining power'. There is no reason to think that bargaining power will be equal on both sides, for it depends on a variety of factors. It may depend on the nature of goods concerned. In our original example, bananas will perish more quickly than pulses and so B is likely to be eager to arrive at a fairly quick settlement. If A knows this 'quality' of bananas and B's position regarding it, it will be to its interest to pretend that there is no urgency about the deal. In such instances the holding power of the two parties differs, conferring a differential advantage to one side. Holding power may differ in other situations as well. In the case dealt with in the previous chapter of households X and Y, where X is interested in getting the use of land and Y is interested in getting the use of labour, it is easy to see that Y will have more holding power than X and consequently also greater bargaining power in order to exert pressure on X to yield.

Along with factors discussed so far, bargaining power will also depend on the number of bidders. If in the village there are more Y households eager to let out land or bid for the use of labour power, they will come to have less bargaining power. The impact of numbers on bargaining power can be seen by considering two different situations, one where there is a single seller, but many potential buyers, and in the other the opposite, where there are many sellers but only one buyer. These instances are referred to as *monopoly* and *monopsony* respectively. In the case of monopoly, the seller will have very high bargaining power especially if the item he has for sale is something that the potential buyers are very much in need of. A landlord who has the only tube well in a village has very high bargaining power as far as the sale of water to his neighbours is concerned. The corresponding opposite case is where a trader in a town is approached by a number of small producers from a remote village trying to sell their grain, or vegetables or mud pots. Obviously the monopsonist will have greater bargaining power under such circumstances. The same will be true where a government sets itself as a monopsonist for the purchase of some goods produced in the country. Under some circumstances it also becomes possible for a party to become a monopolist with respect to some goods and a monopsonist in regard to something else and thus compound the bargaining power. A common example of this kind is where a trader is able to become a monopolist in the sale of yarn to a weaver and a monopsonist for the purchase of the woven cloth, thus exercising bargaining power in both the transactions.

Bargaining power in an exchange may be displayed also by those who are on the same side of the transaction, by buyers among themselves, as is seen in the form of exchange known as 'auction'. An auction is a case where the owner of an item (usually but not necessarily the only one of its kind such as an original painting, a letter written by a celebrity of the past etc.) lets the potential buyers bid among themselves to arrive at its price. The seller (who is a monopolist in most such instances) is exercising his bargaining power passively by letting the potential buyers bid up the price. Among the buyers, the bargaining power will depend partly on their assessment of the worth of the good, but partly also on the resources they have at their disposal to back themselves up in the transaction.

Thus bargaining power depends on a variety of factors, the nature of the commodities transacted, information about the commodities, the urgency of the need, knowledge about alternative possibilities and the resource power of the participants. In barter all of these combine to determine the differential bargaining power of the parties concerned. Is it possible, then, to reduce, if not eliminate, differential bargaining power when exchange is generalised, in particular, where there are many sellers and many buyers? A qualified affirmative answer can be given to that question. If there are many tubewell owners in the village eager to sell water, the high bargaining power that the single seller might have had would be drastically reduced. Similarly, if the peasants who take grain or potters who carry pots to the town have many buyers for their product, they will not have to yield to any of them and can effectively bargain as well as the buyers.

The increase in the number of potential buyers and sellers will, thus, tend to make some reduction in the differential bargaining power of the parties and, consequently, exchange can become a much smoother activity. But increase in numbers alone will not eliminate the differential bargaining power because knowledge about alternative possibilities is but one of the many factors on which bargaining power depends. Increase in numbers may have an indirect influence on other factors, but it is very unlikely that all of them will be neutralised to equalise the bargaining power of the participants. Further, even where exchange is getting generalised, providing alternative sellers for buyers and alternative buyers for sellers, exchange as an activity retains its essential bilateral character: it is always a transaction between just two parties. Under that condition the normal desire of each of the two participants is to see that their own bargaining power is strengthened and it must be assumed that each will do whatever is within his power to confer differential advantage on himself. That being the case, exchange as an activity has a built-in tendency to generate differential bargaining power. A trader, for instance, may try to 'cultivate' a clientele of buyers who become so attached to him that they do not bother to go to a competitor even when there are many competitors. Or, he may try to convince them that his wares are very different from substitutes available, thus making it difficult for his buyers to accurately assess their use value. This is the rationale of what is usually referred to as *product differentiation*. Advertising is a corollary to it. In these and many other ways the trader may try to establish some element of monopoly to enhance his bargaining power so as to influence in his favour the terms of the transaction. Since in generalised exchange the trader becomes the 'professional' as far as exchange is concerned, he is likely to be the one to take the active role in building up differential bargaining power. Other sellers may attempt similar methods, and the buyers too may try in different ways to keep up and increase their bargaining power. Some will be successful and some will not be and it is difficult to say *a priori* what the outcome will be.

Bargaining power and resource power

There is one aspect of bargaining power that generalisation of exchange does not influence and that is the resource power which is a major factor in exchange. Exchange must be thought of as a way of commandeering goods and services, and the force behind it is resource power. The commandeering of goods and services in economies/societies prior to the emergence of exchange was through the power of custom, through the power of authority, through the power of brute force and so forth. In exchange, these have been substituted by the power of resources. This is seen most clearly in the case of auction where the item up for sale is commandeered by the person who makes the highest bid and is able to back it up with the resources he has at his command by which he also excludes everyone else from having that item. Every act of exchange is one of bidding away some item by the exercise of resource power thereby also excluding others from having it. This may not appear so obvious in some instances of exchange as when one buys a loaf of bread from a shop and pays the stipulated price without bidding and bargaining. But even in that instance, it is the power to bid (the ability to pay the stipulated price) that determines whether one can have the bread or not. The point may become clearer if the item in question is a colour television or a car where it is evident that many are excluded from having them because of inadequate resource power or purchasing power. In a country of some 850 million people only a few who can aspire to become bidders for motor cars; television will have more bidders, but still rather limited in number. It is the same principle that makes it difficult for many millions to bid for the daily food they require or the clothing they need. And the principle is clear. Exchange includes those who have resource power. It excludes those who do not have it. This differential in bidding power is not eliminated, not even reduced by making exchange more general.

The generalisation of exchange, however, leads to a regime of prices to become established in the economy. As has been noted already from the treatment of barter, exchange is the changing hands of specified quantities of two qualitatively different goods (goods with different use values). The ratio of the two quantities is an *implicit price*, that is, the rate at which the two goods will exchange for each other. If 5 measures (units) of pulses were exchanged for 10 dozen (units) bananas, the implicit price is the ratio 5:10 or 1:2 which means that the price of *one* measure of pulses is *two* dozen bananas or the price of *one* dozen bananas is $\frac{1}{2}$ measure of pulses. These are, of course, *relative prices*, the price of one good (more accurately one commodity) in terms of another. If there is a common medium of exchange, those relative prices can be expressed as *absolute prices*. Thus if the price of a dozen bananas is said to be six rupees, then from the above example it *must* follow that the price of a measure of pulses is twelve rupees. In other words, if two absolute prices are expressed in terms of a common medium (that is, the price of a dozen bananas is six rupees and the price of a measure of pulses is twelve rupees) then the relative prices can be inferred from it (one measure of pulses for two dozens of bananas). However, from a knowledge of relative prices *alone* it will not be possible to move on to absolute prices. If the relative price of two commodities and the absolute price of one in terms of a particular medium is known, then the absolute price of the other commodity can be inferred in terms of the same medium.

Normally, when we talk about price, we refer to absolute price and indicate it merely as one number, as the price of bananas is *six rupees* a dozen. But, even an absolute price is the ratio of two numbers and is thus a relative price, arising from an exchange transaction. What we should say is that one dozen (units) bananas will exchange for six (units) rupees. The use of a single number is the result of the accepted convention that all price ratios are expressed in terms of units of the common medium, the accepted currency. Sometimes the absolute price is expressed somewhat differently, as 'Two bananas for *one* rupee' which brings out more clearly the nature of price as a ratio or as a relative price.

Prices and costs

What does the price of a commodity signify? It is, of course, the *exchange value* of the commodity, but that does not add anything to what we already know. However, it shows that the price of a commodity may not indicate its *use value*. Here we can see the major difference between use value and exchange value. As we have noted already, any good that enters into exchange *must have* use value, but there is no way of specifying it. On the contrary, exchange value is very specific. Again, use value is subjective, but exchange value is the objective agreement that two parties arrive at because they do not agree on the use value of the two commodities. This does not, however, mean that exchange value, because it is objective, is more important or significant than use value. We can only say that the two are different, but both are involved in exchange as an activity. Exchange is initiated by different assessments of the use value (the 'worth') of goods and culminates in agreement on the exchange value of commodities, as is seen most clearly in barter transactions.

In barter the two parties through their 'negotiations' come to agree on the (relative) price of the two commodities, and to that extent it is objective. But if party A in our example were to find someone other than party B who is also willing to consider exchanging bananas for pulses (let us refer to this entrant as party C) then A and C would bargain about the relative prices of pulses and bananas, and it is very likely that the new relative price that gets established is different from the old one. That will depend on the differential bargaining power of the two parties which is based on both the subjective and objective conditions of exchange as we have already seen. Hence we should not exaggerate the 'objective' status of exchange value as it emerges through the process of transaction. And yet, as more and more parties get drawn into the transfer of pulses and bananas, the relative price (exchange value) will come to have greater acceptance and will appear to be an established 'fact'.

To the extent that it has general acceptance, the price of a commodity may be thought of as the index of the economic significance of that commodity. Again, it is necessary to caution that the economic significance thus emerging through the exchange process is no objective fact, but is premissed on the wide-ranging institutional conditions that lie beneath that process and hence can and will change if any of these arrangements change. All that we can say is that given all those conditions and the subjective evaluations of the worth of that good by the parties to the exchange, the resulting exchange value or price can be thought of as the economic significance of that commodity in relation to other commodities. Price, therefore, may be considered as the worth that exchange assigns to goods in the process of commoditising them.

As exchange spreads, and more and more goods are submitted to its valuation, price authenticated by it will come to find greater acceptance; this is good up to a point because it eliminates all forms of 'private' arbitrariness, not only in the valuation of goods but also in their appropriation. Prices establish an orderly and common procedure for appropriation which is a tremendous advance compared with the many capricious forms of acquisition that are bound to prevail in their absence. Viewed against the arbitrariness and violence on the basis of which many acts of acquisition took place in economies where exchange was not established, the emergence of exchange transactions was a major change and its rapid spread is easy to understand.

With an understanding of what prices are, it is possible to move on to an examination of cost. From day-to-day experience it is evident that there is a close connection between prices and costs. The statement that 'the price of bananas is six rupees a dozen' can be translated straight away into 'bananas cost six rupees a dozen'. Thus while establishing prices exchange provides a notion about costs as well. Though costs are more related to production than to exchange, the statement that 'bananas cost six rupees a dozen' does *not* necessarily imply that 'the cost of producing a dozen bananas is six rupees'. So far we have examined exchange as relating to the pricing of goods that are ready to be transacted. But as exchange becomes more and more generalised it will come to have a bearing on other economic activities including production. We shall now consider some of these wider implications of exchange.

EXCHANGE AND THE TRANSFORMATION OF THE ECONOMY AND SOCIETY

When exchange gets generalised it not only brings more and more goods and services under its sway and commoditises them, but also makes its influence felt on many other aspects of the economy and society. Most importantly it tends to seep into production.

Impact of exchange on production
We have treated production as the generation of use values resulting from human interaction with nature. In the village economy it finds expression as human labour expended on land. In instances of that kind the major part of productive activity is the decision of the kind of labour to be expended and when. We have seen that a good deal of this is decided by nature itself. Thus, when to plough, when to sow, when to weed, when to reap; each one of which calls for different *kinds* of skill, are all largely dictated by nature and over a period of time form part of the thinking and working habits of a community. A prior question—*what* to produce—is

also decided by nature and tradition. Hence productive activity follows some set patterns without major departures except when nature forces changes on those patterns, through droughts, floods etc. To the extent that these calamities too happen from time to time, most communities will also have contingency plans to deal with them.

What happens when exchange emerges? The impact of exchange on production is manifold. In the first place it can lead to an increase in the production of goods. This can be seen most clearly with reference to a rudimentary economy which has 'slack' built into it or which experiences demand-constraint. If the members of such an economy are satiated with the goods they have access to, and the economy, as a result, operates at a low level, the possibility of exchange can enable it to move to a higher level. In terms of the example that we took of rudimentary economies A and B, producing pulses and bananas respectively, exchange can lead to an increase in the production of pulses in A and of bananas in B. And since A desires bananas and B desires pulses, if exchange stimulates increase in the production of both and ensures the availability of the desired goods in the two communities, they can be considered to have become better off through exchange; (although it is not through exchange alone, but through the increase in production that exchange brings about). In this sense, exchange can lead not only to an increase in the production of goods already being undertaken, but also to greater diversification of production. If initially the economy was experiencing 'slack' and if the productive potential remaining unused can be activated into the production of new goods, because exchange results in generating demand for them, diversification of production becomes a possibility. Exchange can influence production in the opposite direction also. Suppose that the units of the village economy were all initially attempting to be self-sufficient with each one producing all the goods it needed—food items, cloth, tools etc. If exchange becomes a possibility among them, each may be able to specialise in the production of that good for which it has favourable conditions, sell some of it and buy some goods that it needs but which it is not producing. Such specialisation which exchange facilitates, can, therefore, also lead to increase in the production of all goods in the village economy. In all these respects, and under the specified conditions, exchange can become a very liberating activity.

Exchange also influences production in a different way. In the absence of exchange, production is simply the generation of use value. But exposure to exchange makes the process of production exchange value conscious. And that brings about many changes in the decisions regarding production. The main feature of these changes is that decisions regarding production, which in a pre-exchange situation are primarily about the coordination of physical aspects, turn out to be increasingly in response to economic calculus, that is, dominated by considerations of prices and costs. Production decisions on a farm, for instance, will have to take into account the costs of inputs to be purchased and the prices that the outputs will fetch. Physical complementarities will continue to play a role in production decisions—such as the proportions of different components of fertilisers or the combination of fertilisers and water—but much more fine-tuning will become necessary. For instance, if successive applications of fertilisers will lead only to less than proportionate increase in the output of paddy, a decision will have to be made as to the amount of fertilisers to be used, for which a comparison of the incremental costs of fertilisers and the incremental receipts through sale of paddy will have to be made. Similarly, if it is likely that increase in production will lead to a fall in prices, a decision will have to be made as to how much should be produced, because an increase in output cannot be considered to be a good thing in itself. This means also that what is required to organise production is not only knowledge about current prices, but also anticipation about future prices.

Changes of a deeper nature may also become necessary. A peasant who was producing paddy mainly for consumption will have to consider whether he should shift to the cultivation of bananas or sugarcane, *sell* these products and then *buy* paddy for consumption. He may have to consider whether part of his land should be taken out of cultivation and used for other purposes. He may also have to deliberate whether part or all of the land should be leased out to somebody else, or even be sold. And he may have to decide whether he should continue to be a peasant or move out to become someone else's paid employee.

These decisions and changes will not have to be made all at once. And yet we can see the tremendous and fundamental changes that exchange brings about in the sphere of production. Making adjustments to these changes is not easy. Some may find new opportunities, but many may find it difficult to cope with them. In view of the variety of decisions to be made in organising production, it may turn out to be more and more a specialised activity with only those who have special skills undertaking it, others preferring to become employees earning a steady income instead of taking the risk of facing the possibility of profits and losses. None of this, however, should be interpreted to imply that the growth of exchange will always be uni-directional. There are many historical instances where the emergence of exchange has led to an intensification of traditional structures and relationships. Such 'reversals of processes' are also a contemporaneous phenomenon as we shall see in our discussion of the Indian economy in Part II.

Exchange and the settlement of claims

In all these ways the social consequences of the spread of exchange are very profound indeed. There is another sphere where these will be even more pronounced. This is in regard to the settlement of claims. In economies with no exchange (as in a rudimentary economy) or with little exchange (as in a village economy) the decisions regarding production and the settlement of claims on the produce are largely independent of one another. Physical aspects dominate the decisions on production and customs; traditions and other social considerations determine the settlement of claims. With exchange and exchange value calculations becoming the prime factors in production decisions, claims are also increasingly brought under the same factors. This is because what are claims from one point of view become costs from another point of view. A worker who is employed by a producer claims wages; wages paid out become costs to the producer. Similarly, leasing-in land results in a cost to the producer as he has to pay rent to the owner of the land, but the rent becomes the claim of the land-owner and so on. With goods and resources such as land, and even the labour power of human beings becoming commoditised and their value getting determined through exchange, claims come to be increasingly defined as part of the production process. Indeed, under these conditions, claims are nothing other than the indices of economic significance that exchange stamps on resources, including labour power; because under a regime of exchange and production organised according to its principles, labour power at best is a resource entering as an input into production. Hence its economic significance (whether referred to as price, cost or claim) is also determined by the exchange process.

This, again, is a radical departure from a pre-exchange situation. In a rudimentary economy we saw that *all* members have a claim on the produce whether or not they participate in the production process. Under such conditions human needs can form one of the considerations in defining claims. Not that it is such a simple matter: recognising needs and providing for needs is not easy. We saw, too, that the worker members can come to resent the fact that they have to slog for the sake of those whom they may consider to be idlers. The point, however, is that the principles and procedures (whatever they may be) of defining and settling claims were largely detached from the decisions about production. In a village economy claims come to have some relation to production, but considerations other than production also have a bearing on the effective settlement of claims.

In both these (and similar) instances, the settlement of claims appears to be subject to some degree of arbitrariness. By contrast, the settlement of claims with reference to contribution to production appears to remove that arbitrariness, since the same principle determines *all* claims. However, if production decisions are based on prices established by exchange, then they are indirectly governed by the prevailing distribution of resources;

and all the arbitrariness of that distribution will, therefore, seep into production and into settlement of claims with reference to contribution to production. There is also the question about the claims of those who are not involved in productive activity.

Be that as it may, with the settlement of claims getting increasingly geared to the pricing principle as determined by exchange there is likely to be an erosion of all other patterns of settlement of claims summed up in the statement that with the emergence of exchange, customs are replaced by contracts. Its social consequences, that is its impact on the lives and livelihood of people to be more specific, are enormous. One writer has tried to capture some of these in a book called *The Great Transformation* (Polanyi, 1957).

That the spread of exchange brings about major changes in the social fabric must be fairly clear. Economies where exchange is absent or is not dominant in economic decisions—particularly decisions about production—are all based on considerations of use values—where the sense of priorities is determined by social considerations of a broad nature. Exchange brings with it the generation of exchange value which because of its quantitative nature provides an opportunity to convert all valuation procedures into a uniform scale. The question no longer is of what value a good is, but of what price it commands and the answer is not provided by any philosophical discourses or social debates but by the market. The social transformation that the spread of exchange brings about is, thus, through the new criterion it seems to offer in deciding social priorities, which is certainly much more operational than anything else that we have known.

Exchange and ownership

The impact of exchange is not merely on or through the economy and economic processes. And so we must trace some of its wider ramifications. Of these one of the most significant is the ownership question to which we have already referred. Exchange brings with it a sharper concept of ownership because it combines within it the three distinct aspects of ownership, the right to appropriate, the right to alienate and the right to exclude. What is significant is that with the growth of exchange each one of these will get accentuated because exchange has a propensity to strengthen the individualising tendencies. We have seen that one reason for exchange to develop is the different assessment that two parties have about the 'worth' of goods. Initially these two parties are likely to be two communities— two rudimentary economies that we considered at the beginning of this chapter—and exchange emerges as an activity *between* them. But as more and more goods are brought under exchange it will be increasingly difficult to preserve the community's assessment about the worth of goods; individuals within the community may come to differ on the worth of goods and exchange may penetrate into the community too. But because exchange must presuppose appropriation, ownership as right of appropriation will enter into the community also. Hence, if initially the distinction was between what is *ours* and what is *theirs*, it will tend to move towards what is *mine* and what is *yours*. This is one reason why exchange tends to break down community ownerships and encourage individual ownerships, posing a problem in many economies where the emphasis is on collective ownership. To what limit the individualising tendency inherent in exchange will be pushed is a major socio-economic question. In most parts of the world the shift initially will be from community ownership to family ownership especially when land remains the major resource. But exchange will change the nature of resources too, and the individualising process may continue further.

Whatever that may be, the change in the pattern of ownership that exchange brings about calls for other changes also. Since ownership is a right, and a social right at that, there must be a social authority to guarantee that right. Here the tendency will be in the opposite direction. Since primordial social groupings tend to disintegrate or at least weaken with the growth of exchange and because exchange tends to burst spatial and social boundaries, the social authority to guarantee rights is likely to be at a much higher level, the State, for instance being well above the tribe, village communities etc.[3] One of the major functions of that authority will be to guarantee the right of appropriation acquired through exchange. At the beginning of Chapter 3 we saw that the earlier forms of appropriation were through conquest and colonisation. If appropriation through exchange is to become acceptable, someone must guarantee that that right (to land, for instance) can be purchased and what is purchased can not only be possessed but can also be alienated. Such guarantees are provided through appropriate legal measures *and* through the assurance that the authority concerned will enforce such measures.

In the context of exchange, apart from ownership another area that requires legal measures and is protected by them is the realm of contracts. Exchange, initially, is a transaction in commodities. But as it develops it will turn out to be transactions in promises—promises to deliver goods or render services in exchange for promises to pay—that is, contracts. Protecting the legality and credibility of contracts therefore will be crucial to exchange and guaranteeing these will be one of the economic functions of the authority. One way in which that authority usually enables transactions through promises is to issue promises of its own as the guarantor of all contracts and promises associated with exchange. The authority can issue promissory notes stating: 'I promise to pay the bearer the sum of ...'. To the extent that the promise of that authority is accepted by those who recognise its authority, these promissory notes become legal tender and the most common medium in all trade and transactions, money *par excellence*. Along with money, credit also emerges and grows to facilitate exchange. Hence institutions to create credit, to administer and regulate credit will also become necessary as exchange progresses. The view that is held and propagated by some, that as exchange expands and increasingly takes over economic decisions, the need for an authority in the system (concretely the state) will tend to be eliminated is not valid. On the contrary, as we shall see in subsequent chapters, the so-called exchange economies rely on the state not only as an external guarantor but very much as an internal participant.

Exchange and traders

Another major change that takes place as exchange expands is the emergence of traders as a specialised group, as we have already seen. We have also noted some functions that traders perform in relation to exchange. But the emergence of traders or merchants as a group or class has much greater significance. For one thing, it opens up a new activity in the economy and a new opportunity for members of a society to make a living. In a rudimentary economy and a village economy the livelihood of people depends very much on productive activity; and involvement in production is the only possible economic activity (to the extent that 'economic' activities can be separated from other activities at all). In both instances too there are those who depend on the surplus generated by the producer group for their livelihood. With the emergence of exchange and traders, a second economic activity is formed where a group of people are not engaged in production (going by our characterisation of production as an interaction between human beings and nature) and yet are involved in an economically necessary activity. A distinction, therefore emerges clearly between production as generating *goods* of use value and trade as providing a *service* of use value. It also brings about a difference in the understanding of 'resources' which, so far, we have treated as material resources, especially physical and natural endowments available to a community to utilise their labour in production. For the traders the resources to utilise their labour is the surplus value ($\triangle M$) that they come to have through exchange.

As exchange expands, therefore, there will be many people who set themselves up as traders to use their labour with whatever surplus values that can be obtained via exchange to make a living. Hence traders themselves will consist of two categories, those who turn to trade to make a living through it (small traders or retail traders) and those who enter trade to acquire and augment surplus value (large traders or wholesale traders). The distinction between these two categories cannot be made absolute (because small traders can become large traders and the reverse can also happen) but because the motivations and operations of the two groups are different it is a useful distinction. As exchange expands, specialisation in production develops and more and more goods become commoditised, there will be a proliferation of both categories of traders, visibly those of small or petty traders. And as traders have an interest in the expansion of exchange, their activities and their impact on production will become mutually reinforcing . A further change, frequently noticed, is for trade to become a supplementary activity of some groups of producers. It may be that a small producer (of cloth, let us say) becomes a trader of his own goods or it may be that a small peasant sets up shop to become a part-time retail trader (of a variety of goods) in his own locality. Big producers may become big traders too, but we shall postpone until the next chapter the close link of this kind between production and exchange that emerges with exchange.

The big traders who come to have a steady increase in surplus value come to play a different kind of role in the economy and society. In the economic sphere they become the first category of people who specialise in the accumulation of exchange value. Surplus generation and accumulation are both possible in pre-exchange economies and some of them have become famous for their accumulated wealth in the form of buildings and other tangible assets. But generalised accumulation, or accumulation in terms of money, becomes possible only with surplus emerging in terms of the surplus through trade. And because of the possibility of easily augmenting it through trade, traders or merchants also become a new wealthy class. One of the wider consequences of this is the new alliance that develops between the merchants and the rulers, the latter always in need of money and the former always having plenty at their disposal. It is easy to see that it is a powerful combination of wealth and authority.

We have dealt with exchange essentially as a form of social relationship, that is, a relationship between persons or group of persons. But frequently exchange may appear to be an impersonal relationship between commodities. The accent on commodities in the exchange relationship is understandable because commodities are the visible part of exchange and what exchange does is to bring about the equality in value of different quantities of two commodities, as in the case of barter. As exchange gets generalised, it becomes a transaction between money on the one hand and commodities on the other. Even so exchange may still appear as a mere transaction of commodities, because money which is a command over goods has a tendency to make social relationships appear as relationship between things. But one acquires money through a complex of social relationships and there are social relationships underlying the production of goods, their display in shops and the manner in which the actual transaction takes place.

By examining different forms of exchange and the social changes that come about when exchange gets generalised we have probed into these more important, but perhaps less visible, aspects of exchange as an economic activity.

EXCHANGE AND MARKETS

Exchange and market are closely associated terms. Normally we think of the market as the *place* where exchange takes place, as when we refer to 'the fruit market', 'the fish market' etc. But the spatial concept of the market is very limited and can be misleading. For instance, the seller of fruits may be willing to sell fruits in his house, but the house does not become spatially a market. Also, it is not always easy to figure out where exactly the exchange takes place. The order for some goods are placed over the telephone or by mail; the goods are delivered at one's residence and payment is made by cheque. In such cases it is not possible to identify the location of the transaction. Hence a more general interpretation of the term *market* is needed. Market may be identified as the institutional arrangements necessary for the activity of exchange to take place. The institutional arrangements will include the provision of space where it is necessary for transactions to take place, provision of the appropriate medium of exchange, provision of protection for contracts where they form part of the transaction etc. Since exchange is not an abstract phenomenon or mere logic, but a real-life activity, it cannot take place without these institutional arrangements.

In fact it is possible, and under certain circumstances necessary, to examine even some of the more remote institutional arrangements required for exchange. As noted already, the distribution of resource power is a major condition of exchange. Hence the pattern of ownership of resources must be thought of as part of the institutional arrangements on which exchange rests. Again, to the extent that money is used in exchange and contracts form part of exchange, a crucial pre-requisite for exchange is the authority backing money and contracts. Sometimes we tend to take these for granted, but their crucial significance for exchange surfaces from time to time. For instance, socialist countries that wish to move into exchange relationships frequently discover that they do not have many of the pre-conditions necessary to launch and sustain a regime of prices. In particular, many of them discover that market relationships are not compatible with the pattern of ownership of resources which they are used to. In countries that experience very high rates of inflation and where currency reforms are being attempted, exchange involving money may come to a standstill until there is clarity about the regime that issues a new currency.

In veiw of this, it is not easy to indicate which are the crucial institutional factors of exchange that define the market. A decision in this matter can only be arrived at contextually.

Since the market is the configuration of conditions necessary for exchange as an activity to take place, sometimes exchange and market are used as interchangeable terms. In particular an economy in which exchange relationships are widespread, and where economic decisions are based largely on prices established through exchange, is referred to as a *market economy* or even as a *free market economy*. While these expressions are normally used to describe the characteristics of some economies, sometimes there is also a tendency to use them to propagate what may be referred to as the *market ideology*, that is the view that an economy in which decisions are made on the basis of signals provided by the unhindered functioning of the market is a superior economic order. And frequently the descriptive and the normative aspects get mixed up. We shall try to keep them separate by posing two different questions: Is it possible to have a fully marketised economy? What is the basis and meaning of the (ideological) claim that a free market system is superior to all other economic orders?

Limits to exchange and markets

The first question arises from a characteristic of exchange noted already—its tendency to increase in frequency once it is established, to spread rapidly once it comes to be mediated through money, and for its influence to penetrate into all areas of the economy and society. Does it now follow from these that once it is set in motion it will bring the entire economy under its sway? It is important to note that a fully marketised economy implies not only that all goods (and services) are commoditised, but that all economic decisions, including all settlements of claims, are in response to market signals. Historically, in both these areas exchange made slow and halting progress for a very long time. Isolated instances of barter as a form of exchange may have increased in frequency over time. Land-related economic units (of the village economy) may have been substantially self-sufficient, with occasional acts of exchange without or with the use of money. The rapid spread of exchange is a fairly recent phenomenon going back just about two or three centuries and, for reasons that will become evident in the next chapter, has been closely associated with the development of capitalist economies.

It is worth considering why, in spite of its propensity to expand, exchange remained limited over much of the long history of humankind.[4] In village economies land and labour were locked up in production, particularly the production of food, to meet the needs of those who were involved in production. The totality of economic activities, therefore, constituted a rather limited circuit without the possibility of it being easily divided into distinct parts. None of it, consequently, could be alienated. Neither land nor labour could be alienated because they were both closely knit in an activity necessary to sustain life. The produce could not be alienated for the same reason. Hence the complementarities necessary for the preservation of life formed a barrier against exchange. The fact that the level of production must have been low added to it. In many traditional societies, therefore, there developed taboos against transactions in the necessities of life and those things that were necessary to produce them. Exchange, therefore, appeared first in goods that were useful, but not essential, such as salt or in goods that were luxuries. For the same reason when trade became established it was more prevalent between regions at a distance from one another than between close neighbourhoods, and traders were adventurers from or to distant areas. Such trade had little or no bearing on the internal organisation of the economy of the unit, whether a household or a village community. A local market may soon develop, too, where the producers themselves exchange their goods, vegetables, fruits, art and craftwares in either a C–C or C–M–C form which would soon come to be accepted very much as part of the local social organisation but, again, with little impact on the rest of the economic processes. As a writer has noted: 'The economic system was submerged in general social relations; markets were merely accessory features of an institutional setting controlled and regulated more than ever by social authority' (Polanyi, 1957: 67).

The tendency for exchange to go beyond this level was ably assisted by the emerging nation–state which removed some of the local boundaries of trade, but did everything to separate national trade from international trade. Thus markets and regulations on markets grew up together. A change in this pattern could come about only when land and labour also began to be commoditised. On both these the process of commoditisation was slow. Land was the pivotal element in the social order and formed the basis not only of the economic set-up, but also of the legal, administrative and military arrangements. Even when on economic grounds its commoditisation appeared attractive and imminent, other social forces operated against it. Labour, too, was slow in getting commoditised because of the possibility that most people had to provide a living for themselves and because of a variety of customs and social practices.

A major change in the pattern comes with the growth of industries which produce goods specifically for sale on the market. But if this were to become operational, each item that went into the production of the goods also should be commoditised: land and labour would, therefore, come increasingly under the commoditisation process. However, with the growth of industries, the organisation of production would have to change and become more complex. Thus while all goods and many services would tend to be commoditised, it would become difficult to get the internal structure of the organisation to follow the principles of buying and selling. The sense of authority could not be maintained solely, or even principally, on market principles. Decision-making and coordination of decisions, too, could not be left to the regulations of the market. And while some labour power could be commoditised, and paid uniform wages, other kinds of skills would have to be compensated on very different considerations. Hence not all settlements of claims would be done according to market principles.

Thus, it would appear, that while there are some built-in tendencies for exchange to expand, there are other factors in operation in societies—from different quarters at different times—working in the opposite direction. We shall see in the next chapter that under the capitalist order these inhibiting factors are substantially overcome by the accumulation of exchange value becoming the organising principle of the economy; but even under the capitalist system the economy does not come fully under the sway of markets.

One reason for this is that as economies develop over time, they find it necessary to produce or provide some goods which cannot easily be commoditised. Let us recall that to commoditise goods or services, they must be liable to be appropriated through exchange by the application of the exclusion principle. Now, there are goods/services that do not satisfy this criterion which have come to be known as 'public goods': street lighting provided by a municipality and national defence provided by the state are among typical examples.[5] In these instances, a user of these services is not able to exclude others from the use of the same and hence would not want to bid for their appropriation. And in the absence of such bidding it would not be possible to bring them under the pricing principle via the operation of the market. Hence the cost of providing these services will have to be met in some other way, usually by taxation. The presence of taxation in modern economies (including capitalist economies) is an indication that not all economic operations can be carried out using the market principle.[6]

Then there are areas where the private calculations (of benefits and costs) which form the basis of market biddings go contrary to social considerations. This problem of 'externalities' received recognition soon after theoretical claims began to be made about 'the fully marketised economy' but was for long treated as a somewhat odd case.[7] But in recent years it has emerged as a widely discussed theoretical and practical problem of environmental consequences of economic activities. A few examples will indicate the nature of the problem. Felling of trees to use wood for the manufacture of many articles is a very profitable activity both for the sellers and the buyers of trees. But over time it begins to affect the temperature levels and rainfall patterns which may have enormously adverse consequences for economy and society. Modern fishing trawlers may increase the catch of fish, but may destroy the ecological balance of ocean life. Constructing a dam across a river may help to irrigate agriculture and generate electricity, but it may also destroy forever certain rare species of wildlife. Application of fertilisers and pesticides may increase yield of output, but may have adverse effects on the soil. In instances of this kind, decisions about economic activities cannot be left entirely to market forces and various forms of non-market social regulations may become necessary. A general problem underlying many such cases is that where current decisions have future consequences, market signals are rather poor indicators to guide policy.

There are also instances where commoditisation is not desirable even if it is possible. We have already made reference to the qualitative attributes of goods. Where it is not possible for an ordinary purchaser to get to know the qualitative attributes of goods, particularly manufactured goods, specialised agencies can be set up to certify that required standards have been met. This is what ISI (Indian Standards Institution) is doing in our country. Such services, of course, can be commoditised, but if that means that the agency sells to the highest bidder what it wishes to have, the very purpose of independent certification will be lost. Or, to consider another example, a driving licence is issued after a competent authority certifies that the applicant possesses the required qualifications. True, sometimes this procedure gets commoditised with some applicants purchasing licences without possessing the skills, although it is considered to be illegal. But imagine the economic and social consequences if those who wish to drive, or fly an aeroplane, or prescribe medicines for illnesses, can simply purchase their certifications without going through an independent authority to have their credentials certified! The same can be said about judicial services which must also not be allowed to become commoditised if the basic criterion is to be effective. Judicial services, after all, are not far removed from the economy, especially an economy based on promises and contracts. Such services can also be commoditised, but if it comes to be known that disputes over contracts are decided in favour of the highest bidders, the usefulness of contracts itself will be in doubt. And, in a way, it will be conceding too that *everything* will be decided on the basis of resource power, which is similar to the law of the jungle, that might is always right.

It may be noted too that the market does not come 'free'. There is a cost to the services provided by the market. If all commodities that are purchased are made to order, it is not necessary to carry stocks of goods. But in order to have the freedom to pick up the goods of one's choice from a shop or supermarket, there must be a stock of goods readily available on the shelf or the warehouse. The cost of holding idle stock is something that a society must be willing and able to meet, to ensure that goods can be picked up as and when desired. The greater this freedom (to the individual purchaser) the greater will be the social cost of the operation. This is specially so when the purchasers' desire for variety is to be respected whether the purchase is of bread, toothpaste, two-wheelers, television sets, transportation, education, health services or whatever. In each one of these instances the larger the scope for individual choice the greater the social cost and social waste. Consequently each society must make decisions about the extent to which it will permit the market to cater to the fancies of the purchasers. There is virtually no society that permits the availability of food to be determined solely by the 'laws of the market' under all circumstances. Even the most affluent societies have had to restrict the freedom that individuals have (depending on their puchasing power) to buy bread, butter, meat, petrol etc. when engaged in war. In many instances the government intervenes to restrict the quantity of goods any individual may purchase, even if some individuals may be willing to purchase more and at a higher price. A quantity restriction of this kind may appear to be a temporary adjustment. But there are other cases where it is the standard practice and not a temporary feature. There is hardly any country in the world where airline or train tickets are sold to the highest bidders; total quantity available is fixed and while there may be no restrictions on the quantity that any individual may purchase, if there are many who wish to purchase tickets they will have to queue for them, and some may not be able to purchase even if they could afford to do so. (A queue consists of those who can afford to purchase the goods and most people in a queue might even be willing to pay a higher price.) Societies which are conscious of their priorities may limit the scope of the market in many areas in order to enforce their priorities. If, for instance, a society decides that more of its resources (physical resources such as steel and electricity and human resources such as engineering skills) must go into the construction of schools, health resorts and public parks, it may decide that fewer of these resources should be made available for the production of motor cars for private use. If so, those wanting to purchase cars may have to place an order, wait in a 'queue' for one or two years and then take a car of very standard features, the only kind that is being made available to the market. In another society which is poorer still, the same decision may have to be made about many other markets also. It may appear that such a society has no faith in the market as an institution, but the fact may be that it cannot afford to let many markets to become 'free'; but when conditions improve, most of these restrictions may also disappear. The point, once again, is that each society decides, depending on a variety of factors and circumstances, not only the areas where commoditisation will be permitted, but also how far it should extend.

We are now in a position to respond to the first of our questions relating to the market, viz. about the possibility of a 'fully marketised' economy. The answer has to be that while exchange and commoditisation may spread rapidly under certain conditions, it is not possible—nor always desirable—for them to bring all economic decisions directly and fully under their influence. Every society makes decisions as to what goods and services will or will not be commoditised. Economic processes themselves sometimes bring up conditions where commoditisation is not possible.

Hence more than markets are necessary for the economy to function and the market itself can function as it is supposed to only when it is set within limits by other social institutions. Among these we have taken note of two institutions which influence most economies. The first is an authority which has responsibility to make many crucial decisions involving society as a whole, including the limits of the market, and the institutions that supplement and correct the market's decision on claims by defining and settling claims according to *non-market* principles. The second is the rudimentary economy component in all economies, principally, but not exclusively households, which retain the generation of use values as their organising principle; hence having principles other than those of the market to decide on the utilisation of the labour power of its members as well as to settle claims. Markets function between these two boundaries and are in a process of continuous engagement with them.

Market ideology

In the light of this conclusion a brief answer may be given to the second question: Why has the market which is a social institution and of high instrumental use given rise to what has come to be known as the market ideology? Its beginning probably can be traced back to the period of the emergence of the M–C–M' form of exchange and of traders as specialists in exchange with their capacity to accumulate surplus value through trade.

In the European continent (and elsewhere in the world too) when traders emerged as a new wealthy group, they had to bear comparison with the upper social group of an earlier period—the landed gentry as they have come to be referred to—whose standing in society was not based on their wealth *per se* but on their long tradition of social status, their valour in warfare, their patronage of the arts, music and culture in general. The social background of those who came to be noted as wealthy merchants was very different. Usually they came from the lower ranks in a highly status-conscious social order, 'drop outs' from the normal rounds of economic and social life and, at best, upstarts showing off their wealth at a time when wealth was not the basis of social esteem. Also since it was part of the professional activity of merchants to buy cheap and to sell dear, they were often suspected of cheating by societies which paid at least lip-service to high moral principles. It was conceded that traders were wealthy, but it was generally believed too that their wealth was ill-gotten.

Under such conditions merchants would receive recognition in society only by propagating the view that exchange and trade were honourable things to be engaged in and that market activities were beneficial to society. The ideology of exchange as a socially beneficial activity and market as a respectable institution arose in that context. In this effort the merchants received full support from a new ruling class.[8] The old feudal system was gradually crumbling and with it the military and civil authority that the lords used to exercise. Internal transport and communication facilities were breaking down; geographical barriers and larger territories were being brought under common authority. Parochial loyalties too were getting eroded and the concept of 'nation' was gradually finding acceptance. 'Authority', therefore, was increasingly being manifested as the nation–state with a new set of leaders emerged as rulers. The new rulers derived their support principally from the merchants. Merchants, too, were rising above local loyalties and boundaries and were willing to support authority at a higher level since that opened up new market opportunities. The rulers, always in need of financial resources, were only too willing to receive support from a rising group of merchants. Hence the combination of wealth and power which we noted earlier.

Once this happened, the ideology of the merchants was projected as the national ideology. The view that the nation could become wealthier and stronger through trade would have greater acceptance than the argument that it would make those directly involved with it richer. Thus emerged what later came to be known as the ideology of mercantilism, which propagated the view that trade makes nations wealthy and which was prevalent in Europe for many centuries, especially in the Seventeenth century.

Adam Smith, towards the end of the next century pointed out the fallacies of mercantilism, especially the claim that it was precious metals earned through trade that made nations wealthy. But he provided greater respectability to exchange as such by arguing that the propensity to enter into exchange was part of human nature, in fact one of those propensities that distinguished human beings from lower forms of animals, and that only by allowing it full play—without let or hindrance—would the productive powers of labour improve so as to contribute to the wealth of the nation. By linking exchange to human nature, particularly self-love which he considered to be the motor for all economic activity, Smith provided the basis to consider markets as part of the natural order of society; and by arguing that production and productivity would grow when markets were permitted full play he provided a special place for markets in the economy.[9]

But the view that markets and the price signals they provide should be accepted as the only criterion for all economic decisions and actions became doctrine or ideology only much later; in fact almost a century later, especially after the French economist Leon Walras succeeded in constructing a model of the economic universe which had prices as the single unifying principle and the only signals to guide action. This view was further strengthened a century later, in the second half of the twentieth century, when formalised and axiomatised versions of 'general equilibrium' were worked out by contemporary economists.[10] What was considered to be intuitively valid now appeared to receive rigorous sanction. Based on this long history there are today many economists (and perhaps many more non-economists who unintelligently swallow the conclusions that are arrived at through a chain of reasoning without examining the basic premises) who proclaim that economies perform best when they are left to the laws of the market. And since capitalism is said to be a market economy what is claimed as the virtues of the market are claimed to be the virtues of capitalism also so that in effect the plea for a market economy becomes a defence of the capitalist system. It is in that sense that the market becomes an ideology.[11]

Some aspects relating to these claims will be taken up in the next chapter. There can be no doubt that exchange, money and markets are among the major and most beneficial of social institutions. But these are to be viewed as instruments to achieve social purposes. This is why we have attempted throughout to set them in their social context, which certainly has changed a great deal over time and is not the same everywhere at any given time. Hence any attempt that tries to legitimise and idealise the claims of the market in abstract terms must be dismissed as misinformed and misdirected. The real issue is how effectively markets can be made use of and that is a highly contextualised problem. In Chapter 6 and many sections of Part II we shall have to address ourselves to it.

NOTES

1. Consider the following illustration of bidding where the offers differ widely in the initial step, but converge to an agreement through subsequent steps.

A's offer of pulses for bananas	B's offer of bananas for pulses
3 measures for 10 dozen	10 dozen for 12 measures
4 measures for 10 dozen	10 dozen for 9 measures
$4\frac{1}{2}$ measures for 10 dozen	10 dozen for 7 measures
5 measures for 10 dozen	10 dozen for 5 measures

No exchange takes place following the first, second or third bids, but after the fourth, exchange can take place because the quantity of pulses that A is willing to offer for (a given quantity of) bananas is the same as the quantity of pulses B is willing to accept for (the same quantity of) bananas.

Note that each offer in terms of the quantities of the two goods also implies a certain exchange rate. The exchange rate that A offers is not acceptable to B and vice-versa in the initial steps, but the agreeable quantities arrived at in step four has an agreeable exchange rate as well, one measure of pulses for two dozen bananas or a dozen bananas for half a measure of pulses.

2. Among the major economists of the past, the most thorough treatment of the transformation of exchange as an activity has been made by Karl Marx. His treatment of this theme lies scattered in many of his writings, but chiefly Capital Vol. I (Marx, 1971) and Grundrisse (Marx, 1973). The section on transformation of exchange relies largely on these writings as well as Hicks, 1969.

3. On the formation of nation–states during the period of rapid commercialisation see Hill, 1969, Part Two, Ch. 1.

4. For a detailed account of these aspects reference may be made to Polanyi, 1957, Chs. 5 & 6.

5. The classic writing on this subject is Samuelson, 1954 and 1955. For a detailed discussion see also Musgrave and Musgrave, 1973, Ch. 3. The latter authors refer to public goods as social goods and say: 'Social goods are goods the consumption of which is nonrival. That is, they are goods where A's partaking of the consumption benefits does not reduce the benefits derived by all others. The same benefits are available to all and without mutual interference', p. 51. They indicate earlier that 'the market can function only in a situation where the exclusion principle applies, that is, where A's consumption is made contingent on his paying the price, while B, who does not pay, is excluded. ....Given such exclusion, the market can function as an auction system', p. 50.

6. The distinction between market and non-market decision-making and transfers referred to here is sometimes misunderstood as the distinction between private and public sector activities. The state, the public authority, is usually responsible for many non-market decisions in the economy, but more often than not, the state or the public sector is also a market participant in the economy making decisions of buying and selling. Similarly in the private sector there may be many institutions which function along non-market principles. A charitable trust which raises funds through voluntary contributions and gives free medical services to those who approach it is an example of this kind. Hence 'nationalisation' does not rule out all possibilities of applying market principles and 'privatisation' does not necessarily mean 'marketisation'. Those who are not clear about this distinction and those who have vested interests in privatisation may tend to identify privatisation and marketisation, but that is not accurate. As we shall see in the later pages of this chapter (as also in the next chapter) every society has to decide which decisions in the economy will be left to the market and which will be carried out by the state or the public authority. Decisions regarding 'public goods', obviously, cannot be left to the market and agencies that deal with them must be thought of as performing public functions on the basis of authority that they directly possess or is delegated to them.

7. Till recently the standard example that used to be cited on the problem of 'external economies' was the problem of smoke coming from a factory causing a health hazard to those living in the neighbourhood. It was considered to be external to the pricing mechanism because the price of the good produced did not take into account the deterioration in the health of the people in the neighbourhood as an item of cost. It was recognised that this posed a problem to the allocation of resources based on the market principle, but

was not considered to be a major issue. The mood has changed, however, after there has been world-wide public recognition of the damage that economic activities cause to the environment. On this latter issue see Singh, 1978, in particular the Epilogue.

The following also will be useful: Centre for Science and Environment, 1982; Adiseshiah, 1987, Nadkarni, 1991.

8. On the new rulers of this period see Dobb, 1963, Chapter Three and Hill, 1969.

9. Adam Smith considered 'the disposition to truck, barter and exchange' as a specific human characteristic distinguishing human beings from other forms of animals. He said,

> Each animal is still obliged to support and defend itself, separately and independently, and derives no sort of advantage from that variety of talents with which nature has distinguished its fellows. Among men, on the contrary, the most dissimilar geniuses are of use to one another; the different produces of their respective talents, by the disposition to truck, barter and exchange, being brought, as it were, into a common stock, where everyman may purchase whatever part of the produce of other men's talents he has occasion for (Smith, 1966, BK I, Ch. II).

To Smith it might have been obvious, but it is worth indicating, that for this arrangement, apart from the disposition to truck, barter and exchange, a further necessary condition is that 'everyman' also has enough purchasing power to purchase the produce of other men's talents.

10. The *Elements of Pure Economics* by the French economist Leon Walras originally published in 1874 (Walras, 1954) was the first mathematical representation of the economy as a system of exchanges. The approach and the method were so unconventional that the work did not receive recognition for a very long time. A discussion of the contributions in the mid-twentieth century in this area is given in Koopmans, 1957, especially Essay I. The treatment is essentially mathematical.

11. In his *The Rise of Market Culture* William M. Reddy (Reddy, 1984) argues that there never was a 'market economy' if that meant an economy which was completely commoditised. There was only a market culture which made use of the ideology of the market system. It may be noted that the market ideology is propagated by those (persons and countries) who have enough resource power to enable them to make use of the market to their own advantage.

5

Capitalist Economy

In comparison with the rudimentary economy and the village economy dealt with earlier, the capitalist economy which is examined in this chapter is more complex. Surprisingly, the complexity arises largely from the fact that a single concern, the accumulation of exchange value, comes to dominate all economic decisions—calculations may be a more appropriate term—but its manifestations are different in different spheres. The accumulation of exchange value is primarily the interest of the capitalists—those who own and exercise control over the resources, the means of production—who bring labour power into productive activity on payment of wages. The surplus generated by labour process in production, that is the difference between labour productivity and wages, appropriated by the capitalist owner, becomes the source of his profit and the quest for profit comes to be the driving force of the capitalist economy. It finds expression in the tendency to produce new goods, to change the patterns of production constantly and to expand aggressively into more and more territories.

However, the capitalist path of growth and expansion is not a smooth one. It runs into problems because capitalists are competing amongst themselves to achieve their objective of capturing markets and their attempts to push sales frequently run into difficulties. And although the capitalist economy thrives on generating surplus value using labour power, it also has a tendency to make labour power redundant from time to time, thus excluding its owners from productive activity. This becomes an acute social problem in situations where owners of labour power have nothing other than their labour power to sell, because a capitalist economy is meant exclusively for those who have something to sell.

The chapter also examines the role of the state in capitalist economies especially against the frequently heard claim that the capitalist economy functions best when it is left to its own innate laws and that external interventions interfere with the system's ability to achieve efficiency in the use of resources. At a broader level some aspects of the relationships between a capitalist economy and a capitalist society are also dealt with.

The discussion calls for careful reading. Those who are new to the treatment of capitalist economies may find it rewarding to go through the simple exposition in Jalée, 1977.

The capitalist economy to which we now turn is fundamentally different from the two we have seen already, viz., the rudimentary economy and the village economy. A major reason for this difference is the role that exchange comes to have in it in contrast to the other two: the rudimentary economy has no exchange at all in it, and in the village economy its role is very limited. The great transformation that exchange brings about in economy and society has been outlined in general terms in the preceding chapter.

The capitalist economy is not only based on exchange; the accumulation of exchange value becomes its organising principle. The ramifications of that change will be examined in this chapter.

REPRESENTATIONS OF THE CAPITALIST ECONOMY

The capitalist economy is a very complex entity. We can gather some idea about its complexity by contrasting it with the rudimentary and village economies. Stability of organisational patterns and performance is their hallmark; the capitalist economy is intrinsically dynamic. An increase in the quantity and variety of goods is a feature of the capitalist economy; the other two are characterised by a fairly steady production of a few standard goods. The accent in them is on production for use; in a capitalist economy production is primarily for sale. The processes of production undergo frequent change in the capitalist economy; they remain invariant for long periods in the other two.

How is the totality of these differences to be portrayed so as to gain an understanding of the capitalist system?[1] As in the case of the rudimentary economy and the village economy, the capitalist economy also takes many distinct forms. This is particularly so because some of its features change quite drastically as it evolves over time. The capitalist economy as it emerged first in Great Britain and then in Europe in the eighteenth and nineteenth centuries and about which Adam Smith, David Ricardo, Karl Marx and many others of that period wrote, was very different from what capitalism became in these countries in the twentieth century. The nature of the capitalist economy in the U.S.A., in Japan and in India during the last decade of the twentieth century is distinctly different from one another. That being the case, it is impossible to describe *all* features of a capitalist economy so as to get a total picture. What can be done is to probe into the essential features of an economy that can be described as 'capitalist' which can be seen in any of its many manifestations, both historical and contemporary. In other words, the only way to understand a capitalist economy is to search for a proper representation of it. But then, there is also the problem that something as complex as capitalism will come to have many representations and it will not be easy to decide which one of these is the most appropriate. The adequacy and appropriateness of a representation can be decided only in terms of how it enables one to understand and interpret the variety of the specific aspects relating to the economy that one comes across in daily life. We keep this in mind as we now turn to two different representations of the capitalist economy.

The capitalist economy as an 'all exchange' system

A very common and, in academic circles very popular, representation of the capitalist economy is to emphasise the generality of exchange in it. That exchange, markets and prices have a central role in a capitalist economy is a fact. But the representation of the capitalist economy as a system linked together by markets and integrated by the pricing principle implies much more than that. A version of it presented in mathematical form was worked out by the French economist Leon Walras in the 1870s. Two contemporary economists improved upon it and made the presentation rigorous in the 1950s. In textbook versions this representation has come to be known as *the competitive economy*. In popular language it is also referred to as *the market economy*.[2]

Let us look into the representation in greater detail. As seen in the preceding chapter, one of the things that exchange as an activity does is to establish the (relative) prices of the goods exchanged. As exchange becomes more and more generalised, the relative prices of all goods, or the indices of their economic significance, get established. To the extent that producers who produce goods to be sold must reckon with these prices as their costs, production decisions also will come about in response to prices that exchange or the markets determine. One implication of this is that all resources too (which in the rudimentary economy and in the village economy are principally physical and natural endowments) have the indices of their economic significance defined by the market. For, after all, resources are meant to be used in production. Hence any resource that is made use of in production will come to have its economic significance assigned by the market.[3]

There is a corollary to this also. Only those things that are priced by the market can be considered as resources. Air may be absolutely necessary for life and for production; but if it is not priced by the market through the exchange process, it is not an economic good, but a 'free good'. In the case of air, this may be because there is plenty of it (because it is not 'scarce') that it does not get priced. But consider another example. Both land and rainfall are necessary for cultivation. In most instances land comes to be priced through exchange (that is, it becomes a commodity), but rainfall seldom does—even when it is extremely scarce. In this case the reason why rainfall does not get priced even though it is scarce is that unlike land it is not *owned* by anyone, and hence does not come to be exchanged.[4] A further example will bring out the implication of this more clearly.

Consider a village community that has a tank which serves as the common source of water for all its members; which also has enough water for all their direct needs and for cultivation. Suppose now that one member of the village community (let us say the landlord) appropriates to himself the ownership of the tank and that there is no other change in the village. Now, the landlord will be in a position to sell water to all the others in the village because they need water to live and to cultivate. And if the landlord's claim to ownership is accepted, others will also be willing to buy the water from him. In this case, therefore, it is not scarcity of water that leads to its ownership and pricing. On the contrary, the act of appropriation establishes the right to exclude others and makes it possible to commoditise water. No matter how it is brought about, within an exchange system, only those goods that have a price become resources, and in this sense the distinction between resources and (produced) goods also disappears. Lastly, as we have already seen, when exchange gets generalised, claims also come to be settled on the basis of the pricing principle because the service rendered by labour power in production is viewed by the producer as part of his cost of production which is determined via exchange and pricing. In short, in a generalised exchange economy, prices established by the market through the process of exchange is the basis of *all* economic decisions and activities. On this consideration this representation of a capitalist economy portrays it as a system in which prices established by the laws of exchange or the free market become the coordinating principle of all economic activities.

Implications of capitalism as a system of prices

The contrast between the capitalist system and other economic systems can be seen very sharply in this representation. In other systems customs and/or human interventions of some kind are the guiding principles of economic activity; they can, therefore, become very subjective and arbitrary. Prices determined by the free-play of markets are the basis of economic decisions in capitalism and hence capitalism is objective and rational. This is what the representation indirectly conveys.

In fact, it conveys more. Let us probe further into the representation following one of its most clearly worked-out versions. Since the economic processes can be thought of as a set of decisions, let us think of the economy as consisting of a group of decision-makers. These may be divided into three groups: resource holders, producers and consumers based on the three key decisions. The purpose is to show that the system is an integrated one where the decisions of the three groups are orchestrated entirely through mutual exchange with prices serving as signals.

We may make an entry into the system through the decisions of the consumers, because a claim frequently made about the capitalist economy on the basis of this representation is that in it the consumer is sovereign. It is the personal preferences of the consumers which get translated into economic activity in the system, or so the argument goes. The sequence of decisions and actions may be thought of as follows:

Consumers express their preferences for the goods they desire. In the market these bids get registered as the increase in the demand for the goods so preferred. The prices of these goods, therefore, tend to rise. The changes in prices thus emerging serve as signals to producers who on that basis decide what goods need to be produced. Their decision in this regard does not arise from any desire to satisfy the preferences of consumers, but from their own desire for profit because they know that only by responding to the order of the consumers will they be able to augment their own profits. The preferences of the consumers and the desire of the producers to make profit thus get translated into the kinds of goods to be produced. That decision, in turn, shows the signals to the resource holders as to where their resources are likely to get the highest returns or claims. They, therefore, respond to the production pattern by withdrawing resources from those goods for which demand has declined to those where it has gone up; but, again, not out of consideration for the producers or consumers, but solely from their own self-interest.[5]

Through these processes the quantities of all goods to be produced are determined, the prices of all goods and resources are determined and all claims are settled. All these are achieved through exchange, and the exchange process can go on (will go on) till no consumer or producer or resource-holder has a desire to exchange further, because everybody's independently defined personal preferences are satisfied through interactions in the markets. For all this to happen, there are some additional conditions to be imposed, such as consumers must be consistent with their preference orderings, that the nature of technology must conform to certain stipulations (in particular that production process must be scale neutral, or at least that the costs of production must not decrease as the size of production increases) and so on. Usually these conditions are assumed to be satisfied. On the basis of these assumptions the claim made is not only that the capitalist economy ensures consumers' sovereignty, but that the self-interest of decision-makers who take the market signals as the basis of their decisions and actions results in a socially satisfactory economic situation of 'efficient' allocation of resources. In other words that it will not be possible to make any one better off without making someone else worse off, respecting the preferences of everyone. In this sense the representation features the freedom of individuals in a capitalist economy to make choices and suggests that when individuals act in their own interest, there comes about a socially efficient outcome. Adam Smith had argued that it was as though the system was being guided by an 'invisible hand'.

Capitalism and consumers' sovereignty

The representation of the capitalist economy as an exchange system which is usually traced to the writings of Adam Smith, which was first formally presented by Leon Walras and subsequently developed and reformulated by some of the leading economists of our own time, points to many important aspects of the capitalist economy—the dominance of markets; the role that prices play as signals to decision-making; the freedom that members of the economy have to purchase the goods of their choice etc. But while it may be a throughgoing logical exercise with considerable aesthetic appeal, it has major weaknesses as a representation of capitalist reality. For one thing, although it is possible to set up an 'all exchange' system depicting its logical features, we have seen in Chapter 4 that no functioning economy ever becomes fully marketised. Similarly (as we shall see later in this chapter) no real-life economy can function without an authority which lays down its basic working conditions, and the capitalist economy is no exception. So the attempt to depict the capitalist economy as functioning entirely on the basis of price signals is a misleading exaggeration.

Another weakness is that exercises of this kind are usually 'static' that is, for a given time with the claim that the analysis can be 'dynamised' by comparing present and future markets and prices for every commodity, just as markets and prices for different commodities are dealt with at any given time. But the future is not the present with a time dimension added to it. Knowledge about future markets cannot be as adequate as knowledge about present markets, which itself may not be complete in many cases. It is also well known that producers who plan production for the future are more guided by their expectations about future market conditions in general, particularly the expected purchasing power of different sections of the population than by anticipated prices. A capitalist economy functions a great deal in terms of future expectations and price signals are poor guides as far as the future is concerned. This was one of the major differences between J.M. Keynes (Keynes, 1936) and other economists of his period about the representation of the capitalist economy, and the so-called 'Keynesian revolution' owed much to this perception of Keynes about the investment decisions of capitalists.

The claim made about 'consumers' sovereignty' under capitalism in the representation is also not quite valid. Capitalist producers do not, and do not have to, respond to the needs or preferences of consumers as such. On the other hand, the concern of the capitalist producers is to sell what they produce and so they concentrate their attention on purchasers rather than on consumers *per se*. Because of the interdependence of production through exchange, the vast majority of purchasers in a capitalist system are producers themselves. Of course, the 'final consumers' also provide the demand for the goods that producers make available in the market. Here the producers are more guided by the purchasing power of the consumers, and production decisions are geared to capture the purchasing power of the consumers rather than to respond to their needs or even preferences. Consumers' preferences too can be expressed only through the power to bid for goods because the only language that the market understands is the language of purchasing power. What are referred to as price signals are essentially expressions of purchasing power, and it is to that power and that power alone that the market responds. The market is not a neutral social institution; since it is propelled by purchasing power, it is a close ally of those who have resource-power.

What is the basis of the resource-power itself? It is the manner in which resources are owned and controlled in the system. A major weakness of the representation of the capitalist economy as an exchange system is that it is rather silent on this aspect. The analysis proceeds on the basis of a given initial endowment of resources among the resource holders. Analysis cannot certainly alter the initial endowment. But except in rare instances the analysis does not even bring out the implication of the initial endowment condition on the inferences made. To see what this means, imagine that the initial endowment is such that 90 per cent of the resources are owned by one rich person and the rest are fairly equally distributed among 99 poor owners. If an 'all exchange' economy emerges from these conditions, and going by its laws, it can be seen that production will respond substantially to what the one rich person wants rather than to the needs of the ninety and nine—one luxurious house for the one who can commandeer most of the goods in the economy rather than dwellings for the vast majority. Prices that get established in the system will also reflect this basic condition. And the 'social efficiency of production' that those prices reflect will also be a derivative of the initial endowment of resources. Where this is recognised, analysts point out that if the initial endowment conditions are altered, another configuration of prices supporting another socially efficient pattern of production can be derived. But the analysis has nothing to suggest which among the many possible efficient points is to be preferred. Consequently the 'all exchange' representation of the capitalist economy tends to glide over questions relating to ownership and control over resources which, as we have seen right from the beginning, are among the major issues in *any* economy.

But one aspect of the ownership issue emerges rather subtly from the representation. To the extent that the capitalist economy functions through exchange it is an economy of owners, for, as we have noted in the preceding chapter, exchange as an activity is between owners. The capitalist economy being one of buying and selling, it is confined to owners, to those who possess something which they can sell in exchange for what they wish to buy.[6] Capitalism, then, is an 'owners only' club. The ownership aspects that remained muted in the rudimentary economy, and even in the village economy to a large extent, comes to the fore in a capitalist economy, but subtly garbed in the categories of exchange and markets.

Capitalism as an economy of owners

That being the case we need to turn to a representation of the capitalist economy that brings the ownership issue to the centre of the analysis. To make sure that such a representation is not merely an exercise in logic let us look at the historical conditions under which capitalism first emerged in England during the period from about the end of the fifteenth century to the middle of the eighteenth century.[7]

During this period, several things happened which caused the break-up of the kind of production and social organisations characteristic of a village economy which in England (and most of Europe) took the form of feudalism. One of these was what has come to be known as the 'breaking-up of the lands of feudal retainers', that is, denying the traditional claims of a group of people whose survival depended on their rendering services (frequently military) to the feudal lords. During this period there also took place another major socio-economic process, 'the enclosure movement' which was an attempt to take over open lands used by peasants for culti-vation and to enclose them for sheep breeding which was a response to the rising price of wool and the profitability of the wool trade. Once again, many who were making a living by cultivating land were thrown out of their traditional avocations and into the open. Something similar happened when those who were hereditary tenants and sub-tenants in the lands held by the church monasteries were also deprived of their traditional rights on land. The powerful groups emerging as a result of these processes soon began to take over state lands and common lands to which many people of the lower ranks had access for gathering and pasturing. There was also the process of peasants working on small plots of land finding the land inadequate to support their families and leaving cultivation after transfer-ring land to larger peasants. Indebtedness to traders sometimes imposed the same problem on rural artisans who had to surrender their tools and emerge as 'free labourers'.

The large numbers of proletariat who emerged as a result of these processes were free in two distinct senses. Firstly, they were free of all their feudal obligations to render labour services to those who were eco-nomically and socially above them, which meant that they were also denied all claims that were part of the old socio-economic order and had nothing other than their own labour-power to fall back upon. Secondly, they now became free to sell their labour power to anybody who was willing to bid for what they had available for sale. For the first time, therefore, there emerged a new class of people with socio-economic characteristics entirely different from all that had existed earlier: a class which had no claims on society and owned nothing other than their labour power.

Along with this new class of owners, there emerged another group of owners, those who owned money and thus came to have command over all forms of resources and were eager to have more of it.

Marx was the first to recognise a reciprocal relationship between these two kinds of owners. He said: 'capital presupposes wage labour; wage labour presupposes capital. They reciprocally condition the existence of each other; they reciprocally bring forth each other' (Marx, 1952: 13).

We saw in Chapter 3 how the village economy gives rise to a class of people not directly involved in production coming to appropriate the surplus arising from production, and how that surplus forms the basis of trade. In Chapter 4 we saw how traders as a class emerge and how they use trade to acquire surplus value. These processes too are long term ones; longer, in fact, than the ones we have dealt with above because they are part of the village economy itself. Historically, they too tended to become accelerated in England during the period we have examined. We shall not go into the historical processes in detail. But it should not be difficult to see how merchants turn to purchase land when land becomes the key factor in a flourishing wool trade. Similarly, it is easy to see that merchants who had no special interests in the production activities coming to possess the looms of weavers and the tools of artisans. The socio-economic processes, therefore, bring to the fore a group of people who possess variety of items of wealth—raw materials, tools, land—all useful in production, and all coming to be valued and quantified through exchange. The money value of these commoditised goods may also be designated as capital, capital in the primitive form of accumulation.

We now have two groups of owners—those who *must* sell their labour power for sheer survival and those who are eager to buy labour power in order to make use of their wealth—their capital in production. Frequently these two owners are referred to as *workers* and *capitalists* respectively. While the motivation of the former to sell their labour power is clear, a little more scrutiny is needed as to why the latter are eager to buy labour power.

Capitalism and the appropriation of surplus

In both Chapters 2 and 3 we have seen that workers can and do produce more than what is required to maintain themselves. In the rudimentary economy the surplus that the workers produce goes towards the maintenance of dependants—the young and the old in the community, the infirm and so on. In the village economy the surplus that the workers generate is appropriated by those who claim to be owners of land. This means that in the process of production some surplus is generated which, then, is made use of in different ways. Workers do not become productive without some form of non-labour resources (land, tools etc.) which enable them to activate and realise their labour power. But those non-labour resources do not and cannot generate any surplus. Left to themselves they will remain what they are and nothing more. So, while they are necessary components in the production process, they do not generate the surplus; the generation of surplus, therefore, is done entirely by labour. In the rudimentary economy and the village economy, the inert components of production are under the control of the workers. In the village economy those who claim to be owners of these components, especially land, appropriate part of the surplus generated by workers using the claim of ownership as the justification for this vertical transfer.

Now, in a capitalist economy, the capitalists come to have both owner-ship of and control over the non-labour components in production—tools and machines, all converted into value terms and thus becoming capital. But these things, by themselves, do not produce; neither can they generate a surplus. But capitalists are interested in accumulating their capital because thereby they become more wealthy and come to have further command over resources. To do this they must come to have labour power also under their command so that they can put it to use in production with the non-labour resources they own and control. And because 'free labour' is available, eager to sell labour power, the capitalists need not exert any pressure over labour to acquire the labour power, but are in a position to purchase it. Thus the two owners—capitalists who own the inert components of production and workers who own (nothing but) their labour power—enter into exchange so as to organise production.

The claim of capitalism to be a system of generalised exchange can now be given a different interpretation than what was seen earlier. It does not have to mean that all goods (and services) are commoditised under capitalism. But exchange under capitalism comes to have a new dimension, as it were. Till capitalism emerged, exchange was substantially confined to produced goods, pulses, bananas, and the like. Capitalist exchange spreads into the realm of nature—commoditising land and other natural resources—and into labour power as well. Perhaps there was occasional trading in land and in labour services prior to the emergence of capitalism. But under capitalism physical resources, which are natural endowments, and labour power *must be* commoditised. There cannot be a capitalist system of production unless there is wage labour.

The commoditisation of labour power marks a further transformation of exchange. For, until then exchange simply establishes equivalences (in value terms) between goods exchanged. Through the M–C–M' form of exchange, it is possible (for the trader) to devise some surplus value (ΔM or the difference between M' and M); but as long as the transactions are of produced goods the surplus value is derived only by buying cheap and selling dear, because no produced good *generates* surplus value. With the purchase of labour power, on the other hand, the buyer comes to be in possession of the *source* of surplus (labour power) and through this transaction he is able to *appropriate* the surplus value. In other words, exchange of goods remains at the level of horizontal transfer; when labour power enters into exchange, an element of vertical transfer also enters into the transaction similar to the transfer between the producer and 'owner' in a village economy. Whether in a village economy or in a capitalist economy the vertical transfer from the worker to the owner is an appropriation of the surplus that labour power generates, and this appropriation of surplus generated by workers is defined by the owners as *exploitation*.[8]

In pre-capitalist economic systems exploitation is quite palpable: a share of the goods that the worker produces (let us say grain) is taken from the field, where the worker produces it, to the owner's granary. But the nature of exploitation changes and becomes covert under capitalism. This is partly because of the change in the organisation of production. Because the means of production (non-labour resources) are now owned by the capitalist owner, there is the appearance of the owner being a partner in the production process and hence a claim on the produce by the owner appears reasonable. Further, under capitalism the transfer of the surplus does not take place in the physical form, but in value form because of the conversion of the goods produced, as also of the purchased labour power into value categories via exchange. Hence the appropriation of surplus (exploitation) which is usually achieved through various coercive measures such as the use of physical force in pre-capitalist orders is achieved through the normal exchange process under capitalism.

Production-exchange-ownership nexus under capitalism

But there is a major difference between exchange of produced goods between two parties and the exchange between the owners of capital and the owners of labour power. As parties to an exchange and as owners they stand at 'the same level' (unlike a landlord and a tenant). But in the exchange–cum–production process that the owners of capital and the owners of labour power enter into, the owners of capital also come to have ownership of the (additional) goods produced by virtue of the ownership of the means of production.[9] This is part of the institutional arrangements of capitalism, which confers the ownership of the additional goods to the owners of the means of production rather than the owners of labour power. There is, therefore, a crucial asymmetry of the ownership rights that lies concealed here which makes one of the parties to the trans-action more equal than the other even when both are owners in a technical sense. This special ownership right of the owners of capital, naturally, confers on them greater economic power, a fact which the 'all exchange' representation of the capitalist economy misses or hides.

The fact that the exchange between the owners of capital and the owners of labour power is not merely exchange, but also linked to pro-duction brings about some difference to the understanding of that exchange. It is simultaneously a C–M–C' form of exchange and an M–C–M' form of exchange. From the point of view of the owner of labour power, it is a C–M–C' form, the first C being labour power and C' being other com-modities that are to be purchased after C is converted into money in the first part of the exchange. For the owner of capital it is of the M–C–M' form. But he purchases labour power not merely to sell it; if it were so he would at best be a labour contractor, not a capitalist producer aiming to appropriate the surplus value that labour power is capable of generating in the process of production. In order to activate production, the capitalist must use his initial M for the purchase of not only labour power, but also of the means of production; machines and materials for instance. Labour power and these goods must then be combined to produce additional goods. This production process which is unavoidably linked to exchange can be represented through a modification or elaboration of the M–C–M' form of exchange:

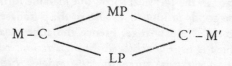

With the initial amount of money the capitalist buys a set of commodities consisting of means of production (MP) and labour power (LP), converts them into a new commodity (or commodities) C' which is then sold for M' with M' > M.

The link-up between exchange and production also shows what the owners of capital are after. Both as capitalist producers and as M–C–M' exchangers their aim is to augment the value of their capital, that is the accumulation of exchange value. They produce goods to commoditise them; they commoditise goods in order to convert them into value cat-egories which become the measure of their ownership and the power that it confers on them over the entire system. The distinguishing feature of a capitalist economy, then, is not that it makes exchange and markets wide-spread; rather, it is that it attempts to convert everything into exchange value which is a homogeneous (and quantitative) index of economic wealth and power. It is in this sense that the accumulation of exchange value becomes the organising principle of the capitalist economy.

The representation of the capitalist economy in terms of its ownership categories,—therefore, is more revealing of its essential features than its representation as an 'all exchange' system. These features are a separation of the means of production from the workers who use it because of the changes that come about in the ownership of non-labour resources through their commoditisation; the commoditisation of labour power and the emergence of a group of owners who have nothing other than their labour-power to sell; the exchange between the owners of labour power and the owners of capital, (that is, generalised command over resources) and the appropriation of the surplus generated by the former by the latter in their quest for the accumulation of exchange value; and the coalescence of exchange and production to facilitate the commoditisation of everything that enters into production.

Capitalism as an exclusive economic system

There is a further essential feature of the capitalist economy that can be captured more clearly by going back to its representation as an 'all exchange' system. We have already indicated that because capitalism functions through exchange, there is place in it only for those who have something to sell. But whether what one possesses is saleable or not is not decided *a priori*, but is determined by the pricing process of the system itself. The working of the system may result in some of the goods not being commoditised because the supply of such goods is in excess of the demand for them which the system determines. In the case of produced goods this happens, for instance, when the availability of a close substitute shifts demand away from them. An example is where the availability of plastic pots and pans makes them substitutes for mud pots and vessels. The producer of mud pots may discover that there is no demand for the goods that he possesses and hence they cannot be sold. In this process the producer himself may become dispossessed, not because he does not possess anything, but because the market assigns nil values to the pots as well as to the skills he possesses. Hence he will also cease to be an owner because what he owns is not saleable, and thus he will be automatically dropped out of the owners' club. He does not have to become a permanent drop-out, however. What the system would demand of him is to shift from the production of mud pots to the production of plastic vessels—if he can, that is. In this sense a capitalist economy is a system of constant, almost perpetual adjustments, each with its set of consequences on the persons involved.

There is one commodity that the capitalist economy has a built-in tendency to make redundant and where the adjustment is not easy. This commodity is labour power. This may appear rather strange because one of the distinguishing features of capitalism is that unlike other systems it commoditises labour power and commoditisation of labour power is necessary for the owners of capital to appropriate via exchange the surplus that workers generate. But what the owner of capital does is to convert part of the surplus that he appropriates into tools and machines which on the one hand become partial substitutes for labour power in production, but on the other hand increases the productivity of labour power in production. If the latter helps the owner of capital to come to have a larger amount of surplus value, he will not hesitate to reduce his demand for labour power. When the system as a whole is taken, therefore, the tendency to make labour power frequently redundant becomes a pronounced feature of the capitalist economy. When this happens, the plight of the owners of labour power (that is, workers) is similar to the owner of the mud pot which the system determined superfluous. Their plight, in fact, will be worse. If labour power is the only good they have for sale, they have no easy way of escaping from this situation. Also, unlike the supply of mud pots which can be reduced when the demand for them shrinks, making adjustments in the supply of labour power is very difficult, because whether utilised or not, it is there, and has to be maintained. The owners of labour power, then, find that the only commodity they possess and can sell is not saleable any more and thus they cease to be owners also. Once this happens, they are thrown out of the membership of the exclusive owners' club that is the capitalist economy. This, then is another crucial attribute of the capitalist economy: *it is an exclusive economic system* with the built-in tendency to make labour power redundant from time to time because the 'worth' of every good is determined by its pricing process, and frequently labour power is shown to be 'worthless', having a zero exchange value. This brings out one of the inner paradoxes or contradictions of the capitalist economy: it cannot function without labour power, and yet it makes labour power frequently redundant.

Labour power being made redundant and its owners being thrown out of the system is what is referred to in day-to-day language as unemployment. Unemployment is recognised as a chronic malady of the capitalist economy. It may be noted, too, that the problem surfaces not only in what may be referred to as labour-abundant countries (such as India); the worst forms of unemployment have occurred and continue to recur in labour-scarce economies such as the United States of America and the countries of Europe. It has been recognised, too, that the problem is one of deficiency of demand either directly for labour power or for the products of labour power which, again, indirectly affects those who are the owners and sellers of labour power.

Capitalists and workers under capitalism
It may be argued that some of the problems discussed above arise because the second representation of the capitalist economy (as consisting of only owners) makes use of a special category of owners, viz., those who have only their labour power to sell. Is this not a case where rather arbitrary and unrealistic assumptions are made for the sake of the niceties of abstraction? For, while such a condition might have been realistic as far as nascent capitalism was concerned, it is no longer true in a typical capitalist economy like that of the U.S.A. or Japan or any of the West European countries today where the workers—and thanks to capitalist development of the past—own much more than their labour power. They possess practically all the necessities of life, many of the luxuries, and in many instances claims on wealth such as bank balances and shares in the capital of industrial concerns, including those which employ them. And their wages are far in excess of what is required for bare survival so that the surplus that they generate is not entirely appropriated by the capitalist. If the features of the capitalist economy have changed so drastically, how useful is it, and how valid, to continue to represent it in terms of its rudimentary version?

This is a very important question and must be adequately answered. First and foremost let us note that capitalist economies have changed, and as we shall soon see, it is in the nature of capitalism to go on changing. Some of its features today are certainly very different from what they were two centuries or even a century ago. But this is similar to the statement that human beings themselves have changed a great deal over the centuries. The issue to consider in both instances is whether there are species-specific characteristics that remain invariant so that a capitalist economy whether nascent or advanced can be considered as *capitalist* economy, and human beings whether primitive or modern can be considered as *human* beings. What we have identified as the essential features of the capitalist economy are its species-specific attributes which are present wherever and whenever an economy is designated as a *capitalist* economy. That is why it is important to recognise that making labour power redundant is an essential feature of a capitalist economy, both early capitalist economies and late capitalist economies; so, also, the other essential features identified, accumulation of exchange value, appropriation by the owners of capital of surplus generated by the owners of labour power etc.

The representation of the capitalist economy which has enabled us to identify these features, therefore, is functionally adequate even when some aspects of it may not be 'realistic'. Let us trace some more functional properties of that representation. It portrays the capitalist economy as consisting of two sets of owners, those who own the means of production and those who own labour power entering into an exchange-production activity. It brings out the crucial significance of the nature of ownership in a capitalist economy. It also emphasises the asymmetry in the power of ownership of the two sets of owners. It also draws a distinction between the earnings of the owners of the means of production (that is, property incomes) and the earnings of the owners of labour-power (i.e., wage income). And by positing the two set of owners as different in ownership as well as in orientation, it brings out the element of conflict that underlies the economic system in contrast to the element of harmony that the 'all exchange' representation of the economy tends to feature.

If these basic features of a capitalist economy are understood, modifications in the representation can be made (and should be made) to take into account the changing reality of capitalist economies. We shall touch upon only one such aspect—the economic progress of workers as a capitalist economy develops. This is a fact that must be accepted whether or not it is compatible with certain theoretical formulations about what is likely to happen to the condition of workers as capitalists go on accumulating capital and wealth. It has happened for a variety of reasons. An important one is the manner in which the State in capitalist countries (especially those that have democratic political structures) has intervened to keep under control the brute acquisitive tendencies of the owners of capital, by prescribing legally binding minimum wages and other conditions favouring workers. It is also due to the organised strength of workers who, through trade union movements have mobilised something of a countervailing power against the owners of capital. But most of all, it is the result of technological progress which was expected to be a feature of the capitalist economy, but whose role in raising the productivity of labour has been immense in advanced capitalist economies. The surplus that the owners of capital appropriate, it may be noted, is the difference between labour productivity and the wage rate. Hence where the former is growing rapidly, appropriation of surplus can continue without pressing the wage rate to the lowest possible level. The owners of capital, therefore, can afford to let the owners of labour power have some share in the rising productivity, ensuring, as far as possible, that the increment in wage rate does not exceed the increment in productivity.

When workers come to have a wage level higher than what is required for subsistence, they usually tend to raise their level of consumption and thus move to a higher standard of living. Subsequently, they may also retain some of the surplus, generally converting it into claims on assets (capital or wealth). Thus while owners of capital tend to convert the surplus accumulated into physical assets, owners of labour power who come to have a share in the surplus usually hold it in the form of financial assets. Even with this sort of sharing of surplus, the representation of the capitalist economy as consisting of owners of capital and owners of labour power is useful because it shows that there is a difference between the earnings of the former which consist primarily of property income and those of the latter which consist essentially of wage income. While individual workers may come to have some property income and in rare cases may even 'graduate' into the rank of the capitalists, a capitalist economy as such can exist and function only if a vast section of the population consists primarily of wage earners. The second representation of the capitalist economy that we have seen is, so to say, the limit case of such an economy and what the representation depicts is not vitiated even if all instances of the capitalist economy do not strictly conform to it. As we shall see in Part II, the main feature of the emerging capitalist economy in India (and many other Developing Countries) is that it functions in the context of many who have nothing other than their labour power to sell. The representation, therefore, is literally applicable in many parts of the world even today.

PRODUCTION IN A CAPITALIST ECONOMY

Having gained some insight into the essential features of the capitalist economy, using two standard representations, we can now turn to some of its specific features. While exchange becomes, of necessity, an all-pervading activity in a capitalist economy, what distinguishes it is not the generalisation of exchange as such, but the exchange–production–ownership nexus that the generalisation of exchange makes possible. In this exchange–production–ownership tie-up, productive activity and the organisation of production in a capitalist economy become distinctly different that in other kinds of economies, especially those that preceded it.

Productive activity in all economies prior to capitalism was organised to fulfil directly specified human needs. And, as we saw in the treatment of the village economy, for thousands of years the main purpose of production was to provide livelihood to the members of society; and so the production of food, or agriculture in general with its close association with nature, was the central productive activity of economies throughout the world, along with the production of cloth which, again, is a basic requirement of human beings. To put it briefly, production in pre-capitalist economies was the generation of use values.

The quest for exchange value
In a capitalist economy the orientation of production changes radically. It is not *directly* concerned with use values any more. Production becomes part of the capitalist's incessant quest for exchange value. Its rationale

turns out to be the accumulation of exchange value, or wealth in the abstract, and not wealth in any specified form. There was place for wealth in all previous societies, but wealth in specified forms, as land, buildings, cattle or even slaves. But the quest for wealth in the abstract—and using production to achieve that objective—emerges only in a capitalist economy. A capitalist economy can be depicted as the capitalists' unending search for the accumulation of capital and more capital. Now, capital as accumulated wealth has existed in many pre-capitalist economies and in the form of tools, at least, it played a part in production. But a capitalist economy is one in which accumulated wealth is used primarily to accumulate more of the same.

It may appear rather strange that it should be so, and it may appear stranger still that practically all major features of a capitalist economy can be shown to be related to this organising principle of that economy. So, let us examine it in some detail.

The capitalist wants to accumulate capital. He can do this only by producing to make profit. In order to do that there must be persons who can be lured or compelled to work for him. Once the goods are produced they must be marketed, which means that there must be a group of buyers who have the ability to purchase them and who can be persuaded to do so. The exchange value of goods thus realised must be enough to meet all the costs of production, to provide for the subsistence of the producer *and* to leave a surplus. It must then be possible to make use of that surplus to get the whole production-exchange circuit going again—in the endless pursuit of more, or in the incessant circuit of capital. These chains are by no means simple processes. At each stage, organisations, institutions and authority are required to back them up and to ensure that they go on. All these processes will have to be gone through for every good produced, and for every good needed to produce that good. These processes are the experiences of all producers. It is the totality of all these activities, arrangements and persons that constitute a capitalist economy. It is a very complex entity indeed.

Let us enter into that complexity through one of its typical production units, a factory.[10] The factory is owned by a capitalist. The factory has within it the machinery and power (electricity, let us say) required for production as also the raw materials (raw cotton if it is a factory producing yarn, or yarn if it is a factory producing cloth, or cloth if it is a factory producing garments etc.). There are also workers in the factory. Hence a factory consists of machines, materials and workers. In the process of production, workers work on materials with the help of machines. From the capitalist's point of view, machines, materials and workers (their labour power, as we saw in the last section) are all commodities that he has purchased and constitute his cost of production. After production takes place, the commodity produced must be sold in the market and the capitalist receives a sum of money as the sales value. The sales value minus the costs incurred becomes the capitalist's profit.

The maximising of this profit is the aim of the capitalist producer. While we have noted this already, we have not drawn out its implications. The first implication is that the capitalist producer has no commitment to produce the particular commodity that he is currently producing (let us say cloth) or any other specific commodity for that matter. In other words, his interest in production is not to generate a good of use value, but to produce a commodity—*any* commodity—that will fetch him the profit, which is his main concern. At the same time, he cannot totally ignore all considerations of use value. In fact, he must be concerned with what his unknown potential buyers will consider to be use value. And, if his quest for profit is to materialise, he must be prepared to shift over to what the potential buyers will consider as use value. To take an example, if he has been producing cloth using cotton yarn, but realises that potential buyers consider cloth made of synthetic fibre to be of greater use value, he must shift from the production of cotton cloth to the production of polyester cloth. Now, this shift would certainly mean that he purchases different kinds of material; he may have to change the machines he has been using; and quite possibly he may have to change some of his workers also. But change he must, if that is what the quest for profit indicates. The change from the production of cloth using cotton to cloth using synthetic fibre may be marginal, but the capitalist producer must be prepared to shift from the production of cloth to the production of plastics, or pencils or powder or whatever it may be that the market shows up as the commodity that will enable him to make profits.

Nature of competition

It is not difficult to see why he will have to do it. He is not the only producer; he is not the only capitalist. A feature of a capitalist economy is that anyone with capital can enter into any sphere of production. Neither custom nor authority comes in the way of anyone entering into a sphere of production in which he perceives opportunities to make profit. Which means that every capitalist producer has to compete with other capitalist producers. In purchasing commodities for production, every capitalist is disbursing his money capital to other capitalists (that is producers of machines and materials) and to workers. And every capitalist is trying to (must try to) win back for himself as much as possible of the money capital that other capitalists have relinquished in similar fashion. This continuous dissolution and recapture is the essence of the process of competition which is another feature of a capitalist economy arising directly from the organising principle of that economy. Of course, capitalist producers do not recapture the money capital of other capitalists directly. It happens through the production-exchange processes. And since in those processes buyers and sellers are involved, it is also the attempt to mop up as much as possible of the general purchasing power that is floating around. In other words, each capitalist producer disburses his money capital first in the form of a series of purchases, generates surplus value by getting labour power to produce more than what it costs to purchase it, and realises that surplus value as profit by selling his commodities to other producers and final consumers. In both the terminal stages of purchase and sale, he is competing with other capitalists who are also trying to achieve the same objective. Competition, in this sense, is rather different from what it is frequently understood to be. As one commentator puts it: 'competition does not simply mean the vying of vendors who sell similar products in a market...but the inevitable exposure of each capitalist to the efforts of others to gain as much as possible of the public's purchasing power' (Heilbroner, 1988:·57).

An implication of competition of this kind is that capitalist producers must be constantly on the watch not only to make use of every opportunity to make profits, but also to create such opportunities to get the better of their competitors. Creation of such opportunities typically takes the form of innovations—new products, new processes, new sources of supply, new markets, new forms of organisation—which strike, not at the margins of the profits and the outputs of the existing firms, but at their foundations and their very lives, 'the perennial gale of creative destruction' as Joseph Schumpeter, one of the well known writers on capitalism describes it. Let us look both at its creative and destructive aspects.

Creation and destruction
The creative aspects of this process strikes the eye whether we look at the historical evolution of capitalism in England first, and throughout Europe later, or at the contemporary penetration of capitalism in different parts of the world. Imagine, for a moment, a catalogue of new products that have been introduced since the·early days of the emergence of a capitalist economy. It will include virtually all the wide variety of manufactured goods that we know of and are used to! And consider the new products that routinely enter into our lives day by day.[11] One may say that these are the achievements of science and technology rather than of capitalism. That is true up to a point. But it is the quest for profit by capitalist producers that has brought science and technology into the daily lives of human beings during the past couple of centuries. Equally impressive is the wide range of new production processes—such as the introduction of

division of labour in the manufacture of pins that Adam Smith wrote about, to the many changes that take place day by day in contemporary life. What Adam Smith could only vaguely anticipate, Karl Marx clearly and forcefully stated a few decades later. Marx was one of the earliest to see why a capitalist economy could not function without constantly re-volutionising the techniques of production and augmenting productive forces. And writing during the early days of capitalism, he recognised that during its rule of scarcely one hundred years it had created more massive and more colossal productive forces than had all preceding generations together. 'Subjection of Nature's forces to man, machinery, application of chemistry to industry and agriculture, steam navigation, railways, electric telegraphs, clearing of whole continents for cultivation, canalisation of rivers, whole populations conjured out of the ground—what earlier century had even a presentiment that such productive forces slumbered in the lap of social labour?' (Marx and Engels, 1971: 37).

It is not necessary to go into the details of all the changes that have come about in production technology in the century and a half since those words were written. Neither is it necessary to document the new markets that capitalist production has brought into being. We may use the words of Schumpeter, once again, to drive home the main point: 'Capitalism, then, is by nature a form or method of economic change and not only never is but never can be stationary.... The fundamental impulse that sets and keeps the capitalist engine in motion comes from the new consumers' goods, the new methods of production or transportation, the new markets, the new forms of industrial organisation that capitalist enterprise creates.' (Schumpeter, 1974: 22–23)

Whether through new products or processes, or through the discovery of new markets or through tapping of new supplies, a capitalist producer who innovates is fairly certain to make profits—short term monopoly profits we may say—till his competitors catch up with him. And when what appeared as new becomes old and widespread, something else has to come out as new again and the gale of creation goes on.

What of the destructive aspect of that gale? One aspect of the destruc-tion is simply a natural corollary of the process of innovation. When something new appears—whether as product or process—what existed hitherto tends to become obsolete and to be discarded. Electric lights make oil lamps outmoded; motor cars displace horse carriages and so on. And, indeed, the latest model car makes previous models obsolete. There is destruction and waste in all of these. Some argue also that affluent capi-talist societies can function effectively, that is, continue to provide profit to producers, and thus sustain production, only through planned obsol-escence and by systematically wasting resources.

But there is another aspect of the destructive thrust of innovation and competition which may not be very obvious. Competition affects production units directly and brings about changes in the organisation of production. We may recall that competition is part of the process of accumulation and that with accumulation the tendency is for production to become more and more mechanised, that is, for the machine component of the capitalist's initial purchases to become proportionately larger. This results in both the concentration and centralisation of capital. Concentration is the process whereby, when capital accumulates, individual capitalists come to have larger and larger amounts of capital under their control. Centralisation, on the other hand, is the process whereby existing capitals tend to merge. Both these processes result from the interaction of technology with economic conditions; and though there can be exceptions, the general tendency in both instances will be for effective control over capital to go into the hands of fewer capitalists. And to the extent that control over capital can be used to bring about technical change and to have easier access to credit, the general tendency will be for the larger capitalists to drive the smaller ones out or to swallow them up, just as in the world of nature the bigger fish tend to swallow up the smaller ones. The destruction, therefore, is of some of the capitalists and their production units whch is seen as a creative opportunity by other and usually the larger capitalists. As Wallerstein says: 'Bankruptcy has been the harsh cleansing fluid of the capitalist system, constantly forcing all economic actors to keep more or less to the well-trodden rut, pressurising them to act in such a way that collectively there has been ever further accumulation of capital.' (Wallerstein, 1983: 18)

This should not be interpreted to mean that capitalist processes will lead to the elimination of small capitalists and small production units. Such is not always the case. Smaller ones may continue; but the larger ones will dominate and frequently use the smaller ones as shock-absorbers in what is essentially an unsteady pattern of development, as we shall see in the next section.

DEVELOPMENT OF A CAPITALIST ECONOMY

A capitalist economy must grow; a capitalist economy must change. Both these arise from its very nature. Having examined the central logic of a capitalist economy in the preceding section we shall, in this section, consider its growth and change.

What basically gives rise to a capitalist economy? Lenin answered this question by saying that 'the starting point of all capital...is the accumulation of free money in the hands of individuals (by free money we mean that money which is not needed for personal consumption etc)'. (Lenin, 1964: 364)

To illustrate this he referred to an episode from nineteenth century Russia (*Ibid.*, 366–68). It is about a group of women lace-makers whose produce was initially consumed by the landlords of their own locality. But the women soon found going from house to house inconvenient and decided to entrust the sale to one of the lace-makers who was compensated for time she lost. She would collect the lace from all producers, take the goods to the nearby city (Moscow), sell them there and return with thread for further production. Soon she would become a specialist in trade. She would bring other wares from the city and sell them to her colleagues and others in the rural area. She would also sell the lace above the set price and pocket the difference. She would take advantage of the monopoly she had over trade to subjugate the lace-makers completely. She would bring back from the city fresh orders, give loans required during the period of production and buy up all goods produced. 'Thus, on the one hand, the tradeswoman becomes the most needed, indispensable person: on the other, she gradually develops into a person who cruelly exploits the labour of others'.

Similar episodes can be found in several parts of Europe in the sixteenth century (and earlier, perhaps) as also in many parts of the world today. Whether of the past or the present, such instances point to one of the commonest patterns of the rise of capitalism, capitalism emerging from trade.

This is not surprising in view of the close connection of the productive process with exchange in a capitalist economy and in view of the fact that accumulating exchange value is the organising principle of capitalist economy. According to Maurice Dobb in his well-known *Studies in the Development of Capitalism*, trade was the soil from which capitalism first grew. He says:

Not only did its impact on the mediaevel village have a potent influence, if only an indirect one by promoting a differentiation among the peasantry into well-to-do peasants and poor, thereby fostering the growth of a rural semi-proletariat from among the latter; not only have markets shaped the moulds into which industry settled....; but one can say that it is periods of rapidly expanding markets as well as of expanding labour supply which are the periods *par excellence* of industrial expansion, of progress both in productive technique and in forms of organisation. (Dobb, 1963: 26)

There is a second, and more straightforward process of capitalist development. A producer himself, or a group of producers, may set himself (themselves) as capitalist producer(s) by using his (their) surplus to employ hired labour. This usually happens when, as a result of changes in the techniques of production, the *physical* capital required turns out to be more than can be obtained through the money capital available at the disposal of an ordinary producer who works with his own labour and the labour of the members of his family. When the physical capital requirement is high only some one who has more than the usual quantum of surplus at his disposal, or those who through changes in organisational structures (such as partnerships, joint-stock companies) can pool their surpluses that can remain in production, and the only way they can remain in production is to hire in labour power.

Thus the emergence of a capitalist economy witnesses a number of changes of economic and social significance—substantial increase in trade and profits through trade; changes in the techniques of production and the organisation of production; the commoditisation of labour power; and the acceptance of change as the normal pattern in society. Maurice Dobb makes the following comparison between a pre-capitalist independent petty producer and the production pattern in a capitalist economy:

> In the old days production had been essentially a human activity, generally individual in character, in the sense that the producer worked in his own time and his own fashion, independently of others, while the tools or simple implements he used were little more than an extension of his own fingers.... Relations of economic dependence between individual producers or between producer and merchant were not directly imposed by the necessities of the act of production itself, but by circumstances external to it: they were relations of purchase and sale of the finished or half-finished product, or else relations of debt incidental to the supply of raw materials or tools of the craft....

Dobb Continues

> Whereas in the old situation the independent small master, embodying the unity of human and non-human instruments of production, had been able to survive only because the latter remained meagre and no more than an appendage of the human hand, in the new situation he could no longer retain a foothold, both because the minimum size of a unit of production-process had grown too large for him to control and because the relationship between the human and mechanical instruments of production had been transformed . Capital was now needed to finance the complex equipment required by the new type of production unit; and a role was created for a new type of production unit; and a role was created for a new type of capitalist, no longer simply as usurer or trader in his counting-house or warehouse, but as a captain of industry, organiser and planner of the operations of the production unit, embodiment of an authoritarian discipline of a labour army, which, robbed of economic citizenship, had to be coerced to the fulfilment of its onerous duties in another's service

by the whip alternatively of hunger and of the master's overseer. So crucial was this transformation in its several aspects as fully to deserve the name of an economic revolution. (Dobb, 1963: 259–60)

Role of credit

One of the consequences of production undergoing a capitalist transformation is the new role that credit comes to play in the economy. Some form of borrowing and lending is a part of economic activity in practically all economies. In Chapter 3 we saw the special role that credit assumes when the production process extends over a period of time. This role of credit becomes more significant when investment decisions turn out to be the most important feature of production as it does in a capitalist economy. Investment, we have seen, is the formation of physical fixed capital anticipating increase in production at some future date. For a capitalist producer it is part of his attempt to accumulate more and more capital. But as accumulation takes place, and more and more people become property owners and thus come to have claims on the surplus generated, there may come about a distinction between property owners to whom surplus accrues and those who wish to convert surplus in its monetary form into surplus in its physical form. To put it differently, some will be eager to lend (their surplus) and others will be eager to borrow (that surplus); when these transactions increase a new market is created for loans or credit. Initially the transactions may be directly between the two parties, but as in the case of any other exchange, soon intermediaries or traders emerge. The trade or the intermediation function may be done by individuals, or more likely, by institutions that specialise in such operations. Banks are the typical institutions in this area and their function is to 'mobilise' the surplus (savings) that owners of property come to have and to lend it to those who wish to convert it into physical capital. Such conversion leads to an increase in output, a part of which will have to be paid to the intermediary for services rendered, of which a part is passed on to those who parted with their surplus. Thus 'everybody' (all property owners and intermediaries, that is) comes to benefit, or comes to have a share in the surplus generated by labour in the production process.

Credit, therefore, plays a very crucial role in a capitalist economy. It enables the capitalist producer to bring labour power into productive activity; it brings together those who wish to lend and those who wish to borrow; it results in the distribution of the surplus among different sections of property owners; and it results in a substantial increase in exchange and financial transactions in the economy. It is a critical link in a capitalist economy.

The growth of credit, in turn, brings about many changes in a capitalist

economy which are closely related to the intermediation function. Intermediation in credit transactions is a kind of trade, and like any trade, it
can become a profit-making activity. Consequently, for individual capitalists it can become an attractive manner of accumulation. There will,
therefore, be a tendency for capital to move increasingly into credit transactions. Secondly, the intermediation function results in the generation of
money and of money substitutes. Banks that receive deposits and lend
them out are holding the money surplus of depositors and at the same
time are making money available to users, thus generating more money
than would have been the case otherwise. In that process they are also
creating their own forms of money. Those who hold deposits with banks
can use cheques drawn against such deposits to pay for purchases and to
settle transactions or claims. A bank deposit, therefore, may be considered as a 'money substitute'. A long-term deposit in a bank is also a
form of money, except that it is not as 'liquid' as currency or coins but,
unlike them, it earns an interest. Other forms of money substitutes also
become available from time to time. A capitalist who borrows may issue
an IOU, and if some intermediaries are willing to do transactions in such
IOUs, they can become money substitutes. Such IOUs are what are
known as *bonds*. Similarly a capitalist who wants to raise capital (from
those who have surplus) can issue documents entitling them to a share of
that capital. A *share* thus becomes a kind of a certificate of ownership.
When many capitalists or groups of capitalists issue share certificates,
those who have surplus may be willing to 'subscribe' to such shares,
and soon a market for shares and intermediation in shares may also get
established.

Activities related to credit, thus, have a built-in tendency to proliferate
and diversify. The different forms of money substitutes that result from
that process are collectively known as *finance*. They are money substitutes
in two different senses. They can be used to settle claims instead of
money, that is, they perform some of the functions of a medium of exchange. Secondly, and more importantly, they become a store of value,
providing to owners of property or capital, a variety of options to hold
their wealth. We may, in a sense, think, of a wide spectrum of alternatives
available to the owners of wealth to hold their wealth, consisting of
money, bank deposits (among them short-term and long-term, for instance)
bonds, shares and physical forms of wealth such as buildings, land, and
machinery. Money is the most 'liquid' of these as it can be used for any
transaction, but it is the least profitable; in fact, it does not get any earnings at all. Other items have different levels of liquidity and profitability,
usually working in opposite directions, that is, the higher the liquidity,
the lower the profitability and *vice-versa*.

A well developed financial structure, financial intermediation and financial markets are, therefore, an indication of the growth and development of a capitalist economy. Sometimes it is considered that financial capitalism is an advanced stage of capitalism and that is a valid claim up to a point. But the important thing to note is that the development of a capitalist economy is a process of interaction among the three forms of capitalism; merchant capitalism, productive capitalism and finance capitalism. Except in the very early stages of a capitalist economy where financial capitalism may not be adequately developed, these three constantly interact. The dynamics of a capitalist economy (both in terms of increase in production and in terms of organisational patterns) is the result of such interaction.

Realms of capitalist expansion

If expansion is an inherent feature of a capitalist economy it is important to consider where, or into what areas, that expansion takes place. The expansion of capital takes place to some extent within the capitalist economy itself. It finds expression as the deepening of capital in each of the production processes which leads to higher productivity of labour power, generation of larger surplus and its appropriation by the capitalists, its ploughing back into production through capital deepening, and so on. The higher productivity that constantly results from this process may mean more and more existing goods, but certainly also the new goods that continuously become available in a capitalist economy.

But a capitalist economy also has an outward expansion. It results partly from the tendency of exchange via the mediation of money, particularly the M–C–M′ form of exchange, to 'burst' its local bonds and to spread to wherever the quest for profit leads it, as we saw in the discussion on exchange. In this sense, the outward thrust of capital is directed into the commoditisation of more and more goods, and in fact to make forays into as much of pre-capitalist economies as possible.[12] But while more and more goods get commoditised and become part of the capitalist circuit as a matter of course, that is not enough if the quest of capital is to reach out to more surplus. The forays that capital makes into pre-capitalist economies have to reach them into their production operations where through labour processes surplus is being generated. But this cannot happen by converting such production processes into typical capitalist production processes whereby the owners of capital purchase labour power. It has to be an indirect operation. Often it is achieved through what is known as the *putting out system*, whereby a capitalist, usually a merchant capitalist, places orders with traditional producers to purchase from them the goods that they produce. Neither the techniques nor the organisation of production undergo any change by this arrangement. Techniques of production remain what they were and the organisation of production is usually of the domestic type with men, women and children participating in different aspects of production possibly according to some conventional division of labour. It could be a 'household production unit' of the kind that we referred to at the end of Chapter 2. But while such production units normally produce goods of use value, in this arrangement their products become commoditised with the merchant capitalist purchasing them. The merchant, in turn, may supply the raw materials required for production and may determine the prices of commodities that are sold to the producers and of commodities purchased from the producers, fixing the prices in such a way that surplus generated by the producers is systematically appropriated. Without converting producers into wage-labourers, capital comes to subordinate them, depriving them of their independence as producers and also delinking them from the network of economic and social relationships within which they used to function.

Reaching out to pre-capitalist forms of production and subordinating them to its hegemony was a common practice of capital in the early stages of capitalist development. It is not confined to the early stages, however. It is part of the inherently aggressive thrust of capital; and wherever capitalist and pre-capitalist or non-capitalist economies coexist, capital has the tendency to bombard the others in this manner. It is, indeed capitalist operation without fixed capital and without wage-labour. Because the productivity of labour is bound to be low in the pre-capitalist production processes, the surplus generated is also likely to be low. But the capitalist operators have the advantage that they do not have to purchase labour-power with their capital in this arrangement, and so they may still be able to make substantial profits through this arrangement. Capital frequently seeks out such arrangements wherever it can be organised and it is a very common pattern of capitalist domination in different parts of the world, including in our country as we shall see in Part II.

There is another form of this expansion of capital which is very widespread wherever capitalist economy is active. As Heilborner says, capital scans daily life for possibilities that can be brought within the circuit of accumulation (Heilborner, 1988). The transformation of activities that also yield profits become another important realm into which capital expands. Common instances are laundering, cooking, cleaning etc. which are normally considered as activities done within households. The taking-over of these activities by capital not only commoditises such services directly, but also introduces a wide variety of commodities such as soaps, detergents, processed foods, and commoditised services like laundries, restaurants, quick meal counters, with production activities organised along capitalist lines. We may say, therefore, that a capitalist economy has a constant engagement with the rudimentary economy component—the repository of the generation of use value that is universal as we saw in Chapter 2.

The outward expansion of capital also proceeds along a spatial dimension. In its incessant desire to move and to grow, capital is no respecter of regional and national boundaries. In search of profit it will go to any part of the world, especially those parts where labour power is available at a comparatively cheaper rate. The history of capitalist development saw substantial movements of capital across countries and continents. And international movements of capital are a regular feature and a major form of business activity in our own time. Capital moves to set up production units in different parts of the world; capital moves to start and sustain trade in commodities; capital moves about in the form of financial transactions. And each one of these is a part of capital's incessant urge to go on expanding.

One more area of capital's outward expansion need to be noted. This is its tendency to bring nature itself under its domain. Nature is humanity's primordial use value, but in its quest for self-expansion capital does not spare nature. But, of course, capital does not convert nature as such into exchange value; it reaches out to nature bit by bit. Every tree will be converted into timber that can be sold to meet some need; every animal will be converted into meat to be eaten or hide to be displayed. Even water will be processed and 'purified', poured into bottles to be sold as drink for civilised people! Once again we turn to Marx's inimitable words:

> Just as production founded on capital creates universal industriousness on one side...so does it create on the other side a system of general exploitation of natural and human qualities, a system of general utility, utilising science itself just as much as all the physical and mental qualities....
> For the first time, nature becomes purely an object for humankind, purely a matter of utility; ceases to be recognised as a power for itself; and the theoretical discovery of its autonomous laws appears merely as a ruse so as to subjugate it under human needs, whether as an object of consumption or as a means of production. (Marx, 1939 : 409–10)

But the fact that capital always strives to move out and keep on expanding should not be interpreted to mean that it has a smooth and steady progression or that it is always successful in its attempts. Far from it. And it should not be difficult to see why.

Internal problems of capitalist expansion

Let us recall that the capitalist process is one that consists of three distinct internal moments which we saw earlier in our schematic representation.

There is first of all a purchase of machines, materials and labour-power which is a transformation of money capital into commodities; then the production of a new commodity and the generation of surplus value; and finally an attempt to convert the new commodity into exchange value and money capital. Now, these three movements or processes could turn out to be quite independent, separate in time and space but for the fact that capital provides them a unity, by linking them up as chains in a single circuit. But taken by themselves there is nothing to guarantee that what is expected to happen will happen. This is most clearly seen in the third process which let us examine in some detail.

The new commodity that the capitalist has produced is not yet a commodity. It is only a good, a product. It will become a commodity only when someone recognises a use value in it and pays a price to purchase it. In a capitalist economy both these can turn out to be problems. In pre-capitalist economies only those things which the producer himself or somebody else recognises as use value will be produced. If it is not the producer himself, then that other person must clearly indicate his need and possibly place an order for it too. In a capitalist economy, in view of the compulsion of capital to go on expanding, production is incessantly being done, and new products are regularly being turned out. There is nothing to say that in all such instances the demand to match the production will immediately or ultimately materialise. Hence in the case of particular goods and therefore of individual capitalists the mismatch between the supply of goods and the demand for goods can occur, and in practice it does occur. If supply happens to be less than demand, it can be corrected through the efforts of the capitalists themselves. But if the reverse is the case, capitalists (and therefore capital) have a serious problem. We are concerned with the attempt of the capitalist producer to sell (that is exchange for money) a new good that he has produced. This exchange is not the exchange of surpluses that two producers happened to have (going back to the exchange of pulses and bananas that producers A and B enter into in our example in Chapter 4). It is the exchange of a producer with buyers who hold money, that is, generalised purchasing power. They are, therefore in no hurry to dispose of what they hold; they can continue to hold it because it does not perish, unlike bananas and pulses; neither does it cost much to store. So, the capitalist producer frequently will have the responsibility of convincing his prospective buyers that they in fact need what he has to offer. Other producers will also be trying to do the same. Then he must make sure that the price they are willing to offer covers his cost of production. If the first condition is not satisfied, he does not sell at all and if the second condition is not satisfied he may have to sell at a loss. In view of this, in a capitalist economy the problem of lack of adequate demand (the condition of over-production) is one that specific goods run into and individual capitalists confront. In extreme cases producers may also have to destroy what they have produced for want of demand, for fear of reducing prices if they place more on the market and the practical problem of meeting the cost of storing the goods. Ironically, a capitalist economy which has a tendency to produce more and more may be able to keep up with that pattern only by destroying what it produces. Destruction does not have to be a physical process always; it can be a technical one of 'writing off', that is, declaring as *not-value*, what has been produced.

Production and adjustments of this kind have their social consequences. First is the waste of physical and human resources. Second, the anticipation of losses of this kind prompts producers to set their prices in such a way that the cost of producing the entire quantity is covered by the receipts from what is sold, that is, to set the unit prices far above the cost of production. And third, production may tend to be more than the market will clear sometimes and less at other times. If and when this happens in the case of different capitalists and commodities, it may be said to affect the economy as a whole, generating swings of glut followed by scarcity or of prosperity followed by depression. These movements in physical output interact with monetary and financial aspects which sometimes mitigate, but at other times magnify the swings. The history of capitalist development in different parts of the world has shown that the capitalist path of expansion is one of fluctuations and business cycles. Those who demonstrate theoretically that a capitalist economy is an epitome of efficiency do not generally step out of their theoretical models to see what is in fact happening in the world around them.

Deficiency of demand and attempts to meet it

A capitalist economy, especially after it has developed for some decades also tends to generate a general problem of demand of a chronic nature. We have seen that, of necessity, the capitalist quest for accumulation leads to the capital intensification of production, that is, for the fixed capital component in production to go up. While this may (but not necessarily always) lead to the displacement of labour, its intention is to increase the production of goods and that usually happens also. But the process is also one of shifting the distribution of income in favour of producers (and property owners in general) and against consumers (or workers as a class). What was, therefore, seen above as the problem confronting particular capitalists can turn out to be the problem of the system as a whole as well—a general and chronic deficiency of demand to sustain the level of output that the system is capable of producing. When this happens, production units will have excess capacity (machinery and equipment remaining inadequately utilised) and workers may remain unemployed even if they are willing to work at the going wage rate. Such an unfavourable business climate may prevent producers from undertaking fresh investment which further tends to aggravate the situation. This is the kind of problem that Keynes dealt with in his famous *General Theory of Employment, Interest and Money*. It can be seen also why Keynes rejected reduction of wages as a measure to solve this problem because if deficiency of consumers' demand is the crux of the problem, it cannot be solved by further reducing their purchasing power!

But temporary set-backs and even chronic maladies do not deter capital from its quest for expansion. It always attempts to be self-correcting. In order to ward off demand deficiencies, capitalist production is invariably accompanied by efforts to persuade consumers to keep on purchasing. That is why advertising becomes an essential component of a capitalist economy. The techniques of advertising and its intensity has changed enormously since the early days of capitalism but it is to the credit of Marx that even during the nascent stages of capitalism he was able to perceive the logic of advertising in all its ramifications.

> Exploitation of all of nature in order to discover new, useful qualities in things; universal exchange of the products of all alien climates and lands; new (artificial) preparation of natural objects, by which they are given new use values. The exploration of the earth in all directions, to discover new things of use as well as new useful qualities of the old; such as new qualities of them as raw materials etc; the development, hence, of natural sciences to their highest point; likewise the discovery, creation and satisfaction of new needs arising from society itself; the cultivation of all the qualities of the social human being, production of the same in a form as rich as possible in needs, because rich in qualities and relations—production of this being as the most total and universal possible social product, for, in order to take gratification in a many-sided way, he must be capable of many pleasures, hence cultured to a high degree—is likewise a condition of production founded on capital. (Marx 1939: 409)

That a cultured person is one capable of many pleasures and hence needs many more things than his primitive predecessors did; science has made it possible for these to be made available through human ingenuity and a more thorough use of nature; capitalism is a system that delivers these goods—such is the essential logic of advertising in a capitalist economy, old or new. The logic remains invariant; its communication has become more glamorous if less authentic, that is all!

Another, and more recent, way of ensuring that demand is kept up in a capitalist economy is through extending credit for consumption. All measures of 'buy now, pay later' are manifestations of the application of credit to the realm of consumption and are meant to ensure that demand never sags and does not tend to curb or even slow down production.

Capitalist economies, nascent and advanced, have had another very dependable measure of creating and sustaining demand—military expenditure. Military expenditure is never a mere economic factor and in the next section we shall look into its broader ramifications. But since we are dealing with demand or consumer expenditure we may note that even in economies where every family or local group tried to be self-sufficient (that is, producing the goods they needed to consume) a professional army emerged as the first major segment in society consisting entirely of consumers. They not only required large quantities of goods, but also gave the impetus to go in for uniformity in consumption goods. Both these aspects would have served as stimulus for the development of exchange and for production being undertaken for exchange. To the extent that this was the case, military expenditure should be considered to be among the factors that contributed to the development of capitalism.

Be that as it may, there is no doubt that military spending is a major sustaining factor in all recent and contemporary capitalist economies. It stimulates and sustains production (and thus contributes to profits and accumulation) not only by creating demand for consumer goods. A great deal of productive activity including employment of skilled labour (scientists and strategists among them) and investment in most advanced capitalist economies is now related to military considerations. In fact in one of the leading capitalist economies recently the political leadership gave up a series of social welfare expenditure, to show commitment to a capitalist system without state intervention, but boosted military expenditure allegedly for 'strategic reasons', thus combining ideological commitment with pragmatic manipulation![13]

'Can capitalism survive?'

Can a capitalist economy go on surmounting the problems that it confronts, most of which are the results of its own logic and operations? The track record of capitalist economies during the past two or three centuries suggests that it has done it so far. It has survived many a crisis, some confined to individual capitalist economies such as the great depression of the 1930s in the United States as also global ones of which one of the most prominent was the financial catastrophe associated with the break-down of the gold standard, also in the 1930s. Even in more contemporary periods it has shown exceptional resilience and the capacity to survive threads of unemployment and depression on the one hand and continuing inflation on the other. But then we must remind ourselves that the past few centuries of capitalist development represent a very short period in the history of humankind. In many parts of the globe different forms of village economies have survived for many many centuries. Even their decay was a process that extended well over three centuries. So it is too early to say what the future may have in store and it seems best to be open-minded about the possibilities.

But there is an important question, a question of a theoretical nature, regarding the future of capitalist economies (or capitalism in general) that we may acquaint ourselves with. Practically all major writers on capitalism—whether in the early stages or more recently, whether considered champions or opponents of capitalism—have represented it as having a bounded future. A recent writer sums it up thus:

> Adam Smith describes the system as reaching a plateau, when the accumulation of riches will be complete, bringing about a deep and lengthy decline. John Stuart Mill expects the momentary arrival of a 'stationary state' when accumulation will cease and capitalism will become the staging ground for a kind of associationist socialism. Marx anticipates a sequence of worsening crises produced by the internal contradictions of accumulation each crisis clearing away the obstacles of the moment but hastening the day when the system will no longer be able to manage its self-generated tensions. Keynes thought the future would require a somewhat comprehensive socialization of investment, Schumpeter though it would evolve into managerial socialism (Heilborner, 1985; 143–44).

Of these, all except Marx are considered to be generally supporters of capitalism. 'Can capitalism survive?' asks Schumpeter and goes on to answer 'No, I do not think it can'. But he clarifies his position too. He says, 'Prognosis does not imply anything about the desirability of the course of events that one predicts. If a doctor predicts that his patient will die presently, this does not mean that he desires it'.

We too shall approach the question in that manner, not to give a verdict about the future of the capitalist system, but to consider whether there are *internal* factors that curb its future.

The future of capitalism is the future of its growth, of its accumulation which is related to investments and investment opportunities, technological change and the cost of labour. The issue to be considered is whether the interaction of the three will tend to push down the rate of profit so low that capitalists will not find it worthwhile to undertake production and investments any more. Let us note that if we consider each of the three separately, there is not likely to be any major problem. For instance, cost of labour may go up, but if investment opportunities are also going up, the capitalist may not have to worry about his profit. Or, investment opportunities may be receding, but technological change may neutralise this and so on. But for how long? Is it possible to envisage the system going on expanding and reaping profits, or will there be secular stagnation reducing the rate of profits and restricting further expansion? That is the question. But the response to the question should not be a prediction about the future. Rather, it is to understand two related, but somewhat contradictory, aspects about the nature and working of the capitalist system. The first is that it has an *internal* dynamics which is centred on the accumulation of capital which means that the prospects and problems of a capitalist economy are both closely associated with its thrust for accumulation. We have seen earlier how the achievements of a capitalist economy can be seen to arise from its propensity to grow and expand. The problem we have examined now suggests that the limits of the capitalist economy are also related to its internal dynamics. As Marx puts it tersely, but appropriately: 'The true barrier of capital accumulation is capital itself'. Secondly, however, for its working a capitalist economy depends also on a variety of factors and forces outside it. The cost of labour depends partly upon the growth of population and that growth is but little related to the accumulation of capital; investment opportunities are assessments made by capitalists interested in accumulation, but their assessments depend on a whole range of psychological, political and sociological factors. Technological progress too is crucial for accumulation and is to a great extent influenced by the level and rate of capital accumulation, but science and technology and inventive minds are not invariably bound up with the accumulation process. That being the case we can, at best, talk about some possibilities— perhaps distinctive possibilities—for the future of the capitalist system, but we are not dealing with a system whose future is already programmed and only remains to be scientifically discovered.

CAPITALIST ECONOMY, STATE AND SOCIETY

One of the claims about a capitalist economy is that it is a self-regulating system with specific laws of its own. If that is the case a capitalist society can be thought of either as consisting of two distinct regimes, one of economics, and the other of politics, ethics etc., or a combination of these, or, alternatively that all other aspects of society, whether it is politics or, culture, will be determined by the dominant and dominating economic factor. In this concluding section we shall examine these contentions.

There is no doubt that compared with the other two kinds of economies we have dealt with, the capitalist economy is easier to comprehend. It constitutes a distinct realm of its own and within that realm there appears to be a neat orchestrating arrangement. Similarly, it seems reasonable to suggest that the passion for accumulation is not confined to capitalists alone, or to the economic realm alone. Within the economy all participants, whether resource owners, producers or consumers (to go back to the partition of the participants of the economy in the representation of the capitalist economy as an all-exchange system) appear to be or may be represented as maximisers. Or, if it is true that producers are interested in accumulation, households too appear to be prompted by the same motive, and if capitalists are supposed to be making profits through investment, it is the households which are seen to be accumulating savings. Outside the realm of economics too, other realms, especially politics, appear to be alternate avenues for accumulating wealth. Even culture can be cashed in for the same purpose.

Whatever may be these appearances, we must insist that the economy, including the capitalist economy, is an intellectually conceived notion. However, it too functions within a larger social context. It influences and is influenced by other realms of society.

Role of the state in a capitalist economy

In order to argue this point further we shall confine ourselves initially to just one other social sphere—the state. The choice of the state for this purpose is partly because it is the embodiment of authority in society, and we have already examined the role of authority in other forms of economies. But partly it is also because the state is, in a very meaningful sense, the epitome of society. The choice of the state has the additional advantage that some of those who speak about the autonomy of the capitalist economy define that autonomy with reference to the state; it is the absence of interference by the state that makes possible the autonomy of the economy; it is the state that is asked to leave the economy to function according to its own logic and laws.

To trace the relationship between a capitalist economy and the state, let us first look back into history. We recall the close association between the merchant class and the evolving national state as exchange got established into the M–C–M' form. The inception of the capitalist economy is historically and theoretically located in that milieu. It may not be inappropriate to think of the merchant class as the mother and the state as the father of the capitalist economy. Capitalism has seldom disowned the maternal link. But when it comes of age, it has a tendency to assert its independence by disowning the paternal connection.

But perhaps during infancy, it is the state that has systematically nurtured the capitalist economy.[14] It is for this reason that every capitalist economy has its specific *national* history, starting with English capitalism, then with French and German capitalism, Japanese capitalism, American capitalism and so on. And if capitalism as an economic system has certain central features which are common to all capitalist economies, capitalist economies in different nation states have their distinct features too. A reading of the history of capitalist development in any two countries will make this abundantly clear. But once again we shall draw attention to some of the common nurturing that states provided (and continue to provide) to capitalist economies in their early stages.

The most obvious of these are the legal supports that states extended to the kind of property rights that a capitalist economy required in the beginning, and continued to extend whenever its changing features necessitated them. After all, property rights and relationships did not always exist in the manner in which a capitalist economy needed them. Changes had to be made and legally sanctioned. For instance, in England open lands whose ownership issue remained muted and which were used for cultivation by peasants had to be enclosed for sheep raising by merchants to whom the state gave *exclusive* ownership of those lands, thus bringing in a legally recognised regime of private property. Later, when joint stock companies had to be floated for overseas trade, legal recognition had to be given to that form of organisation and the legal concept of limited liability had to be enacted to ensure the pooling of capital for productive purposes while restricting the liability of those who managed the concerns. A series of legislative measures had to be brought in to mobilise and administer credit too. Many more examples can be cited. This is not to say that the state merely rubber-stamped what capitalists wanted. States have also brought in legislations to protect the rights of workers, but wherever capitalist economies have flourished the states have done what is required for the effective working of the system, recognising that it has different components which had to be held together even when their specific interests were in conflict.

Adam Smith on 'duties of the sovereign'

Surprising as it may appear, it was Adam Smith whose reference to the working of the capitalist system on the basis of the self-interest of the participants, that free enterprisers are fond of invoking, clearly laid down the crucial economic role of the state in the day-to-day working of a capitalist economy. He prescribed three duties of the sovereign or the state (Smith, 1966, Bk V, Ch. I). The first was, 'that of protecting the society from the violence and invasion of other independent societies'. The second was 'that of protecting, as far as possible, every member of society from the injustice or oppression of every other member of it, or the duty of establishing an exact administration of justice'. And there was no doubt in his mind that the administration of justice was essentially one of protecting property. He said:

> It is only under the shelter of the civil magistrate that the owner of that valuable property, perhaps of many successive generations, can sleep a single night in security. He is at all times surrounded by unknown enemies, whom, though he never provoked, he can never appease, and from whose injustice he can be protected only by the powerful arm of the civil magistrate continually held up to chastise it. The acquisition of valuable and extensive property, therefore, necessarily requires the establishment of civil government.

The first two of Adam Smith's duties of the sovereign may be thought of as providing the basic conditions for the working of a capitalist economy. The third duty, however, is specifically related to the functioning of the economy

> that of erecting and maintaining those public institutions and public works, though they may be in the highest degree advantageous to a great society, are, however, of such nature that the profit could never repay the expenses to any individual or small number of individuals, and which it therefore cannot be expected that any individual or small number of individuals should erect or maintain. The performance of this duty requires, too, very different degrees of expense in the different periods of society.

Adam Smith's 'three duties of the sovereign' or of the state are sometimes referred to in the discussions about capitalist economies, but its rationale, especially of the third duty is seldom spelt out. The statement of the third duty gives the impression that the sovereign has some responsibilities to society at large and so it is. But if the sovereign or the state can undertake public works it follows that the physical resources and the labour power required for them are available. That is, the projects concerned are feasible. But then why is it that capitalists who undertake many other productive activities in the economy shun them?[15] Smith himself provides the answer: Capitalists will not find them profitable enough. And why? We must assume that the physical resources required to carry out a particular piece of (public) work, let us say an irrigation project, will remain the same whether it is undertaken by the capitalist or the state. We shall assume that the labour power required is also the same. Hence, the costs involved in taking on and completing the project are seen to be the same whether it is done by the state or by private capitalists.

What then is the difference? The state meets the costs out of the revenue it obtains through taxation etc. Hence for the state it is expenditure out of revenue, and provided the revenue can accommodate the expenditure on the project it will be done. But the calculations of the capitalists are quite different. For them the costs of the project must come from their capital and they will take up the project only if their calculations show that they will be able to get an expected profit from it. The crux of their calculations is two-fold. First, they must be sure that the costs incurred on labour will be less than the productivity of labour so that they are sure of surplus value being generated. Secondly, they have the 'realisation' problem to look into. Can the good that is produced be priced in such a way that the quantity sold at that price will bring in enough receipts over costs incurred to realise the profit? This second question is not a simple one. We saw in Chapter 4 that there are certain goods (which are described as public goods) where the principle of market pricing may not apply and goods generated through public projects are usually of this kind. There is also the problem that the quantity to be sold may be too large for 'any individual or small number of individuals' to handle. From all these angles, private capitalists may decide that the project concerned does not measure up to their profitability calculus and so may decide not to take them up. That is, a project that is physically feasible may not be financially profitable.

Let us look closer into the meaning of that distinction. There is a project that is considered to be socially desirable, 'in the highest degree advantageous to a great society'. In fact, it may be advantageous even to the capitalists in that society, who may derive indirect benefits through it. But carrying out that project is not a profitable proposition to them. Hence they do not take it up. Adam Smith's 'third duty' makes it an imperative for the state to accept responsibility to carry out the project. Adam Smith would have argued that in any 'civilised society' there are always goods that need to be produced, but which will not pass the profitability calculus of the capitalists. Hence the duty of the state is to do for capitalists what they will not do for themselves. Note too that Adam Smith recognises that what these goods are will be different in different societies and in different periods. It may be physical infrastructure in one period, training of labour in another period, maintenance of public parks to escape from the pollution of day-to-day productive activity in a third and so on. To put it differently; there is a role—and a crucial role—for the state in a capitalist economy *always*, whether the hand of the state becomes visible or remains invisible. Far too often the hand of the state is made invisible by describing its economic role as social responsibility lying outside the realm of economics!

But there are situations where that hand cannot be invisible. Keynes dealt with a typical case. He was dealing with a situation where the capitalist countries of the world were confronting the problem of chronic and acute deficiency of demand with productive capacity remaining idle, workers remaining unemployed and capitalists exceptionally diffident and nervous about new investments. It was one of the worst crises that capitalist economies had faced. Keynes invoked Adam Smith's injunction about public works (before he as a theoretician did it, Roosevelt had done it in America as a pragmatic politician) and argued that the deficiency in spending should be compensated by the state, if necessary by the state spending more than its revenue. He found in deficit budgets and monetary policies a way by which the state could bail out the capitalist economy from its own misdeeds. From then on for a while the visible hand of the state had become quite respectable in capitalist economies. But capitalism's rule is that the state must come out when and only when it is needed, and then must retreat into the green-room waiting there, ready to come on to the stage when required.

Properly interpreted, therefore, Smith's duties of the state are wide-ranging. More than that they are crucial to the functioning of the capitalist economy with the basic injunction to the state to absorb the losses of capitalism in one sense. In another sense it is a recognition of the fact that while a capitalist economy relies considerably on private enterprise for its functioning, many things that need to be done will not get done if there is no public authority to attend to them.

With that comment we can proceed to list the major functions of the state in a capitalist system. First and foremost the state determines the territorial jurisdiction of the economy. We have stated earlier that a capitalist economy does not respect national boundaries and bursts out of its locational specification. This is true. But since a capitalist economy functions, and has to function, within a legal framework, the state defines for it its homeground. It may become transnational in its functioning,[16] but seldom chooses to renounce its citizenship completely, partly because other nation states may not permit it unrestrained operations within their territories. Secondly, the state substantially influences the social relations of production particularly because of its power to determine conditions of labour, and in that sense directly intervenes in the accumulation process. Thirdly, the state through its power to tax enters into the realm of the utilisation of resources and through its spending patterns influences a variety of production patterns. Very often the state also becomes a direct participant in economic activity. While it has the obligation to attend to public works, that does not limit the scope of its economic activities. Fourthly, through the control it exercises on money and finance, it makes its presence felt on all economic transactions in a capitalist economy. And fifthly, the state becomes a big employer and purchaser particularly through its military responsibilities.

In view of these wide-ranging and deeply entrenched economic functions of the state, anyone who claims that a capitalist economy is one that functions without any external props and influences, or that a capitalist economy functions best when all state interventions are removed, is either fooling himself or trying to fool others. So crucial indeed is the dependence of a capitalist economy on the state that a writer bluntly but rightly says: 'Remove the regime of capital and the state would remain, although it might change dramatically; remove the state and the regime of capital would not last a day' (Heilborner, 1988: 105).

Private and public realms

Sometimes the role of the state in a capitalist economy is recognised, but with a clear and sharp distinction between what is private and what is public; and an insistence that at least in the private sphere economic laws (the laws of the market) reign supreme, while the public sphere (including public works) may come under political considerations. We have noted already that there is an element of political decision-making as far as public works are concerned. But to pretend that the private sphere is solely under economic laws is not right.[17] The laws of the market, we have seen, are predicated on the distribution of property in the system, more than on the preferences of the buyers and that distribution is very much a matter of political decisions, active or passive. Also, without the public works the private economy cannot function. Transport, communication and other infrastructural facilities will clearly indicate that.

Such a distinction between the private and the public, of economics and politics, is part of the attempt to show that a capitalist society has two distinct *loci* of authority—the economy and the state. It will be noted that this is partly an attempt to show that a capitalist economy and society are distinct from what preceded them. In the two economies that we examined earlier, there is no distinct economic realm. In such societies authority and power, however they may be exercised, show no clear separation between economic and political realms. The apparent emergence of an autonomous economic realm under capitalism had two reasons. The first was the political recognition of the equality of individuals before law. This principle of *de jure* equality was closely associated with the *de facto* right of private property and the associated functioning of the market and the process of accumulation. Thus it looked as though in a capitalist society the state withdrew from some of the spheres and surrendered its powers to the new realm that was emerging with its own laws. Secondly, there was the gradual loss by the state of its rights of direct access to the surplus, because capitalist production and exchange—substantially independent of political authority—came to take over the function of the appropriation of surplus through its own 'natural' operations. In other words that coercive political power which was necessary in earlier societies to appropriate surplus, now passed on into the normal functioning of the economy.

If the autonomy that the economy seemed to acquire through these processes was apparent, they gave the 'economic realm' enormous power. Property and capital came to dominate society and their homeground, the economy, thus came to be in a position to exert influence, if not power, over the political processes and the state. Hence, if we showed earlier that in a capitalist society the economy is dependent on the state, the state can be said to be dependent on the economy too. But it will not be right to interpret this dependence as the subordination of the state to the economy, or to the capitalist class within the economy as it is often argued.[18] In a capitalist society both the economy and the state have relative autonomies. The relationship between them is of mutual dependence and interpenetration in such a way that often the boundaries tend to disappear. At times, it may appear that the economy is dominating the state; at other times the state is seen to have the upper hand.

What form of polity?

In the relationship between a capitalist economy and the state, there is one more aspect that needs to be examined. Is there any specific form that the state in a capitalist society is likely to take? Historically capitalist states have taken different forms, monarchy, parliamentary democracy, dictatorships and so on. At present also capitalist societies have different forms of state. And so the answer to our question is that there is no inevitable or necessary relationship between the economy of a capitalist society and its form of state. However, there is something of a conceptual link between a capitalist economy and liberal democracy based on adult franchise. This is mainly because both the capitalist economy and liberal democracy consider the individual as the ultimate entity in society. Market economics and a polity based on universal franchise are often seen as twin expressions of the liberal social philosophy. An author who has examined this aspect says:

> The first formulations of liberal democracy came to its advocacy through a chain of reasoning which started from the assumption of a capitalist market society and the laws of classical political economy. These gave them a model of man (as maximiser of utilities) and a model of society (as a collection of individuals with conflicting interests).... The general theory was clear enough. The only rationally defensible criterion of

social good was the greatest happiness of the greatest number, happiness being defined as the amount of individual pleasure minus pain. In calculating the aggregate net happiness of a whole society, each individual was to count as one. What could be more egalitarian than that as a fundamental ethical principle? (Macpherson, 1977: 24–25)

We have seen that by commoditising all goods and monetising all wealth and by seeing all members of the economy as participants in the exchange process the capitalist economy creates an image of the economy and society as consisting of independent individuals. And by assigning to every individual a single motivation of attempting to maximise pleasure or profit from resources and by projecting that motivation as economic rationality, capitalism also conveys the impression that those independent individuals are essentially homogeneous. The philosopher Bentham was one of those who projected society as consisting of pleasure-seeking individuals. His philosophy of utilitarianism let each individual decide what pleasures he would pursue, including many non-material ones, but the worldly philosopher was clear that the possession of material goods was so basic to the attainment of all other satisfactions that it alone could be taken as the measure of them all. ' Each portion of wealth has a corresponding portion of happiness' he stated and 'money is the instrument of measuring the quality of pain or pleasure'.

Assuming society to consist of such individuals who try to maximise pleasure or utility and use money as a measure of it, it was considered that the proper thing to do was to give each person a portion of political sovereignty too via universal adult franchise thereby making the individual sovereign, both in the realm of the economy and of the polity. It is because of this correspondence of the treatment of the individual as sovereign both in a market economy and in liberal democracy that it is usually claimed that liberal democracy is, or ought to be, the counterpart of a capitalist economy.

The importance that liberal democracy gives to the individual *qua* individual and the treatment of all individuals as equal in law are no doubt to be cherished and defended. But the real question is whether it is liberal democracy's 'individual' who constitutes the basic unit of a capitalist economy. It is not. In the representation of the capitalist economy as an all exchange system (which gets closer to the individual being considered as the basic unit of the economy) the decision-makers are not merely individuals *qua* individuals, but resource owners, who have enough resources to make a living on their own (as peasants, for instance) and use their surplus to enter into exchange with others, as was clarified in a rigorous version of that representation. To put it bluntly, the basic units in a capitalist economy are commodity owners, and (as already noted) the economy *excludes* all those who are not commodity owners. But at least can a capitalist society with a liberal democratic state and its championing of the individual *qua* individual enable those who are excluded by its economy to share in some of the material benefits that it produces? Can it make every individual an owner of property through appropriate legislation? These are important questions being discussed in many parts of the world today, especially in many of the developing countries. We shall not attempt theoretical answers to these questions. What has been happening in our country since Independence is an enacted debate of these issues. In Part II we shall present the evidence from that experience as answer to the questions posed.[19]

The 'acquisitive society'

In concluding our tour into the capitalist economy let us look into one more aspect. Whether the rest of society can influence a capitalist economy or not, there is plenty of evidence to show that a capitalist economy greatly influences the rest of the society in which it operates and of which it is a part. The craze to go on accumulating exchange value which is a requirement of a capitalist economy as a *capitalist* economy and thus becomes the behavioural pattern of the capitalist *qua* capitalist tends to percolate into and rapidly spread through the rest of society making it, as an author aptly puts it, an 'acquisitive society' (Tawney, 1982). It is easy to see how that happens. Let us once again look at our abstract representation of a capitalist economy depicting it as consisting of two classes—capitalists and workers. While initially the workers have nothing other than their labour power to sell (that is they own no physical or financial property) and by selling it they earn only a subsistence wage which does not permit them to spare or save anything from what they earn, the situation begins to change when their wages tend to go up as a result of capital accumulation, and the capital intensity of production going up raising productivity. Soon workers may come to retain part of the surplus they generate, and they may also convert these into different forms of wealth, especially financial assets. And as this tendency spreads, workers also may wish to accumulate. Once financial intermediation becomes generally established, wealth will accumulate *automatically* as long as owners are willing to part with it for a while. Thus little surpluses left in a bank grow into larger surpluses and these larger surpluses can then be used to purchase shares in capitals of productive units; this may be riskier than leaving money in a bank but has the possibility of higher returns and faster accumulation. With a variety of financial assets becoming available, and all forms of wealth getting denoted in terms of their money value, anyone who has a surplus will soon come to have easy opportunities to augment that surplus. 'Making money' can then become the behavioural pattern of everyone in the capitalist economy including the workers. In fact, since the earnings and wealth of the workers can and often do increase, the workers may come to have the feeling that the capitalist economy and all social institutions that sustain it are beneficial to them also. This is how the acquisitive spirit spreads and gets transformed from an *economic* condition into a *social* characteristic. And we may say that one of the major factors responsible for the tenacity of capitalism is the widespread support it gets from its enlarging circle of beneficiaries.

There are some who argue that the acquisitive spirit is inherent to human nature, that every human being at every period in history would wish to have wealth and more wealth, but that it is only capitalism that made it possible for such large numbers of people in all parts of the world to realise their innate desires. But this is not a correct argument. For one thing it is not possible to verify whether all human beings at all periods in the past and present as also in the future have the desire to go on piling up material wealth. On the contrary, there is historical evidence to show that there have been human communities (and there still are) who were mainly concerned with the generation of use values rather than the unlimited accumulation of material wealth. That it is possible to describe economies rooted in such a principle has been the thrust of our account of the rudimentary economy. Again, the special feature of capitalism is not the desire for wealth as an abstract yearning, but the organisation of production in such a way that the purpose of productive activity becomes the ceaseless quest for the accumulation of wealth. We have seen that specific historical conditions are necessary for this to happen and the issue under discussion is the acquisitive spirit under such conditions:

There is one more related issue or debate. Was it the acquisitive spirit that gave rise to capitalism when it did emerge as a historical entity? Those who support this view draw attention to a number of changes in the realm of thought and social practices that took place in Europe prior to the period that is generally acknowledged to have witnessed the origin of capitalism. In particular, attention is drawn to the Renaissance which brought in the emphasis on reason against the background of Europe's adherence to tradition and subservience to superstition; and to the Reformation which is said to have discovered the 'individual' and his rights in contrast to mediaeval catholicism with its emphasis on authority and community.[20] We must recall that the capitalist economy did not spring up suddenly and that its emergence was a process that spread over several centuries. In that process certainly a variety of social factors would have contributed to the shaping of the new economic system. There can be no doubt that human reflection and imagination do play a decisive part in all processes of social change whether such changes are described as evolutionary or revolutionary. To deny this would be to conceptualise society as a physical mechanism which it is not. Society is the fabric of human relationships and hence human thoughts and actions contribute enormously to social processes. But thought does not result in action except when it gets embodied in and finds expression through institutions. This is the reason why in studying social processes it is important to understand institutions, their working and metamorphosis much more than abstract thoughts (including value systems) and the deeds of individuals. We shall keep this in mind as we turn now to an understanding of economic systems which are post-capitalist.

NOTES

1. We shall use the expressions capitalist economy, capitalist economic system and capitalism interchangeably, although it can be argued that 'capitalism' refers to more than the capitalist economy.
2. Reference to the work of Walras has been made already at the end of the previous chapter. The two contemporary economists referred to in this paragraph are Kenneth J. Arrow and Gerald Debreu, both of whom have received the Nobel Prize in economics for their contributions in this area. A popular text book that brings out the features of 'the market economy' is Dorfman, 1964. For an advanced treatment see Dorfman et al., 1958.
3. The logic of the market economy is captured in simple language by Schumpeter in his History of Economic Analysis (Schumpeter, 1954), Ch. 6, sec. 3.
4. Refer to the interconnection between ownership and scarcity in Ch. 3.
5. That self-interest is the basis of economic activity and how exchange gives expression to it goes back to Adam Smith's famous declaration, 'It is not from the benevolence of the butcher, the brewer, or the baker that we expect our dinner, but from their regard to their own interest. We address ourselves not to their humanity but to their self-love, and never talk to them of our own necessities, but of their advantages...' (Smith, 1966; Bk I: 13).
6. It is not necessary that ownership has to be of material things; it can be, and very frequently is, just labour power as long as it satisfies the condition that there is someone willing to purchase it. In fact, as will be seen from the paragraphs that follow, the commoditisation of labour power is one of the essential features of capitalism. We shall also see that capitalism, however, has a built-in tendency to make labour power redundant which means that those who have only labour power to sell find that they cannot sell what they have.
7. For details regarding this transformation see Marx, 1971, Vol. I, Part VII: Dobb, 1963, Ch. 6; and Polanyi, 1957.
8. This technical definition of exploitation comes from Marx. Note that the expression is not used in the same sense as when one talks about the 'exploitation' of nature. In the technical sense in which Marx uses the term, exploitation occurs when one section of the population produces a surplus whose use is controlled by another section. Underlying this meaning of exploitation is the contention that no matter what the nature of the organisation of production, only the human component (but *not* the cooperating

factors whether land or tools) is capable of generating the surplus. Under certain forms of the organisation of production, the workers themselves may decide how the surplus is to be used; in other forms, those who work may have to yield part of the surplus to those who make claims on the produce via the right of ownership. Under the capitalist organisation of production, the owner of capital appears to be the active agent in production who employs workers and pay them so that the flow appears to be from top to bottom which, as Marx pointed out, is just an illusion that capitalism generates. It may be added, too, that if the owner of capital puts in his own labour power, whether physical or mental, in the actual process of production, he too must be considered to be a worker capable of generating a surplus. If so, his share in the produce must be decided as is done in the case of any worker, and not as profit due to him as owner of capital. Another thing to note is that unlike in most pre-capitalist economies where the owners had to appropriate surplus using physical force, exploitation under capitalism does not have to be, and seldom is, naked and brutal. The special feature of capitalism is that the organisation of the entire economy, especially the production–exchange link-up, makes it possible for exploitation to become a smooth affair, very much a part of the natural processes of the system, and so it goes unnoticed.

9. On the production–exchange–ownership nexus and its implication see Renner, 1949, especially Ch. III.
10. As a capitalist economy grows and changes, the organisation of production also will undergo changes. For different views on this theme see Baran and Sweezy, 1966; Galbraith, 1967; and Braverman, 1974.
11. A very graphic account of the creative aspects of capitalism can be seen in Schumpeter, 1974, Ch. V.
12. Among the early followers of Marx it was Rosa Luxemburgh who insisted that a major avenue of capitalist expansion would be non-capitalist systems. See Luxemburgh, 1968.
13. This happened in the United States of America under the presidency of Ronald Reagan in the 1980s. In fact so widely discussed was the strategy (the part dealing with capitalism without state intervention) that it came to be known as 'Reaganomics' projected as an anti–thesis to Keynesian economics which asked for an active role for the state to enable capitalism to function well. But it would appear that it was just a passing show.
14. Holland, 1987, Ch. 2, deals with the role of the state in the development of capitalist economies, including the United States.
15. In *Grundrisse* (Marx, 1973, esp. pp. 531–33) Marx raises this question and takes the construction of roads to indicate the nature of the problem.
16. For a discussion of the modern manifestation of transnational capitalism see Ch. 12.
17. On the nature of public and private sectors see also note 6, Ch. 4.
18. Kurien, 1987b, deals with this question and provides a selected bibliography to the literature.
19. See Ch. 11 for the Indian experience and Chapter 12 for a more general treatment.
20. On this issue see Weber, 1976; Tawney, 1972.

6

Post-Capitalist Economy

The achievements of the capitalist economy during the few centuries of its functioning have been enormous. It had led to unprecedented increase in production and the capacity to produce. And by making its organising principle effective in many parts of the world it has, for the first time, created something like a global economy.

But the capitalist economy has another side too. Because of its systemic tendency to exploit labour power and to make labour power redundant, its achievements have remained confined to a small minority who own and exercise effective control over non-human resources required in production. For the same reason it cannot also become an economic system that includes all members of society.

Hence the need to explore possibilities of devising a post-capitalist economic order which can inherit the positive features of the capitalist system but bring it under an overall social direction so as to provision the material needs of all members of society.

Starting with the Russian Revolution in 1917 and the establishment of an economic order radically different from the capitalist system, there have been many experiments in different parts of the world in designing a post-capitalist economy. By the middle of the 1980s about a third of humankind (in the Soviet Union, Eastern Europe, the People's Republic of China, North Korea, Vietnam, Cuba and so on) came under such dispensations. But by the end of that decade practically all East European countries rejected the economic arrangements and the political systems that were trying to implement them. There are rumblings in the Soviet Union also. These historical experiments in 'socialism', therefore, must be treated as early enactments of what still remains an inspired but yet distant goal, for humankind.

This chapter makes a critical assessment of historical socialism, its achievements as well as its systemic weaknesses. Realising that these weaknesses arose from the mistrust of exchange leading to bureaucratic commands becoming the coordinating method in the economy, making both economy and polity non-participatory, the concluding section of the chapter provides the essential guidelines for a functioning post-capitalist economy. Such an economy calls for major departures from the capitalist system in terms of the ownership and use of non-human resources and hence it is very unlikely that it will get established without a substantial transfer of political power to the mass of the people. But the section may be useful to demonstrate the feasibility of a genuine post-capitalist economic order which is yet to come.

Capitalist economies are prevalent in several parts of the world; there are some who would argue that if there is such a thing as a global economy, it is essentially capitalist. In any case there is no doubt that it is a contemporary reality. And its track record, in terms of making available a substantial increase in material goods, is excellent. Then why are we considering a post-capitalist economy or post-capitalist economies?

One reason must be fairly obvious. In the Soviet Union in 1917, there was a revolutionary overthrow of the existing regime and the capitalist economy and a bold attempt to replace it with something very different. Several countries in Eastern Europe also accepted the Soviet model immediately after the Second World War. In 1989 many of these countries brought about major changes in their political and economic systems; it is not yet clear whether they plan to return to a capitalist economy or reconstruct their economies.* In 1949, the People's Republic of China was established with a clear commitment to an economic order radically different from a capitalist system. Major changes have taken place in the economic sphere in China in the 1980s, but with the commitment to an economic system other than capitalism. Cuba, in the American continent, too has an economic system which is not capitalist. There are other countries such as Vietnam and North Korea which are also trying out alternatives to capitalism. In the middle of the decade of the 1980s, approximately a third of humanity had come under economic organisations distinctly different from capitalism. There are major variations in their economic systems, and yet they would claim that their economies are post-capitalist. As is well known, the common name given to these economies is 'Socialist economies'. Hence if we are turning to an examination of post-capitalist economics, one reason is that post-capitalist economies too are a contemporary reality.

There is another reason as well. A capitalist economy has certain inherent weaknesses as we saw in the last chapter. Hence it is important to consider whether humanity has any possible alternatives. The question, therefore, is also about the *feasibility* of a post-capitalist economy because there are many countries in the world where people are aware of the limitations of a capitalist economy and would be willing to try alternative arrangements. We may recall that our country, too, claims to be a socialist republic.

FEATURES OF A POST-CAPITALIST ECONOMY

What must be the main features of a post-capitalist economy? Let us remind ourselves about the inherent weaknesses of a capitalist economy because a post-capitalist economy should certainly be able to overcome them. In the broadest sense, the main weakness of a capitalist economy is that (unlike other economic systems that we have examined) it is an *exclusive* economy. It is exclusive because only owners of commodities can be participants of a capitalist economy. It has no place for those who have nothing to sell; and it is the operation of the system that determines whether what

* This chapter was written in mid-1990 and no modification has been made since then.

one has, such as one's labour power, can be sold at all. We have seen also that it has a tendency to make human beings redundant. Secondly, within the category of owners, a capitalist economy gives special power to those who are owners of physical resources manifested in the form of capital. Decisions about what will be produced, how production will be organised and how the produce will be distributed are all made by the power of the ownership of capital, and the ownership of capital tends to get concentrated in fewer and fewer hands. So, capitalism has a tendency to make even the bulk of the owners mere passive participants in the system. Thirdly, capitalism confers on the owners of capital the special power to claim the ownership of the entire produce by which they are able to siphon off the bulk of the surplus value that workers generate. In this sense the capitalist economy is intrinsically exploitative.

If these are the principal drawbacks of a capitalist economy, a post-capitalist economy must be one which removes them or overcomes them. A post-capitalist economy must be an *inclusive* one; it must give the actual producers—the labourers—the decisive say in matters relating to production and the settlement of claims; it must not have the exploitation of workers as one of its systemic features.

How is it possible to have such an economic order? Superficially, it may appear that the one possibility is to go *back*, to a form of village economy or of some kind of rudimentary economy. But it does not take much of an effort to see that setting the clock back is not an easy option. It may be possible for a small group, but not for a country and certainly not for humankind as a whole. And, let us recall, that a capitalist economy has certain strong positive aspects which should not be given up. The most important among them is the possibility of increasing production, which is surely a blessing. The clue to increase production is to increase the productivity of labour, and technology and increase in the availability of physical capital are the ways to achieve it. The capitalist economy has shown humankind how these are to be brought about and a post-capitalist economy must certainly inherit and enrich these possibilities. In saying this, we are making some value-judgements. We are affirming that an increase in production is a good thing and that humankind must strive for it. A post-capitalist economy must not only be one where an *increase* in the availability of material goods becomes a reality for *all* its members, but where the members will rationally discuss the required limits to material goods. For, if a low level of material goods is not a virtue in itself, neither is an abundance of material goods. Hence, members of a post-capitalist economy should have the capacity to decide what goods will be produced and how much will be produced. An economy that imitates a capitalist economy's mindless expansionist thrust is not one where decisions regarding production are made with *deliberation*.

A further feature of a capitalist economy that must be preserved in a post-capitalist economy is the greater social division of labour that it makes possible through reliance on exchange. In Chapter 3 we saw how exchange removes some of the basic constrictions of a village economy. In fact, if an increase in the quantity and variety of material goods available to everyone is a desirable thing, that will be scarcely possible if everyone (or every small group of persons such as a family) must produce all that he (they) require. This means that a post-capitalist economy *must* be a commodity economy. But here again, its difference from that of a capitalist economy can be easily indicated. A post-capitalist economy must be a commodity economy, but where social decisions will be made consciously regarding the *limits* of commoditisation.

An economy which does not accept the pursuit of growth as its objective, and sets social limits on commoditisation is distinctly different from a capitalist economy. And if such an economy also provides for a steady increase in production in order to meet the rising needs of its members, it is not a pre-capitalist economy. Only an economy that combines these features can be considered a post-capitalist economy.

An economy concerned with use values

From what has been stated above it must be obvious that a post-capitalist economy must have as its organising principle the generation of use values. It will have exchange as an activity, and consequently will have exchange value also, but accumulation of exchange value will not be its organising principle. In fact, accepting the principle of generation of use value and treating exchange as a form of social activity is the major task of a post-capitalist economy. It is not easy.

Since a post-capitalist economy has generation of use values as its organising principle, it shares some of the characteristics of a rudimentary economy and the village economy. First and foremost, it must be embedded in a community and the provisioning of the material needs of *all* its members should be the responsibility of its economy. But the community within which a post-capitalist economy functions is not likely to be a natural community like a family or tribe, or a traditional and local community as in the case of a land based village economy. In the post-capitalist situation that community is likely to be the nation in the foreseeable future.

We shall not enter into a detailed discussion of all the conditions necessary to give a nation a sense of community. Shared traditions and aspirations are likely to be the most important among them. But these cannot be taken for granted. They must be convincingly articulated, frequently restated and from time to time visibly celebrated. A community is always one in the making.

However the community is constituted and held together, it has enormous responsibilities. Decisions taken by the community are the basic premises of a post-capitalist economy. And these decisions are not merely abstract. They include a detailed assessment of the physical resources of the community and how they are to be placed at the disposal of its members. Since these physical resources are the gift of nature, one of the decisions will have to be the extent to which nature is accepted as a use value by itself and how much it should be appropriated to generate other use values. For instance, how much should mountains, forests and rivers be accepted for what they are and enjoyed as such, and to what extent may they be considered as productive forces to be subjected to human decisions? A similar decision will have to be made about human beings too. To what extent should they be drawn into productive activities (and how) and to what extent should they be left to design their own activities. Decisions will have to be made about the kind of organisations required for productive activity, including the types of social control over resources. Decisions will be required on what goods are to be produced and the extent to which markets and prices will be accepted as signals in this regard. Another important decision is the extent to which productive capacities will be used to satisfy today's needs and how much will be set aside for future requirements. And, of course, there is the crucial decision to be made about defining and settling of claims—decisions regarding the distribution of goods and the patterns of payments, that is. To what extent should these be based on needs and to what extent on deeds? Granted that this distribution is not likely to be absolutely equal among all members, what is the degree of inequality that can be tolerated and how is it to be confined to that limit?

These are crucial and difficult decisions. The strength of the capitalist system is that these decisions get *integrated* through the capitalist' quest for profit and accumulation; its weakness is that all these decisions become *subordinated* to that quest. The advantage possessed by a post-capitalist society is that these decisions are not all based on any single consideration so that choices become possible; its weakness is that decisions regarding the criteria of choice are not easy.

But one aspect emerges clearly. If a post-capitalist economy is not to drift into pre-capitalist forms of authority—decisive but dictatorial on the one hand as in most rudimentary economies, anarchist and chaotic as in most village economies—these decisions must be arrived at through the maximum possible participation of the community at large. In other words one of the basic requirements of a post-capitalist economy is authority deriving from genuine participatory deliberation. *A post-capitalist economy is possible only in a participatory society.*

HISTORICAL SOCIALIST ECONOMY

If what we have indicated in the previous section can be taken as the *essential* pre-requisites and features of a post-capitalist economy, the world has not seen one yet, but only approximations of, or rather approaches to it. This is not surprising either. For, all economic systems up to capitalism have had a kind of natural evolution which we saw most clearly in the case of the capitalist economy which, in a very meaningful sense emerged from the ruins of what preceded it. A post-capitalist economy would be the first economic system to be brought about through the deliberate intervention of human beings. The significance of the Soviet revolution of 1917 is that it was the first concrete affirmation of the determination and the possibility of humankind to consciously design an economic system. But it happened less than three quarters of a century ago, and in the long history of humanity it is too short a period to be described even as an 'experimental stage'. So, what humanity has witnessed so far can only be considered as experiments—very bold experiments certainly—towards a post-capitalist economy of the kind indicated in the previous section.

We shall first look at this experiment (experiments in the plural, to be more accurate as they have been tried out in different countries and under different conditions) in terms of the efforts made, and shall also make a brief assessment of the experiments in relation to what in the previous section we have set up as a sort of 'ideal type'.

We may note that the urge for a post-capitalist 'socialist' economy was expressed by many writers even as capitalism was in its early productive stages.[1] These visions about a socialist economy (or 'Utopian socialism' as Marx's colleague ad collaborator Engels described them) came from those who perceived the barbaric and inhuman features of a capitalist economy when the factory system was converting erstwhile independent producers into wage workers driven 'by the whip alternatively of hunger and of the master's overseer' as Dobb expressed it. The sentiments behind these visions were, therefore, very noble indeed, but an economic system cannot be produced merely by providing a blueprint for it. While human beings have the capacity to dream about the future and to work out alternatives, a functioning economic system is not something produced out of thin air, or in a vacuum. One has to understand the working of the existing economic order, its logic and structure, and on the basis of that understanding decide where interventions are possible to provide a decisive turn.

This was the answer that Marx and Engels gave to the dreamers of the past, of their time and of the future. They saw clearly that a socialist economy had to emerge from the capitalist economy; that is out of its collapse after it reaches maturity. Hence, instead of providing blueprints for a future economic order they considered it their task to analyse and understand the capitalist economy. And they, more than anybody else, understood and communicated the essential logic of the capitalist economy.

Their understanding of the logic and working of capitalism led them to make two related observations about the future. The first was about the system itself. They anticipated that the capitalist economy would grow, making tremendous increases in the productive forces at the command of humanity and in the process substantially 'socialising' productive activities: socialising, that is, in contrast to the personal productive activities of peasants, artisans and the like who were responsible for production in pre-capitalist economies. But they anticipated, too, that because of the innate logic of capitalism it would generate more severe crises as it grew, and that as the rate of profit tended to decline it would get caught in its own trap.

But they *did not* expect that these factors would lead to the *automatic* collapse of the capitalist economy. On the other hand, they kept urging the workers, the proletariat, to get ready to give the fatal blow to capitalism when its internal forces would carry it to a vulnerable position. Marx and Engels believed too that the growth of capitalism would be accompanied by the spread of the democratic spirit, and of democratic institutions, providing a participatory form of polity which was to be a training ground for workers. They, thus, expected the collapse of capitalism to be brought about by the workers who, they saw, had no stake in the capitalist order and who, they were eager, should recognise this fact and should prepare to take over when the appropriate moment arrived. Thus, according to Marx and Engels, it was the proletarian revolution that was to pull down the citadels of capitalism and to usher in a socialist economy and society. A socialist economy was to be established, according to this view, after the capitalist economy fully realised its productive potential and after society had gone through democratic and participatory arrangements.

If this were to happen, many of the pre-requisites for a socialist economy would have already been provided and members of society would have the necessary economic and social conditions to build up a socialist economy. It was because of this anticipation that Marx and Engels concentrated more on the road towards socialism than on providing a blueprint for a socialist economy.

Some common features of historical socialist economies
In 1917 in Russia, under the leadership of Lenin a revolution did take place and a party of workers captured political power and the authority to design a socialist economy. But Russia did not have an *advanced* capitalist economy. It was the most poorly developed capitalist economy in comparison with

England and the European capitalist countries or America or Japan. There were even doubts and debates as to whether Russia was a capitalist country at all, although on that point Lenin and his close associates were quite clear that it was. The proletariat, the industrial workers, were a minority in Russia with the vast majority of the labour force being engaged in agriculture, household industry and trade. Neither could Russia claim to be a democracy. The political system was extremely authoritarian, oppressive and, thus, far from being a participatory one.

But Lenin, inspired by Marx and Engels decided to proceed with the task of building up a socialist economy. The first experiment in socialism, therefore, started without two of its basic pre-requisites.

Subsequently attempts at building socialist economies came under circumstances not favourable for the task. In Eastern European countries socialist regimes were established through military interventions during and after the Second World War. And China which turned to socialism in 1949 certainly had an ancient civilisation, but at that time it was one of the poorest countries of the world, ruined by the Japanese assaults during the war and perhaps more so by a prolonged civil war. And politically, although the overthrown regime had come to power through a national liberation movement, it had not built up any democratic institutions and had converted the polity into a means of building up private wealth for a handful of people. It is under such circumstances that Mao Zedong dared to construct a socialist economy. The background to the building of socialism in other parts of the world (Vietnam, Cuba etc.) has also been similar.

It is against such backgrounds that we must appraise the functioning of historically concrete socialist economies. We have already indicated the rationale for a post-capitalist economy and its essential features and have now seen also the background to the limited experiments that have been undertaken. In order to compare the 'ideal type' and the actual ones, we shall briefly examine how the actual ones have performed. We shall not examine every single case. We shall begin with some common observations and then take up a couple of illustrative cases.

We shall see in what sense the concrete cases of socialist economies can be considered to be departures from the capitalist economy. First and foremost, wherever socialist societies have been established, they have officially proclaimed (by appropriate provisions in the national constitutions, for instance) that their economies will be *inclusive* ones; accepting responsibility for the material provisioning of *all* the members of society, young and old, able and disabled, and without insisting on any economic eligibility condition (such as ability to sell something as under a capitalist economy). Not only have such proclamations remained simply as directive principles for policy but have been accepted as the norm in restructuring the economies. Secondly, and as an operational counterpart of the first, the states in such societies have assumed direct responsibility for production in many areas to ensure that production and distribution are organised in such a way as to be responsive to the needs of its members. And, as a matter of fact, in socialist economies *every member* has been assured of the basic needs of life, food and clothing at least. Quite significantly, the basic needs were not narrowly interpreted as material ones. Again, *all* socialist economies have attached the highest importance to education and health, setting aside resources to provide free and compulsory education for children, for adult education and for health services. Consequently, literacy rates have rapidly gone up and there has been substantial improvement in health conditions as witnessed, for instance, in the sharp decline in infant mortality rates. These must also be considered as evidence of the importance that socialist economies attach to labour, or more accurately, to human beings as such. Thirdly, *all* socialist economies have succeeded in bringing about substantial increase in production and in productive capacity to ensure that the increase in production is sustained. In their early phases socialist economies had rates of growth of production considerably higher than international standards and in many instances were among the top in the world. Socialist economies have demonstrated clearly that the usually held view that poor economies cannot step up production is erroneous, thus showing that socio-economic factors and the will to act are just as important in determining the pace of growth as physical and technical factors. Further, they have shown that the abundance of goods is not a pre-condition to make an economy effectively inclusive. Fourthly, by substantially eliminating private property incomes they also succeeded in reducing inequalities in the distribution of income and established a greater sense of equality among all members.

All these have been significant departures from the manner in which earlier economies, especially capitalist economies have functioned. What were the factors that made it possible for historical socialist economies to effect such major departures?

Social control over resources

The most visible aspect in all instances of historical socialism has been their emphasis on the *social* control over the resources available to society. In capitalist societies resources are privately owned and the control over them is so exercised that they are put to private use, specifically, to enable the owners of resources to accumulate more resources. Consequently, the abolition of the private ownership of resources, principally the means of production, has had highest priority in all socialist countries. Not that the private ownership of resources was abolished by a single decree. In fact hardly any socialist economy has achieved the abolition of the private ownership of resources. In the sphere of agriculture, particularly, some land has continued to be under private ownership. This was especially so in the Eastern European countries, Poland, Hungary etc. under the socialist order. But even in these instances, the overall thrust was quite clear: socialisation of the means of production was, and has been the most distinct feature of historical socialism. In all instances large-scale industries and the banking system were completely taken out of private ownership.

A clarification is in order here. In the view of some commentators on socialism, especially those who are eager to bring out its weaknesses, the abolition of private property under socialism would imply that those living under socialism are prevented from possessing anything at all, including personal belongings. This view arises out of ignorance or out of the deliberate intention to distort socialism. The socialisation that takes place in a socialist economy is as a means to the social orientation of production in contrast to what happens in capitalism which has been described as 'the dictatorship of the private ownership of the means of production' (Huberman and Sweezy, 1968: 7). This is what socialism tries to undo by bringing the means of production under social control. As far as personal belongings are concerned (as distinct from means of production) such as clothes, furniture, domestic appliances, consumer durables and in most instances even houses, these remain the possession of those who own them.

Production under social direction

A second common feature of socialist economies, then, is the bringing of production substantially under social control. Here again, the distinction between capitalism and socialism is quite striking. To the standard question: 'What to produce?' the response in a capitalist economy is (has to be) 'whatever is profitable to the owners of resources.' It may be argued that the capitalist response to this question is: 'whatever consumers require' and this is true in a strict sense. But under capitalism consumers are only those who have the resource power to consume or, more accurately, to *purchase* what the market offers. And goods are produced, not in response to the needs of the consumers, but to the differential intensity of the purchasing power of buyers. In a socialist economy, on the other hand, production genuinely responds to social needs. This can be shown most clearly with reference to the manner in which socialist economies have been responding to the social need for education and health facilities, recalling that even at rather low levels of resource availability and production, all socialist economies have set aside resources to meet these social needs. Capitalist economies also devote resources for education and health, but our own experience shows that these are generally neglected areas, and that on the whole these services become available only to those who can afford them, and in proportion to what one can afford, as is cruelly evident in the case of health-services. In sharp contrast, in socialist economies these are recognised as human needs and society makes provision for them to be accessible to all its members. This is the *principle* underlying production in socialist economies, that it is socially informed, and responding to social needs. We shall see subsequently that there are problems in operationalising this principle, and that some of them are not easy to overcome, but that should not divert our attention from the principle itself.

An important aspect of the social orientation of production is the conscious attempt to decide how much of today's production must be devoted to meet today's consumption, and how much to enhance tomorrow's consumption. We have noted that one of the tasks of a post-capitalist economy is to ensure the material levels of consumption are rising over time. Devoting part of production to augment the capacity to produce is, therefore, a necessity and all socialist economies have paid special attention to this aspect. But it is necessary to point out that a reduction in the consumption level of the present is not a requirement to increase productive capacity in the future. In view of the fact that countries that have actually turned to socialism have all been at rather low levels of production when it happened, any attempt to reduce the level of consumption would have been very unfair and intolerable. What socialist economies did was to regulate the composition of production in such a way that the *increase* in consumption goods was less than the *increase* in overall production; so that as production increased, the capacity to increase production moved up faster. The record of the socialist economies in augmenting capital formation in this manner has been very commendable indeed.

Socially oriented production is achieved not only by bringing all resources under social control. It is also accompanied by a tremendous mobilisation of the human potential. One of capitalism's internal contradictions, as we have already seen, is to make human beings redundant in the production process. In a socialist economy, on the other hand, since production is organised to meet social needs, human beings can always actively participate in it. Indeed, the imagination and ingenuity of the human beings and the manner in which the human element is co-ordinated become the main considerations in production. The socialisation of the means of production can be thought of as an enabling pre-condition to achieve this liberation of human energies. All socialist economies, therefore, have paid a great deal of attention to the mobilisation of the human factor in their production programmes. The active role assigned to women in the common tasks in society has been a true indication of the emphasis on the human element.

Nature of consumption

When production is organised on the basis of social priorities, it will have some implications on consumption, in particular if consumption in socialist economies is compared with consumption in capitalist countries. The difference is that the abundance and variety of consumer goods seen in capitalist economies is absent in socialist economies. This difference is partly the result of faulty comparisons, like comparing an affluent capitalist country such as the United States and a very poor socialist country such as China or Cuba. But while comparing a socialist economy and a capitalist economy at roughly the same economic level—let us say, China and India—the impact of a socially oriented production pattern on consumption in the former is quite striking. In China till approximately the middle of the 1980s, about the only means of private transportation was bicycles whereas India could 'boast' of motorised two-wheelers and also four wheelers. But while these were *available* in India, they were *accessible* only to very few Indians, the vast majority being denied access because of the very nature of the distribution of resource power in the Indian economy. We may recall that not only cars and scooters, but even the basic necessities of life such as foodgrains, are not accessible to a large number of people in India, even when foodgrains can be said to be plentifully available in the country.

A socialist economy substantially avoids this problem by orienting production to social needs. Transportation is a social need and, in the first instance, it is provided through public means. But that is somewhat restrictive and hence in the next stage private modes of transportation is made available through production such that it is accessible to most people. At that stage, for instance, it would be quite common to see the head of a big production unit (or public institution) and the lowest paid in the same establishment both riding to work on bicycles. The former may be in a position to afford a scooter or even a car, but because of the social priorities in production they are not available to him. It is by denying the abundance and variety in the private modes of transportation that resources are found for other (and more important) *social* needs such as housing, education and health. In other words, some social regulation of consumption is a natural corollary of the social orientation of production, until at least the resource constraints are sufficiently overcome.

This, however, does not mean that socialist economies have a regimented consumption pattern, as in some military barracks where items of consumption are standardised and doled out to members. In practically all socialist economies consumer goods are commoditised and are purchased by consumers on the basis of the incomes they earn through work. This results from the fact that while production is substantially socialised (both in terms of the social control over resources and the social decisions on what and how much to produce) the claims on the produce are largely privatised in the sense that each individual who cooperates in production comes to have a claim on the produce in relation to the work he performs. That is, the principle of distribution in a socialist economy is *not* 'To each according to his needs', but 'To each according to his work'. This has certain implications.

The first, and most crucial, is that all who are capable of working must work. A significant difference between a socialist economy and a capitalist economy can be seen here. In a capitalist economy, a sizeable proportion of incomes generated is property income (or unearned income) accruing to a small section of the population, who can afford not to work in the sense that they can have all their requirements met through the incomes they derive from their property; and even when they do work, their unearned incomes are much more than their earned incomes. In contrast, the dictum in a socialist economy is: 'If one does not work, neither should he eat'. The rationale of the abolition of private property (means of production) in a socialist economy is both that no one should be permitted to exploit the labour power of another by making use of the means of production to employ others *and* that no one should be made to shirk his responsibility to work by relying on property income. Secondly, the principle of 'To each according to his work' implies that as individuals differ in their activities and skills to do work, their claims on the produce will also differ. To put it differently, socialist economies are not 'egalitarian' if that means that there is an equal sharing of incomes (or goods) among all its members. However, they are egalitarian in the sense that they are committed to providing equal opportunities to everyone in respect of the acquisition of skills, mobility in jobs etc. The distinction between these two meanings of the concept of an egalitarian society must be borne in mind in understanding and evaluating socialist economies.

With inequalities in earning on the one hand and the commoditisation of consumption goods on the other, there is both the need and the scope for earners as consumers to exercise some personal choice of their own. The range of choice (both in terms of variety of goods and differentiation of products) may be rather limited which, as seen above, is the result of social decision to use resources to meet social needs; but the freedom to choose is respected. Here again there may be perceptible differences between the market for consumer goods in capitalist and socialist economies. In one sense capitalism survives by persuading people to go on consuming, and in order to overcome the realisation problem, capitalist producers and traders must constantly court the consumers. On the other hand, in a socialist economy, and particularly in its initial stages, the priorities, as mentioned above, are much more in terms of genuine needs to be satisfied immediately and of building up production capacity for the future. This means, for instance, that the total quantity of any good being produced becomes a 'planning' decision. Within a planning context, there may also be a decision not to vary the price of a good once it is put into the market. The market clearing process, therefore, may be more in the nature of a quantity adjustment, than a price adjustment unlike in the case of capitalist economies. One concrete manifestation of the quantity adjustment process is the formation of queues (which is not uncommon even in capitalist economies with respect to goods in fixed supply and fixed price as, for example, seats in a cinema theatre) so that those who come first get served and those who are late in showing up may have to go back disappointed. If long queues persist for some particular good or service, there may be a decision to increase its supply in the next round, but till then the quantity adjustment by the buyers will have to go on.

This tendency to rush for goods when they become available, and to queue up may be augmented because of another factor, the greater equality of incomes. In capitalist economies too a quantity adjustment takes place (which goes usually unnoticed) when those who know that goods (or services) are not accessible to them do not queue up for the available goods. In both instances what happens is quantity adjustment, one through queues (because of greater equality of incomes) the other through the 'automatic' elimination of queues (because of the greater inequality of income).

The discussion of the settlement of claims—the distribution of incomes and of goods and services—has to be supplemented by a couple of additional comments. The basis of claims on the social product, we have seen, is work done. This does not mean that those who are not able to work are denied any share. Socialist economies make special provisions for children and old people, for women who are child-bearing and the infirm. That is one manifestation of an inclusive economy. Earnings on the basis of work done are also supplemented by a variety of provisions of 'social consumption' on the one hand, such as free education, medical aid, and health facilities, and vacations and subsidised private consumption like very low rents, low priced basic food articles and fuel on the other.

It can be seen that the organisation of a socialist economy—or orchestration of its economic activities, to go back to a terminology we used in the discussion of the rudimentary economy in Chapter 2—is a very complex one and and a very difficult task. Resources and labour have to be mobilised (essentially a social task); a variety of decisions about production have to be made (involving political, technological, geographical, social and economic considerations); the pattern of distribution has to be determined taking into account the principle of inclusiveness on the one hand, and the principles of fairness and incentives on the other; decisions at different levels and by different agencies (production units, administrative bodies etc.) have to be coordinated and so on. Certainly, not all of these can be on the basis of a single criterion (unlike what a capitalist economy claims) or be left to a single institution such as the market. The task is essentially one of orchestration, of holding together disparate elements; of balancing opposing tendencies, of coordinating diverse decisions, of managing different kinds and different levels of institutions; of replacing some old ones and of evolving some new ones—all for the welfare of the people, something not very easy to define or to agree upon. A capitalist economy also has many of these tasks, but the profitability calculus of the owners of resources appears to give it a single unifying principle similar to the role of gravity in Newtonian physics. A socialist economy is more like an entire constellation, where the search for a single unifying principle may not be the best procedure to understand it.

SPECIFIC SOCIALIST ECONOMIES

Because the concept of socialism or a socialist economy, thus, is inherently nebulous, historical socialist economies have not all been alike. Each one has designed its own procedure to tackle the task as it saw it, and each one has changed its procedures and patterns over time. There is an element of groping in these efforts. In order to capture some of these aspects we shall now take a quick look at the actual experiences of three socialist countries, the U.S.S.R., Yugoslavia and the People's Republic of China representing three different kinds of socialist experiments.

U.S.S.R. : the early phase
In as much as Russia (later to become the Union of Soviet Socialist Republics, also referred to as the Soviet Union) was the first to launch into a post-capitalist economic order, the Great October Revolution of 1917 must be seen to be just as significant (and indeed just as experimental) as the first human venture into space beyond the sphere of the earth's gravity—a great leap forward for humankind. The Revolution took place during the First World War, when Russia, as an ally of Britain and France was at war with Germany.[2] Although Russia in the early part of the twentieth century styled itself the Russian Empire, Japan in 1905 had shown how weak was that Empire. The First World War showed its hollowness

further. Not being able to cope with the war and its destruction, the Tsar, abdicated in March 1917 and a Provisional Government came into existence. The Provisional Government tried to take over the wholesale trade in grains, mainly to feed the army, and the peasants had risen up against this. By the middle of the year peasant revolts had become widespread. Unrest soon spread into industry as well which in a short while turned out to be a major political turmoil. It is under such circumstances that Lenin took over power in spite of the warnings by some of his colleagues that it was a dangerous adventure. Lenin pulled Russia out of the war by negotiating with the Germans. This angered his War Allies who decided to take on Russia along with Germany. Among his countrymen too Lenin faced opposition. In particular the big landlords (whose lands had been taken away without compensation according to the Land Decree signed the day after the Revolution) rose up against him. Thus, soon after Lenin and his Bolshevik Party took up power, they were confronted by a civil war and a war against countries opposed to the new regime.

Socialist economic reconstruction had to be initiated under such circumstances. Lenin's own inclination was to have some kind of state directed capitalism as the initial step towards socialism, but to consolidate political power certain key economic positions had to be taken over. There was also the infantile enthusiasm of some of his followers to convert Russia instantly into a communist society by eradicating all capitalist institutions and practices—especially money and exchange which they considered to be the main vestiges of capitalism. By the middle of 1918 further taking over of enterprises and establishments had become necessary. In the meanwhile the civil war was continuing. Goods, including foodgrains had become scarce, especially in Moscow and other urban centres. Prices were soaring. There was a general collapse of economic order. Requisitioning and rationing, which even capitalist economics resort to during wars, could not be avoided and had to be increasingly resorted to. The chaotic conditions that emerged have come to be described as 'War Communism'.

The economic crux of this 'system' consisted of compulsory procurement of surplus grains from the peasants in order to get grain for use in the cities and for the government's employees. Some procurement did take place, but many peasants, including the bigger ones decided to reduce production to avoid the compulsory levy. The government had to retaliate by declaring that those who could produce a surplus but failed to do so would be deprived of the right of citizenship. But the programme had economic consequences too. Procurement and its counterpart, administrative allocation of goods, especially grains, soon led to economic activities coming largely, if not entirely, under the domination of the administrative bureaucracy. Though this was the result of concrete historical circumstances, since this was how socialism was launched, many who favour socialism and those who oppose it have tended to identify it with bureaucratic administration and 'command' performance. In fact the crisis of socialist economies that emerged in the 1980s culminating in the overthrow of many regimes by the end of the decade arose from the failure of command economies to perform.

While one section of Lenin's Party welcomed 'the dying out of money' and the emergence of a command economy as heralding the dawn of communism, Lenin himself held the view that War Communism was thrust on the country by war and ruin, and that it was not the kind of programme meant to initiate a new economic order. After the civil war was largely curbed and the threat of aggression from outside receded, Lenin, therefore, introduced what he described as a 'transitional mixed system', transitional towards socialism and a mixture of capitalism and socialism, which has come to be known as the New Economic Policy (NEP) in vogue from 1921 till the commencement of the First Five Year Plan in 1928.

The NEP was built on restoring market relationship between agriculture and industry. Instead of the compulsory surrender of surplus by the peasantry a tax in kind, assessed as a proportion of the net produce above minimum subsistence need of the family, was introduced with the peasants being free to do what they liked with the rest of the output. That served as an incentive to produce more and to sell a good portion of the output. The revival of the market in agricultural produce was also accompanied by the creation of commercially autonomous industrial enterprises called 'Trusts' and with the exception of fuel and metals (which were retained by the state) practically all of industry was changed into this category. Both in agriculture and industry the formation of cooperatives to work along commercial lines was encouraged. There was also a denationalisation of small industrial enterprises and a revival of the banking system. Private trade too was permitted and picked up momentum quickly.

During a short period of five to seven years the economic order changed drastically from what immediately preceded it and what had existed before the Revolution. And yet there were problems, especially in relation to the working of the price system. During the NEP, agricultural production began to recover fairly rapidly, but industry ruined by war and adjusting itself to new organisational patterns was slow to pick up. Hence the relative price (or the terms of trade as it is technically referred to) began to move against agriculture with more quantity of agricultural goods having to be exchanged for a given quantity of industrial goods. Once again, there was quite a bit of discussion on how the situation was to be dealt with. Fairness to agriculture was necessary to win the support of the smaller peasants and workers for building a socialist economy; but it was also necessary to curb the power of the bigger farmers who were not sympathetic towards the establishment of socialism. There was also the view that a socialist economy would be built up only by the rapid growth of industry.

After Lenin

Lenin died in 1924 and after his death the industry lobby within the Party assumed the reigns of power, and when the First Five Year Plan was launched in 1928 it was quite explicitly the first step in the rapid industrialisation of the country. But rapid industrialisation could be brought about only on the basis of a growing quantum of agricultural surplus, mainly in the form of grain, becoming available. However, although agricultural production was increasing, marketed surplus of grain was not, and this was attributed to the kind of changes that had been brought about in the organisation of agriculture, especially the abolition of large farms which were primarily responsible for generating and marketing surplus grain. Hence a decision was made that independent peasants should be encouraged and induced to form large-scale cooperative farming. Subsequently under the leadership of Stalin there was an intensive drive to form collective farms in which, unlike in the cooperatives, individual farmers would not retain their ownership rights over land. This, it was felt, was necessary to socialise the ownership of land, one of the principal means of production and an important form of property, and hence where there was resistance to the collectivisation drive. Compulsion was used resulting in considerable human suffering and loss of lives. Along with collectives, state farms, giant mechanised 'grain factories' as they came to be referred to, were also set up, all in an effort to increase the availability of grain to facilitate rapid industrialisation. Industry did grow rapidly with an accent on heavy industry, but the changes brought about in the successive Five Year Plans also changed the social structure in the rural areas with the institution of the independent peasant, the backbone of Russia's social system for several centuries, being almost completely wiped out.

With the disappearance of the multitude of independent peasants, it looked as though the entire economy had become a huge big factory or farm, complex no doubt, but entirely under the control of the State; thus making it possible to have 'the greatest possible concentration of the whole economic activity of the country in a unified plan worked out for the whole State', as was expressed in one of the decisions of the Party in the early years after the Revolution. On this basis the accent turned out to be on a 'unified plan for the whole State'. Now, with practically all physical resources brought under the command of the state and with the party having the right (on behalf of the entire population) to determine the pattern of production, it would have been not too difficult for some specialised agency with the necessary skills and technical information to draw up such a comprehensive plan. But how was it to be carried out by a multiplicity of implementing agencies consisting of industrial enterprises, cooperatives and collective farms, banks and trading organisations? What was to be the nature of conveying the inputs that they needed for their production? On what basis were they to make their decisions regarding production? And what were they to do with their outputs?

In a sense, these have been the issues in Soviet economic organisation from the time of the launching of planning to this day, and they have not been satisfactorily resolved. Not that there have been no answers at all. As a matter of fact, part of the problem has been that there has been one ready-made answer frequently: 'Leave it all to the administration', and that has been taken to be the correct answer often. And even where it could be shown that that was not the right answer, it would still be resorted to, if not relied upon, for want of viable alternatives. The problem could be rephrased as the search for the appropriate way to reconcile the need for some form of centralised decision-making on the one hand and for decentralised implementation on the other. And the answer indicated above has been more authoritatively described as the 'centralised command model' of planning which has been the Soviet pattern of socialist economic organisation and activity for over half a century from the end of the 1920s.

We shall not go into details of how it has been executed except to say that there have been attempts from time to time to loosen what can easily be recognised as essentially a rigid one-way control mechanism. From almost the very early days the production units (we shall use the term 'enterprises' to refer to them, irrespective of the nature of their activities, their internal administrative structure and the size of their operations) were given a blueprint of their production plans, but were provided an opportunity to work out 'counter plans' which would be taken into account, to the extent possible, in finalising the 'unified plan'. A major reform measure came in 1965–66 which consisted of the recognition of the need to increase the share of consumer goods in industrial production and also attempted to provide greater autonomy to the enterprises. The reforms of 1965–66 brought about some modifications, but following the *perestroika* (structural reorganisation) thrust of two decades later, it can be seen that these could have been only marginal. An ardent supporter of Gorbachev's perestroika proposals wrote in 1988: 'We know from the press that economic activity in our country is regulated by some 200,000 different instructions. Twenty thousand of them have already been cancelled, but when will the other 180,000 odd instructions, which stand in the way of restructuring the economic mechanism, be abolished?' (Hasbulatov, 1989: 23). No further comments are needed on that issue! How to change the pattern of the centralised command system; how to provide greater autonomy to the enterprises; how to use the market to coordinate the inter-enterprise transactions; how to use prices and costs to make the operation of the enterprises more efficient—these were the questions being discussed in the Soviet Union's socialist economy at the beginning of the 1990s.

Yugoslavia's 'market socialism'

The significance of the Yugoslavian experiment in socialist organisation of the economy is that from the time of its break with the Soviet Union in the early 1950s, it had accepted a programme whose emphasis was on the relative autonomy of the enterprise, the opposite of what the Soviet thrust has been.[3] A principle adopted by Yugoslavia was that *state* ownership of resources was not necessarily the way to ensure the *social* ownership of resources and that wage employment of workers by the state was just as exploitative of labour as the capitalist's employment of wage labour although the former certainly avoided the *private* exploitation of labour. Hence it was decided that the proper approach to a socialist economy was to enable workers in an enterprise to assume collectively the ownership, or resources of the enterprise, and as owners formulate the enterprise's plan including investment, production and distribution. To make this pattern universal, the collectivised farms were decollectivised ensuring through appropriate legislation that there was no return to the pre-socialist large farms. In essence, farming became substantially independent peasant farming. The Yugoslav pattern, therefore, has been one of decentralisation, with the central issue being how to coordinate the independent decisions of the multitude of enterprises and to weave them into something of a plan for the economy as a whole. For this coordinating purpose the Yugoslavs did not hesitate to make use of the market mechanism permitting enterprises to trade with one another, and for prices to be formed on the basis of such exchanges. The distribution of consumer goods, of course, remained almost completely through the market. For these reasons the Yugoslavian model of socialism is often referred to as 'market socialism'. And yet it is not a 'free market' economy on the basis of the ownership of resources by the workers. The state actively intervenes in the decision-making processes of the enterprises by providing overall guidance about investment decisions so that production decisions are not *solely* in response to market signals, and the state also intervenes in the market processes by keeping a fairly strict control over interest rates as well as on foreign trade and the external value of the currency.

But 'market socialism' generated its own problems. While productive activity was left to the farms and enterprises and the principle of self-management was accepted, there was no commitment in Yugoslavia (unlike in the USSR and other East-European socialist countries) to provide employment to every employable person as the utilisation of labour was left to the supply–demand forces of the market. The performance of agriculture was rather poor in Yugoslavia and it was not enough to absorb all the available labour in the rural areas. Hence open unemployment became visible leading on to very high rate of rural–urban migration with all its social and economic consequences for which the economy was not prepared. Unemployment problem has continued to be one of Yugoslavia's main worries, and but for the fact that Yugoslavia's laws and international relationships permitted the migration of Yugoslavs to other countries, which enabled many unskilled workers particularly to seek jobs in other parts of Europe, the situation could have easily turned explosive.

'Market socialism' also had to bear the brunt of price fluctuations. The poor performance of agriculture was initially responsible for a rise in prices which imposed heavy burdens on those with low levels of earnings and to the backward regions in Yugoslavia's economy with very pronounced regional disparities. Inflation and rising domestic costs also affected Yugoslavia's trade with other countries, especially western capitalist economies, and led to a balance of payments crisis. The situation was so bad that the government had to attempt corrective measures through various forms of controls which, however, affected the prospects of enterprises and led to a recession.

These problems showed that self-management and market forces were not enough to keep the economy on the socialist path and that 'market socialism' could easily degenerate into *laissez-faire socialism* if some kind of macro directions were not available. However, the Yugoslavs have set themselves against a return to the centralised command model; they have also been eager to maintain a distinction between directions by the *state* and decisions by *society*, abhorring the former and showing a willingness to accept the latter wherever necessary. One of the measures adopted was to bring about an association of labour (Associated Labour) which was to be entrusted with the ownerships of enterprises in the hope that this would lead to inter-enterprise cooperation and coordination. It was expected too that the communist party would be able to play a more positive role in coordinating the economy through the association of worker-owners. However, since the workers' remuneration continued to be determined by each individual enterprise, the workers of each enterprise stood to gain more by identifying themselves with their enterprise than with the larger association of workers. A further measure of social coordination was attempted after the country adopted a new constitution in 1974, which was followed by the Law on Planning in 1976. According to the 1976 Law, planning was to consist of two distinct components, self-management and social planning. From a constitutional amendment of 1971 the Associated Labour was renamed Basic Organ of Associate Labour (BOAL) with each enterprise containing a BOAL working unit. The 1976 Law set up a Complex Organisation of Associated Labour (COAL) as an apex body of all·worker organisations including BOAL, and in social planning an important role was given to COAL. Social planning was responsible for making the major macro decisions relating to the economy such as overall rate of accumulation, technological improvement, balance of payments issues, regional development etc. and self-management by enterprises was to be within such a frame. This arrangement has succeeded to some extent in redeeming the near-chaotic conditions that prevailed in the 1960s and early 1970s but problems of coordination and performance have continued to persist. But we must not overlook the fact that many problems are also being solved and the Yugoslav socialist experiment has many achievements in relation to the material provisioning of the people of that country. The accent of the socialist experiment in Yugoslavia has been to evolve a workers' participatory economy to overcome the problem of exploitation based on the conviction that from the point of exploitation, there is little to choose between capitalism's private exploitation and the public exploitation that remains in state capitalism which frequently but wrongly gets identified with socialism.

People's Republic of China: early phase

We turn now to the Chinese experiments in socialist transformation of the economy. The Chinese experiment deserves attention for a variety of reasons. Till the People's Republic of China was established in October 1949, socialism had remained confined to Europe. With the Chinese entry into the socialist movement, socialism had to take into account Asian realities, particularly the problems of building a socialist economy mainly with the support of the peasantry. Capitalism in pre-revolutionary China was in its infancy and confined largely to the east coast. In 1949 China was also among the poorest economies in the world using per capita income for the comparison. And, of course, for us in India there is the additional factor, the close resemblance between the two countries in many respects.

Unlike Lenin who came to power somewhat unexpectedly, Mao Zedong had waged a war, through the Communist Party of China and through the People's Liberation Army to capture power.[4] And since the prolonged civil war had driven out many of the landlords to Taiwan and the industrial capitalists to Hong Kong and Taiwan, Mao was a national hero when he took up power and could count on more popular support than Lenin could in his country immediately after the revolution. Till it was ruined by war the Chinese economy had a well-developed commerce, and a sophisticated monetary system. The Chinese also had a relatively high degree of literacy and considerable experience with complex social organisations. But there were initial disadvantages too. The civil war and the Japanese invasions during the Second World War had resulted in severe strains on the economy. And in the international sphere the Cold War was on; international capitalism under the leadership of the United States was doing everything possible to 'curb Communism', and so Red China which had driven out Chiang Kaishek, a staunch ally of the Americans, was naturally included in the list of enemies. By siding with North Korea in the conflict that emerged in the Korean Peninsula, again against American interests, Communist China risked retaliation by the capitalist countries.

Under such circumstances, the Chinese decision initially was to stay as closely as possible to the Soviet Union and its model of socialism. The rehabilitation of the economy was important, and the slogan during those early years—and slogans have played a major role in economic reconstruction and social reorganisation in China—was 'let's be modern and Soviet'. The Soviets had, by this time, evolved measures for centralised planning and these were readily accepted by the Chinese who had little specialist knowledge about macro policies. But Mao had a basic mistrust of bureaucratic procedures and it did not take time to realise that the highly capital–intensive approach adopted in the First Plan following the Russian experience and advice was hardly suited to China, whose central problem was the utilisation of its labour.

And so came the decisions to change the strategy. The new thrust, initiated in 1956, was called The Great Leap Forward. Its aim was to avoid both centralisation and the heavy-handed bureaucratism associated with it as well as dependence on the market principle. It was felt that a feasible third alternative and the correct one for China was to aim at local self-sufficiency. The strategy was centred on the peasantry and on agriculture.

A campaign for cooperative farming was started already in 1954 with emphasis on voluntarism, gradualism and considerations of material benefits. By the end of 1955 nearly 60 per cent of peasant households had been organised into elementary cooperatives. During the Great Leap Forward the emphasis shifted to collectivisation. A collective usually consisted of about 200 households, although there was considerable variation in size from region to region. It owned the land, draught animals, major farm implements etc. Within the collective, brigades consisting of some 20 to 30 households constituted the unit of work organisation. The brigade also determined the distribution of the produce among the members on work-point basis, each kind of specific job being assigned work points. Depending on such job specification and the actual number of days worked, claims would be settled after the harvest, the net produce being distributed according to the work points accumulated by each on the 'to each according to his work' principle. The collective had the right to redistribute some share from more productive to less productive brigades. By 1957 Chinese agriculture consisted of some 740,000 collectives. After that was achieved, the collectives were regrouped into some 26,000 'people's communes' which came to assume some administrative responsibilities as well because they incorporated the townships, the lowest level of state administration. The commune brought under its umbrella small scale industries as also educational and health services. The commune, thus, was to be the basic unit of decentralised administration and local self-sufficiency, although not all communes were able to achieve that objective. But there is little doubt that the communes became the instruments for the massive mobilisation of China's enormous labour potential and for building up a great deal of capital formation, especially in the rural areas, such as bunds, irrigation projects and the like. By bringing together agriculture, industry and commerce, education and culture it was also to be the means to eliminate the distinction between manual and mental labour, and between town and country and thus to be the tool of China's great socialist transformation. The expectation was that social mobilisation and the intense propaganda of correct ideological values would ensure desirable production, effective incentives, appropriate distribution, the right use of local resources and powers, and adequate overall control. It was to be China's model of decentralised democratic and socialist set-up.

The decentralisation mania—or, to be more accurate, the desire to carry out the slogan of decentralisation—was so intense that it was taken to some absurd limits. What came to be known as 'backyard iron and steel factories' was one such instance where decentralised production was attempted, ignoring all technical considerations. But these were probably extreme cases and the policy towards industries was quite different, one of 'walking on two legs' with centralised control over major, large-scale and modern industries while smaller ones, especially China's wide variety of traditional industries, were brought under local control, linked up with the communes to a large extent either administratively or through fairly well defined exchange relationships.

The success of the commune system also threw up some problems, one of the most difficult ones being the work-point principle itself. As long as the allocation of work-points was to be confined to agricultural activities, conventional wisdom could be relied upon to arrive at the relative weights of specific tasks. But when other activities also had to be taken into account—industries, administration and capital works—the allocation principle, that is the determination of relative claims or shares, became more and more difficult and controversial. The procedure of taking care of those who could not work also had to be defined; that is, a principle of sharing beyond the norms of work, and more in terms of need had to be devised. An attempt made in this direction was to provide some goods and services freely to all members. In some places community kitchens provided some free meals, mainly to release women from some domestic chores so as to participate in commune-related works; in other places clothing was freely distributed; elsewhere wedding, funeral and such other personal expenses were met by the communes. However, team work and the possibility of free provisions gave rise to a problem we had noticed in the discussion of the rudimentary economy—that of 'free-riding'.

Since work-points were given for days of work put in, people would become slack at work and take advantage of free meals and other services, for all of which the community was incurring costs. How to link up remunerations and productive work—the incentives issue—was to emerge as a major problem in the Chinese economy fairly soon.

Another crucial issue was inter-commune disparities arising from regional geophysical factors. After all, no matter how intense and intelligent human effort is, the success of agricultural operations depends to a great extent on the nature of the terrain, climatic conditions etc. This was cruelly brought home during the famine of 1959–61 when as a result of crop failure in the interior regions, and in the absence of proper arrangements for transferring surplus from one region to another, and indeed from one commune to another, almost 15 million lives were lost.[5]

For these and other reasons rethinking on economic policies started in the early 1960s. A decision was made that the communes would concentrate on agriculture. The little private plots that households had even in the early stages of collectivisation, but which were taken away during the community experiment of the communes were restored so that households could produce something of their own—vegetables, fruits, poultry etc.—and *sell* in the 'free markets' which were allowed to operate. Many other measures were also taken in the first half of the 1960s for 'readjustment, consolidation, filling out and raising standards'. But major changes had to wait till after the turbulent period of the Cultural Revolution (second half of the 1960s), Mao Zedong's death in 1976, the turmoils of the immediate post-Mao period and the ascendancy of Deng Xiaoping.

Reforms after Mao Zedong

Deng was of the opinion that the major task of the Chinese economy in the two last decades of the century was increase in productivity all around and the modernisation of the economy. For this purpose, within the overall socialist orientation of the economy and under control of the Communist Party, material incentives for production were to be substantially encouraged, market relationships were to be re-established, inequalities in income distribution were to be tolerated, and China's economy was to be opened up to international influences and interactions. 'To become rich is great' became the new slogan.

The new reform measures were started in 1979 with a phased dismantling of the commune system and a move towards farming by households. In 1984 the Household Responsibility System was introduced whereby households could lease out land for 5 to 15-year periods from the collectives and use it and family labour to produce what they like and sell the produce at market prices, subject only to a quota to be given to the collective and the state who retained the ownership of land in this new socialised tenurial system. Agricultural prices were revised upwards and farm households were encouraged to diversify their production, moving not only into different kinds of crops including vegetables and fruits, but also into piggery, poultry and fishing. Households were also permitted to purchase and own motor vehicles and farm machinery. These were measures to encourage the intensive utilisation of land and labour in the rural areas and it led to enormous increase in output and diversification. Tremendous encouragement was also provided to small industries located in rural areas, and the accent here was on labour absorption and phased mechanisation to increase productivity. Work in these factory-cum-dormitories utilising mainly young women from the rural areas was organised on the basis of specified jobs, with teams working on each job on a piece rate system, to link productivity and earnings.

In the urban areas private small-scale production and trade were permitted subject to certain overall regulations and the production and trade of consumer goods were encouraged. The Chinese economy which remained substantially isolated from the rest of the global economy till then was suddenly opened up to international trade and foreign investments, primarily investment by capitalist countries on a joint-venture basis. Tourism, the hotel industry, were also encouraged. In an attempt to obtain foreign exchange through the incentive system Chinese were permitted to get foreign remittances and to use the foreign exchange certificates issued against them to purchase imported consumer goods like colour televisions, cameras, refrigerators, motor cars etc.

Under the impact of these reform measures the Chinese economy did indeed boom in the second half of the 1980s with the rural people, especially farmers as well as traders all over the country becoming the major beneficiaries. But new problems have emerged too. Instability of prices has come about with inflation making serious inroads into the earnings of the fixed income groups—for example the administration and educational services. Inequalities have perceptibly increased and in the urban areas those who are able to get foreign remittances have become almost a separate class. Unemployment is beginning to become open. Corruption and social unrest have increased. There is also some evidence that during the decade of prosperity, there has been a deterioration of health standards, a noticeable increase in the infant mortality rates, for instance.

But to say that a socialist economy faces problems is nothing new. They always do! What is different in a socialist economy is the *conscious* attempt to resolve problems as they arise and the ability to make mid-course corrections. These corrections themselves may give rise to new problems which, in turn, must be corrected. It is a little too romantic to dream about a social order in which no problems emerge, or of one where the emerging problems are *automatically* resolved.

Our discussion of specific socialist economies centred on their functioning mainly to understand their differences from other type of economies especially the capitalist economy. One of the major differences that we noted at the beginning of this chapter between a capitalist economy and a (post-capitalist) socialist economy is that while the former is inherently exclusive the latter deliberately strives to be inclusive. In the People's Republic of China this thrust on inclusiveness was spelled out in terms of the 'five guarantees'—food, clothing, fuel, education and health care. And it is a measure of the seriousness of that commitment that in spite of the many set-backs and problems those have become a reality to practically *all* of the over one billion people. A very creditable and unprecedented record indeed.

CRISIS OF HISTORICAL SOCIALISM

In the sixties and seventies of this century—hardly fifty years after the first post-capitalist economy was launched—historical socialism had appeared as an alternative to capitalism and a distinct model for the so-called Third World countries of the world (that is, with underdeveloped capitalist economies such as ours) to emulate. But in the eighties, especially late eighties, practically all socialist countries had to confront serious internal problems and the regimes in many of them were overthrown as a result of popular uprisings. The fall of regimes came not only in Poland and Hungary which had extensive private sectors, but also in what were known to be the staunchest among the socialist countries, particularly the German Democratic Republic and Romania. Those who have always opposed socialism have interpreted these events as the end of socialism and the triumph of capitalism. Among those who have been sympathetic towards socialism, there has been a tendency to be somewhat dismissive about these events; either on the ground that the basic factors that led to the fall of socialist regimes had little to do with socialism (the desire for German reunification, for instance, has been seen as the explanation for the tearing down of the Berlin Wall and the overthrow of the regime in East Germany) or on the grounds that only those who have not been truly following socialist principles have been rejected. A further explanation has been that the fall of socialist regimes has been brought about by the conspiracy of international capitalism.

We are too close in time to these events to be able to critically evaluate them and the explanations offered by opponents and defenders of socialism. But if a number of socialist regimes have been overthrown, following the clear demonstration of disenchantment by those who till recently have been considered as the chosen beneficiaries of a new socio-economic order, we must infer that there are systemic factors underlying what has happened. The fact that there are evidences of crisis in the People's Republic of China, far from the European scene where major changes took place in the late eighties, and that even the Soviet Union has been running into problems lends support to this inference. Hence in the light of recent experiences it is necessary to explore whether some underlying systemic weaknesses of historical socialism can be identified. We shall concentrate on one major issue which, however, has diverse manifestations.

Centralisation, the systemic weakness of historical socialism

Historical socialism has shown a built-in leaning towards centralisation. To some extent the tendency towards centralisation was forced on the newly emerging socialist regimes by the very circumstances of their start—opposition from within and threat of foreign aggression in the case of Russia, for instance. Even regimes that claim to have great faith in democracy and decentralisation swing towards centralised authority under conditions of war and internal disorder. In the case of the socialist regimes this natural tendency was reinforced by other circumstantial factors. The first is that in all instances, the installation of the socialist regimes was brought about only by rather limited sections or groups in society, by the capture of State power by a popular leader, a party or a section of the armed forces. A small group trying to bring about radical changes in the socio-economic structure will tend to be particularly sensitive about forces opposed to it, and doubtful about the support it will get even from those on whose behalf it took over power. The need to defend its position and to assert its authority has been one of the circumstantial factors that has led all socialist regimes, including Yugoslavia (which has shown the most consistent inclination towards decentralisation) to be heavily centralised and palpably authoritarian in the early stages. This has been buttressed by an economic consideration. One of the primary tasks of the regimes was to achieve economic results, to increase the production of foodgrains, and other basic consumption requirements on the one hand, and to strengthen the infrastructure on the other. The former required immediate mobilisation of resources and labour and the latter was very much of a technocratic and administrative function. In either case a 'command' performance was thought to be the appropriate procedure.

The command mobilisation appeared to be successful too. For one thing, under the circumstances, it did not require much deliberation to decide what the economic priorities were. Both leaders and the masses were clear as to what had to be done. In China, for instance, foodgrains production in 1949 had gone down to a low of 108 million tonnes compared to a pre-1949 peak of 138 million tonnes, and by 1952, output was raised to 154 million tonnes. The peasants responded splendidly to the call of the leadership. On the other hand where there was opposition to the leadership, as in Soviet Russia there was no choice except to rely on commands.

The consensus on economic priorities at low levels of production and the urgency of the tasks to be done, thus provided an almost natural tendency towards centralisation. Another factor too must be taken note of. One of the problems that practically all socialist regimes faced was that the economies that they took over had substantial pre-capitalist elements in them characterised by local self-sufficiency, and lack of economic integration. Most of them had markets of various sorts, but the market forces were not sufficiently strong to link industry and agriculture, for instance, or different regions of the country. Hence, administrative commands appeared to be the only possibility for the coordination of the economy. 'War communism', we may recall, was necessitated in order to get the grain from the peasants to feed the armed forces and government employees.

There were, therefore, circumstantial justifications aplenty for the emergence of a centralised command system. But there were deeper forces underlying the centralisation bias. The first is a view shared by many Marxists—for which some Marxists in the past and some contemporary Marxists also have provided the theoretical rationale—that exchange and markets are intrinsically individualistic, and are thus activities closely associated with capitalism, and are, therefore, not compatible with socialism. Our analysis of the evolution and metamorphosis of exchange as an activity (and market as an institution) has shown that this is, strictly speaking, not a valid proposition. We know, for sure, that exchange, even exchange through the medium of money, had existed long before capitalism emerged as a functioning economic system and, therefore, an identification of exchange, markets and money with capitalism is not correct.

But theoretical arguments, both in favour of markets and against markets, have a tendency to overlook concrete historical experiences and, thus become ideological in nature. In socialist societies the ideological antipathy towards money and markets has been a strong factor strengthening the tendency towards centralisation. It is accompanied by another erroneous view that socialism does (or must) convert the economy into a single giant factory or farm in which particular functions are to be performed on the basis of a line control, that is, commands from above sent down to functionaries below.

This conception of the economy under socialism has a corresponding view about the polity too. The polity in historical socialist countries has been invariably under the control of the respective communist parties. Communist parties have been terribly conscious of their understanding and interpretation of historical processes and have been equally sure of their right to *lead* the processes of change and reconstruction. Thus, whatever may have been their views about the procedures for coordinating the economy, there never was any doubt about controlling the polity: it had to be by the Party. As an organisation meant to bring about change, the Party tended to emerge as a hierarchical structure even when on deliberative matters there was recognition of the need for democratic participation. And since in a socialist system it is not possible to draw any neat distinction between the polity and the economy, the command structure of the party tended to be the dominating feature of societal organisation in general. With the nationalisation of enterprises, this rather inherent tendency towards centralisation was matched by the bureaucratic need for administration and thus the centralised command model appeared to be the right order in socialist systems.

Centralisation and bureaucratic controls

To be sure it played a useful and possibly inevitable role in the initial stages. But a centralised command system has a tendency to perpetuate itself, and even to intensify it. A command system becomes, by definition, a bureaucratic system which must, therefore, lay down in some detail the rules of procedure. Once the rules are codified, it is easier to add to them than to delete them, and so they continue to grow and become less flexible. And, in view of the close link between the polity and economy, the rules and codes become 'affairs of state' with the bureaucracy developing a vested interest in protecting and interpreting the codes. Thus secrecy is added to inflexibility and the distinction between suggestions and orders soon disappear. Everything emanating from above becomes a diktat, thus killing any initiative from below. The steady emergence of centralised control, however, can remain hidden because with the number of people administering the system increasing, there will be semblances of discussions and consultations going down even to the lowest levels and it may appear that a system of centralised control with decentralised deliberations and implementation is indeed being evolved and perfected.

Those who have effective control over the evolving machinery will tend to perpetuate it partly because of their conviction that they are in the right direction and partly because vested interests easily develop in a closed hierarchical system. Under historical socialism these tendencies have been further reinforced by the 'mission' that communist parties have assigned to themselves to lead, which comes to be quite easily interpreted as the right to rule. It is not difficult to see why personality cults are the natural outcome of processes of this kind.

What impact does this sort of set-up—normal, if not inevitable under the conditions described—have on the performance of the system? The gap between formulation of plans and their implementation with power effectively resting with those responsible for the former imposes severe strains on the implementors who constitute the lowest rung in the hierarchy. A good deal of their energies and ingenuities have to be devoted to 'fulfilling the targets'.[6] Which among these are legitimate and which are dubious cannot easily be established: a vast area of grey is sure to be the case. For instance, contacts with key persons above may have to be established to ensure that inputs arrive on time. In due course this may develop into a system of intermediaries which, in turn, can pave the way to all kinds of corrupt practices. Since targets are set in quantitative terms, there is a built-in tendency to sacrifice quality to fulfil the targets. This is particularly so when the producers in this kind of system do not have to worry about the 'realisation problem' which is what really disciplines producers under capitalism. Horizontal arrangements and 'deals' between enterprises may be resorted to, first to be faithful to the orders from above, but later on even to thwart them.

Secondly, as performance improves and the low-level threshold is crossed, the need for decisions about the next step which will include greater variety and therefore diversity of views will become necessary demanding greater flexibility in the system. But as noted above, over time the tendency of the command system will be to become more rigid. There may be genuine appreciation of the need for reform, greater flexibility and some attempts will be made along these lines. Such was the setting of the 1965–66 Reforms in the Soviet Union, and in most of the European socialist countries around that time or immediately thereafter. But the internal proclivities of the control system (the Party-bureaucracy set-up) and the performing system (the economy, for instance) will now be moving in opposite directions that marginal measures of reform suggested from above may not meet the real requirements. On the contrary, the suggested reform measures may threaten the very fabric of the control system and may be reversed, again as it happened in the Soviet Union all through the 1970s and beyond. Hence, a new 'scissors crisis' of sorts may emerge in socialist systems with the view from above and the needs from below diverging and moving rapidly in opposite directions. Its consequences would be serious, as later developments would show.

The third, and most serious, consequence of the centralised command system is that it precludes a participatory form of economy and polity. In the economy the distance between the plan formulators and implementors creates problems not only for enterprises as noted above, but also tends to alienate the workers. Workers who may have some influence on shop floor decisions will soon discover that effective control over the enterprise and consequently over their labour power is in the hands of a few faraway agencies or persons which generates the gap between 'them' and 'us'. It would appear that 'they' own and control the enterprise (the means of production) and 'we' work for 'them'. A sense of alienation, suspicion and hostility very easily springs up once this situation emerges as became evident between the establishment and the workers united under Solidarity in Poland. Even where it does not lead to organised movements of that kind, it will certainly have a bearing on the incentive to work. To some extent it will be countered by moving on to a regime of material incentives and differential payments. But it also has a systemic component. Rising wages and incomes as such are of little consequence unless more consumer goods become accessible and, in fact, unless some variety is available so as to exercise choice. Once this stage is reached, comparisons between one's socialist economy and the neighbouring capitalist economies become quite natural. Thus, workers in East Germany watched with jealousy and admiration the economic conditions in a booming West Germany and the consequent material affluence of workers there. Hungarians came to accept neighbouring Austria as their point of reference. The Chinese and the North Koreans started giving expression to their desire to share the experiences of their counterparts in South Korea and Taiwan, if not of Japan.

Socialist economies, it must be admitted, have provided much more scope for workers' participation in matters immediately relating to their work. But the worker is also a citizen and he is frequently told that socialism is not only an economic programme, but an attempt to reconstruct society as a whole. In this larger social and political process, however, socialist societies have not designed institutional channels for participation by the members of the society at large. On the other hand, the institutional structures in socialist countries have effectively hindered participation. Political processes have all been under the domination of the communist parties; criticisms of the party line have been interpreted as opposition to socialism and have been systematically suppressed; intellectual efforts have been closely tied to the regimes and their requirements; organisations even outside of the political realm were either not permitted or kept under close surveillance.[7]

Not that all of these have gone unchallenged. There have been many individual critics of the deviation of the socialist experiences from the socialist urges. There were organised uprisings too against the system, the most widely known among them being the Czechoslovakian uprising of 1968 which was suppressed at that time, but hailed in retrospect now.

We shall not enter into a discussion here of why serious popular opposition became possible in the late 1980s and why a number of regimes collapsed in 1989. The more important question to consider is whether the collapse has been only of the regimes or of socialism itself in the countries where major changes took place in 1989. Even that is too early to say. But we must accept both possibilities. If the people in those countries are genuinely convinced about the need for and the possibilities of evolving post-capitalist economic systems, but were disenchanted with the non-representative regimes that failed to achieve that objective, they will try again to move in that direction. If they succeed, the events of 1989 and early 1990s will, in retrospect, come to be known as one more instance of mid-course corrections that those who are serious about establishing post-capitalist economies are capable of. But building up a post-capitalist economy and society is a very difficult task which calls for a great deal of clarity in thinking and a great deal of investment of effort. If these are not forthcoming, the events of 1989 will become the first step in dismantling the social experiment. There cannot be too much indecision about the course to be taken. Any modern society must have a functioning economy. If such an economy is not deliberately and effectively steered in a post-capitalist direction, the normal tendency will be for it to turn out to be a capitalist economy. For capitalism is even now a live and aggressive force, ready to take advantage of any opportunity that presents itself. Socialists have frequently misdirected themselves by interpreting the historical nature of capitalism to mean its imminent collapse and by thinking that once a socialist regime has overthrown a capitalist order, there will be no backsliding at all. There can be little doubt that in the attempts to evolve post-capitalist societies and economies, some socialist experiments will fail. The significance of historical socialism is not that it has displaced capitalism, but that it has demonstrated the *possibility* of making post-capitalist economies a reality. The guiding principle for the future, therefore, is that post-capitalist economy is a possibility, not that it is a historical inevitability.

Towards a Functioning Post-Capitalist Economy

Our analysis of historical socialism has shown that unlike all previous economic systems, wherever historical socialist socio-economic arrangements have emerged they were the result of conscious human interventions. In that sense the establishment of a post-capitalist economy is evidence of the growing maturity of the human race, a demonstration that it is possible for human beings to emancipate themselves from the domination of the economy that capitalism had brought about and to make the economy subordinate to social decisions. The restoration of the instrumental role of the economy is, therefore, the rule and a major task of a post-capitalist order. Or, as we have already noted, a post-capitalist economy explicitly recognises that it is embedded within a larger social order, that it is a structure of human relationships set within a totality of human relationships that constitute a community. The emphasis in a post-capitalist economy shifts away from the management of resources into the human factor where resources, and therefore the management of resources, become a means to facilitate human development.

This means that the essential feature of a post-capitalist economy is a conscious and continuous striving to make it function. That does not, however, mean that there are no guiding principles for the operation of a post-capitalist economy. In the first section of this chapter we have already touched upon some basic conditions necessary for its functioning. The discussion of historical socialism spelt them out. more specifically. We also saw how historical socialism failed to follow some of the crucial principles of a post-capitalist economy, participation, for instance.

In this section we shall once again deal with the operating principles of a post-capitalist economy. A preliminary remark is necessary. If a post-capitalist economy does not have its own independent laws, and if it has to be specific in each historical context, an *a priori* blueprint of its working cannot be attempted. To put it differently, a post-capitalist economy cannot be converted into a purely logical or theoretical system. This is not to deny the possibility of any kind of logical analysis of such an economy. What it does mean is that the logical analysis is possible only in relation to the historical context. In the exercise in this section we shall, therefore, indicate only the broad pre-conditions for a functioning post-capitalist economy, in particular to differentiate it from a capitalist economy.

Dual relationship between labour and resources

Let us, first, take up a few conceptual issues. Because one of the central features of a capitalist economy is the private ownership of the means of production, the abolition of the regime of private property becomes a major prerequisite of a post-capitalist economy. We have already seen that the socialisation of the means of production became a priority issue for most instances of historical socialism. But it is important to give careful thought as to how the socialisation of the means of production and of physical resources as a whole is to be brought about. Far too often it is considered as a mere transfer of the ownership of the means of production from individuals and other private agencies to the state, the process widely known as nationalisation. Nationalisation per se, however, does not amount to genuine socialisation for a variety of reasons. First of all, nationalisation is only a legal process whose economic consequence *may be*, but need not always be, conducive to socialisation. Consider, for instance, the nationalisation of. an industry or the banking system as a whole, whereby the legal ownership is taken over by the state. But if that legal transfer does not lead to any change in the operation of the industry or of the banking system, it is doubtful whether the move can be thought of as leading towards socialisation. A similar issue may come up in a different context. Suppose that immediately after the establishment of a post-capitalist economy in a predominantly agrarian society, a legal decree is announced to the effect that all land belongs to society at large. What will be its implication for agricultural operations? Will the farmers who were previously owners as well as cultivators continue to be cultivators without the right of ownership, or will land be taken away from them denying them even the right to cultivate? These two examples show that ownership (as we have already seen in earlier chapters) consists of different kinds of rights and so bringing means of production and resources under social control calls for much more than a legal transfer of ownership. In a post-capitalist economy, the central problem as far as property and ownership goes, is to decide how best to *use* property and resources so as to achieve the social objectives.

In this regard a few considerations are relevant. The first is to recognise the close connection between property as means of production and work. In our discussion of the rudimentary economy we saw that work or productive activity takes place through the interaction between nature and human labour. In a village economy the connection between natural endowments and human labour in productive activity becomes more explicit as land yields produce when labour is expended on it. In practically all stages and forms of production, work becomes possible and 'productive' because human beings use tools of varying degrees of complexity and sophistication. In these respects resources and property indeed become the means of human productivity. But the means of production are also the result of human labour. This is clear in the case of all tools produced directly by the worker. Even natural resources undergo substantial changes as they are worked on by human beings. Land, for instance, becomes more productive when it is cleared, levelled or terraced, and most visibly when it is irrigated. To that extent today's land is as much the gift of nature as it is of past human effort. Capital goods too are stored up human labour.

In view of this dual relationship between resources and labour—resources helping labour *in* productive activity and resources becoming available *through* productive activity—the worker comes to have a special attachment to what he works on and what he works with.[8] Possession or ownership is one form in which this attachment manifests itself. In this sense possession or ownership is a form of relationship between human beings and material things. But possession and ownership take various social forms also and then they emerge as different forms of property *rights*, that is, relationships between human beings. Thus, in the village economy some people put forward a claim on ownership of land which is a form of property right. In a capitalist economy, the capitalists through their ownership of the means of production make it obligatory for the workers to work *for* them and claim the entire produce to be theirs. Alienation of workers from their means of work and exploitation of workers by owners are the result of that form of ownership.

What emerges from these considerations is that the meaning and implications of ownership (of the means of production, of property, of resources, whichever way one looks at it) becomes manifest not only by the legal form that it takes, but primarily through the manner in which work or productive activity is organised. Hence, what is required in a post-capitalist economy is not merely a (legal) *transfer* of ownership from private hands into the public domain, but a *transformation* of ownership through appropriate organisation of work recognising the nature of relationship between human effort and material things in the process of production. Social ownership of and control over things (natural resources, land and produced means of production) is thus a means to ensure that work comes to have its proper place in human affairs and that productive activity becomes genuinely creative and humane. It is much more than what a legal act can achieve although legal changes may be necessary as enabling conditions.

The major issue in a post-capitalist economy, then, is the organisation of work or productive activity. This can be expressed making use of our characterisation of the economy given in Chapter 1. A post-capitalist economy is a set of arrangements, especially control over resources, so that resources and labour can be brought together in truly humane forms of productive activities to satisfy the material needs of all the members of society. Herein also lies the difference between the capitalist and post-capitalist economies. In a capitalist economy the control over resources has to be such that the organisation of production ensures the continuing accumulation of resources for those who own them. Even where attempts are made to improve the conditions of work—and there is no need to deny that in capitalist economies such attempts are made—the *objective* of the organisation of production remains the same, and only those who own resources (in that context only those who possess something that has a positive price resulting from the exchange process) are the constituents of the economy.

We have seen also that in the capitalist economy workers become its constituents by selling their labour power. This has a further implication. 'Work' gets identified with those human activities that are paid for and the 'worker' as a person whose claim on the product depends on expending labour for others, in contrast to those whose claims on the product depend on their ownership of resources (or property).

Organisation of Work

In view of the differences that a post-capitalist economy comes to have, both these terms have to be given new meanings. The latter is fairly simple to deal with. A post-capitalist economy's ownership characteristics and its principles of defining and settling claims, ensure that it does not have the class of people whose claim on the product depends on ownership. The dictum in a post-capitalist economy is (as has been noted already): 'If one does not work, neither should he eat'. A post-capitalist economy has no place for those who *can* work, but *do not* work. Of course, as in a rudimentary economy, it will have those who *cannot* work (children, the aged and the infirm) but its inclusive principle recognises their claims on the product.

Indicating the meaning of 'work' in a post-capitalist economy is more difficult. By recognising as 'work' those forms of human activity that get paid for, capitalist economy provides an identifiable, but arbitrary, criterion to distinguish the two. In a post-capitalist economy there is no such visible criterion to draw the distinction. However, a conceptual distinction is possibly based on the manner in which we distinguished economic relationships and economic activities (in Chapter 1) from other human relationships and activities, by linking the former to the provisioning of the material needs of the members of a society. We shall, therefore, consider all human activities related to the provisioning of the material needs of the members of a society as 'work' recognising that some forms of work will call for physical and other for mental effort, and that some kinds of work may result in tangible goods while others may be in the form of services. In effect, what is being indicated is that in a post-capitalist economy work gets identified with productive activity and, therefore, a worker is anyone who is engaged in productive activity.

This clarification of the meaning of work is necessary in order to turn to an examination of the organisation of work which we must now take up. From what has been said about the nature of a post-capitalist economy some characteristics of its organisation of work are already evident. The organisation of productive activity must be worker-centred, meant to cater to the needs of the workers; conditions of work must be satisfactory from the workers' point of view in terms of safety and health considerations; workers must be in possession of their means of production so that they are not exploited; productivity of workers must increase over time and the drudgery of work must be reduced. What now needs to be considered are the specific forms that the organisation of productive activity must take to achieve these objectives.

The specific forms that the organisation of production will take will depend very much on the historical conditions under which the transformation of the economy is attempted. As was noted at the beginning of this chapter, the original expectation was that the transformation or transition would take place in advanced capitalist economies. But in reality all instances of the attempts to bring about post-capitalist economies have happened in economies which were in the early stages of capitalism, or indeed, where the economies were still passing through the transition from pre-capitalist to capitalist economies, and no economy which was in an advanced stage of capitalism has so far moved into a post-capitalist order. Whatever may be the explanation for these facts, it seems more realistic to say that the post-capitalist transformation takes place in economies which are in the lower levels of capitalist structure rather than in the higher or advanced levels. On that basis the initial conditions we must postulate in examining a post-capitalist transformation are similar to what we noted at the end of Chapter 4 relating to the transformation of the village economy. Specifically these conditions are the predominance of land-based economic activity (agriculture) effectively carried out by households as the primary unit of production, but under various forms of domination by non-cultivating landlords; the prevalence of traditional and low productivity non-agricultural activities, once again organised as household production units and local non-market links, or under the domination of merchants; some capitalist connections and financial intermediation, but with strong links with international capitalism. How is a post-capitalist transformation to be effected under these conditions?

We must repeat what we have already stated: a post-capitalist economy does not emerge through a natural process of evolution; where it is initiated it is through deliberate human intervention, and its evolution and transformation requires constant attention and effort. Hence a functioning post-capitalist economy requires a directing authority. That is the role that is expected of the state, in such an economy. As the state in this regard is the proxy for society as a whole, the overall functioning of the economy becomes its responsibility. It is, therefore, a declaration of the state that brings resources under overall social ownership and control, as a precondition for a reorganisation of productive activity. A natural corollary of such a declaration is to eliminate all forms of property incomes accruing to individuals or groups of people such as landlords, money lenders, owners of industrial capital in their physical or financial forms etc. The immediate aim of the socialisation of property and resources, therefore, is to require that, in the case of all who are able to do so, claims on the product will be only through involvement in productive activity.

However, the socialisation of property need not be followed by an integration of all productive activity under a single centralised authority as it is usually assumed. In most instances, especially under the kind of actual initial conditions that we have postulated, such a step will not be possible or desirable. For one thing to centralise all productive activity is also to assume direct responsibility to provide the requirements of all members which may not be a feasible task. It may also lead to all problems related to a centralised command model. In relation to the organisation of productive activity, therefore, the socialisation of resources is to be regarded as a procedure to enable all to engage in work and to be able to meet the basic necessities of life.

Heterogeneous production units

In most specific cases it will call for different forms of the organisation of production. A common condition governing all of them, however, is that no person or group of persons should be permitted to employ anyone else as a wage labourer. Once this condition is imposed, three forms of the organisation of work are likely to emerge. The first is a continuation of the most widely prevalent form, viz., the household production unit which relies on activating and utilising the family labour at its disposal. This is likely to be the major form of organisation of work in agriculture as well as in many kinds of small-scale manufacturing activities. The responsibility of the state in respect of these production units is to *lease out* to them the land and the tools which they will be able to *use* as their own, but without the right to sell. A second form of organisation of productive activity will be where a group of workers take over the responsibility to run an enterprise as a corporate activity. We shall refer to such production units as 'cooperative enterprises'. These will (or can) emerge where workers on wage employment existed before, and who also will now come to have the right to use the socialised means of production, (land and implements in agriculture, factories and machinery in industry, for example) but again without the right to dispose of through sale. The organisation of work in these enterprises will certainly be more complex than in the case of the household production units, and for this purpose the services of former owners and managers may be retained provided they are willing to accept the principle of work-sharing and product-sharing along with their former employees without any proprietory rights of control or of claims.

The household production units and the cooperative enterprises together will constitute the bulk of the production units in a post-capitalist economy. These units will have two operating principles in common. The first is that they exercise control over resources through contract and not through any absolute ownership. The contract will be between the units and the appropriate organs of the state, which are the guardians of the social ownership of resources. In return for the use of social resources these production units will be subjected to some levies which will also be part of the contract. The second principle is that subject to the levies which are transfers from the units to the state, the definition and settlement of claims of the members will be an internal decision of the units themselves. This is obvious in the case of the household production units, but will be applicable also to the cooperative enterprises.

Apart from the household production units and cooperative enterprises there will also be a third kind of production units which will be specifically state owned, and hence may be referred to as state enterprises. The need for state enterprises arises for a variety of reasons. They perform what may be described as residual functions: to provide work opportunities to those who do not become own account workers, or members of work teams, as also to ensure that all necessary productive activities other than those taken up by the other production units are carried out. They also become instruments to discharge the obligation of the state to provide overall direction and coordination to the economy. In this sense their function may be much more than to play a residual role. State enterprise, may, indeed, come to control the 'commanding heights' of the economy producing some crucial goods such as energy or steel and controlling some key services such as banking. State enterprises also have the responsibility to generate enough surplus to discharge the obligation of the state on behalf of society, to provide for the needs of those who cannot work. In this regard the surplus generated by the state enterprises must supplement the share of the produce that the state will come to have through fiscal transfers. State enterprises will not be 'owned' by workers as are other production units, and yet workers must have a great deal of say in their operations, and suitable principles of sharing will have to be worked out for the settlement of claims.

Coordinating the production units

The production units in a post-capitalist economy are subeconomies in the sense in which we have used the term in Chapter 3, each kind with its own internal principles of labour utilisation and settlement of claims, but also interacting with other production units under the overall coordination of the state. Coordinating the activities of these subeconomies so as to translate the essential principles of a post-capitalist economy into action is the central economic task of the state.[9]

We shall refer to this coordinating function as planning. It consists of two aspects. The first is technical and is what is referred to in modern socialist literature as 'material balances'. A few examples will indicate what this means. If clothing is required as final output, yarn and dyes will be required as inputs in fairly well specified quantities. If the total output of clothing is to increase steadily, textile machinery will also have to be provided for. In order to do that, the production of steel will first have to increase. Similarly, a sustained increase in agricultural production will make it necessary to increase the production of fertilisers which, in turn, can be done only if the basic chemicals are produced in desired quantities at the appropriate time. Thus material balances have to ensure the appropriate input-output links at any given time (usually referred to as inter-sectoral balance) as also the proper alignment of sequential production activities (referred to as inter-temporal balances).

Apart from the coordination of the material or physical aspects of production, planning must also address itself to what may be called economic coordination. If the goods mentioned in the previous paragraph are produced by different production units, they must also move from one unit to the other for production to proceed smoothly. Apart from the physical movement of goods (which form part of the material balances consideration) there is the more important and more complex task of sales and purchases, of exchange, that is.

We have noted earlier, that from certain theoretical considerations it has been argued that exchange and markets are not compatible with socialism. But in the kind of post-capitalist set-up that we envisage, exchange, market and money have very legitimate and very important roles to play. Their roles, of course, will not be the same as in a capitalist economy. But we have seen that exchange as an activity and market and money as institutions function within broader economic and social milieu and that they get metamorphosed as their associative conditions change. Consequently, their role in a post-capitalist economy can be, and needs to be, different. As resources get socialised in a post-capitalist economy, exchange, market and money, too, must be socialised in order to perform their roles in the new set up. With reference to exchange we shall indicate how this is achieved.

Socialised exchange

To some extent the socialisation of exchange follows the socialisation of resources because it sets social boundaries on exchange as an activity. Land and other resources, the means of production and labour power are not bought and sold in a post-capitalist economy. This is because all these together form the basis of society, and within society there is no 'other' and hence there is neither ownership nor exchange. In this respect a post-capitalist economy is fairly close to a rudimentary economy: the members of a post-capitalist economy (like the members of a rudimentary economy) possess together, or together exercise control over, what is available and accessible to them. In a post-capitalist economy it is the multiplicity of production units that necessitates exchange, a major part of which is in the nature of inter-enterprise transfers. Such transfers can be thought of as corresponding to inter-departmental transfers within a large multi-product firm. Consequently, these transfers can be worked out on the basis of commonly agreed criteria without resorting to any bargaining based on the resource power of the parties concerned. To the extent that the inter-sectoral material balances are carefully worked out, they indicate the technical coefficients of input-output relationships which can be used to derive the ratio of transformation between goods. Such ratios also indicate the relative cost of goods, that is, the cost of one good in terms of other goods providing an objective basis for inter-enterprise transfers. In fact in a post-capitalist economy it is possible to go a step further. In as much as labour power is an input into all production processes and all output is ultimately meant to produce, preserve and develop labour, something like a unit cost can be evolved to assess all costs. For instance, the goods equivalent of the subsistence of a human being, or of 'decent living' can be used as the unit cost. Not that such calculations can be precise or that they will remain invariant over time. But it is possible to arrive at a generally recognised *social norm* for costing. Costs thus arrived at can be the objective criterion to guide all inter-unit transfers. The procedure also makes it possible to socialise exchange in a post-capitalist economy.

Production units would want to cover a little more than costs in their transactions with other units. This too can be accommodated by accepting the principle of 'cost plus mark up' as the basis of exchange and pricing. All produced goods used in further production can be brought under this principle of transaction whose basis is the technical input-output relationship, which, therefore, can be common knowledge to all parties that wish to enter into exchange. We shall refer to these inter-enterprise transactions as the exchange of intermediate goods. A substantial share of all exchanges taking place in a post-capitalist economy (as also in a capitalist economy) will be of this kind, and because they can be based on objective criteria, the subjective element in exchange can be set aside, and inter-enterprise transaction can be standardised. In this respect the post-capitalist economy has a distinct advantage over the capitalist economy. The technical nature of the transaction of intermediate goods is common to both. However, in a capitalist economy this exchange (as the exchange of all commodities) takes the M–C–M form, and since that form is under the domination of traders, either as specialised traders or as capitalist producers-as-traders, whose purpose is to acquire ΔM through exchange, the transactions will come to be governed by more than technical considerations. For instance, the trader, who realises ΔM by buying cheap and selling dear, will have an incentive to distort the technical information and to refuse to reveal the extent of the mark-up in the transactions to turn them to his advantage. This is an essential part of capitalist competition as we saw in the previous chapter. Competition may make it difficult to impose too high a mark-up, but capitalist producers and traders will constantly strive to hide and distort information regarding their cost structure, and so subjective factors can still dominate the exchange of intermediate goods.

In other words, to the extent that information asymmetries prevail in a capitalist economy and the generation and maintenance of the information gap is a systemic requirement of capitalism, not even the exchange of inter-mediate goods of an inter-enterprise nature can be expected to be firmly based on objective cost considerations. On the other hand, in a post-capitalist economy, one of the basic principles of socialised production is universal access to technical information pertaining to production. One of the responsibilities of the state in organising production is to have something like a Bureau of Costs and Pricing (BCP) which ·,ï'l continuously gather information about the technical aspects of production from all types of production units (households, cooperative enterprises and state enterprises), help in the conversion of technical data into standard costs, monitor and regulate all mark-up and make all this information available freely to anyone interested in it. All inter-enterprise transactions must be made to conform to the norms of the BCP. In arriving at the norms the BCP can also take into account the inter-temporal variations in production that can be one of the considerations in mark-up differentials, spatial considerations, cost differences arising from specific regional factors etc. Subject to these norms and the legal requirements to conform to them, producers must be permitted, and indeed encouraged, to have non-price competition, parti-cularly regarding the quality of the product and promptness of delivery. By having and making available information about the standard cost of goods the BCP can encourage enterprises to strive for technical efficiency in production; through non-price competition enterprises can also be brought to some measure of economic efficiency.

The state will have to be active in at least two other areas in the organi-sation of production. The first is in research and development (R & D). We have seen that the capitalist system has a built-in imperative to bring about improvements in techniques in production, but the scientific effort that goes into it is of necessity privatised by keeping the procedures con-fidential and by patenting the outcome. In a post-capitalist economy, research meant to improve techniques of production can be and must be open. A Bureau of Research and Development (BRD) where professional scientists and technicians will continuously try to improve production techniques with the awareness that their labours will benefit society as a whole (and not only some private concern as in a capitalist economy) is a further requirement for the socialised organisation of production. It is not difficult to see that the BCP and the BRD will have to function with close coordination. The BRD can perform a further social function. It can receive suggestions from the public about new goods required and new processes necessary and bring them to the realms of possibility.

Secondly, the state will also have to assume responsibility for upgrading the technical skills and the overall competence of workers. These will relate to a wide variety of situations. For instance, workers in a household farm may require training not only in the use of farm machinery and farming practices, but also in cost accounting if they buy some inputs and sell some of their output as is likely to be the case. Workers engaged in traditional industries may need training to improve their techniques if these can be done and seen to be desirable, or may have to be trained in other skills if their traditional skills are becoming obsolete. Workers in enterprises also may require periodic upgrading of skills. And since, 'workers' are also functioning as 'managers', they will need training in these areas as well.

These considerations give us a different understanding of the nature of planning in a post-capitalist economy to organise production and to make it respond to genuine social needs. Socialisation of production must refer to this kind of orientation and the organisational aspects necessary for it rather than to the conventional nationalisation of the means of production and centralised control over all productive activities. Recalling the specific historical context in which post-capitalist economies have been tried out so far, we must note too that one of the major tasks of the reorganisation of production is to ensure that the goods and services required by the vast majority of people are increasingly becoming available and accessible to them. Involving the masses in productive activity (reversing the tendency of the capitalist economy to make labour redundant) and ensuring that production and productivity are going up are, therefore, the central tasks. The organisational structures of production are means to achieve those objectives. A post-capitalist economy must also recognise the fact that the organisation of production will and must undergo change over time. For instance, household production units which may be necessary in the initial stages for the effective use of labour power as well as of the means of production (especially land in countries where land is scarce in relation to labour) may tend to give way to cooperative enterprises subsequently. At the same time technological changes may encourage the formation of household production units in other areas.

Distribution of goods

We must note too that the organisation or reorganisation of productive activity is only one aspect of planning in a post-capitalist economy, a very important aspect to be sure. We shall now turn to some of its other dimensions. One of them, clearly, is the organisation of the distribution of goods produced to the final consumers. In some of the production units such as household farm producing goods for the consumption of its members, both the organisation of production and the organisation of distribution become the internal decisions of the unit. But in other instances, some intermediation is required for goods of final demand (as distinct from intermediate goods meant to go into production again) to reach their destination. The destination, of course, is the consuming unit, usually the household. This transfer of goods, from producers to consumers or from enterprises to households, is part of the overall transactions taking place in the system, an aspect of exchange. But exchange here will have some features other than what we have already seen when we dealt with the exchange of intermediate goods between enterprises. The exchange between enterprises and households is the exchange of labour power for (final) goods. Since the unit cost in the system is based on labour, there is a technical component to this exchange also. But this exchange cannot be confined to the technical component alone. The subjective preferences of consumers play a role in it. The demand for the goods will depend to a large extent on the preferences of the consumers. A post-capitalist economy must recognise, and subject to some limits, respect these preferences. This does not mean that unlike in the case of intermediate goods where exchange is based on considerations of cost, and hence of supply, the exchange of goods of final demand will be based solely on considerations of demand. The decisions regarding the quantum of goods of final demand to be produced will continue to be part of the overall planning decisions although the demand factor will be given due recognition in arriving at such decisions. Since property incomes have been eliminated and, in the initial stages, there is likely to be consensus on the final demand goods required, for a while at least the production of such goods can be decided on the expected increases in the general levels of income. But even at this stage consumer preferences can be respected by following a policy of simultaneous quantity and price regulations. A very common practice is to make available a fixed quantity of essential goods at fixed prices leaving it to the supply-demand factors to determine the distribution of the rest. Similarly, variety in goods can be provided for by having a standard type (with a few more varieties reflecting higher quality and at higher prices) leaving it to consumers to make their choice. These practices do not amount to giving full freedom to consumers; the scope of free choice can be increased as production and productivity increase, but at no stage does a post-capitalist economy propose to become entirely guided by 'consumers' sovereignty' as it is understood in a capitalist economy, where it effectively amounts to production responding not to consumer preference as such, but to resource power. The aim will be to respond more and more to needs as recognised by society as a whole.

On the basis of such principles of distribution, a post-capitalist economy must also attend to the organisational pattern for the distribution of final goods. The state will have to play a major role in this area as well; but as in the case of the organisation of production, it does not require that the state be solely responsible for the distribution of goods of final demand among the households. Let us recall that the major item of final demand, foodgrains, may be produced by household production units who owe levies to the state. Cooperative enterprises producing foodgrains too are subject to state levies. Some agency of the state is necessary to collect these levies. The marketing of the product may become an important consideration for most of the small units such as artisans producing goods of final demand. Some agency like a State Trading Corporation, therefore, will be required to procure and purchase goods of final demand from the production units. The distribution of these goods can be entrusted to a variety of agencies. The state itself will have to accept responsibility for some retail trade, especially if (as it may become necessary) some essential goods have to be sold below production costs. The rest of the trade may be left to cooperative organisations and even to households that wish to set themselves up as retail traders. In the case of the cooperatives and individual traders the cost plus mark-up principle can be followed, once again the costs being widely made known to the purchasers. Even where the forces of demand play an important part in retail trade, the market clearing mechanism will be largely quantity adjustment.

Both in the case of the exchange of intermediate goods and of the goods of final demand, the principle of socialisation is achieved to a large extent by the objective process of costing and by making information widely available with the cost involved in these processes being met by the state on behalf of society. Once this is done, trade can be substantially decentralised without opening up the possibility of the trader making excess profit through trade. A post-capitalist economy, therefore, has the possibility of using exchange as a useful social activity, basically of the C–M–C form without permitting it to become a traders' activity to accumulate exchange value.

In concluding our discussion of the subeconomies within a post-capitalist economy and their interactions, we must note too that they differ in their internal organisations, especially in relation to the principles of utilisation of labour and the settlement of claims. The distinction here is primarily between the households and the enterprises and the basis of the distinction is that as a subeconomy the household's organising principle is the direct conversion of labour power into use values. This is possible only because of its informal arrangements for the utilisation of labour and for the settlement of claims. In most instances the direct conversion of labour power into use values is performed by the female members of the household in a wide variety of ways. In a capitalist economy work of this kind is not even recognised as work because it is not 'paid for'. A post-capitalist economy will recognise the productive activities of females done within the household as work. How this is to be done requires careful consideration. A necessary step in this direction is to ensure that within the household the sexual division of labour does not become inflexible. Males performing some of the household chores usually considered the responsibility of females, must become common in a post-capitalist economy. Another suggestion that has been made is that the need for the conversion of labour power directly into use values must be recognised as a *social* necessity and so socially desirable forms of direct conversion of labour power into use values must be organised making it obligatory for all workers to devote part of their labour time for voluntary services of this kind, either within the household or elsewhere. Over time, what is household work itself will undergo change narrowing down the areas specifically reserved for females.

No equality of claims

Another fact to note is that a post-capitalist economy does not aim at bringing about equality of claims. As was discussed earlier, it removes one of the major societal factors contributing to inequality of earnings by abolishing all forms of property incomes. But interpersonal differences in earnings will continue as between subeconomies and even within them. In cooperative and state enterprises, for instance, specific rules for defining and settling claims will have to be worked out, and differences will exist, the broad principle being 'to each according to his/her work'. To the extent that in state enterprises workers are 'employees' the post-capitalist economy will also continue to have some elements of exploitation. What it succeeds in doing is to abolish *private* exploitation, and the exploitation of workers as the basis of the organisation of production.

Finally, we must note that the planning of economic activities in a post-capitalist economy cannot be done merely at the level of its subeconomies and in terms of their interactions. A number of important macro decisions will be necessary. The extent to which resources will be used to meet current needs, and set aside for future needs is one of them which will affect the composition of production. The magnitude of a common fund at the disposal of the state, to meet collective needs and the manner in which it is to be raised, is another. If price parities are to be changed between the major sectors of the economy (for instance, agriculture versus manufacturing) that will be a third macro decision. Monetary policies including the administration of credit will be a fourth, and so on.

To deal with these questions and to make decisions affecting the essentially decentralised production units, something like a Council of Economic Affairs must become an important organ of the state. It must consist of representatives of workers from the different kinds of productive units as well as those with specialised skills in dealing with the issues. The Council's task will be to consider the relationship between macro decisions and micro activities, to define the specific economic functions of the state, to overview the functioning of the BCP, the BRD and such other agencies, and thus to institutionalise the essentially participatory orientation of the system. The issues that the Council will deal with cannot be said to be purely economic, but will overlap considerably with what are often treated as political. That is but the reflection of a post-capitalist economy's inseparability from the wider society of which it is but an important component. A post-capitalist economy will become participatory to the extent that the larger society and its political processes are also participatory and conducive to genuine human development.

The building up of a post-capitalist economy is not an easy task. Any process of conscious social reconstruction is somewhat like the attempt to replace the wheels of a moving train. The process of the post-capitalist reconstruction of an economy is even more complex and hazardous. It will be resisted by powerful forces from within and without, because while a post-capitalist order can undoubtedly be beneficial to the vast majority of the members of an economy under capitalist domination, it cuts out the privileges of a minority who wield economic and political power in the existing arrangement. Removing the claims to property income has to be a major and preliminary step in the attempt to establish a post-capitalist economy. It will certainly be resisted by those who consider property rights to be natural and eternal and who may also feel that the properties they possess were acquired by their personal efforts or the efforts of their immediate predecessors. Even those who are to be beneficiaries of a post-capitalist order may be ambivalent about what may appear to be the processes of disruption that usually signal a change in the socio-economic order. They may fail to extend support to the attempt to bring about change. Because of the international spread of capitalism, the internal resistance is fairly certain to get external support too. Consequently what we have described as post-capitalist in terms of characteristics will not be post-capitalist in a chronological sense, but will have to be attempted in the context of strong capitalist (and pre-capitalist) forces within the country and all around it. It is impossible to overlook these aspects and to produce a blueprint for a post-capitalist economic order as though one was working on a clean slate. There can be no doubt also that the failure of historical socialism can be attributed as much to 'environmental hostility' as to internal weaknesses.

Crucial role of political processes

It is in such contexts that we must consider the role of the political processes in bringing about a post-capitalist economy. Mobilising the support of those who favour the change-over to a post-capitalist order from whatever exists, and convincing them about the feasibility of the new order, is the essential task of the political processes. That mobilisation calls for leadership. For reasons that are not difficult to understand the leadership comes from a party of workers. Constantly striving to capture political power which is necessary to bring about the change-over into a post-capitalist social order and economy and working out the major steps for that transition once power is captured, are the responsibilities of that leadership. How political power is actually captured depends on the specifics of each case. Even after that there is need for a group committed to the transformation with clarity of vision and resoluteness in action. From all these perspectives the vanguard role of a small group is not only necessary but is unavoidable. But the experiences of the past have shown that it is very easy to interpret the responsibility to lead as the right to rule. To a considerable extent the claim of the group to rule—to exercise power without submitting to effective scrutiny—can be rationalised as the response to the exigencies of the situation. However, in that process the need for participation and demo-cratisation gets neglected and relegated to the background. Often blind belief in the superiority of the post-capitalist order and in the ultimate withering away of the state makes those who lead and rule insensitive to the abuses of power. We have seen what such tendencies can lead to. Working systematically for the democratisation of state power and of social relationships, while providing effective leadership, is certainly no easy task. And yet the possibilities of organising a functioning post-capitalist economy depend more crucially on the success in this sphere than on the variety of arrangements of a specifically economic nature. For, as in the case of a rudimentary economy, so in a post-capitalist economy 'the economy' is a structure of human relationships embedded in and mentally carved out from a larger network of social relationships.

NOTES

1. Prominent among these early socialist writers were Robert Owen, Charles Fourier and Saint Simon.
2. Standard works on the Russian experience are Dobb, 1966 and Nove 1969.
3. On the socialist experiment in Yugoslavia see Vanek, 1971 and Dasgupta, 1989.
4. The account on the Chinese experiment in socialism is based on Riskin, 1987.
5. The loss of life during this period remained unknown for a long time. In the early 1980s the numbers became a matter of controversy among scholars. A careful scrutiny of available evidence has been undertaken by Ashton et. al., 1984 from which source the figure quoted in the text is taken.

6. Janos Kornai's two volume study (Kornai, 1980) deals extensively with these issues.
7. Bahro, 1978 gives a detailed account of these problems. Another writer from an Eastern European country said: 'Socialism stands before us not as a free community, but as a totalitarian state.' (Vajda, 1981: 64).
8. See Erazim V. Koshak's, 'Possessing, Owning, Belonging' in Howe, 1986.
9. On the issues of coordination of production in a post-capitalist economy see Elson, 1988.

Part II

The Indian Economy

7

The Indian Economy: An Analytical Description

We turn now directly to the Indian economy. The *Indian* economy is identified in terms of the geographical territory of the country and the domain of authority exercised by the Government of India. All *national* economies are bounded, similarly, by the respective features of geography and authority. These, however, are inadequate to describe their economic aspects. During the pre-colonial period the geographical territory identified as 'India' was very much the home of the village economy and even now the Indian economy retains many of its characteristics. In the second half of colonial domination, the Indian economy began to come under the sway of the capitalist system. The capitalist proclivities have increased and intensified since independence though the Constitution declares India to be a 'socialist' republic. A clue to the understanding of the Indian economy at present is, therefore, the interaction between its village economy and capitalist economy components.

In this chapter we try to capture the nature of this interaction through an identification of the heterogeneous units of the economy and their various links, constituting what are described as 'activity chains'. The empirical aspects of this analytical frame are also indicated.

In Part I we surveyed four different types of economies: rudimentary economy, village economy, capitalist economy and post-capitalist economy. They were in the nature of what has come to be described as 'ideal types'; each one constructed to represent what were considered to be the essential features of the type concerned. Thus the rudimentary economy was meant to typify the characteristics of a small, primitive and isolated economy functioning without interaction with others. The village economy denoted one where the primary productive force is land and where there are limited kinds of interactions among the units that constitute the economy. These include the interaction between those who labour and those who put forward a claim to a share in the produce based on ownership rights. With exchange gradually emerging, and then rapidly spreading, the functioning of an economy undergoes major changes. These take place due to the increase in the division of labour it facilitates, the concept of ownership that it makes more definitive, the greater inter-action between units that it gives rise to (especially after money comes to mediate in these interactions) and the appearance of specialists in trade—for whom the accumulation of exchange value becomes the main consideration. While the rudimentary and the village economies have the generation of use values as their organising principle, the capitalist economy which functions through exchange has the accumulation of exchange as its organising principle. The nature of the ownership of resources and the organisation of production in it gives rise to a clear distinction between the contribution of labour, on the one hand, and the claims of the resource owners on the other; with the latter being the appropriated surplus, via exchange, of the surplus generated by labour in the production process. The capitalist economy is also seen to be an 'exclusive' one whose participants can only be owners of commodities as well as one where constant changes in technological features of production become a systemic necessity in the continuing quest to augment exchange value.

The post-capitalist economy was shown to be an 'inclusive' economy subject to overall social decision and control aiming to provision the material needs of *all* its members with also a growing availability of goods and services to everyone over a period of time. In order to achieve these objectives, the post-capitalist economy would have to socialise ownership and exchange and have units with·different kinds of organising principles and patterns, as well as a body such as the state to coordinate inter-unit relationships.

Although the four economies examined in Part I have been 'ideal types', we have selected them in a way so as to also represent historical categories—*historical* in two different, but related senses. First, they are representations of real economies, economies that have existed and continue to exist in the world of experience. That is, though we have examined the inner logic of each type, they have not been merely logical constructs. Secondly, they also indicate a kind of chronological sequence and of evolution or transformation over time.

This second historical dimension requires some clarification. The process of evolution and transformation does not imply that later types immediately and totally replace the former; on the contrary, the chances are that there will be considerable overlapping of the different types and for fairly long periods too. Since (as we have already seen) the capitalist economy is the contemporary reality in most parts of the world (including our country) we may use it as our point of reference to illustrate this aspect. In a chronological sense, therefore, we may refer to three broad types of economies—pre-capitalist, capitalist and post-capitalist, recognising that there can be major variations within each.

The capitalist economy is intrinsically dynamic and expansionary in the sense that constant change and expansion is a requirement of its logic. Hence it has a tendency to wipe out (or absorb or transform) earlier types of economies and, in some parts of the world (especially Europe where it first started and in North America where it was transplanted), the capitalist transformation of the economy can be said to be substantially completed. But we know that that is not the case in other parts of the world where both pre-capitalist and capitalist types coexist and function simultaneously. This is what is happening in our country. In fact, what are commonly referred to as Developing Countries share this feature. If we take the global economy, we know that the emergence of post-capitalist economies in some of its units has not eliminated capitalist economies in other units; they too coexist. And we have seen that just as economies'can undergo post-capitalist transformation, some post-capitalist economies may revert back to capitalism or transform themselves into capitalism.

What emerges from this discussion is that real world economies will not be as simple and neat as the ideal types which, after all, have been 'cleaned' and structured through abstraction. This is not to say that ideal types are of no use in understanding the real world economies such as the Indian economy. We could, for instance, situate the Indian economy in the transitional stage of a village economy of the kind that we examined at the end of Chapter 3.[1] Alternatively, we could understand the Indian economy in terms of the interaction between capitalist and pre-capitalist economies touched upon in Chapter 5. However, this approach to a national economy has its limitations. To understand a real economy as a mixture of two ideal types can, at best, be a beginning. It provides only an external view of form, but does not provide a procedure to probe into its internal structure and functioning which calls for an understanding of the inter-action *between* types; the types themselves do not show how that can be captured. Two pure types cannot be combined to provide the features of a 'mixed' type of economy. What is needed is to construct an abstract version of the mixture itself. That is what we shall be concerned with in this chapter. We shall first consider how a national economy is to be approached, remembering that each national economy will have its own specific structure. Our interest is in a national economy such as ours whose features have been broadly indicated above.

A NATIONAL ECONOMY AS AN INTERACTING SYSTEM

A national economy is usually identified in terms of the geographical territory within which its economic activities take place and of the state under whose political and legal domain it functions. These territorial and political dimensions of the national economy are important, but they only define the boundaries of such an economy without yielding any clues about the manner in which it operates. In order to enter *into* a national economy much more information about its internal structure is needed.

To obtain that information let us recall our initial statement of what an economy is:

An economy is a structure of relationships among a group of people in terms of the manner in which they exercise control over resources, use resources and labour in the production of goods and services, and define and settle claims of the members over what is produced.

The statement indicates three basic functions of (or in) an economy: exercising control over resources; using resources and labour in production; and settling of members' claims. Each economy will have specific (institutional) arrangements to discharge these functions. These arrangements also constitute the 'structure of relationships' among the group of people. But who are the group of people who perform the functions in a national economy such as ours? A moment of reflection will show that these functions are carried out by a large variety of groups.

Control over agricultural land is exercised by the millions who own land and/or cultivate it; urban land is controlled by owners and users of different kinds; the government exercises control over some lands. Similar arrangements exist for exercising control over other resources also. Combining resources and labour in production is also done by households, farms and firms and by the government. Claims of the members are also settled by a variety of measures. The multiplicity and variety of units that perform the basic functions is a characteristic feature of national economies.

National economy in terms of its units and their links

Hence one possibility of understanding a national economy is to approach it in terms of its units. That is necessary to get an internal view of the economy. The units, too, have their internal structure which consists of the specific arrangements they have for carrying out their functions. In this respect the units are not all alike. For instance, the manner in which a peasant household exercises control over its land, uses land and labour power of its members for the production of paddy, and distributes the produce among its members is distinctly different from the way in which a household dependent on fishing does these tasks. It will also be different from the way a large farm or factory performs these functions. The internal structure of an agency of the state engaged in economic activities is likely to be different from the others indicated, and so on. Consequently, to get acquainted with the units of a national economy is to familiarise oneself with the internal structure of the variety of units that constitute the economy.

But except rarely, the units do not exist in isolation. They interact with other units. We may say that they are linked to other units. Thus, a household may lease-in land from another household and pay rent for so doing. The other, then, has a reciprocal relationship as leasing-out land and receiving rent. Another household may use the labour power of its members to make goods and sell its produce to several other units. The state may collect taxes from households and enterprises. Factories purchase their inputs from other factories and sell their outputs to households, to other factories, to the government and/or to merchants. Merchants buy from and sell to many other units. Banks receive deposits from households and enterprises and lend to a variety of units. Just as the units themselves are multifarious and heterogeneous, so also are the inter-unit links.

It is not difficult to see that except in the case of totally isolated units (that is, units that exist and function without links) the internal structure of units cannot be independent of the kind of links they have or can have. Just a few examples will suffice to bring this out. If a farm household has access to land that it does not own or if its members can work on other people's land, the manner in which it combines land and labour power will be different from what it would be otherwise, and so its internal structure will also be different. Or, a household which can sell its produce will function differently from one that cannot. The relationship between links and internal-structure exists in the opposite direction as well: the nature of inter-unit links depends on the internal structure of the units. If most units are nearly self-sufficient, the inter-unit links will be limited. If some units have more land than they can cultivate and other units do not have enough land for their needs, inter-unit links emerge as we saw in Chapter 3. Units and links, therefore, are mutually determining.

In view of these relationships we may say that a national economy (such as the Indian economy) consists of a number of heterogeneous units with a variety of links among them. The units and the links that relate them to other units may together be designated as *Activity Chains*. A unit may be linked to a number of and different kinds of units and the links it has with them may be of different kinds. Thus there are likely to be several and different kinds of activity chains of which a designated unit or specified link forms a part. This means that the activity chains themselves are overlapping and interacting. The 'structure of relationships' that our statement of the economy refers to can, therefore, be thought of as consisting of these overlapping and interacting activity chains.

A national economy, thus, is a very complex entity. But that is what makes it fascinating and not always easy to understand. Let us then describe a national economy as a complex network of overlapping activity chains consisting of a large number of heterogeneous units and a variety of links expressing their interactions. Now, the units themselves, in some instances, and the activity chains constitute sub-economies in the manner in which we defined the term in Chapter 2. Hence a national economy may also be thought of as a system of different kinds of sub-economies, each with its own internal structure and patterns of interaction with others. In Chapter 3 we had referred to the micro and macro views of the economy. What we have here is neither of these views but what may be described as a *micro-global* view, that is, an attempt to understand a totality in terms of the interactions within it. Because the totality is viewed in terms of the interactions within it, it is more than a mere sum of its units or a mere aggregation of the flows that are represented by the links. Its special features will become more evident as we go along.

Studying changes in the national economy

Apart from throwing light on the functioning of a national economy at any point in time, this frame can also be used to understand *changes* that are experienced by the economy over a period of time. In terms of the frame, changes over time can be seen as consisting of three components:
1. Changes in the internal structure of units.
2. Changes in the unit-mix of the system.
3. Changes in the activity chains, or in the pattern of interaction among the units.

This means that changes that come about in an economy are the result of changes taking place *within* the units as well as changes that come from *outside* the units, and the way in which the two interact. This is true whether the units are the micro units or the macro unit. To be more specific, households, enterprises etc., change because some changes are taking place within them, and because some changes are imposed on them from outside. Similarly, a national economy changes because it generates some changes within and because it experiences changes from outside.

Changes from within and changes from without are unlikely to be of the same kind. The internal changes (or the 'internal dynamics' to use a more technical expression) arise from the internal structure and function-ing of the unit itself and hence can be anticipated or predicted from the knowledge of these aspects. External changes cannot be clearly anticipated. They come as 'shocks' from outside, but impinge upon the internal struc-ture and functioning. Consequently, the total change that a unit experiences cannot be fully anticipated, and may be quite different from what its internal dynamics may indicate. But the situation is not as hopeless as may first appear. This is because the external shocks are not merely random phenomena; what a unit may consider to be external to it may emanate from the internal structure and dynamics of other units and hence can be anticipated and understood at least to some extent. If we now take a second look at Chapters 3 and 5 it will be seen that our discussion of the two different types of households in the village economy (X–type and Y–type), of the transformation of the village economy and of the dynamics of the capitalist economy have all been informed by this kind of an approach to the analysis of change, although the procedures were not explicitly spelt out in those instances. We shall press this method into service to understand the changes that take place in a national economy too.

One more observation is needed in our approach to a national economy. We have suggested that a national economy can be viewed as a network of interactions among its heterogeneous units *at any given time*, as well as a process of change in these interactions taking place *over time*. The separation into these two aspects is only for convenience of exposition for the two are not independent. As changes are always going on, an effort must be made to keep the two aspects as closely connected as possible. Hence what is required is a *dynamic macro-global* analysis. It is going to be an even more challenging task than we had indicated earlier. We would need to combine analytical insights with empirical evidence.

We shall now move to a micro-global profile of pre-capitalist and capitalist economies as a prelude to a micro-global analysis of the Indian economy.

MICRO-GLOBAL PROFILES OF PRE-CAPITALIST AND CAPITALIST ECONOMIES

We have already noted that the Indian economy is in a transitional phase from a village economy to a capitalist economy. Therefore its essential feature is to be understood as the transformation resulting from the interaction between these two major types. We have also seen that this kind of change is best captured in terms of the changes in the internal structure of units, the unit-mix and the patterns of interactions, that is, a micro-global analysis.

We shall examine this process through a classified listing of the units of the Indian economy (which will also give an indication of its unit-mix) and by reviewing the changing pattern of activity chains. For this purpose we shall rely on the insights we have gained from Part I as also on what we know of the Indian economy through experience.

The first issue to consider is what must be thought of as the lowest unit of the Indian economy. It is true that individuals enter into economic activities, but, as we saw in Chapter 1, individuals do not become economies because our understanding is that an economy is a 'structure of relationships among a group of people'. We shall, therefore, accept as the lowest or primary unit of the Indian economy what may be designated as an *establishment* (e). An establishment is a group of people who either through their existing structure of relationships, or through relationships that they specifically enter into for that purpose, attend to the three basic functions of an economy, that is, they exercise control over resources; they combine resources and labour in production; and they decide on the claims of members on the produce.

Pre-capitalist economy in terms of units

The distinguishing feature of a pre-capitalist economy is that its primary units are 'natural' units, that is, economies functioning on the basis of existing structure of relationships whose organising principle is the generation of use values. We shall designate them *households* (h). To begin with we shall consider households that *do not* interact with others at all or where such interaction is so limited that analytically we can afford to ignore it. They must be self-sufficient in terms of all material needs. If a unit of this kind is not to become extinct, it must also be able to re-produce itself over time. Analytically, it is the prototype of the rudimentary economy and hence our discussion about it can be related to Chapter 2. Its real life counterpart is a household that has land to cultivate and is able to produce to meet the needs of all its members by utilising the labour power of its members on the land at its disposal.[2] We shall designate it as a self-sufficient producer household and for purposes of identification denote it as h–1.

Since units of this kind do not, by definition, interact with others, we must try to understand them solely in terms of their internal structure. We already know one of the crucial aspects of the internal structure, the P/W ratio which, as we saw in Chapter 2, has a value greater than 1. The second aspect of the internal structure is the extent of land the household has at its disposal. We must assume that it has enough land to enable it to be self-sufficient. Whether it has or not, does not depend solely on the extent of land at its disposal in a physical sense (let us say in terms of hectares). First of all, it will also depend on the quality of the land, for instance, whether it is wet land or dry land. On the assumption that wet land is likely to be more productive than dry land, we may say either that wet land will support a higher P/W ratio than dry land, or that given a P/W ratio, the W members will have to put in more effort on dry land than on wet land to provision the needs of its members. This means that another important aspect of the internal structure of a unit of type h–1, viz., the manner in which it combines resources (land) and labour for production depends on the type of land that is available to it. Similarly, and for the same reason, the unit's internal structure will also depend on the kind of technology that it has. Another crucial factor is how the unit perceives its 'needs' to be. We know that a lower limit can be set here, the survivor limit. There is also a notional upper limit, the maximum that can be realised by exerting the labour power of the W members to the maximum, given the extent and quality of the land and the technology. The actual that it attains will be between these two limits and closer to the former as we have noted in Chapter 2. A further aspect of the internal structure of a self-sufficient producer household is the decision-making process which will have a bearing on the kind of division of labour it will practise as well as how the claims of individual members will be settled.

While these are the major issues relating to the internal structure of the unit at a given time, to get to know what is likely to happen to the unit over time we should know what its long-term perspectives are. We can speak with confidence only about the lower limit: we will assume that the unit is interested in its survival and reproduction. But we do not have to insist that self-sufficient producer households are interested only in sub-sistence. They may wish to have a rising level of living over a period of time. Whether that will materialise or not will depend on the resources it controls, the technological changes it can generate and most crucially on how the P/W ratio varies over time. Without detailed empirical studies there is not much more we can say about the internal structure and dynamics of the h–1 type of units.

Nature of h–2 units and their links

We shall, therefore, move to producer households which are not self-sufficient and which, consequently have (have to have) interactions with others. We shall designate them as h–2 units. Concrete examples are farm households that lease-in or lease-out land, use hired workers or work for others, sell output and/or buy inputs; households that interact with others mainly through the exchange of their produce (fishing households, artisan households).

A large number of units of the Indian economy belong to this category. Although they all share the characteristics of producer households and are primarily concerned with use values by the direct conversion of labour power, their economic activities (unlike the h–1 units) are not confined to that process. In order to provision the material needs of their members they have to interact with others. These interactions take many forms, but may be grouped into three broad categories, vertical, horizontal and mixed. The vertical links constitute a regular feature of the village economy where producer households pass on a share of the produce to those 'above', who put forward a claim to the produce on the basis of ownership rights. It is a transfer of the surplus generated by the 'lower' households to the 'higher' ones.

Arrangements that households enter into for the exchange of the goods that they produce (transfer of grain for cloth either of the C–C form or the C–M–C form) are examples of horizontal interactions. While vertical and horizontal interaction of these kinds are widely prevalent among h–2 units, most of their interactions turn out to be of the mixed type, that is, horizontal ones which have vertical components built into them. Two kinds of examples may be noted. The first is the practice that used to prevail widely in the past and which continues in some form in many parts of the country, whereby the specialised services of some households are put at the disposal of other households; not on any regular quid pro quo basis, but for periodic fixed payments. These services could be work on land in connection with cultivation to be rendered as and when requisitioned by some other household who, in return, would give certain stipulated quantities of grain, clothing etc, or the services of carpenters, smiths, barbers; rendered as and when required, in return for which they would receive either a specified quantity of grain or a portion of land where they could produce grain using their own labour. The horizontal link in these instances is obvious, the exchange of services for goods; the vertical link is the requisitioning of services (labour power, that is) on the basis of customary obligations. The second example is where a household (a master weaver, for instance) 'advances' goods (such as yarn) to another household which converts these goods through the application of their labour power (into woven cloth) and returns them to settle the advance given. There is a horizontal component in this link (it is as though the weaver household first buys yarn from the master weaver and then sells the cloth) but there is also a vertical component in as much as the master weaver is usually in a position to requisition the services of the weaver who has no say on the terms of the exchange. Another variant of this mixed type of link is where the advance is in the form of credit or a loan which is settled by selling the manufactured goods.

Within these three or four major kinds of links or interactions a variety of variations in terms and conditions are possible and come to be established. Thus land leasing could be of different forms. The payment by the lessee to the lessor could be either a share of the produce or a fixed quantity of the produce; the payment could be in kind, it could be in cash. Remuneration for labour services rendered could also take a variety of forms; it could be a piece rate or a time rate; it could be a specified amount settled at regular intervals or unspecified amounts at irregular intervals. The distinguishing micro-global feature of pre-capitalist economies, therefore, is that the units, though natural ones are of different kinds and there are a wide variety of links among them which cannot be reduced to a single form. However, we may note that in the activity chains thus generated, the units are more important than the links. This is because pre-capitalist economies concentrate largely on production which is essentially *internal* to the units and because most units are able, through their internal activities, to provide for the needs of their members. The nature of the links is also decided largely by the characteristics of the units. Some units, especially those whose claims on ownership are strong, are in a position to determine the nature of their links with others. In their links with others they make full use of their monopoly power in the sales transactions and their monopsony power in the purchase transactions whether of goods or services. They are, therefore, frequently in a position to convert all links into bilateral ones which is another reason why the activity chains in pre-capitalist economies turn out to be multifarious and heterogeneous. Such activity chains are a feature of many spheres of the Indian economy.

Capitalist economy in terms of units and links

We shall now turn to the capitalist component of the Indian economy by first attempting a micro-global profile of an ideal type capitalist economy. The standard micro-global profile of the capitalist economy partitions it on a functional basis connected through a single (and homogeneous) link, exchange. The two functions usually recognised are *production* which is considered as the activity of units called enterprises or firms on the one hand, and *consumption* which is recognised as the activity of units designated as households. It can be seen that in the activity chains thus produced the emphasis is on the link, exchange, with the units being considered merely as agents facilitating it. The attempt is to convert the economy essentially into a commodity flow (of goods and services or goods *for* services), and to be able to measure the flow at any given time and over time.[3]

Whatever may be the merits of such a representation, it can be seen that it is a very partial one leaving out crucial aspects such as the ownership and control over resources, the internal structure of units and the metamorphosis of the units and, consequently, of the economy over a period of time. Some of these, such as ownership, are perhaps implicit in the frame (resources are owned by households, but leased out to and controlled by enterprises) and are made explicit by other related representations. We shall modify the standard representation in terms of its own logic and then see how it can be made use of for an understanding of the structure and transformation of the Indian economy.

Let us start with exchange. Because of the intrinsic commoditisation thrust of a capitalist economy, exchange as an activity will tend to become widespread as we have seen in Chapter 5. But from Chapter 4 we know that exchange to become widespread and generalised, it has to be mediated for through money, and that the C–M–C form of exchange which is the first form of exchange involving money will transform itself to the M–C–M form and that the M–C–M form gives rise to new agents in the system, merchants who are specialists in exchange. If so, a generalised exchange system cannot be adequately represented without incorporating merchants also as agents (or units) in it.[4] Secondly, with resources taking monetary and financial form, the system cannot be represented correctly without bringing in financial intermediaries also into it. Thirdly, we have seen that a capitalist economy cannot function without the support of the state Hence, the state also must find a place in a micro-global representation of a capitalist economy. And fourthly, if households are treated basically as suppliers of labour power a distinction must also be made between households that own resources (and hence can become producer units if they so desire) and households that have nothing other than their labour power to sell, and so do not have the option of becoming producer households and *must*, therefore, enter into exchange relationship with the producer units. In Chapter 5 we saw the crucial significance of such households in understanding the essential feature of a capitalist economy.

In the light of these considerations we shall provide an alternate micro-global profile of a capitalist economy in terms of units and links. We shall depict a capitalist economy also as consisting of establishments as its primary units. But we shall divide them as follows:

Households with financial resources and labour	(h–3)
Households with only labour	(h–4)
Firms or enterprises	(f)
Merchants	(m)
Financial Intermediaries or Banks	(b)
State	(s)

We shall consider that these units are all linked through exchange although with the state brought in as a unit we shall also have to recognise links which are of other kinds (taxation, subsidies etc.).

In a sense the units in a capitalist economy (with the exception of the state) can all be thought of as similar because in exercising their functions they must all respond to exchange, and the accumulation of exchange values may become their organising principle. This homogenising tendency of capitalism is one of its important features, but it should not be made absolute. One would imagine that households even within a capitalist system are 'natural' units and will attach importance to the direct conversion of labour power into use values. To the extent they do, they will have an internal structure which will have a bearing on their economic function. Firms are units set up to concentrate on production, but since production is essentially an activity internal to a unit, it will have to have an organisational structure and hence an internal structure which will determine the manner in which they will combine resources and labour power in production and the way they will settle the claims of their members.

Differentiation and segmentation

There are other factors that bring in elements of heterogeneity into the working of a capitalist system. One of them is what is referred to as product differentiation which has two distinct but related aspects.[5] The first is related to the income differentials represented by the h-3 and h-4 households. Granted that the former has a higher level of income than the latter, the goods that its members use are likely to be different from the goods used by the members of the latter. Of course, the h-4 households will not have access to some of the goods that become available in the system, but even in what may be considered as goods in common use differentiation can be seen. For instance tables and chairs, vessels and plates etc. are all likely to be differentiated on the basis of purchasing power differentials of customers. If so, firms and production processes may be differentiated too. This basic tendency is reinforced by the activity of merchants which is the second aspect relating to differentiation. As we saw in Chapter 4, once merchants come to specialise in trade, exchange is no longer between those who have excess produce to dispose of and those who are looking for others in a similar situation, but with other goods. It will be between those who purchase to sell, store what they purchase, sell once again to buy and then to sell (merchants) on the one hand; and on the other, those who store purchasing power (whether firms or households) and wish to purchase what they want when they want. Of these the former are the more active participants because they must buy and sell to make a living and also to accumulate surplus value (Δ M). A capitalist economy, there-has a tendency to be dominated by merchants or merchants' activity.

But the merchants do not have it easy under capitalism. What we saw in Chapter 5 as the 'realisation' problem is essentially the merchants' problem, or the problem of anyone who has to sell, whether merchant or producer-cum-seller.[6] The merchants as capitalists are in competition with other capitalists in the quest for the accumulation of surplus value. They have expended their initial capital to purchase commodities (just as the producer capitalists do, except that they do not expend it on labour power) and they come to have surplus value only to the extent that they are able to *sell* the commodities they have purchased. It is in this respect that they have to compete with other capitalists. As merchants they have a limitation in that they do not have direct access to the generation of surplus. Consequently, they have to concentrate on measures to appropriate surplus value in competition with all the others trying to do the same. To protect his interest in this situation, each merchant must attempt to protect 'his' market—his constituency. To a large extent this is done by creating his own market and by cultivating his customers to stay with him. Part of the strategy is to appear to be catering to some specific group of customers. Purchasing power differentials among customers and differentiation of products become the objective factors in this effort. But these are hardly enough. Customers must be persuaded that their specific needs, preferences, standing etc are being catered to. Very often it must appear too that on these grounds they are becoming a distinctly different group.

A striking example of this kind of differentiation or segmentation is a cup of tea being served for Rs. 20 in a posh restaurant to rich customers while in a tea shop just outside the gate a cup of tea is sold for a rupee. Of course, this is not an instance of the 'same' commodity being sold at two different prices. The price of the cup of tea in the restaurant includes the expenses connected with better crockery, uniformed waiters, channel music, and a variety of overheads. But that is an important aspect of market segmentation. We saw in Chapter 4 that the qualitative attributes of a good can be quite wide-ranging and that this has a bearing on exchange as an activity. Part of the process of commoditisation under capitalism is to stretch that range and to package each good with different combinations of real or put-on qualitative attributes. This is how substitutes and near-substitutes become available along with advertising strategies to persuade different groups of customers that there is a specific commodity to match each taste and each pocket. Since these efforts involve producers and products and customers of different levels, they also result in the formation of multiple activity chains. For instance, it is possible to think of clearly drawn activity chains involving standard steel furniture, steel furniture with brand names and luxury steel furniture; each with separate producers, possibly with different kinds of technologies and workers, merchants with different kinds of showrooms and customers with different kinds of purchasing powers and preferences, thus constituting three different activity chains. On the other hand, it is possible that all three are produced by the same enterprise, but sold by different merchants; or that three different producers are involved and different kinds of customers, but they are all brought together in a department store that specialises in catering to 'all' customers. Whether the activity chains get sharply differentiated or vaguely mixed, what is important to note is that from a micro-global perspective a capitalist economy is a system of multiple and overlapping activity chains and merchants play a decisive role in making it what it is.

We may now sum up our discussion of the micro-global profile of a capitalist economy. The units in the activity chains are not autonomous entities, but functional complements of one another, each performing a designated function so that together they achieve the accumulation of exchange value, the motivating and integrating principle of the system. To this extent all units become subservient to the one link that connects them all, exchange. It may, therefore, appear that the units get submerged into the chains thus losing their identities, but this is only an optical illusion because the two principal functionaries, households and firms, both have their internal structures; the former because the search for use values that cannot be derived through exchange is the basis of their unit structures and the latter because the organisation of production cannot be solely on the basis of the exchange principle. A second illusion that is widely prevalent about a capitalist economy is that since exchange is the only link in it (apart from links emanating from and related to the state) and because in exchange the parties are considered to be at the same level, the transactions in a capitalist economy are all horizontal. But to the extent that a capitalist system makes labour power also a commodity, the exchange process has a concealed vertical transfer from those who generate surplus to those who appropriate it as surplus value through the mediation of exchange. Thirdly, it is often assumed and argued that exchange brings about certain uniformities in the system, primarily the uniformity of prices.

But this is only a partial view. If exchange as an activity has a tendency to unify and standardise, exchange mediated through merchants has the counter-tendency to differentiate and segment. Consequently, a capitalist system is not (cannot be) a fully integrated system, but a segmented-and-connected one. And fourthly, it is necessary to note that as a capitalist economy does not remain confined to national boundaries, its activity chains also will extend beyond the geographical and political domains of a nation. Where this is the case, it will be necessary to bring into analysis extra-territorial units and links between them and domestic units in which again the merchants play an important role. Merchants themselves are not a homogeneous group, but among all the units they are the most homogeneous and as specialists in exchange they tend to become merged with exchange as an activity. They, thus, become the dominant functionaries in a capitalist economy, and hence it is surprising that there are theoretical representations of the capitalist economy which do not even recognise their role in it.[7]

THE INDIAN ECONOMY: ITS STRUCTURE AND FUNCTIONING

Our knowledge of the Indian economy from day to day experience suggests that many of the micro-global features of both pre-capitalist and capitalist economies are prevalent in it. This has seldom been in doubt.

The crucial issue is how it is to be interpreted, or how it is to be made use of in order to gain an understanding of the structure and functioning of the Indian Economy.

A standard procedure is to treat economies with pre-capitalist and capitalist components as *dual economies* consisting of two distinct and separate segments.[8] These segments are identified as pre-capitalist and capitalist respectively by those who do not find such terms offensive, or as 'traditional' and 'modern' by those who find ideologically neutral terminologies more acceptable. There are also some versions of dual economies which depict the long term absorption of the pre-capitalist (traditional) sector by the capitalist (modern) sector without going into details of the structure of either, especially of the pre-capitalist sector.[9] Such treatments, naturally, do not provide much insights into the contemporary functioning of a 'dual economy'. A more fruitful line of enquiry has been what has come to be known as the analysis of *multi-structural* economies.[10]

Activity chains in the Indian economy

We shall make use of the units–and–links activity chains analysis developed in the earlier sections to probe into the structure and working of the Indian economy. We shall make a quick comparison of the activity chains of the pre-capitalist and capitalist economies. The major similarity between them is that they are both connected–and–segmented. But they are not alike. The main difference between them is that in the pre-capitalist sector the accent has to be on the units because of the heterogeneity of their internal structures, although in one sense they are all h–2 type households. In contrast, in the activity chains of a capitalist economy the units are related in terms of their functional complementarities which reduce their autonomy considerably and so the emphasis shifts to the link, exchange. This, however, tends to segment the economy. The link continues to be strong and prominent because all units have to resort to it for their functions. We may, therefore, say that in a pre-capitalist economy the segmentation is intrinsic because of the very nature of the units and the connections, especially the horizontal connections, are rather weak. On the other hand, in a capitalist economy the segmentation is functional and the connection is strong. There is a second similarity between the two activity chains. It is that in both there is a vertical transfer of surplus. It is palpable in the case of the pre-capitalist sector, but concealed into the horizontal structure of transfers in the capitalist sector. However, even in the pre-capitalist sector there is the mixed link which combines the vertical and horizontal while superficially appearing as horizontal. That link is propelled by merchant or money-lending activities. In the capitalist sector too, the concealed vertical component is the more aggressive one.

Capitalist units rely on exchange partly because of their functional necessity, but also because it is the only conduit for some of those who generate surplus value (h–4 households) to make a living, and for those who do not generate surplus value to appropriate it.

The comparison of the micro-global profiles of the pre-capitalist and capitalist segments in the Indian economy shows that attempts to depict them as entirely different (the former consists of self-sufficient units that do not interact with others; they do not generate or appropriate surplus etc.) or essentially similar (both consist of rational decision-makers) are both inadequate, if not inaccurate. In any case, if they are interacting segments what needs to be done to understand the Indian economy is to trace the nature of those interactions.

The links between the two segments come initially through the activity of merchants. Wherever there are interactions between units there is the possibility of intermediation and the role of intermediation increases with the increase in the interactions. In Chapter 4 we saw that as the basis of the emergence of merchants, who are specialists in trade. The pre-capitalist economy has different forms of exchange and many exchange-like links. The emergence of professional traders is, therefore, a natural pheno-menon in it. It is further strengthened by the geographical distance and the physical inaccessibility between parties to trade where the presence of a professional trader may not only be useful, but quite necessary also. But since the productive activity in a pre-capitalist economy is at a low level and a slow pace and because the units in it generally sell only small pro-portions of what they produce, the activities of the merchants also will be limited.

However, as merchants derive their surplus value by increasing their turnover they will always be on the look-out for opportunities to increase their activities. They will naturally get attached to a capitalist economy (or segment) if that is possible at all because capitalist enterprises have a larger quantum of production (in comparison with the h–2 units of the pre-capitalist segment) and they *must* sell all that they produce. While production units in the capitalist and non-capitalist segments differ on the basis of the objectives, processes and quantum of production, the objec-tives and activities of merchants are common in both. The merchant, *qua* merchant, has the same objective and the same functions whether he is dealing with pre-capitalist or capitalist production units and their objectives of production are immaterial as far as the merchant is concerned. To him they are both buyers and sellers. For instance, a typical h–2 unit may sell more by producing more converting its slack into productive activity; or by changing its production from the kind of goods it uses directly to the kind of goods it wishes to sell. These are of no concern to the merchant as long as it is willing to sell some goods and buy some other goods. This may be a C-M-C exchange for the unit, but from the merchant's point of view it is a M-C-M transaction which yields him some ΔM.

However, the h–2 unit cannot be indifferent to the manner in which it responds to the merchant's activities. Every kind of response that it makes will have a different kind of impact on its internal structure and the kind of links it will have with other units. In short, responding to accelerated merchant activities may change the internal structure of the pre-capitalist units, the unit-mix in the pre-capitalist segment (and hence also of the entire economy) and the activity chains as well. These changes start a dynamic process that begins to alter the pre-capitalist segment itself and the economy as a whole.

Transformation of h–2 units

The changes in the internal structure of a h–2 unit in the context of merchant activity and the presence of a capitalist segment can transform it to a h–3 or h–4 household or into an enterprise (f). When many h–2 units undergo transformation of this kind, the unit-mix of the entire system also changes and along with it the activity chains in the system as well. When these happen, the system itself undergoes change.

Is it possible to anticipate the direction of the processes of such changes set in motion and their speed? To answer this question let us examine a few typical cases.

One of the simplest is the case of a h–2 household whose command over resources is such that it has plenty of 'slack'. The demand by the merchants for the good it produces (let us say grain) leads to the slack being put to use to increase production. It may appear that other than the increase in production there need be no other adjustment. But such is not the case. The internal structure of the unit undergoes change partly because the manner in which resources and labour is combined in production will change, and partly because the settlements of claims may also change. Secondly, in return for the sale of grain the unit receives some other good or money. In the former case further changes in the internal structure may come about. In the latter case links with other units may also change, as for instance when the unit has to decide whether the money is to be converted into financial assets. Over time, if the processes continue, the unit will have to decide whether to continue as a h–2 unit at a higher level of performance, or to specialise in production and move towards becoming an enterprise (f) or to convert itself into a h–3 household.

A second case worth considering is where merchants' activities impinge directly on what was described as the mixed link between units in a pre-capitalist set up. Consider that merchants succeed in purchasing the cloth produced by weavers which till then was entering into a well-defined activity chain. The chain gets abruptly disrupted necessitating adjustments by other units associated with the chain. In that process some h–2 units may become h–3 units and some others h–4 units. The h–4 units may then have to get attached to a h–4 <—>f type of chain.

As a variant of the above consider a further case where merchants were supplying yarn to weavers and taking back cloth from them. Imagine now that the merchants decide to do business with a capitalist enterprise producing cloth and hence abandon their link with the pre-capitalist weaver households. In this case the weaver households may either enter into a vertical link with a farming household by leasing in land and thus continue to be h–2 type households or become h–4 type households linking themselves with capitalist units.

As a final illustration let us look at two pre-capitalist units that had an activity chain involving vertical links. Typically, one of the units permitted the other to cultivate its land claiming a share of the produce. But land comes to have alternate use and the landlord deprives the tenant of a customary right that he had enjoyed and evicts him from the land. The vertical link that existed between two h–2 households snaps. One of them could become a capitalist enterprise and the other a h–4 household.

Micro-global profile of the Indian economy

These instances show how transformation at the unit level takes place and how links across the two major (and different) segments take place. They show also that the system as a whole—the Indian economy—comes to have new activity chains as a result of the transformation of units and changes in existing activity chains. At any given time, therefore the Indian economy can be thought of as a complex network of criss-crossing activity chains of heterogeneous units and a variety of links. The links are the transactions in labour power and goods, the transfer of surpluses and the fiscal policies of the state and are brought about by merchants, financial intermediaries and the state. We provide a chart which depicts something of the structure of the economy that results in these activity chains. The chains themselves are not easily represented partly because on a two-dimensional surface it is not easy to indicate the vertical and horizontal links, but mainly because the criss-crossing of the links, is far too complex to be neatly laid out.

The chart shows many interesting features. Contrary to popular (and some theoretical) views, the h–2 type households have one of the largest network of relationships with other units. In the last column among the units that they are connected to we have included h–2 also to point out that any given h–2 household usually has a variety of interactions with other units of the same type. This is one of the significant features of the

Micro-global Structural Profile of the Indian Economy

Units	Non-labour Resources	Links	Connected to
h–1	Nature	Nil	None
h–2	Land, Capital goods	Leasing in/out	h–2; h–3; h–4;
	Financial Assets	Purchase/Sale of labour power	f; m; b; s
		Purchase/Sale of goods	
		Lending/Borrowing	
		Taxes/Subsidies	
h–3	Financial Assets	Purchase/Sale of labour power	h–2; h–4; f;
		Purchase of goods	m; b; s
		Lending/Borrowing	
		Taxes/Subsidies	
h–4	Nil	Sale of labour power	h–2; h–3; f; m; s
		Purchase of goods	
		Borrowing	
		Taxes/Subsidies	
f	Capital goods	Purchase of labour	h–2; h–3; h–4; f;
	Financial assets	Purchase/Sale of goods	m; b; s
		Borrowing	
		Taxes/Subsidies	
m	Stock of goods	Purchase/Sale of goods	h–2; h–3; h–4; f;
		Borrowing	
		Taxes/Subsidies	m; b; s
b	Financial Assets	Lending/Borrowing	h–2; h–3; h–4;
			f; m; s
s	Land, Capital goods,	Purchase of labour power	h–2; h–3; h–4;
	Financial Assets	Purchase/Sale of goods	f; m; b
	Power to tax	Borrowing/Lending	
		Taxing/Subsidising	

typical unit in the pre-capitalist sector, although we should now stop dividing the system into pre-capitalist and capitalist. That distinction is not particularly useful at the units level. One way to demonstrate this is to point out that while h–3 and h–4 units are the ones complementary to the f units, the f units should have no problem in accepting labour power from h–2 units. Similarly, h–3 units are typically units that supply labour power and in that sense their connections are mostly with the f units, but they may also use labour power from h–2 and h–4 units. The h–2 units are shown to be connected to h–3 units also, but usually it will be in the form of sale of goods rather than of labour power. In other words while the h–2 and h–3 households are interrelated, the relationship is not symmetrical. We may also distinguish between h–2 households, and h–3 and h–4 households. The former is connected to other units through the sale (or purchase) of labour power as well as sale of goods whereas the other two (h–3 and h–4) do not *sell* goods. The h–4 households have a distinct feature too. They are the only ones which *must* sell labour power; it is immaterial to them whether their labour power is purchased by the f units, the h–2 units, the h–3 units or by the state. Consequently, along with the f, m and b units and the state, they reach out to all units and are available to any unit that will care to use their services. In this sense they are similar to the f units which are willing to purchase labour power from wherever it becomes available.

There is a further point that we should note. In a capitalist economy surplus generated by labour can be appropriated only by directly employing labour in production, typically by f units purchasing labour power from h–4 or h–3 units. But in economies of the kind which the chart represents, productive activity takes place in (at least) two different kinds of units; the f units and the h–2 units. Some of the h–2 units purchase labour power and use it in productive activity. In this respect they must be treated as being close to the f units. But in many h–2 households productive activity meant for the sale of the produce takes place without purchasing labour power. However, surplus value is appropriated from them through the exchange process in which, therefore, exploitation is done by merchant capital. The possibility of such appropriation of surplus value gives merchant capital a special role in the economy.

Dynamics of the system

With this understanding of the structure of the Indian Economy we can now take up the question we had flagged earlier; is it possible to anticipate, to predict, the outcome of the dynamics of the system? The tendency towards a transformation of the economy as a full capitalist system is clearly indicated. It is the result of the internal dynamics of a capitalist economy to go on expanding and in that process to transform production units into capitalist enterprises and to compete out those that do not undergo such transformation. The internal dynamics of the pre-capitalist segment also suggests the same: that is what the metamorphosis of h–2 units into capitalist enterprises (f–units) and h–3 and h–4 household implies. However, these tendencies should not be interpreted to mean that a capitalist transformation of the economy is inevitable. There may be other forces in operation that may slow down and prevent that possibility.

First, the formation of h–4 households may be too fast for all of them to get linked with capitalist enterprises. We may recall that apart from economic factors causing the emergence of h–4 households, fairly autonomous demographic factors may also cause movements in that direction.[11] At the same time the increase in and growth of enterprises may not be fast enough to absorb fully the labour power that becomes available from h–4 households. Where merchant capital is active in leading to the emergence of h–4 households and retards the growth of enterprises this is a distinct possibility. Under such circumstances where some h–2 households do not have the possibility of becoming h–4 households, they may be forced to continue as h–2 households simply to make a living. The overall changes taking place in the economy may be conducive for such people to 'set up shop'.

Where h–2 households continue or emerge in this manner, frequently the only way in which they will be able to compete with better-off h–2 households and/or enterprises is by taking lower earnings, the proverbial 'tightening of the belt' strategy. This situation provides an opportunity for merchants (merchant capitalists, to be more accurate) to buy cheap. If the merchants succeed in linking these units to enterprises, they may become cheaper alternative sources of supply of inputs, semi-manufactured products etc. In a way, this is the continuation, revival and intensification of the 'putting out' system which is a common feature in situations of this kind. In the Indian context, the commonest examples of this phenomenon are in the sphere of the manufacture of *bidis*, in the footwear industry and in some forms of handloom weaving in all of which the labour component is a major item in the cost of production.[12] By skilfully manipulating the supply of material inputs for these products (leaves and tobacco in the case of *bidis*, leather in the case of footwear and yarn in the case of cloth) and by purchasing the outputs, merchant capitalists are in a position to appropriate a great deal of surplus value generated by the actual producers of these goods. Some capitalist enterprises can buy these goods, affix their brand names on them and market them as 'their' differentiated products. Thus the need of a large number of labourers to survive may provide an excellent opportunity for merchant capitalists and enterprises to accumulate surplus value. Where this is the situation, capitalists themselves will have no incentive to bring about a full capitalist transformation of the economy.

Thirdly, the state may lend support to the continuation of h–2 households. What is described as the transformation of h–2 households into h–4 households involves the survival and welfare of a sizeable proportion of citizens (and voters where the polity, as in the Indian case, is based on universal adult franchise) and the state may not be able to remain passive when a process of such economic, social and political implications is going on. Preservation and protection of h–2 households that face the threat of disintegration may become an unavoidable economic measure for political and humanitarian reasons. Thus, the survival requirements of a section of the population, the opportunities that it provides for accumulation and the mixed political and economic considerations of the state may all coalesce into the uneasy preservation of the h–2 households.

Features of the analytical frame

The analytical framework we have developed in this chapter is not an end in itself. It is meant to be used in understanding a variety of issues pertaining to the working and on-going transformation of the Indian economy. That will be the attempt in the subsequent chapters. But before we do that, two concluding observations are necessary for a fuller appreciation of the frame itself.

The first is to note that the boundaries of the units used in the frame are not rigidly drawn; in fact several of the units can easily merge into one another. This is particularly so in the case of the four household categories. The distinction between h–1 and h–2 is only that the former does not interact with others. We have also conceded at the outset that within a national economy it is very unlikely that one will be able to come across units of that kind. If and when these units come to have interactions of any kind with anyone else they become h–2 types. In other words the distinction between h–1 and h–2 is an *analytical* one, and not an empirical one. So is the distinction between h–2 and h–3. As households, they must both be using the resources under their control and the labour power of their members in production, and both must be concerned with the generation of use values not available through exchange, or use values that cannot be purchased. The difference between the two is that h–2 households enter into relationships with other units through what they produce, which h–3 households do not do. Again, it should not be difficult for h–2 units to metamorphose themselves into h–3 households. The distinction between h–4 households and all other households too is analytical, that the h–4 households do not have any non-labour resources while the others do. But it is difficult to see how a household can be a household without having *some* non-labour resources over which it exercises control. Once again, what is important is the analytical distinction—that h–4 households do not interact with other units through resources that they control and only through the sale of their labour power. We note too that the distinction between the h–2 and f units too is not very sharp; after all they are both production units, and h–2 units can (and often do) transform themselves into f units. The distinction between producers (h–2 and f) and merchants (m) is also functional. Often producers become merchants especially in a capitalist economy. And it will not be surprising if some producers and merchants take on some of the functions of financial intermediaries (b). The only distinct unit in the system is the state which analytically and empirically combines all the functions.

The hazy unit boundaries we have used is partly a reflection of what obtains in the world of experience. Economic agents *are indeed* frequently composite entities, combining in them functions that can be analytically distinguished. Consider the following description of some typical household units in the Indian economy: 'The same family, for example, flays dead cattle, tans the hides, cuts and stitches the leather into sandals, carries sandals to the bazaar and sells them, and subsequently repairs them when necessary. Members of a fishing family make their own nets, take their boats out to sea for the catch, cure the fish and hawk it. Owners of milk cattle not only breed and raise the animals but also deliver milk daily to their customers. In addition they may utilise milk to prepare sweetmeats for sale' (Thorner, 1962: 72–73).

We must add that these families consume what they themselves and others produce, cook their meals, look after their children etc. So, what kinds of units are they—producers, merchants, labourers, consumers...? This kind of composite feature is not confined to the poorer households either.

> The bigger people like to keep their fingers in many pies. For the land which they cultivate themselves (that is, through hired labour), they may buy a small tractor and introduce other improvements. Simultaneously they may be getting handsome rents by giving out a sizeable portion of their land...to tenants or cropsharers.... They may also be doing some moneylending or trading.... (In some places) the principal landowners are at one and the same time the largest employer of agricultural labourers, the chief traders, the main moneylenders, the shop keepers, and the village officials. (Ibid: 9).

We may also add that they become the office-bearers of the cooperative societies, the panchayats and, not infrequently the MLAs and MPs too. So, what are they?

The composite nature of these units certainly presents some analytical problems, but it has at least one major advantage. It enables us to capture 'the transformation of the economy' which is, in a sense, too abstract a concept. But once we realise that the transformation of the economy is the transformation of its units and their interactions, we have an empirical procedure to give content to that abstract concept. We must note too that since the transformation is an on-going process, in the empirical sphere the units may seldom appear as pure types; they will appear as different shades of the units we have analytically described. For instance, the h–2 and f units may be thought of as two ends of a spectrum with several shades between them, one tending to merge with another next to it. Also, just as at one end of the spectrum (the h–2 end) one may see distinctly shrewd economic calculations, at the other end (f units) one may see many hidden and not so hidden household characteristics! The h–2 <—> f is not the only spectrum that can be thought of either. The h–2 <—> h–3 is another and h–2 <—> m a third and so on.

The second comment that needs to be made about the frame is that the amount of (non-labour) resources that the unit will have command over is one of the crucial aspects relating to the structure and the transformation of the economy. Resources have a stock and a flow aspect. The stock aspect is the quantum of resources that a unit can be said to have at any given time—such as so many hectares of land, so many rupees worth of capital assets etc., and thus indicates the asset position of units. The flow aspect refers to the resources it can expend over a period such as the purchasing power at its disposal during a year. Obviously the flow arises from the stock although not all forms of assets can immediately yield a flow. But whether as stock or as flow, resources indicate power, aptly captured in the expression 'purchasing power'. In the h–2 units it is the control over resources that to a large extent determines the kind of links that a unit can have with others as we have already noted. In Chapter 4 we had seen how exchange is directed substantially by the distribution of purchasing power. In our frame the significance of the h–4 units is that they represent units with no resource power (just as h–1 units represent units with no interaction).

As the structure and transformation of the economy depend crucially on the distribution of resource power in the system, we shall pay special attention to it in the chapters that follow.

EMPIRICAL ASPECTS

For reasons which we have just seen it will not be easy to find the empirical counterpart of the micro-global structure of the Indian economy outlined above especially shown in the Chart on p. 230. The first is related to the frame itself. We have noted that a crucial aspect of the frame is that it consists of overlapping units, and that therefore, the unit boundaries cannot be clearly identified. That poses a problem for empirical enquiry because in order to compile statistical data it is necessary to have well-defined units—or 'boxes' as they are sometimes referred to—into which information gathered can be put. Thus, if one is interested in the empirical (as against the conceptual) classification of households, it should be possible to indicate in terms of empirically identifiable attributes how h–1, h–2, h–3 and h–4 households differ. Similarly, if one is mainly concerned with a classification of production units, it will be necessary to specify the characteristics that distinguish between h–2 and f units. We shall soon see that the problem here is not with the frame we have used; lack of clear unit boundaries is very much an aspect of the empirical reality we are dealing with, viz., the Indian economy.

The second reason why the empirical account will not strictly correspond to the frame of analysis is that statistical data presently available have not been compiled according to the specifications of that frame. In the wide variety of official statistics relating to the Indian economy, the need to distinguish between different types of households is not adequately recognised. Some statistical data draw a distinction betwen h–2 and f types of production units, but that distinction is usually in terms of a single attribute such as whether the units concerned do or do not function solely on the basis of household labour. That is an important distinction, but we know that that is not the only difference between h–2 and f production units.

In view of these difficulties we shall not attempt a definitive empirical identification of the analytical frame. Instead, we shall use the available statistical information relating to the Indian economy to gain an empirical understanding of the characteristics of the economy as portrayed in the earlier sections of this chapter. Even then our knowledge of the Indian economy will be only partial because at best we will get acquainted with its unit-mix without adequate information about the links that connect them into different kinds of activity chains, not to mention the internal structure of the units. Our understanding of those aspects must come from the subsequent chapters.

We shall now move to depict an empirical account of the structure of the Indian economy in terms of its units making use of statistical information pertaining to the decade of 1980s.

THE ECONOMY: PROFILE OF LABOUR FORCE

For some basic information about the economy we shall rely on the Reports of the 1981 Census.[13]

According to the Census the total population of India (excluding Assam where the Census was not conducted) in March 1981 was around 665,288,000 consisting of 343,930,000 males and 321,358,000 females. The total population was divided on the basis of 'work' into three main categories, ie, main workers, marginal workers and non-workers. 'Work' was defined as participation in any 'economically productive activity' whether physical or mental. Main workers were those who had worked for the major part of the year preceding the date of enumeration, that is for 183 days or more during the year. Marginal workers were those who worked any time at all in the year preceding the enumeration, but worked for less than 183 days. Non-workers were those who had not worked anytime at all in the year preceding the date of enumeration. Infants and those who were too old or too infirm to work would have certainly figured as non-workers. But 'work', it may be noted, was defined as any 'economically productive activity', a term which was not defined, and not very easy to define. On this basis those who were primarily active as students (even if they occasionally engaged in economically productive activities) were classified as non-workers and that may be considered as legitimate. However, those (especially women) who were engaged primarily on one's own household duties were also treated as non-workers, and that is clearly arbitrary or at least questionable. We had dealt with this aspect in Chapter 2.

On the basis of these definitions, 222,517,000 persons or 33.5 per cent of the total population consisted of 'main workers'. In view of the definition, while 51.6 per cent of men were classified as main workers, only 14.0 per cent of women were brought under that category. 22,088,000 persons were classified as 'marginal workers'.

With a total population of 665,288,000 and 222,517,000 main workers, the P/W ratio of the Indian economy would be 2.9:1 and if the marginal workers are also included in the denominator, the ratio would come down to 2.7:1.

Four-Fold classification of 'workers'

The Census also classified 'workers' into four broad categories, cultivators, agricultural labourers, those engaged in household industry, and other workers. This classification reflects the predominance of agricultural activities in the Indian economy. A person was considered a cultivator if he or she was engaged either as employee, single worker or family worker in cultivation of land owned or held from the government; or held from private persons or institutions for payment in money, kind or share of crop. Cultivators, therefore, could be those who cultivated the land they owned or those who leased-in land from others. They could be those who applied their labour power in cultivation or those who used hired workers, but exercised 'supervision or direction' of cultivation. It is thus a very miscellaneous category. However, most of them could be considered to be h–2 type of units although some of them (those who hire workers and supervise or direct cultivation) would have to be treated as f-units. In Chapter 9 we shall see that finer differentiation of h–2 units will be necessary to understand many of the problems relating to agriculture in the country. Of the total main workers, the Census treated 92,523,000 or 41.6 per cent as cultivators. It must be noted that those who were engaged in growing fruits or vegetables or keeping orchards or groves or working on plantations were *not* included in the category of cultivators, but would be brought under 'other workers'.

The second category of main workers, 'agricultural labourers' were defined as those who worked in another person's land for wages in cash, kind or share of crop. According to the Census, agricultural labourers, unlike cultivators, had no risk in cultivation; neither did they have any right of lease or contract on the land on which they worked. 55,500,000 main workers, or 24.9 per cent of the total, were classified as agricultural labourers. Agricultural labourers may or may not have some land of their own, but it is presumed that the major part of their earnings come in the form of wages and so this group must be thought of as consisting of h–4 type households.

The third category of main workers were those who were engaged in household industry. Household industry was defined as an industry conducted by the head of the household himself/herself or by members of the household at home or within the village in rural areas, and only within the precincts of the house where the household lived in urban areas. A household industry is one that is engaged in production, processing, servicing, repairing or making and selling (but not merely selling) of goods. The main criterion of a household industry is that the larger proportion of workers in it should consist of members of the household including the head. If so, most of them will be of the h–2 type, but in as much as household industries would also have hired workers, some who were classified as belonging to household industries would also be the h–4 type. Altogether, 7,711,000 workers (that is 3.5 per cent of the total) were classified as coming under household industry.

The rest of the main workers, 66,783,000 or 30 per cent of the total were grouped under 'other workers', and included 'factory workers, plantation workers, those in trade, commerce, business, transport, mining, construction, political or social work, all government servants, municipal employees, teachers, priests, entertainment artists etc.' That, indeed, is a miscellaneous category. However, it may be noted that in terms of the number of workers involved it constitutes only a little more than agricultural labourers and household industry workers put together and much less than cultivators. At first it may appear that in contrast to the first three categories, most of whom may be thought of as belonging to the 'traditional' sector of the Indian economy, the residual fourth category may be considered as representing the 'modern' sector. But many units in trade, transport, construction etc., may have closer resemblance to the traditional sector, and hence it is not a tenable distinction.

'Other workers'

The Census itself divides the 'other workers' into further categories as livestock, forestry, fishing, hunting, plantations, orchards and allied activities; mining and quarrying; manufacturing, processing, servicing and repairs; construction; trade and commerce; transport, storage and communications and other services. Except the total numbers involved, however, not much information is available about them from the main Census Reports.

To get to know a little more about the characteristics of the 'other workers' category, we shall, therefore, turn to another source. In the preliminary stages of the Census of 1981, an Economic Census was conducted as part of the overall Census enumerations. One of the main reports of the Economic Census 1980 became available in 1988 and we shall make use of it for a further probing of the 'other workers' category. In the Economic Census, the basic unit is an *enterprise*. An enterprise is described as follows:

> An enterprise is an undertaking engaged in production and/or distribution of goods and/or services not for the sole purpose of own consumption. The workers in an enterprise may consist of members of the household or hired workers or both. The activities of an enterprise may be carried out at one or more than one distinct location. The activity of the enterprise may also be carried on only for a part of the year but on a fairly regular basis... An enterprise may be owned or operated by a single household or by several households jointly (on a partnership basis) or by an institutional body.[14]

This description of the enterprises shows that they include the household industries also apart from 'other workers', but that other forms of organisations are also included in them. The Report under reference does not go into what the specifics are of these other organisational forms. Instead, enterprises are divided into two broad categories: 'Own-account enterprises' which are owned and operated with the help of household labour only and 'Establishments' which are enterprises engaged in economic activities with the assistance of at least one hired worker on a fairly regular basis. It is, therefore, clear that the former consists of our h–2 units while the latter will have h–2 units and other kinds of organisations as well. The establishments, thus, will have the h–2 <——> f spectrum that we discussed earlier. In order to avoid terminological confusion, we shall refer to the two types of enterprises as 'own-account units (h–2)' and 'all other units' noting that the latter may include h–2 units that make use of hired workers also.

As the units covered by the Economic Census include 'household industries' and 'other workers' of the main Census Reports, the total number of workers covered should be 74,494,000 (7,711,000 'household industry' plus 66,783,000 'other workers'), if the enumeration were to be exhaustive. But the total number of workers covered by the Economic Census is only 53,667,000 or 72 per cent of what might have been expected. We rely on the Economic Census, then, not for total coverage, but for the additional information that it provides about the characteristics of predominantly non-agricultural workers and units in the economy.

The Economic Census divides the economic activities represented in it into the following groups:

1. Agriculture, hunting, forestry and fishing (other than agricultural production and plantation)
2. Mining and quarrying
3. Manufacturing and repair services
4. Electricity, gas and water
5. Construction
6. Wholesale and Retail Trade
7. Hotels and Restaurants
8. Transport
9. Storage and Warehousing
10. Communications
11. Financing, insurance, real estate and business services
12. Community, social and personal services
13. Unspecified

Hence there is a fairly detailed break-down of units and workers in the 'other workers' category. The 53,667,000 workers are organised into 18,362,000 units of which 13,379,000 or 72.9 per cent are own-account units which, however, account for only 37.6 per cent of the workers. Even so, it is significant that over 70 per cent units in this segment of the economy are h–2 type units. Table 7.1 shows that the h–2 types range from as low as 0.9 per cent in communications to 84.4 per cent in primary activities (agriculture etc). Segments where the own account units are above 70 per cent are primary activities, manufacturing and repair services, construction, wholesale and retail trade (which has the highest share among the non-agricultural activities) and transport.

Table 7.2 shows the size of the units (by number of workers) in the units which are not own-account ones starting out with 1 to 2 workers all the way to 100 workers or more. It is striking that the units that have 1 to 2 workers really dominate the scene; their lowest share is 24.7 per cent of the total units in the unspecified category, but the highest is 65.0 per cent in communications. Other activities that show over 50 per cent for this category are electricity, gas and water, trade, storage and services. There is no definite information as to whether these units are households which use hired workers also, but it must be presumed to be so. If so, these will also be of the h–2 type. In fact, many of the other smaller units also must have household characteristics, possibly partnerships. Where such units are likely to end is difficult to say, but if the cut off is drawn at units with up to 5 workers, then it will be seen that they account for from 55 to 90 per cent of the total units. This shows how dominant numerically are the

Table 7.1 *Unit Structure in the 'Other Workers' Sector of the Indian Economy*

Activity Groups	Own-Account Units (h–2)	All Units	2 as p.c. of 3
1	2	3	4
1. Agriculture, hunting forestry & fishing	1,230,105	1,457,784	84.4
2. All other activities	12,149,081	16,903,767	71.9
3. Mining & quarrying	18,869	29,886	63.1
4. Manufacturing and repairs	4,646,476	5,968,159	77.9
5. Electricity, gas & water	4,079	33,729	12.1
6. Construction	123,375	151,942	81.2
7. Wholesale & retail trade	5,013,648	6,046,252	83.0
8. Hotels & restaurants	541,901	807,013	67.1
9. Transport	253,889	352,342	78.0
10. Storage & Warehousing	56,740	122,459	46.3
11. Communication	867	98,918	0.9
12. Finance, insurance, real estate and business	109,907	273,465	40.2
13. Community, social & personal services	1,359,568	2,997,670	45.3
14. Unspecified	19,762	48,932	40.3
15. Total	13,379,186	18,361,551	72.9

h–2 units in this segment of the economy which accounts for over 30 per cent of the workers. If we take into account the agricultural production segment (consisting of cultivators and agricultural labourers according to the general census) and on the assumption that most of the cultivators belong to the h–2 units (of various kinds) then it may not be wrong to say that of the total number of establishments(e) in the economy anywhere between 50 and 60 per cent may be of the h–2 type. Since we have taken agricultural labourers who constitute about 25 per cent of the workers as belonging to the h–4 type, it may be assumed that they also account for about the same per cent of the establishments. In the segment covered by the Economic Census also there must be h–4 type of units that supply hired workers. It is, however, difficult to calculate the share of such units in that segment. Hired workers constitute 55 per cent in the segment

Table 7.2 Units (other than own-account units) by Size of Employment

Activity Groups	Percentage share of units by size of employment								
	1-2	3	4	5	6-9	10-19	20-49	50-99	100 or more
1. Agriculture, hunting forestry & fishing	53.8	15.7	10.6	6.4	9.7	3.0	0.6	0.1	0.05
2. All other activities	47.6	15.2	9.2	6.0	10.7	6.9	3.2	0.8	0.5
3. Mining & quarrying	30.8	10.3	8.1	6.2	16.2	13.3	8.9	2.7	3.3
4. Manufacturing & repairs	34.0	16.9	11.4	7.8	15.1	9.3	3.6	0.9	0.7
5. Electricity, gas & water	54.7	9.4	5.4	3.3	8.3	8.4	6.9	2.1	1.4
6. Construction	41.4	10.6	7.7	5.8	12.0	12.0	7.2	1.9	1.3
7. Wholesale & retail trade	52.0	20.3	10.6	5.9	7.8	2.7	0.5	0.1	0.05
8. Hotels & restaurants	37.2	21.3	13.4	8.6	12.5	5.4	1.3	0.2	0.1
9. Transport	42.6	17.3	8.9	6.0	11.1	7.3	3.6	1.2	1.9
10. Storage & Warehousing	62.2	11.5	6.6	4.6	7.2	5.0	2.2	0.5	0.3
11. Communication	65.0	17.2	4.8	2.6	4.0	3.1	2.0	0.7	0.5
12. Finance, insurance	40.0	14.5	10.6	7.5	14.9	11.5	5.7	1.2	0.6
13. Community, social & personal services	58.0	9.7	6.1	4.2	8.6	7.4	4.1	1.0	0.5
14. Unspecified	24.7	13.9	10.9	9.0	18.4	12.4	6.8	2.0	2.0
15. Total	47.9	15.2	9.2	6.0	10.6	6.7	3.1	0.7	0.5

(19.4 per cent in agriculture and related activities, and 57.1 per cent in non-agricultural activities) but then these hired workers may come from h–2, h–3 or h–4 units. We had indicated that the distinguishing feature of the Indian economy is the presence in it of h–2 and h–4 units and their predominance in the system. We have no way of assessing precisely what share of the total establishments they account for, but on the basis of the figures given above, they may constitute some 75 per cent to 85 per cent of all establishments in the economy.

We may recall too that the boundary between h–2 and h–4 is not very distinct and that there is considerable 'mobility' between them. The h–2 units (households with some resources) can easily become h–4 units (households with no non-labour resources). The reverse mobility is also possible, though not as easy as the former. The h–4 units with very minimal resources can 'set up shop' whereby instead of selling their labour power directly to some employer (as h–4 units must do) they may be able to sell some 'services' or labour-intensive goods to customers directly. For instance, with a very small amount of financial resources, a h–4 unit can become a retail trader; with a sewing machine it can become a tailoring unit; an agricultural labourer with a buffalo can become a milk-seller, and so on. The fact that in Table 7.1 there is a crowding of own-account units (h–2) in such areas as manufacturing and repairs (where possibly the h–2 units concentrate on repairs), trade, and transport points to this possibility. Table 7.2 shows that these activities also have a high proportion of units with a worker strength of up to 5 which, again, we have suggested may be units of the h–2 type.

The main feature of the h–2 and h–4 units is that their primary concern is to provide the livelihood of its members. They use the resources over which they have control and the labour power they have, to achieve this objective. They also use any and all opportunities that the economic system as a whole offers for the same purpose. In other words, *the Indian economy has a large segment where the economic motivation of the participants is sheer survival which they cannot afford to take for granted. Day in and day out they must strive for it.* In the chapters that follow we shall try to bring out how this factor influences the working of the system.

In passing we may also point out that Table 7.1 indicates that among the non-agricultural units about 36 per cent are in trade (m units) and a little less than 2 per cent in finance (b units).

This quick empirical survey brings out the predominance of the h–2 units in the Indian economy principally in terms of the utilisation of labour power. The presence of a variety of other units in the system, especially h–4 units, has also been noted. The important thing, however, is not to get a static view of the structure of the economy, but to use it for an understanding of its working and transformation over time. We take up these aspects in the chapters that follow. While we shall be concentrating on the post-independence period (Chapters 9, 10 and 11) we take up in the next chapter the evolution of the Indian economy during the pre-colonial impact. The discussion in Chapter 8 provides the setting for the more detailed analysis of contemporary issues in the subsequent chapters.

NOTES

1. This would imply an increase in exchange as an activity, the disruption of some kinds of production units and the emergence of others, and changes in the relations of production.
2. The nature of such households is dealt with by Chayanov who, in dealing with peasant farm organisation said: '....The basic economic problem of the labour farm is a correct and joint organisation of the year's work, stimulated by a single family demand to meet its annual budget and a single wish to save or invest capital if economic work conditions allow' (Chayanov, 1966: 60). In other words, such an household is a producing-consuming-saving-investing unit and its decisions in these aspects are bound to be interrelated.
3. The commodity flow depiction of the economy consisting of households and firms (or 'public' and 'business' as some modern versions have it) and its use in national income analysis can be seen in most Western text books on economics such as Paul A. Samuelson's *Economics*.
4. We had identified units as subeconomies which carry out the three major functions of any economy. But with the introduction of exchange and the specialization in functions that it makes possible, the nature of some units undergoes change. Merchants and financial intermediaries, for instance, attend only to some specific functions. And, of course, the state as an economic unit has some special features of its own.
5. Product differentiation came to be formally recognized in economic literature only with E.H. Chamberlin's *Theory of Monopolistic Competition*, published in 1933. Its significance in understanding the nature of markets, is largely ignored because of the power of the theory of perfect competition as the basis of market studies. Chamberlin himself missed the point because of his concentration on the product, instead of seeing product differentiation as an essential aspect of the sellers' attempt to segment the market to establish some element of monopoly.
6. Reference may be made to the discussion of the 'realisation' problem in Chapter 5, esp. pp. 140–43 and 148–49.
7. The studies following Walras's general equilibrium analysis (as cited in note 10 of Chapter 4) do not provide a place for merchants although they are representations of the capitalist economy.
8. For literature relating to dual economies see Higgins, 1959, especially Ch. 12.
9. The classic work on this problem is Lewis, 1954.
10. The characterisation of economies in the process of transition from pre-capitalist to capitalist formations as 'multi-structural' economies is essentially a contribution of Soviet scholars. For a good account see Levkovsky, 1987.
11. Reference may be made to the discussion on X–households in Chapter 3.
12. This aspect is further developed in Chapter 9.
13. The Census Reports are an important source of empirical information regarding the

Indian economy. We are relying on the 1981 Census Report because though the 1991 Census is over, only its preliminary findings have become available at the time of writing. The material contained in this section is from Census of India, 1981, Series—1, Part II–B (i).

14. Census of India, 1981 (Economic Census)—Instructions to Enumerators for filling Enterprise List.

Notes to Tables

The source of Table 7.1 and Table 7.2 is Government of India, Central Statistical Organisation, *Economic Census, 1980—Number of Agricultural and Non-Agricultural Enterprises and Employment therein in States/Union Territories according to Major Activity Groups* (1988).

8

The Evolution of the Indian Economy

This chapter presents a thumbnail sketch of the evolution of the Indian economy. The main features of its pre-colonial village economy set up are first described. From the early sixteenth century India's contacts with European countries increased, initially India being a supplier of a variety of goods, especially luxury goods that European traders were looking for. Territorial interests of the traders and their home countries emerged in the seventeenth century especially with the arrival of the (British) East India Company. The struggle for territories by the competing traders in which the local rulers and merchants took an active part provided the first major factor for the transformation of the village economy set up. After the East India Company succeeded in driving out the European competitors and established political authority in India, more changes came, particularly in the land settlement patterns. The Industrial Revolution was going on in England at that time and the character of relationship between India and England began to change with India soon becoming a colony of the British. After the Crown took over the administration from the Company and India was made part of the British Empire, the Indian economy's role was envisaged as supplying raw materials to Britain and providing a market for British manufactured goods, especially mill-made cloth. This led to the village economy being battered in different ways. Towards the end of the British rule, the British gave some support for the industrialisation of India and for the growth of capitalist units of production. On the eve of Independence, therefore, the Indian economy had become a very complex entity.

In approaching the evolution of the Indian economy, there is a preliminary question to be settled: Where does one begin? In a country like ours with a long history behind it, this is an important issue. But in an analytical sense deciding on a benchmark which is not altogether arbitrary appears to be a distinct possibility. We have noted that even today the village economy form, as we discussed it in Chapter 3, is a widely prevalent feature of the Indian economy although it is undergoing change under the impact of capitalism. The capitalist impact on the Indian economy was initiated during the colonial period, especially during the couple of centuries of British domination culminating around the middle of the present century. Since it is the transformation that the economy has been experiencing under the impact of capitalism that we wish to study (as was stated in Chapter 7), we shall concentrate on the colonial period in this chapter. In the next chapter we shall examine aspects of the ongoing transformation since Independence.

PRE-COLONIAL STRUCTURE OF THE ECONOMY

In order to discuss the changes that the economy experienced during the colonial period, we shall take the pre-colonial period, that is, India's village economy phase as the benchmark. It is generally considered that the village was the primary unit of that order and that the villages were, by and large, self-sufficient and self-perpetuating. Marx, in an oft-quoted passage, described them thus:

> The simplicity of the organisation for production in these self-sufficing communities that constantly reproduce themselves in the same form, and when accidentally destroyed, spring up again on the spot and with the same name—this simplicity supplies the key to the secret of the un-changeableness of Asiatic societies, an unchangeableness in such striking contrast with the constant dissolution and refounding of Asiatic States, and the never-ceasing changes of dynasty. The structure of the economical elements of society remains untouched by the storm clouds of the political sky. (Marx, 1971, I: 338–39).

A more recent account reflects a similar view: 'The outstanding feature of the economy of India before the advent of British power was the self-subsisting and self-perpetuating character of its typical unit, the village. India's villages functioned as little worlds of their own.' (Thorner, 1962: 51)

If the reference to 'unchangeableness' in the former passage and to 'self-subsisting and self-perpetuating character' in the second passage are taken literally, neither of these two passages would be correct depictions of the pre-colonial economy of India. But compared with the rapidity and magnitude of the changes in the 'political sky' of the period, and the nature of changes in the economy itself in subsequent periods, there was a certain stability to the pre-colonial economy. Let us look at the way in which the economic activities within the village have been described.

Within the villages, social and economic relationships were governed by customary patterns and conventions of great antiquity. The cattle were tended and the soil was tilled by peasants whose fathers had been cultivators and whose sons would take their places when they come of age. Cloth for the garments of the peasants generally was spun and woven by families whose ancestors had been weavers long before the living memory of man. The other crafts were carried on by families which in effect were servants of the village. These occupations passed on traditionally from father to son: the blacksmith, potter, and carpenter, who made and repaired the implements and utensils of the village; the silversmith who made the village jewellery; and the oilseed presser.... The village itself consumed most of the foodstuffs and other raw materials it produced. Its needs for handicrafts were satisfied by the families of craftsmen associated with the village. It was this tight union of agriculture and hand industry which made the village economically independent of the outside world except for a few necessities like salt and iron. The share of the village crops which went to the local magnate and moved from him in diminishing stream upward to the highest political overlord sustained the structure of government and provided subsistence for the urban population. (*Ibid.*:51)

This detailed account presents a picture which is quite familiar in many villages even today. It also shows that the villages could not have been 'little worlds of their own'. They existed in a wider world of government structures and of an urban economy which they *economically* sustained as also from which they obtained some necessities like salt and iron. In fact, historical research of the more recent years has shown that whatever might have been the *internal* structure of the villages, within the Indian economy as a whole exchange and commodity production were widely prevalent.[1] Hence, even if the villages were largely self-sufficient, it would not be correct to say that the pre-colonial economy of India consisted entirely of such units. Do we then reject completely the characterisation that 'unchangeableness' was the main feature of the typical unit of the pre-colonial economy? A more accurate statement would be 'continuity, rather than change characterised most aspects of economic life over very long periods up to the colonial period.... The movement from one period to another before British rule consisted of changes within a broad framework of continuity in the fundamentals of economic life...' (CEHI, 1984, I: xii). In the discussion that follows we shall try to bring out this element of long-term stability of the pre-colonial economic order. It is because of this long-term stability that we can use the pre-colonial period to understand the changes and transformation of the colonial period.

Role of geo-physical factors

To enter into a closer examination of the pre-colonial economy, let us recall a general feature of village economies that we dealt with in Chapter 3, viz., that as economies concentrating on primary production, they depend crucially on geo-physical factors—soil types, temperature, availability of water etc. That being the case, one of the distinguishing features of the pre-colonial economy of India must be visible regional and locational patterns involving not only different kinds of production activities as may be expected, but also practically all aspects of human relationships. A concrete example of this can be seen from the classical works of the early period of Tamil literature (around the third century AD) when the basic unit of human settlement was the *nadu*, and which were divided into five basic types on the basis of natural sub-region and related occupational patterns.[2] These were:

1. The ploughmen inhabiting fertile, well watered tracts and living in villages.
2. The hill people living in forest areas.
3. The pastoralists.
4. The fishing people living in large coastal villages.
5. The people of the dry plains who were essentially hunters.

It is not difficult to see that the economies of these different groups would show very distinct features. Even within basically settled agricultural communities differences of economic organisations and activities could be seen based on whether the land was irrigated or not, whether it depended solely on rainfall etc. These 'wet'–'dry' distinctions appear to be crucial even in contemporary times and there are several studies that use this aspect as one of the key analytical variables.[3]

This fact of the geo-physical diversity of economic activity needs to be emphasised because in a sense any attempt to make general statements about the 'pre-colonial economy of India' ignoring the specificities of the many variations can be misleading.[4] At the same time the variations were too numerous and too distinctly different even to provide a reasonable typology. We shall try to get out of this dilemma (not always successfully) first by concentrating on communities primarily dependent on land-related activities and within that restricted subset by featuring locational variations where these make a major analytical distinction. The first volume of the (recent) *Cambridge Economic History of India*, which deals with the pre-colonial period, it may be noted, deals with the North, South, West and East quite distinctly.

Apart from the ecosystems, there is one other factor that is of general significance in understanding the economies of this period, viz., the social organisation based on considerations of caste. There were, no doubt, close interactions between the two and the pre-colonial economic structure could be examined making use of these two factors. Together they defined what is frequently referred to as the 'village community'.

Rights on land and vertical transfers

As was noted in Chapter 3, village economies which had land as the main productive force gave more prominence to land *holding* than to land *ownership*. Ownership of land, in fact, remained ill defined, while the holding of land which formed the basis of the right to use and of the right to enjoy the produce in the case of most members of the community, was fairly clearly regulated. In most instances, land holding was also a hereditary right. The lack of precise concept of ownership has sometimes led to the interpretation that land was owned by the community as a whole. There were probably isolated instances of this kind. However, if individual ownership rights were ill defined, there is no reason to imagine that collective or communal ownership would be clearly indicated. For the issue was not whether the ownership was individual or collective; rather, it related to the very concept of ownership which is usually (especially in its present day meaning) understood as the right to alienate or sell. When land transactions were, on the whole, very limited such a right would not have been a major issue. The point is that for a long time in the past land was territory, not property. It has been stated also: 'The question whether the land was owned by the Raja, the talukdar, Zamindar, the cultivator or the king was not a real question. Each had claim based upon custom or upon grants made by the king or a raja, or upon grants made by a talukdar or zamindar. But in addition to these claims each did or did not have the power to enforce his claims or enlarge his claims. There was no appeal if a usurper had the power to usurp.' (Neale, 1962: 37). The rights on land were thus determined by custom and the ability to defend them.

Conferring and receiving land rights was a very common practice. From the fourteenth century at least there were people in North India who were known as zamindars, *zamin* being the Persian word for land and the suffix *dar* implying a degree of control, but not necessarily of ownership. The zamindar's main right over his estate was to a share of the produce customarily determined. But where his power was strong and custom was weak, he could extract from the actual cultivators more than what was customarily due. In the South there were inamdars and mirasdars. Some of them at lower levels were also actual cultivators even while they claimed their share from those who were still lower. The Mughal conquerors recognised the rights of the variety of local chieftains in return for a claim of land-rent collected. They also provided a firmer pyramidal structure to the rent claimants. At the top were mainly the Muslim elites with the biggest holdings or jagirs; then came the big, mainly Hindu, landholders who largely retained their hereditary right to their lands; and below them were the influential landholders in each locality who probably added to their traditional lands various wastelands from time to time. The relationship between these groups, and these groups and the central authority, were complicated. It is, therefore, clear that rural society in Mughal India was highly differentiated. It was a spectrum of powerful chiefs at one end and lowly peasants and menials at the other. The land system was based on a welter of claims and rights enforced by custom and might. There was also a tendency for these rights to become property rights, transferable and saleable. For a long time, therefore, though land itself did not become a commodity, rights on land such as zamindari became inheritable and marketable. The basis of all these rights, it may be noted, was the 'vertical' transfer referred to in Chapters 3 and 7.

From the point of view of the village community below, these transfers were significant for two reasons. First, the village communities were seen as 'communities' more by these higher and external agents than by the villagers themselves. For purposes of revenue collection, for instance, it was very convenient to treat the village as a single unit and to have dealings with the headman or a small stratum of upper peasants. This external view also led to the overlooking of the village as an economic unit which, in turn, led to it being represented as an internally cohesive and undifferentiated entity. We shall soon see that it was a misrepresentation. Secondly, and more importantly, the vertical transfer led to anywhere from a third to a half of the gross produce of the village being siphoned-off. The Mughals had perfected a system of collection of rent tax on the basis of their claim as holders of state property which was the economic basis of their rule. Aurangzeb's declared land tax was around Rs. 35 crores of which some 60 per cent was actually collected (Pavlov, 1979: 33). The tax collection, it may be noted, was not done directly by the administrative personnel of the state. The procedure was one of 'tax-farming': the proprietory right to claim rent given or recognised by the state which carried with it the responsibility to surrender a part of the collection to the state as tax. There was, therefore, no effective control over tax collection: it became a standard instrument for exploitation and harassment of the peasantry. Non-payment of taxes elicited different forms of punishments, enslavement, torture of various forms and even massacres.

The Mughal Empire, it has been observed, was established on 'the uncomplicated desire of a small ruling class for more and more material resources—an almost primitive urge to consume and acquire'. And there was reason for it too.

A cavalier indifference to economy characterised every branch of the administration and the army. The tent which took a thousand men one week to erect with the help of machines, the employment of five or more persons to look after each elephant in the imperial stable, the production of increasingly large-sized canon which were often disfunctional, all suggest an emphasis on grandeur at the cost of efficiency. The army on the march—a moving city with 100,000 to 300,000 men and vast quantities of tents, baggage, furniture, etc., carried by some 50,000 horses and oxen was as much a display of imperial life-style as a purposive instrument of state power.... The Mughal state was an insatiable Leviathan: its impact on the economy was defined above all by its unlimited appetite for resources. (CEHI, 1984, I: 172–73)

It is not necessary to go into further details. Suffice it to say that in under-standing the pre-colonial economy of India the state must be accepted as one of the major units.

The structure of the village economy itself must be seen against this background. Except in regard to taxation, as seen above, the village was not a single economic unit. It is best to think of it as a territorial unit with a number of h–2 economic units in it. The cultivable land in the village was held individually and cultivated individually by these units. They were not alike in respect of land holding either. An authority on the economic life of the period says:

Economic differentiation had progressed considerably among the peasantry. There were large cultivators, using hired labour, and raising crops for the market; and there were small peasants, who could barely produce food grains for their own subsistence. Beyond this differen-tiation among the peasantry, there was the still sharper division bet-ween the caste peasantry and the 'menial' population, a primitive land-less proletariat, which served as the reserve for supporting peasant agriculture.[5]

Communitarian elements

But there were some communitarian elements too in the village set up. A foreign visitor had noted that some particular fields were set apart in each village for public purposes and the produce on such fields was appropriated for the maintenance of the Brahmins, and other functionaries in the village such as smiths, barbers and watchmen, but also of the lame, blind and helpless.[6] The social division of labour—into cultivators, smiths, washermen, barbers, accountants, artisans, priests, astrologers et al., was determined strictly according to caste and denoted very clear principles of hierarchy. The social organisation of the village in many places followed what has come to be known as the *jajmani* system. This system meant that the non-cultivating professionals in the village were remunerated not with the payment of work done, but with a fraction of gross agricultural produce, usually at harvest time. The record of a Deccan village, for example, showed the following kind of distribution of the produce:

Table 8.1 *Distribution of Produce to Village Functionaries in a Deccan Village*

Functionary	Annual Remuneration (converted into Kgs)
Headman	680
Official	2,160
Carpenter	1,500
Smith	1,360
Harness-maker	1,360
Potter	1,020
Washerman	1,140
Servant	680
Temple servant	780
Teacher	680
Goldsmith	560
Watchman	680
Water-carrier	780
Servant	560
Servant	3,600

These payments, it is estimated, claimed about 10 per cent of the gross produce. In some places, there was another variant of the *jajmani* system whereby instead of giving a share of the produce to the functionaries they were given a parcel of land which they could cultivate free from taxes or bearing a reduced tax. The functionaries were considered as servants of the community as a whole. As a rule they were of lower castes and hence of lower social status than the landholders. But their responsibilities to the community and their maintenance by the community were considered as social duties.

A further form of community in the village set up was via the 'commons' where all members of the village could send their cattle for grazing and from where, in most instances, any member could gather reeds for the thatching of their roof. Providing labour for maintenance of irrigation systems (particularly tanks) was another collective responsibility of the village.

Among the artisans in the village the position of weavers and oil pressers was somewhat different. For one thing while the carpenters and smiths, for instance, had functions related to agriculture, the weavers and oilpressers performed services resulting in specific goods which could be used in the village itself, or could be sent out of the village. They were, therefore, not as fully integrated into the village economy as were the other functionaries. In some parts of the country such as the north-eastern region perhaps spinning and weaving were parts of the activities of all households. Even where this was not the case, and there were special weaver castes, they could also be partly engaged in agricultural operations of their own. But in most instances weavers and oilpressers were among the first to enter into commercial activities. They could produce (cloth or oil) specifically for their village; but they could also produce for the remote urban markets.

Horizontal activity chains

These arrangements show different kinds of horizontal activity chains among the h–2 units of the village. Some were confined to the village and were organised according to collective principles as was the case in the *jajmani* system; others, as for instance, transactions between grain producers and cloth producers, could have been exchange either of the C–C form or the C–M–C form; there were also trade between some of the h–2 units of the village and units outside, and such trade could be mediated by merchants.

Most villages also had agricultural workers who did not, and, according to caste principles, could not have any land holdings. Their presence was necessitated partly because some landholders (especially those belonging to the higher castes) could not, according to tradition, perform most of the agricultural operations, in particular ploughing. Since some members of the village could not hold land, and others could not operate land, they tended to come together via 'reciprocity in unequal obligations' which in Chapter 3 we saw as a characteristic feature of village economies. Those who were prevented from becoming landholders were, thus, obligated to supply their labour power to those who had land and could not operate it. They would become 'attached' to some landholders, or more accurately to some land, because they would be transferred along with the land to some other holders if the land itself was transferred. In return the landholders were required to compensate the workers for the services they rendered. Such 'attached labour' households (belonging to the untouchable caste groups) existed in many parts of the country, especially in the paddy growing areas of the south.[7] They were not h–4 households of the kind discussed in Chapter 7 because they were not free to *sell* their labour power. Since they were maintained at the barest subsistence level and could be sold (usually along with the land) they could be considered as slaves. Indeed in the south they were frequently referred to as *adimai* which was the word in the regional languages for slaves. What is significant is that the village economy of pre-colonial India had the category of landless agricultural labourers.

These accounts show that the tendency to take a romantic view of the village economies of the past in the belief that they consisted of landholders and producers of equal status functioning on a basis of mutual sharing is hardly valid. The village economies were highly differentiated. There were rentiers and peasants; landlords and tenants; cultivators and artisans; free workers and attached workers. They were certainly not communities of equals, but an assemblage of hierarchically ordered and palpably unequal groups. But they were 'inclusive' communities in the sense that custom had assigned a place for each group in the total structure with a right, however meagre, on the produce.

The urban economy

In Chapter 3 we saw that village economies almost naturally give rise to an urban component resulting from the vertical transfer of surplus from the actual producers to the rentiers. Pre-colonial India was not an exception.

An urban centre is essentially an assemblage of people engaged in non-agricultural activities, but heavily dependent on agricultural activities elsewhere. Such centres arose for various reasons. Traditionally, places of religious significance would attract pilgrims and though the pilgrim population would be temporary, such places would attract persons who would stay there on a more or less permanent basis to cater to the needs of the visitors. Varanasi, Bhuvaneswar, Tirupati, Kancheepuram and Madurai were such centres. There were also centres of trade and manufacture such as Agra, Lahore and Kozhikode. With the arrival and rule of the Mughals the seats of administration also emerged as urban centres. The Mughal period saw the accelerated pace of urbanisation for various reasons, especially in the north. The political unification of a major part of the sub-continent stimulated commerce and urban life in general. We have already seen how large the Mughal militia was. There was an even larger entourage. One account for the mid-seventeenth century has it that 'taking into account the large number of non-military personnel in the service of the army, the nobles and the imperial establishment and the families of all the people thus employed, the total number dependent for their livelihoods on employment in the armed services and associated activities has been estimated at some 26 million, a remarkably large figure for a population estimated at a mere 100 million...' (CEHI, 1984, I: 179). The bulk of these people were maintained at a bare subsistence level. But there were also members of the nobility noted for their fabulous lifestyles. A contemporary writer had noted that in Delhi's bazaar a young nobleman could expect to buy only the barest necessities with Rs. 100,000! (CEHI, 1984, I:180)

Apart from these large religious, commercial and administrative centres there were many smaller urban centres throughout the country where a nobleman, a zamindar, a raja or a local chief—all, however, being rentiers—would live with his retinue consisting of bodyguards, artists and artisans. The producers of the traditionally famous luxury goods of India were artisans of this kind living under the patronage of some nobleman. This implied that based on the vertical activity chain distinctly different from anything we have seen so far, there arose a further one essentially the activity chain that linked the nobility and their retinue including a different group of artisans. Commerce between such centres (or between such centres and centres in other countries) also developed, giving rise to a number of merchants and their activities. While the merchants were primarily active within and between urban centres, the collection of revenue in cash introduced by the Mughals provided the merchants entry into the rural economy as well. A characteristic feature of the pre-colonial economy, therefore, was 'layer after layer of market networks, often, though not always interlinked with one another' (CEHI, 1984, II: 28). And yet it should be noted that the bulk of economic activity in the rural areas did not get affected by these transactions and belonged to quite different activity chains.

But the activities of merchants became significant for other reasons. Merchants soon got access into the tax business. 'Merchants who undertook the collect tax in a given area paid the Treasury a sum of money fixed in advance, collected the tax in kind from the agricultural population and then sold the products for a profit in the towns and army camps' (Pavlov, 1979: 85). The big merchants as tax-farmers acquired very strong influence in the early eighteenth century when the fiscal functions of the Mughal Empire were largely concentrated in their hands. As they began to accumulate wealth through these activities they also started taking on the function of moneylenders. They would lend to zamindars who had to pay tax to the state; they would lend to artisans who had to make a living while they were in the process of making their goods; they would even lend to the rulers who were constantly in need of resources and cash. Whether it was their role as traders or as money-lenders that was more significant is difficult to say.

We may now sum up our discussion of the pre-colonial economy of India and say that it was a system consisting of a wide variety and range of h–2 units, some bordering h–4 units, many m units and the state(s).

Transformation in pre-colonial period
It is from this kind of a structure of a village economy that its transformation begins and we saw in Chapters 3 and 5 that in many parts of the

world that transformation led to the emergence of capitalist economies. This, obviously, did not happen in India and it will be worth considering why. It is not possible to give a definitive answer to that question, and any explanation put forward can only be in the form of informed speculation.

We have noted that physical and social factors greatly influenced the pre-colonial economy of India. They have, to a large extent, also accounted for the stability of that set-up for a long time. The physical features of the country, especially the tropical climate made it possible for human beings to survive at very low levels of consumption of material goods and the relative abundance of land enabled those limited material needs to be satisfied with few tools and implements. The combined effect of these two was to keep productive activity at a low level depending largely on human effort and skills of a traditional kind. Within such a basic situation the caste system ordained a fairly elaborate, but also strictly rigid social division of labour. The caste system, by preventing some from engaging themselves in manual labour and others from holding land, also provided a basis for dividing society into rentiers and workers. By defining the social position and economic role of the members, including their claims on the produce, the caste system laid strong foundations for the temporal stability of the system. Thus from generation to generation the same process got repeated with the same arrangements for the organisation of production and the distribution of the produce being preserved. This set-up also gave rise to a system of mutual dependence which could not easily be broken. These aspects had a particular bearing on non-agricultural production which served as the main area of change in other parts of the world. As already mentioned, a major part of the productive force in India consisted of personal skills which could not be easily augmented because they were, in many instances, closely guarded family secrets and were, therefore, communicated only from father to son. Further, 'in striking contrast to India's pre-eminence as an exporter of manufactured goods, her technology was remarkably backward in comparison with the other advanced civilisations of the period, especially Western Europe and China. Her world famous textiles were produced without the aid of multi-spindle wheels known to China from at least the fourteenth century and, of course, she had nothing to compare with the water-powered throwing-mills with 200 spindles of the Italian silk industry.' (CEHI, 1984, I: 291).

Again, in contrast to the splendour of the product, the producers themselves were of rather low estate. Not only were they lower in the caste hierarchy than those who were involved in agriculture, but their earnings were low, and they were subjected to the extortions by the village headman, the nobles who were their customers, and the middlemen. What was perhaps most critical was the fact that 'it was virtually impossible for an artisan to aspire to a higher social status and, one imagines, like the untouchable who accepted his untouchability as part of a God-given order, the manufacturer accepted his economic as well as his social situation as unalterable facts.' (CEHI, 1984, I: 278).

While, therefore, the pre-colonial economy of India generated surplus, it was siphoned-off from the producers into the hands of the rentiers who used it mainly to enjoy a luxurious life and to maintain a retinue, and into the hands of merchants who certainly went on accumulating wealth and more wealth. In both cases the surplus appropriators were not interested in utilising the surplus to augment productive forces and capacity. The pre-colonial economy, therefore, continued for centuries with but minor changes of redistributive nature. The disparities in distribution were very striking indeed. Foreign travellers who visited India during the sixteenth and seventeenth centuries have portrayed a picture of a small group, especially in the ruling class, living a life of immense luxury, in sharp contrast to the miserable condition of the masses—the peasants, the artisans and domestic attendants. The Mughal nobles, for instance, received salaries which were probably the highest in the world at that time. These disparities, however, were very much a part of India's traditional economic order. They did not affect the underlying structure of the economy. Changes affecting the basic structure were yet to come.

TRANSFORMATION OF THE ECONOMY UNDER COLONIAL IMPACT

While the bulk of the population of pre-colonial India lived in the villages and their material needs were substantially met through production in their own localities, there were other sections of the population whose economic activities were primarily geared to supplying goods to other parts of the world. Thus as a country, India had for many centuries economic relationships with several other countries, especially the emerging commercial nations of Europe. These relationships became stronger and of a more sustained nature from the time Vasco Da Gama, the Portuguese trader set foot in India towards the very end of fifteenth century. Traders from many European countries came to the Mughal courts to establish and increase trade with India attracted by the variety of goods this country could make available to European markets. The East India Company made its entry in the early seventeenth century. For a long time the British had to fight battles on Indian soil against other European traders, in particular the French. By the end of the eighteenth century, they succeeded in driving out their rivals and in establishing their presence as an economic and political power in the void that was left by the decay of the Mughal empire. The Indian economy which had experienced but minor ripples from the end of the fifteenth to the end of the eighteenth century began a perceptible process of transformation from then on.

About the same time, major changes were taking place in the British economy also. The process of the capitalist transformation of the British economy was going on and by the middle of the eighteenth century Britain was entering into what has come to be known as the phase of the Industrial Revolution. From then on for about two centuries, the Indian economy was closely linked with the British economy. It is the nature of the transformation that the Indian economy experienced during that period that we shall examine now.

The first phase

In the beginning, at least, the intentions of the British, especially of the East India Company, were commercial; mainly to make use of its exclusive right to import Indian goods to Britain to sell them in both British and European markets, making a profit on the difference in prices of these goods in India and Europe. England was to be 'the emporium for supplying all other countries of Europe with the productions and manufactures of India' as Warren Hastings, one of the Governors-General during the days of the Company's administration of India put it. The assistance that the foreign merchants needed for their operations in India were readily provided by Indian merchants—on the basis of a commission, of course, usually 2 per cent of the transactions. The first major changes in the structure of the Indian economy were initiated, therefore, on the basis of increased merchants' activities, foreign and Indian. The urban component of the village economy of India, thus, came to play its expected part in the transformation.

There was another factor to be taken into account. While the Indian merchants, as seen above, had close contacts with the Mughal and local rulers, they did not have political power. The English merchants, on the other hand, had the full backing of their government. And they made full use of the disorder and unsettlement that followed the fall of the Mughals to gain political power in India also. They set up and knocked down local rulers and indulged in all forms of intrigues, cunning and treachery to establish themselves on Indian soil. 'Theft, bribery, confiscation, taxation—every conceivable method of squeezing money and goods out of the inhabitants was open to them', says a writer, 'and was used with a freedom and ferocity of greed not equalled perhaps even by the Japanese in Manchuko'. (Shelvankar, 1940: 147). The success of the East India Company in establishing power in Bengal whipped up its appetite, he continues: 'It saw how much better, how much more profitable, sovereignty was, than mere trade; and like a tiger that had tasted blood it pursued its hunt for territory with a new zest until, in the end, the whole continent lay under its domains'. (*Ibid.*: 148)

During the first phase, therefore, the transformation of the Indian economy was brought about by the combination of merchant power (m) and state power (s). One of our economic historians has given the following account of an English eye-witness on how this power was put to use:

It may with truth be now said that the whole inland trade of the country, as at present conducted, and that of the Company's investment for Europe in a more peculiar degree, has been one continued scene of oppression; the baneful effects of which are severely felt by every weaver and manufacturer in the country, every article produced being made a monopoly; in which the English, with their Banyas and black Gomastahs, arbitrarily decide what qualities of goods each manufacturer shall deliver, and the prices he shall receive for them.... Upon the Gomastah's arrival at the Aurung, or manufacturing town, he fixes upon a habitation which he calls his catcherry; to which, by his peons and hircarahs, he summons the brokers, called dellals and pykars, together with the weavers, whom, after receipt of the money despatched by his masters, he makes to sign a bond for the delivery of a certain quantity of goods, at a certain time and price, and pays them a certain part of the money in advance. The assent of the poor weaver is in general not deemed necessary.... The roguery practised in this department is beyond imagination; but all terminates in the defrauding of the poor weaver; for the prices which the Company's Gomastahs, and in confederacy with them the Jachendars (examiners of fabrics) fix upon the goods, are in all places at least 15 per cent, and some even 40 per cent less than the goods so manufactured would sell in the public bazaar or market upon free sale.... Weavers, also, upon their inability to perform such agreements as have been forced upon them by the Company's agents, universally known in Bengal by the name of Mutchulacks, have had their goods seized and sold on the spot to make good their deficiency; and the widers of new silk, called Nagodas, have been treated also with such injustice, that instances have been known of their cutting off thumbs to prevent their being forced to wind silk. (Dutt, 1960: 17–18)

Of course, tyranny as such was not uncommon before the arrival of the Company. But there was a major difference as noted by our historian:

The people of Bengal had been used to tyranny, but had never lived under an oppression as far reaching in its effects, extending to every village market and every manufacturer's loom. They had been used to arbitrary acts from men in power, but had never suffered from a system which touched their trades, their occupations, their lives so closely. The springs of their industry were stopped, their sources of wealth were dried up. (*Ibid.*: 18).

The treatment meted out to the weavers was not individual aberration either. According to Thomas Munro, who had been an administrator under the Company's rule such treatments were beginning to get legal sanction also by the early part of the nineteenth century. Deposing before a committee of the British House of Commons set up to examine the East India Company's activities in India, Munro stated:

> In Baramahal the Company's servants assembled the principal weavers and placed guard over them until they entered into engagements to supply the company only. When once a weaver accepted an advance he seldom got out of his liability. A peon was placed over him to quicken his deliveries if he delayed, and he was liable to be prosecuted in the courts of justice.... The whole weaving population of villages were thus held in subjection to the Company's factories, and Mr. Cox deposed that 1500 weavers, not including their families and connections, were under his authority in the factory over which he presided. (*Ibid.*: 181–82).

The control under which the weaver population was held was not merely a matter of practice, but was legalised by regulations. It was provided that a weaver who had received advances from the Company 'shall on no account give to any other person whatever, Europeans or Natives, either the labour or the produce engaged to the Company'.

Disruption of traditional activity chains

Apart from what it was doing to the weavers themselves and other producers whose goods the Company was eager to 'purchase', the practice followed by the Company had a direct impact on the system itself because it pulled out these production units from the activity chains of which they were parts, thereby disrupting those chains. Disruption came about in other ways as well. Elsewhere, the disruption came because groups of consumers withdrew from the activity chains. Many of the traditional handicrafts were maintained, as noted earlier, by the rich consumers in the urban areas who began to become part of the new establishment and to change their habits. According to Kipling: 'No sumptuary regulations to restrain extravagance in gilded shoes, and enforce the use of plain black leather could be half so potent as the unwritten ordinance, which permits an oriental to retain a pair of patent leather boots on stockinged feet and requires him to doff shoes of native make, when in the presence of a superior.[8] The superior, of course, was an Englishman. Another writer observed: 'To wear silk is not the fashion it used to be in Sikh times or to the extent it still is in the Native States. European cotton goods, printed calicoes and cheap broadcloths have turned silken garments out of the field'.[9] Many upper class Indians were extremely ready to accept European standards and to pour scorn on everything Indian.

At a later stage, after the British cotton industry was largely mechanised, the Indian producers had to face the competition of the substantially cheaper British goods that started flowing into India. The first to face this problem was yarn. After spinning was mechanised in England in the early decades of the nineteenth century, the increase in labour productivity brought down the prices of yarn, especially of the most popular grades while the prices of Indian yarn continued as they were, thus causing a major price differential between the two. The prices of English and Indian yarn of various counts in 1832 are shown in Table 8.2.

Table 8.2 Price of a Pound of Cotton Yarn in England and India, 1832

Grade No.	In Britain	In India
40	2s. 6d	3s. 7d
60	3s. 6d	6s. 0d
80	4s. 4d	9s. 3d
100	5s. 2d	12s. 4d
120	6s. 0d	16s. 5d
150	9s. 4d	25s. 6d
200	20s. 0d	45s. 1d
250	35s. 0d	84s. 0d

The prices of cloth were in a similar state. By the end of the 1830s, good shirting made in Britain was sold in India at 10 annas a yard, whereas the corresponding Indian pieces were offered at double the price. Consequently, India which was a large exporter of textile goods became a net importer within a period of a couple of decades. Exports which were of the value of Rs. 5,281,000 in 1813/14 went down to Rs. 823,000 in 1832/33 while imports shot up from Rs. 92,000 to Rs. 4,265,000 during the same period (Pavlov, 1979: 281).

The consequence of this on the artisans in India and the Indian economy were manifold. To withstand the competition from imported factory produced goods, the local artisans were forced to offer their goods at prices below their cost of production, thereby substantially reducing their already meagre earnings. Increasingly, they also became indebted to the merchants who were able to take full advantage of the plight of the poor producers. Many of the artisans were also forced to give up their traditional occupations and fall back on agriculture in what Nehru has tellingly described as 'the compulsory back-to-the land movement of artisans and craftsmen'.

Among those destroyed were those who had already moved out of the traditional village barter arrangements and, consequently, were the more advanced in a technological sense. Those who remained had to make major changes in their production patterns. Hand spinning of yarn was considerably eliminated and so weavers, to a large extent had to depend on factory made yarn, imported at first, and then manufactured in India after the factory sector of the cotton textile industry developed in the country. Factory manufactured metals, dyes etc. also became standard inputs in Indian handicrafts. In turn these brought about changes in the organisation of production and in the kind of activity chains that these units were linked to.

Land settlement patterns

We have started our discussion of the transformation of the Indian economy under the colonial rule with its impact on the handicraft producers because it was there that the impact was first felt and quite prominent. Other sectors of the economy also experienced the impact of colonial rule, though, perhaps, not as glaringly as in the case of the artisans. In the sphere of agriculture the policy of the British conquerors was mainly to get the support of the rural elites as a political necessity and to get as high a land revenue as possible. The British found the ill-defined ownership pattern over land in rural India confusing and decided to fashion it in the manner they were familiar with. Emerging from the somewhat chaotic feudal patterns, British land system had, by this time become well established in individual ownership which appeared to have raised agricultural productivity quite significantly. As a means to raise land revenue, the colonial administrators were interested in increasing agricultural productivity in India also and they believed that conferring definite private ownership of land would lead to this end.

With this in view, and in order to gain the support of the influential people in the rural areas, the British set out on a programme to convert the tax farmers and revenue collectors into private landlords, conferring upon them some, but not all, of the rights of private property in land. The land settlement system effected in Bengal in 1793 came to be known as the zamindari system. The zamindars were given the ownership of large areas of land on the understanding that they would be responsible for collecting greatly enhanced land revenue from the cultivating peasants and pass it on to the state. In this process the zamindars lost the judicial and administrative powers they had traditionally enjoyed, which were taken over by the state. The Permanent Settlement (as the new land system was referred to because it fixed the revenue payable to the government from each state on a permanent basis), thus, removed a group of people who exercised considerable local power, but converted them into firm supporters of the new regime because of the new economic prosperity they were assured. Thus the political objective of the settlement was achieved.

However, the expectation that the private property right would lead to an increase in productivity did not materialise as the zamindars were quite content with playing the role of intermediaries between the actual cultivators and the state, for that itself assured them a substantial income without having to bother about cultivation. The British also came to realise that the Permanent Settlement resulted only in the enrichment of the inter-mediaries and were more cautious in their dealings in other parts of the country. In the Madras Presidency, for instance, very little land was converted into zamindari land. For the rest, the state decided to deal directly with individual peasants. The proprietory rights of each peasant (ryot) over the lands he occupied were recognised on condition that he would pay a stipulated amount of money every year as revenue to the state. This land system known as a ryotwari settlement, with minor modifications was later applied to the Bombay Presidency as also to areas in North-Eastern and North-Western India. Comparing the two major land settlements effected by the British, it has been observed:

Whereas the zamindari system made the landlords masters of the village communities, the ryotwari system cut through the heart of the village communities by making separate arrangements between each peasant cultivator and the state.... Under both of them, the old body of custom was submerged by the formidable apparatus of law courts, fees, lawyers, and formal procedures. For, with the introduction of some of the rights of private property in the land, the purchase and sale of zamindaris' holdings were explicitly sanctioned by law. All of this was too much not only for the humble peasants, but also for the new landlords'. (Thorner, 1962: 53).

The formal sanctioning of and encouragement for commoditising land was one of the fundamental changes brought about by the British. We shall see that its *de facto* implications may not have become visible immediately, and would wait till after Independence, when for a variety of reasons what remained dormant so far began to become explicit. In the meanwhile, even soon after the settlements were effected, the direction that the course of events would take later on became evident. Many of the landlords could not raise the heavy revenues required by the government (in the ryotwari areas, for instance, land revenue was generally fixed at half the net-produce on unirrigated 'dry' lands and three-fifths on irrigated 'wet' lands, and even higher on the so-called 'garden' or improved lands growing high-value crops) and so had to sell their lands to merchants, speculators and persons from the cities; few of whom had any interest in cultivation or the cultivators, but were eager to extract as much rent as they could from them. Thus began an era of middlemen, speculators and absentee landlords. The legal rights conferred on some also began to erode the traditional rights of many, although, this again did not become manifest with full vehemence immediately. We must note also that the state itself took over the ownership of some lands over which the ownership rights in the traditional order were particularly vague.

Commercialisation of agriculture

The jolt that the traditional agrarian system of India received from the new land systems was further aggravated by a process of the commercialisation of agriculture which gathered momentum from the mid-nineteenth century. Traditional agriculture was mainly production for local use, and for a long time rent and taxes were also paid in kind, although we have seen that changes in these respects had come in even during the Mughal period. But the British were more demanding about payment of revenue in cash and so it became necessary for a part of production to be systematically undertaken for sale. The British also had another reason to encourage cultivation of land by commercial crops like cotton, jute, and indigo. By the middle of the nineteenth century these were required as raw materials for British industries. The Crown had taken over the administration of India from the Company in 1857 and so India could be viewed as part of the Empire. It was held by many politicians that the Indian economy should be dovetailed into British economy for the benefit of Britain and some economists were ready to argue that British specialisation in industry and the Indian specialisation in agriculture would be advantageous to both.

The manner in which the commercialisation of agriculture took place is seen most clearly in the case of cotton. India was a producer of cotton for many centuries and the Deccan region was particularly noted for its production. But the cotton produced there was largely used within the country itself. In the second half of the nineteenth century, however, there was a sudden increase in the British demand for Indian cotton mainly because the Civil War in America resulted in a reduction in the export of cotton from there to England, and the mechanised textile industry of England was frantically searching for alternate sources of supply. The price of cotton in the Indian market shot up immediately from around $2^{1}/_{2}$ annas per pound in 1859 to about $10^{1}/_{2}$ annas in 1863, that is a fourfold increase in four years! In what was then the Central Provinces (which included the Deccan region) the area under cotton cultivation increased from 376,000 acres in 1861–62 to 6,91,000 acres in 1864–65, and the export of cotton from India to the U.K., increased from around 500,000 bales in 1859 to close to 1,400,000 bales in 1864. It is recorded also that in the single district of Bellary (in the Madras Presidency) the ryots made $1^1/_2$ million sterling by the sale of cotton during the three years of cotton boom. These changes were dramatic. They were not sustained, nor were there many instances of this kind in case of other crops. And yet what happened in cotton and on a much smaller scale in other crops was quite significant in terms of the new signals that they gave to the cultivators: they brought home to the cultivator 'the fact that causes other than local needs were beginning to govern the nature and extent of the crops he sowed'. (Gadgil, 1971: 18).

And the commercialisation of agriculture continued to gain momentum. Reliable time series data are available only from the tail-end of the nineteenth century, but they may be indicative of what may have been going on at least from the middle of the century when the process was dramatically triggered off. Table 8.3 gives information on the relative performance of food crops and commercial crops (mainly cotton, jute, groundnut, sugarcane, tobacco and tea) from 1893–94 to 1945–46.

Table 8.3   *All-India Estimates of Food Crop, Commercial Crop and Total Crop Production, 1893–94 to 1945–46*

	Indices of average annual crop output			Non-food to food crop output ratio
Years	Food	Commercial	Total	
1893–94 to 1895–96	100	100	100	0.22
1896–97 to 1905–6	96	105	98	0.24
1906–7 to 1915–16	99	126	104	0.28
1916–17 to 1925–26	98	142	106	0.32
1936–37 to 1945–46	93	185	110	0.44

This Table reveals many interesting aspects. The first is that the period of half a century covered was one of very little increase in agricultural production, in fact one of virtual stagnation, with the index of total crop production increasing only from 100 to 110. Secondly, this was accompanied by a *fall* in food crop production, whereas commercial crops kept steadily rising from 100 to 185. Consequently the ratio between the commercial crops and food crops increased from 0.22 at the beginning of the period to 0.44 at the end of the period. That is, towards the end of the British rule in India commercial crops in value accounted for almost half the value of food crops. That can be taken as an indication of the commercialisation that had taken place in the agrarian economy.

Food grain production had declined, from 73.9 million tons in 1893–94 to 69.3 million tonnes in 1945–46. But the period was one of increase in population, by around 6 per cent per decade (which is negligible by the increase of over 20 per cent per decade in the more recent period, but a 'high' figure in comparison with what was happening prior to it) and on that basis it has been calculated that per capita food crop production declined from 587 pounds per year to 399 pounds during that period (Thorner, 1962: 106). Not surprisingly, famines had become a regular feature of the Indian economy. That must also be noted as another feature of the economy during the British period.

Private property and commercialisation—their impact

As we noted above, the two major changes that came about in agriculture during the British period were the introduction of private property rights and the commercialisation of agriculture. The combined effect of these two, along with the revenue system may now be summarised.

The Indian cultivators, of course, were used to surrendering a part of their output to 'authorities' outside in the form of rent and/or tax. The British regime added two aspects to these payments, especially the land revenue payments: a demand for payment strictly in cash; for payment in full each year, and both these in the context of a private property land system. One of the consequences of these changes was to make the peasants heavily dependent on credit which added to the role of the money-lenders and traders in the rural areas, and increased their numbers and power. Because of the inflexible demand for the payment to the state each year, the peasants had to default or to borrow further in years of poor agricultural performance. To default meant facing consequences from the state; to borrow meant to fall into dependence on the money-lenders from which it was not easy to escape. Under these conditions either the state or the creditors could dispossess the peasants of their land, and this used to happen not infrequently. 'In effect, the new forms of land tenure and legal procedure introduced by the British afforded to the landlords and the providers of credit a set of unprecedented mechanisms for drawing away from the peasants everything but a bare minimum required to keep cultivation going. In no other period of Indian history can we find so large, so well-established, and so secure a group of wealthy landholders as that which grew up and flourished between the 1790s and 1940s'. (*Ibid.*: 109).

The increase in population led to an aggravation of the situation. The increase in population resulted from the reduction in the death rate brought about by controlling some epidemic diseases. It began to exert pressure on land and reduced the options available for those in the rural areas. It also led to an increase in the landless labourers.

Along with these changes, new developments were also taking place. Of these the most important was the emergence of essentially capitalist forms of production; that is, production on a large scale for profit-making based on the use of wage labour. It took two forms, plantations and industrial production organised in factories and using inanimate power. Among plantations the first to take shape were the indigo plantations. Indigo was cultivated in India from ancient times and formed the major raw material in the production of dyes. The East India Company found the production of indigo a profitable enterprise and brought planters from the West Indies and settled them in selected districts of Bengal by the first decade of the nineteenth century. But the prosperity was short-lived and a decline in export started from the third decade. Tea plantations were taken up in Assam, again with the support of the government around 1840. For over a decade they did not register much progress, but from the late fifties there was a phenomenal growth in the number of estates, in the quantum of tea produced and exported. But while the Government could make land available and could show other forms of concession, the supply of wage labour was far from assured. The people of Assam were not particularly interested in taking up wage labour in the plantations, and inadequate transport facilities stood in the way of bringing in labourers from other parts of the country. But as establishments based on wage labour, these and other plantations were the pioneers in the country. They also made a contribution towards the commercialisation of agriculture.

Beginnings of factory production

The British rulers were also interested in trying out factory production in India as the factory form of production had become quite established in England by this time. But the early experiments in this direction were failures. A company to start a cotton spinning and weaving mill was started in 1851 and the mill went into operation in 1854. Some more mills came up in quick succession including some started by Indian entrepreneurs, mostly in and around Bombay. But progress was slow till about 1875 mainly because of the demand for cotton from outside the country. After the cotton export boom collapsed, and cotton cultivation continued, the mill industry started picking up. In 1874 the number of mills in the Bombay Presidency was 19, in 1875 it had risen to 36, and by the end of the decade there were in all 56 mills in the country, three-fourths of them still in the Bombay Presidency. The jute industry in Bengal was also started in 1854 and was largely under European control. By the beginning of the eighties there were 20 jute mills employing nearly 20,000 people. Coal mining also commenced during the middle of the century.

By 1890, there were some 300,000 people employed in factories and mines of whom 200,000 were in cotton mills, jute mills and coal mines with the cotton mills alone employing some 110,000 (Buchanan, 1966: 139). By the turn of the century the total employment in factories and mines had gone up to 540,000 and by 1917 it crossed the 1,000,000 mark. That may look like a big figure, and so it is important to note that it was out of a total population of some 285,000,000 and that the total number engaged in the (decaying) traditional industries at that time would have been around 12,000,000 with those in spinning and weaving alone probably 2,500,000! The British administration was not particularly keen to see modern industries growing in India, but after the First World War, some kind of protection was given to new or infant industries; but even so total employment in the factory sector was not more than about 1,550,000 till 1931. That year is significant because that is the last one for which census classification of occupations is available during the British period as the occupational data of the 1941 census were not tabulated in full. The 1931 census data provides the following broad picture. The total population of the country was 338,200,000 of whom 154,000,000 were enumerated as workers. Industrial workers (including those in the traditional industries and modern industries) were 15,400,000 or around 10 per cent, so that the employment in the factory sector noted above was just 10 per cent of 'industrial workers' and 1 per cent of total workers. The most numerous industrial workers were in textile production numbering 4,100,000. Carpenters numbered over 900,000 and potters 870,000. Tailors, milliners etc., were 650,000; basket makers and similar workers were also about the same size. Rice pounders numbered 560,000 and oilmen 550,000. Included as workers in 'industry' were also nearly 110,000 washermen and 700,000 scavengers. All other categories (masons, stone-cutters, metal-workers, leather-workers etc.) accounted for the rest. On the basis of these figures we may conclude that while the British period saw the emergence of f–units in the economy, they were not large enough or strong enough to absorb any significant proportion of even the small non-agricultural segment of the labour force whose traditional occupations and means of livelihood were disrupted by other changes that were taking place in the economy.

Impact of British administration

The British administration in India had a major share in the kind of changes that were going on. As we have seen, a number of the changes were initiated by the state; others were consequences of the actions of the state. A role—even a leading role—for the state in economic aspects and economic transformation is not a matter of surprise. But in the case of the British administration in India, the nature of the state, to a large extent, also determined the nature of these changes. What then were the distinguishing features of the British administration that accounted for the kind of transformation that took place in India during their regime?

The fact that the British were outsiders is obvious. Prior to the British too, India had come under the rule of those who came from outside. Their immediate predecessors, the Mughals, too were foreign invaders to begin with. But there was a major difference in the case of the British. All previous invaders had come to settle in India and to make the country their home; this being particularly true of the Mughals. This is where the major change came. As a recent writer puts it: 'With the arrival of the British, India found herself placed in an entirely new political situation, with the 'centre of gravity' located outside her land, and in this way she was subjected to a class of rulers who were permanently alien in origin and character.' (Ambirajan, 1978: 3–4). It was not only that the alien rulers came to view Indian problems in the light of English ideas and notions, but the rulers, especially after the administration was taken over from the Company by the Crown in 1857, thought of India as a land of primitive culture which stood in need to be brought into the realms of modern civilisation. In any case, both during the administration of the Company and that of the Crown, policy decisions were made, not in India, but 'back home', by the court of Directors in the former case and by the Secretary of State in the latter. Thus, under the British, it was not only that the destiny of India was being decided by the British, it was also being decided away from the country.

There were two factors shaping British society and opinion at this time. The first was that Britain was passing through its capitalist transformation, and during the heyday of colonial rule in India Britain had also become the leading industrial and economic power in the world. Hence the relationship between Britain and India was not only that of rulers and the ruled, but also of a capitalist economy and a pre-capitalist one. In this sense the British were the first 'superior' power to rule over India. Secondly, British public opinion at this time was dominated by the economic philosophy of the English classical economists, Adam Smith and David Ricardo, and also by James Mill and James Stuart Mill. In the domestic sphere, it was known as *laissez-faire* which, in effect, meant that the economy performed best when it was left to its own devices and that the role of the state was essentially to provide the infrastructural and institutional conditions for free enterprise. In the international sphere, it called for specialisation by each country in those areas where it had comparative advantage and to enter into free trade on that basis. Both these—Britain's role as a rapidly industrialising capitalist country, and the wide acceptance of laissez-faire philosophy—had their impact on the British administration in India.

As we have already noted, during the early days of the East India Company's contacts with India, it was in the nature of two countries entering into trade, something that India was quite familiar with. It is better to say that that relationship, in fact, was very little between two countries, but between merchants of two countries. The Company's political and administrative role came later and gradually becoming prominent after the collapse of the Mughal empire. Towards the end of the eighteenth century, the Company established its administrative power over different parts of the country, particularly centring around the three major ports, Calcutta, Bombay and Madras which became the capital cities of the three Presidencies. But with the Crown taking over the administration, India became a part of the British Empire and from then on the assumption was that India's economy would become complementary to that of Britain. There was no attempt to thwart the development of the Indian economy. On the contrary, in order to secure benefits from possessing India, it was thought necessary that some development should take place in the Indian economy. What was official policy could be best summed up in the words of an unofficial spokesman who said: 'We have machinery and steam power for weaving; India has the cultivators and land for growing cotton without limits. Why should our looms ever stand idle, or the Indian expose his bare back to the sun?'[10] This meant that India should specialise in agriculture—not agriculture in general, but of industrial raw material arising from agriculture, raw cotton, raw silk, jute, tobacco, indigo etc.— and trade her produce with Britain in return for her manufactured goods. Thus the growth of commercial crops seen earlier was very much part of a well thought-out pattern of economic growth. Other policies supplemented it. Among them the most prominent was the opening up of the country through a network of railway lines and roads. The early railway lines were all from the major ports to their immediate hinterlands, and even the rate structure initially was in favour of carrying the raw materials to the ports. Many of the roads constructed were feeder lines going into the interior to carry British manufactured goods into all parts of the country. That the British administration in India would be more concerned about British interests than Indian interests is hardly surprising, but some of the measures taken saw the state sacrificing 'principles' to promote British interests. Thus, although the laissez-faire principle wanted the state to refrain from the economic sphere, the British administration in India took a keen interest—selectively—in economic affairs. As noted already, great deal of official encouragement and support was given to the plantation industry. For the construction of railways private companies were given a guaranteed return on investment. At one stage the state took a direct part in railway construction. Similarly the 'principle' of free trade did not stand in the way of imposing tariff duties on Indian goods imported into Britain, at one stage as high as 75 per cent.

From time to time, principles were also given up in favour of India, however haltingly and grudgingly it was done. After Tata started the iron and steel industry in 1907 and it was followed by some other industrial enterprises by Indian entrepreneurs, there was considerable pressure in the country for a positive programme of industrialisation. During the First World War it became clear also that the industrialisation of India was a strategic necessity as well. So the government set up an Industrial Commission in 1916 which called on the government to initiate a policy of energetic intervention in favour of industrial growth. Subsequently a Fiscal Commission in 1921 recommended that some form of protection had to be provided if India's infant industries had to have a chance against powerful competition from established industrial concerns in other parts of the world. Consequently a policy of discriminating protection was initiated in 1923 from which several Indian industries benefited.

But imperial interests were not to be sacrificed. After the First World War the British share in imports by India began to decline, a major reason for which was the new Japanese competition. Unable to defend her position by competition in the open market, Britain was obliged to use her political power and force India to give preference to British goods. In order to hide its true intentions and convey the impression of reciprocity and mutuality, the proposal carried the imposing name of 'Imperial Preference'!

British rule—detrimental or beneficial?

A question that has been discussed for a long time and continues to be debated even now is whether the British rule in India was detrimental or beneficial to the Indian economy. As early as 1871, Dadabhai Navroji linked up the poverty of India to the *un*-British rule of the British.[11] Nationalist sentiments later made it clear that Britain was exploiting India and that British capitalist development was built in no small measure on the drain of resources from India. 'The Drain Theory' had played a powerful role in the nationalist argument against the British.[12] But in more recent times some scholars, especially foreigners, have tried to show that whatever may have happened to food production and to the traditional artisans, India showed considerable industrial progress during the days of *pax Britannica*, and did fairly well overall.[13] Another argument has been that since under the British India was essentially a private enterprise economy, the British administration could not have been responsible for whatever happened in the economy, and that if economic progress was retarded, Indian entrepreneurship (or the lack of it) should bear the responsibility.[14]

We shall not try to settle this issue, but shall draw attention only to some facts and factors which have a bearing on it. Let us note first that the British did not generate poverty in India. We have seen that even before the colonial period the vast majority of the people of the country lived on the borders of subsistence, though there were a few whose affluence and luxury were well known in the country and outside. Secondly, the British were in India not to help the development of the Indian economy. Britain was a colonial and imperial power, and the main interest of the British administration in India was to strengthen and develop the British economy. And as an imperial power Britain certainly did not hesitate to use India, its economy and people for imperial purposes. India may have been thought of as a jewel by some, but it was to be a jewel in the Crown. To give just one example, the cost of the British administration included, as was pointed out by a British observer, 'the cost of a ball for the Sultan of Turkey when he came to London in 1868, a lunatic asylum in Ealing, gifts to members of the Zanzibar mission, diplomatic expenses of the Mediterranian fleet and the communication between Britain and India. The net result of all this brought into existence a home debt of £30,000,000 between 1857 and 1860 alone'.[15] And an Indian observer was to point out: 'The single city of Manchester in the supply of its inhabitants with the single article of water has spent a larger sum of money than the East India Company has spent in the last 14 years from 1834 to 1848 in public works of every kind throughout the whole of its vast dominion'.[16]

Thirdly, there need be little doubt that even if it could be shown that the living of an *average* Indian may have improved during the British period, such an average hides the fact that the lives of many, possibly the vast majority, would have become poorer and more precarious while a few could have definitely become better off also as a result of all the changes that took place during the British rule.

Fourthly, while the aggressive commercialisation of the colonial period threw out many from their traditional patterns of livelihood, the British administration was not active enough to encourage the growth of modern industries to absorb even a fraction of those who were thus displaced. It is a poor argument to say that if industries did not develop, the blame must rest with the native industrialists alone.[17] With the possible exception of Britain itself where the Industrial Revolution first took place, there is no other country in the world (including the United States of America, for instance) where modern industries took roots and grew up without sustained and active support of the state.

And lastly, because India became subservient to Britain, India's international trade also came to be linked too closely with that country. India had the potential to have a diversified and multilateral pattern of international economic links but was forced into restricted bilateralism by the British.

From the point of view of the present study, the more important issue is to decide how the transformation of the Indian economy that came about during the colonial period is to be interpreted. The first thing that strikes us is the enormous increase in merchant and commercial activity that took place throughout that period. The British (or any other earlier colonial groups) did not introduce trade and commerce into India. On the contrary, one of the main reasons why the European colonialists turned to India was because the Indian economy already had a flourishing trade and, under the Mughals had also become quite monetized. However the commercialisation of the British period brought about two major changes.

The first was that prior to the colonial period trade was primarily an activity chain based on (the non-commercial) transfer of surplus from the producers to the rentiers. In other words, the activity chain that manifested itself as the horizontal transaction of buyers and sellers arose from the vertical activity chain linking producers and rentiers. Another way of putting this is that the day to day activities of most of the producers remained outside commercial activities. This began to change quite visibly during the colonial period, especially in the case of many non-food necessities of life as witnessed by the collapse of the non-commercial arrangements for the provision of clothes and the services of the village artisans. Secondly, even where (as we have already noticed) weavers and oil producers had moved into the commercial realm before the colonial era, these were rather limited and more in the nature of the search for the acquisition of use values by entering into exchange. These groups, in other words, remained primarily producers becoming traders only to a limited extent. If we combine these two aspects of commercialisation we can see that one feature of the transformation that took place during the colonial period was a shift in emphasis from use value as the organising principle of the economy to exchange value as the main quest. Some, like the cultivators were forced into it; others like those who ceased to be producer-merchants to become merchants did it because they found the change in the economic environment conducive to do so; yet others, like the traditional artisans became its victims.

Now, the increase in commercialisation—or the growth of trade and markets—is not a socially neutral phenomenon. Even if we grant that those directly involved in an exchange transaction must benefit by it (otherwise why should they enter into what is, after all, voluntarily participated in activity), when commercialisation spreads in an economy some obviously benefit by it, but others may stand to lose. The latter consists of those whose customary claims come to be displaced by the commercial principle and those who find that they own virtually nothing that can be commoditised. In particular, when commercialisation is accompanied by changes in the ownership concept which makes it exclusive, rather than inclusive, as happened (or was deliberately brought about) during the colonial period, many become the victims of commercialisation. The colonial period initiated this process which has continued into the post-Independence period also, as we shall see in subsequent chapters.

There is another aspect of commercialisation that makes it socially non-neutral. Even among those who have resources, not everyone can take advantage of what may be described as 'market opportunities'. The 'tastes and preferences' of British textile manufacturers led to an increase in the demand for Indian cotton. But not all Indian cultivators could respond to that situation. Only those who had land suited for the cultivation of cotton, whose land was fairly close to a port and who could get the credit to take up a new line of cultivation could benefit by it. Thus resource specificities and resource strength are important to take advantage of commercialisation and where these, particularly the latter, are uneven, the benefits that can be obtained through commercialisation could also be uneven. In the case of the Indian cotton boom of the second half of the nineteenth century, for instance, those producers who could afford to take their produce to a bigger market could expect to get a higher price than those who had no option but to sell it to the village trader. Those who could afford to get the cotton ginned and graded could expect to do even better.

We have seen also that once trade becomes generalised, it becomes the natural avenue for the growth of merchant capitalism; exchange leads to specialisation in exchange and that leads to accumulation of exchange value through exchange. Within merchant capitalism there is no equalising tendency at all, and generally, the one which has larger resource power to begin with is at an initial advantage which is easy to perpetuate and augment. In a traditional economic system with disparities in resource power, the acceleration of commercialisation, therefore, sets in motion a simultaneous process of disruption *and* accumulation which ruins many and benefits some. The transformation of the Indian economy that took place during the colonial period was of this kind. It left behind an economy battered by commercialisation but not strengthened by industrialisation.

But a more unified Indian economy emerged than was ever the case before. The railways and roads constructed had not only opened up the economy, but has linked it up territorially and functionally. The movements of people and goods gave the economy a coherence that it had never seen before. A well organised monetary and banking system contributed further to the closer linking-up of units and activities in the economy. And, of course, it was also brought much more into the sphere of international economic forces. But the economy was far from fully integrated. Though the British currency system was clearly dominant, several of the major native states had currencies of their own. The movement of goods across these internal political boundaries was not completely free either. There were different kinds of weights and measures in different parts of the country. And while the banking system was widespread with a central bank (the Reserve Bank of India) to control and coordinate them, indigenous credit institutions and agencies were far more important as far as the bulk of the producers and traders were concerned. In spite of the introduction of modern technology and production organisations, the age-old technologies and production patterns also continued. Altogether, what had emerged over a period of some two centuries was indeed a very complex and cumbersome entity.

NOTES

1. See CEHI, 1984 and Pavlov, 1979.
2. Refer Burton Stein, 'South India: Some General Considerations of the Region and its Early History' in CEHI, 1984, I.
3. Reference may be made to Washbrook, 1976, Kurien and James, 1979, Baker, 1984.
4. On the significance of specificities in understanding traditional economies see Pandian, 1990.
5. Irfan Habib, 'Agrarian Relations and Land Revenue' in CEHI, 1984, I: 247.
6. James Forbes, an official of the East India Company quoted in Pavlov, 1979: 53.
7. See Kumar, 1965.
8. Quoted in Gadgil, 1971: 42.
9. H.C. Cookson quoted in Gadgil, 1971: 41.
10. Quoted in Ambirajan, 1978: 219.
11. Dadabhai Navroji published his classic work *Poverty and Un-British Rule in India* in 1871.
12. See Ganguli, 1977, esp. Ch. Six for a discussion of the 'Drain Theory'.
13. On this aspect see W.I. Macpherson, 'Economic Development in India under the British Crown, 1858–1947' in Youngson, 1972.
14. This view is expressed by Morris D. Morris, 'The Growth of Large-Scale Industry to 1947' in CEHI, 1984, II.
15. Quoted in Davey, 1975: 82.
16. R.C. Dutt, quoted in Davey, 1975: 67.
17. See Bagchi, 1972.

Notes to Tables

The source of Table 8.1 is Pavlov, 1979: 61; the source of Table 8.2 is Pavlov, 1979: 280; the source of Table 8.3 is Thorner, 1962: 105.

For different views on the colonial impact on India see Dutt, 1947 and Baker, 1984.

9
Indian Economy since Independence

The ongoing capitalist transformation of the Indian economy under the leadership of state power is taken up in this chapter. The nature of that transformation is concretely illustrated with the help of the experience of some selected villages for which information is available from the early twentieth century. It is seen that till Independence there were no major changes in these villages, but that since independence, especially from the early 1960s, they came to have many changes each in its own specific ways. An increase in production, a greater diversification of production and a pronounced differentiation of the members of the villages are seen to be the common features.

Against that background and making use of the frame developed in Chapter 7, the transformation is analysed in terms of the changes taking place in the units–and–links activity chains in the system, featuring the dominant role of capitalist forces, especially of merchant capitalism. The nature of market relationships emerging is described and examined. The 'unorganised sector' of the economy which provides employment for the bulk of the labour force and accounts for a substantial proportion of the output is studied showing its connections with the 'organised sector'. The role of the state in the economy is also brought out.

The division of the treatment of the economy into two distinct periods, pre-Independence and post-Independence is based, in a sense, more on political factors than on economic considerations. No sudden change came about in the Indian economy during the early hours of August 15, 1947, or in the months and years immediately following that date. But there was a transfer of political power and administration from the British to the Indian people, and in that sense, the centre of gravity was shifted back into India. And while that could not have altered the structure of the economy, it must have given a shift of emphasis. In this chapter we shall examine that aspect. The discussion will only be initiated in this chapter; many of the manifestations of the transformation will be taken up in the subsequent chapters.

TRANSFORMATION AT THE VILLAGE LEVEL

In order to get acquainted with the process of transformation as concretely as possible we shall first look into the experience of three villages. Obviously these villages have been selected not because they represent what has been going on in the hundreds of thousands of villages in the country. In fact a truly representative account is virtually impossible. But the experiences of the three villages may indicate something of the diversity of patterns of change, even though the three belong to a single state in the country. They will show also that the Indian economy must be viewed not only in terms of its global aggregates—as is frequently done—but also in terms of its many components, their elementary units and groupings at different levels and according to different criteria. Our attempt in this chapter and the chapters that follow will be to unscramble what is described as the Indian economy in different ways so as to understand and appreciate its complexity; this will not be seen if it is approached only as a consolidated entity, though that too serves some purpose. For the unscrambling we shall keep in mind the guidelines given in Chapter 7, as also the availability of information and data.

The choice of the three villages discussed below has been determined by the kind of information available about them. They belong to what have come to be known as the *Slater villages*. Gilbert Slater was appointed in December 1915 to head the newly started Department of Economics in the University of Madras. He found it distressing that the learning of economics in Madras at that time consisted of 'a series of unintelligible theories to be learnt parrot fashion from Marshall's *Principles*' and felt that the central object of the study of economics in the country should be to understand 'the causes and remedies for Indian Poverty'; and that this could be achieved by directing the attention of students towards the study of particular villages—their own villages to the extent possible. Slater succeeded in conducting such village studies from 1916 to 1918 in different parts of what was then Madras Presidency and brought them out in a publication with the title *Some South Indian Villages* (Slater, 1918). These villages were resurveyed in 1936–37 and also in the late 1950s, and there was a kind of quick reappraisal in 1961. Five of these villages, which are now in Tamil Nadu, were again studied between 1981 and 1983 under the auspices of the Madras Institute of Development Studies and the three villages we have chosen are from among them.[1] What we shall attempt is to reconstruct the 'initial conditions' of these villages based on available information and then concentrate on the kind of changes they have experienced since independence.

Iruvelpattu

Iruvelpattu, about 12 kms south of the commercial town of Villupuram in South Arcot district, was the first to be surveyed by Slater and his students as well as the first to be resurveyed in the 1981–83 period. In the early decades of the century its population was around 1,000 divided (as most villages in those days were and continue to be) into a main section, the residential area of caste Hindus and a *cheri* of Harijans. The high castes were mainly Reddiars who were originally from the Telugu region and constituted about 5 per cent of the population. The cultivating castes of Vanniars and others were some 60 per cent, the rest being Harijans.

The village relied on rainfall (about 90 cms per annum received mainly during the N.E. monsoon period) and tank irrigation for cultivation and ne rly 80 per cent of the cultivated land was under paddy. Some millet and groundnut were also cultivated and sugarcane cultivation started in 1920. Out of the total cultivated area of some 650 acres, close to 400 acres belonged to one wealthy family which also owned 200 acres in adjoining villages. The family directly cultivated about 200 acres with the help of workers who were dependent on its land and let out the remainder to tenants. Most of the other owners had less than five acres of land. Details of tenancy are not available for the early decades, but when the village was resurveyed in 1937, about 400 acres had been leased out to 161 tenants of whom 37 owned some land of their own and 124 were landless. Fixed rent was the dominant form of tenancy accounting for 64 per cent of leased land, and the rest was under share-cropping, for which the landlord gave seeds on loan which was repaid in kind at the time of the harvest with interest amounting to 100 per cent.

The village had some carpenters, blacksmiths, potters and goldsmiths who were probably given some land for cultivation. There was a sense of community in the village which was partly expressed in the *Kudimaramat* system whereby all families owning land contributed labour for the upkeep of the tanks and the channels. There was also a 'common fund of the village' which arose from the sale of the right to fish in the village tank and to gather fruits from the tamarind trees. Village festivals were financed out of the common funds.

But the village life was dominated by the one wealthy family which in 1916 had a house which was 'imposing, with two storeys, a flat roof, a covered approach, ornamental gates and pillars adorned with paintings'. This must have stood in striking contrast to the other dwellings in the village, especially in the *Cheri* where the huts were 'made of a framework of sticks, the roofs thatched with palm leaves, and the walls also woven, as it were, of leaves and twigs'.

Changes in the village were rather slow till the early 1960s after which they were very rapid and quite visible. Electricity was brought to the village in the late fifties. New roads connected the village to the neighbouring town. When the village was resurveyed in 1981 there were 78 wells in private ownership of which 65 were electrified and 13 were operated with oil engines. With the availability of well water, agricultural practices had also changed. Hardly any commercial fertiliser was used in the village, at least till the resurvey of 1937 when organic manure was estimated to account for Rs. 4 in the total cultivation cost of Rs. 22 per acre of paddy (of which Rs. 10 went as wage payments). By 1981 total cost of cultivation per acre of paddy had gone up to Rs. 1841 with wage accounting for Rs. 456, fertilisers and pesticides Rs. 587 and electricity Rs. 503. With the use of 'miracle' seeds also total output of paddy increased from 1110 kgs. in the earlier period to 2330 kgs.

There was other evidence of progress in the village—a couple of tractors, cars and a truck, an upgrading of the village school and the beginning of a primary health centre. But if the change that came about in the village is unscrambled, it can be seen that what appears as the prosperity of the village is largely the affluence that the descendant of the wealthy family had come to have. At the time of the 1981 resurvey he owned 39 per cent of the land (although a large part of it was registered in the names of the servants, attached labourers and tenants). He also owned 35 houses in the village other than his own residence, and 28 of the 78 pumpsets in the village. The tractors, cars and truck seen in the village belonged to him. He also had a rice mill, urban properties, shares and other financial assets. The affluence did not come all of a sudden and was achieved through a variety of ways. The family kept buying land whenever someone in the village was in distress, and had to sell. That the landlord was also village munsif from 1950 to 1967 certainly helped in this as also to persuade the State Government to 'acquire' some of his land at market price just on the eve of the land ceiling act of 1960. When electricity came to the village in 1958 he was, naturally, the first to get connection both for domestic purposes as well as for cultivation. This early start enabled him to escape subsequent restrictions about ground water utilisation and thus came to have effective control over the ground water that was available in the village and which had now become his private property. In turn he was able to put this control over ground water to his advantage. He came to be in a position to make 'his' surplus water available to neighbours who were in need of water for their cultivation, especially after the tank in the village came to be neglected as the landlord did not have much interest in it any more. He was able to combine the modern ground water facility with the traditional share-cropping principle and charge one of his tenants rent not only for land leased out, but also for water made available, 400 kgs. of paddy as land rent and 780 kgs. as 'water rent' out of a gross output of 2300 kgs. As he, thus, emerged as both traditional landlord and new water-lord, his influence in the village and the neighbourhood increased, and he was elected to the Legislative Assembly in 1967, and was able to use the new position to retain effective control over the Village Panchayat and the

Cooperative Society. He was also in a position to corner the rights on the common tank and over the reeds and encash them for about Rs. 13,000 per annum. However, he was not totally selfish. He was responsible for getting the public health centre and a veterinary sub-centre established in the village and got a new building constructed for the village school. He also makes a liberal contribution to the annual temple festival. Hence as the authors of the 1981 resurvey have observed he has, 'more or less, become a one-man version of the common fund that Slater had taken to be a striking evidence of village solidarity in the process replacing solidarity with hegemony'. What this hegemony can do when the need arises was shown in early 1982. At the time of the harvest, the labourers in the village planned to have a strike to press for higher wages. Getting to know about it the landlord imported labour from outside the village and got his harvest done in record time without any 'help' from the rebellious workers!

While the landlord and his family, thus, came to benefit immensely as a result of development, modernisation and all the changes that came about, there was no major change in the earnings and living conditions of the agricultural labourers in the village. Between the mid 1930s and the early 1980s harvest wages might have gone up in real terms but real wages for transplanting and weeding either stagnated or declined. And on the basis of two adults per family taken as workers and on the rather heroic assumption that they would find work all through the year, the families of the agricultural labourers would still be below the nationally recognised poverty line. Cultivators operating less than two acres of land without access to pumpsets would also be in the same plight.

Vadamalaipuram

Vadamalaipuram, located some 5 kms away from Sivakasi town, now well known for its match and fireworks industries, was in the early part of the present century a village consisting of about 250 households and a total population of close to 1200. It was an agricultural village which depended on rainfed tanks for the water required for cultivation. Because of scarcity of rainfall (about 75 cms a year obtained mostly in the months of September, October and November) cultivation was essentially dryland farming with paddy, ragi and cumbu being the main crops, but with some cotton, chillies and tobacco also being produced. The first survey of the village in 1916 noted that it was '...very difficult to find in the village people who own no land except the actual labourers and some of the artisan classes'. Among these labourers there were 53, all males, who were permanent labourers; there were also some 45 male and 50 to 60 female casual labourers. There were also 8 who were tied to their landlord employer by debt-bondage. Land was very unequally distributed. Foodgrains were produced mostly for own consumption. The permanent labourers were provided three meals a day and an annual cash payment while the casual labourers were generally paid in cash. The cotton produced was taken by the cultivators to the neighbouring town of Sattur and Virudhunagar to be sold to the agents of ginning companies. Chillies and tobacco were sold to merchants who visited the village regularly.

Even in 1916 Vadaimalaipuram was a progressive village with an elementary school offering free education which enrolled 30 pupils including five girls with even a few Harijans. There was also a flourishing cooperative society and functioning village administration.

The set up of the village continued more or less in the same manner till the late 1950s with the 1958 resurvey noting that agriculture—either own cultivation or agricultural labour for others—was almost the sole occupation except for some traditional arts and crafts. But by 1958 the population of the village had come down to around 800 indicating that there must have been a flow of people out of the village.

Between 1958 and the resurvey of 1983 there were many striking changes in the village. The occupational structure changed as can be seen from Table 9.1.

Table 9.1: *Vadamalaipuram—Occupational Profile, 1958 & 1983*

Occupation	Share of workforce male (p.c.)		Share of workforce female (p.c.)	
	1958	1983	1958	1983
Cultivator	40.74	18.30	18.56	23.35
Ag. Labourers	30.56	25.77	73.20	31.14
Arts & Crafts	3.24	2.62	0.0	2.69
Manufacturing, Processing & Repairs	3.70	28.61	1.03	33.23
Other Services	21.76	24.69	7.22	9.59

This shift out of agriculture (cultivation in the case of males and labour in the case of females) into manufacturing came about because a spinning mill was started near the village in 1967 and four match factories also came up. By 1983 the mill was employing 70 male workers from Vadamalaipuram and the match factories 124 workers, of whom 101 were females. Similarly 106 men and 41 women were employed in construction, trade and commerce, transport, storage, communications and other services. Within agriculture, the proportion between cultivators and agricultural labourers changed only marginally. But agricultural technology experienced a major change. Bullocks in the village came down from 96 in 1958 to 43 in 1983 and ploughs from 57 to 23 and carts from 18 to 15. But electric pumpsets increased from 20 to 87 and three tractors had also been bought. Chemical fertilisers and pesticides were also in common use by 1983. As a result the yields increased markedly: paddy from 980 kgs. per acre in 1958 to 1670 kgs. in 1983; cotton from 157 kgs. to 503 kgs.; chillies from 301 kgs. to 683 kgs.; ragi from 603 kgs. to 1010 kgs. and cumbu from 300 kgs. to 910 kgs.

Marketing of the produce also increased. While in the case of paddy only 10 per cent of the total output was sold, in the case of cumbu and ragi 50 per cent of the produce found its way to the market. Onion became a commercial crop of considerable importance, with the quantity sold increasing enormously between 1958 and 1983. A new cash crop, sunflower also entered the scene.

Land distribution had already become quite concentrated by 1958 with the top 14 per cent of households each owning 20 acres or more accounting for nearly 40 per cent of the area owned while 28 per cent of households owning less than five acres each had only 7.6 per cent of the land. The number of holdings exceeding 15 acres declined from 21 in 1958 to 15 in 1983. But there was a great proliferation of holdings below 5 acres from 26 in 1958 to 70 in 1983. Land prices also increased as also transactions in land. Because of the demand for land from the industrial concerns it was the price of the near-useless land along the roadside that came to fetch fancy prices.

Wage payments had become substantially monetised by 1958 and although wages in money terms had gone up, in terms of purchasing power the 1958 wages were significantly lower than in 1916 and 1937. But wages moved up by 1958, but they were no higher than what they had been in 1916 and for casual labourers, definitely lower than in 1916. There was definite increase in agricultural wages between 1958 and 1983 due mainly to the growth of non-agricultural employment opportunities. However, because the duration of agricultural employment was limited, the per capita earning of agricultural labour households in 1983 was considerably below the rural poverty line.

Dusi

Dusi is a village in North Arcot district in the neighbourhood of Kancheepuram town, noted for its temples and silk sarees. It is a very old settlement which can trace its history as far back as the sixth century AD when the Pallava kings used to station their cavalry in the area giving the place its name which in Tamil means 'dust'.

At the beginning of the present century it was a habitation of some 1200 people dominated by the Naicker caste but also with a sizeable presence of Brahmins and some Muslims, but with no Harijans. It must have been a village of above average means considering that out of 251 houses at the time of the 1916 survey, 71 were tiled or terraced. There was also an elementary school with 61 boys, 22 girls and two teachers.

Dusi receives a rainfall of a little over 100 cms per annum of which 47 per cent comes during the North East monsoon and 43 per cent during the South West monsoon. It .was a predominantly agricultural village. 'No industry at all in the village excepting agriculture and the minor crafts of the carpenter and other smiths', noted the first survey. Agriculture too was mainly paddy cultivation which claimed 93 per cent of the gross cultivated area, the other crops being millets and pulses. Paddy cultivation was partly rain-fed and partly dependent on tank irrigation. Paddy was marketed in the village to commission dealers who came to the village to buy the grain and sold it in the neighbouring town market.

Brahmins were the main land owners with a share of 64 per cent of the land. Naickers came next to them. More than 500 acres or over 70 per cent of cultivable land was under tenancy of which 80 per cent was share-cropping. The standard arrangement was that the tenant would contribute the labour and the landlord all other inputs with one-sixth of the produce going to the tenant and the rest to the landlord.

Changes in the village started in the 1920s and 1930s when some weavers came to settle there. But it was from the early 1960s that the character of the village began to change. There was an out-migration of the Brahmins who sold their land to their tenants. Naickers are now the major land owners who by the early 1980s came to have over 70 per cent of the land. There has been a general reduction in the inequality in the distribution of land. Between the period of the first survey of the village and the latest resurvey, households owning 10 acres or more decreased in number from 15 to 8 and their total share in land ownership went down from 25 to 9 per cent. The largest owner in 1913 held over 70 acres while his counterpart in 1983 had about 31 acres. At the same time, marginal farmers (owning less than 2.5 acres) increased from 59 per cent to 80 per cent of all owners with their share of land going up from 17 per cent to 40 per cent. The landless now constitute 58 per cent of the total households, but most of them are weavers and engaged in other non-agricultural operations. Tenancy too has continued, though not as widespread as was the case in the early period.

The most striking change in the village has been in terms of occupational pattern. In the early 1980s out of a total workforce of a little over 1500, only 42 per cent were engaged in agriculture. Weavers constituted 36 per cent and non-agricultural activities other than weaving accounted for the rest. This last category included 84 traders, 49 salaried people, 35 in cattle tending, 28 in traditional crafts, 24 in bidi manufacturing, 17 in repairs and maintenance, 16 in tailoring and 92 in other activities—a very remarkable diversification indeed for a village which less than a century ago had only agricultural activity. But this diversification did not imply economic prosperity as between 60 and 70 per cent of the non-weaving households and a very large proportion of the weavers too are below the poverty line.

One of the major aspects of the transformation of Dusi has been the emergence of weaving especially since about the early 1960s. A major reason for this, of course, is the propinquity of the village to Kancheepuram which, as mentioned already, is a well-known centre for silk weaving. Weaving, in a sense, is a traditional caste industry, but the weavers in Dusi are predominantly from non-weaving castes, especially Vanniar Naickers, who found silk weaving an attractive avenue. Many of them sent a member of the family—usually a child—to train as a silk weaver so that the family could combine agriculture and weaving. Many of the weaver families do not possess looms, but work for a wage on looms belonging to others. Practically all weavers operate under master-weavers in Kancheepuram. The master-weaver purchases yarn, has it warped and dyed to a prepared design and gives the warp to the weaver who is then paid a piece rate. The marketing of the woven material is done by the master-weaver. Weavers with looms of their own do better than those without their own looms, and as many belong to the latter class they are very dependent on the master-weavers for work and livelihood.

The experience of the three villages gives us a feel of the kind of transformation at the ground level since Independence characterised by larger interactions with 'others', technological progress and modernisation, increase in production and productivity, greater diversification and differentiation. The three villages, although within one State, show different patterns of change and there are bound to be a great many more differences of experience. But underlying most of these are some common threads.

These can be conveyed by the concluding observations of the Report of the 1983 Resurvey of the Vadamalaipuram village:

The overall picture that one gets is thus of some major structural changes in the economy of the village, of which the most important are the modernisation of agriculture and the rise of manufacturing activity. However, these changes have taken place within the constraints of a highly unequal distribution of land and other assets, and of political and social power as well. The new technology has made agriculture profitable for the dominant landowners while the small cultivators have been caught in the trap of increasing costs on the one hand, and unremunerative and sharply fluctuating prices for the produce on the other. The bigger landowners have also been able to cushion themselves to some extent against the vagaries of nature and product market by diversifying into professional employment. The biggest among them have found a lucrative new source of income in the business of hiring out tractors. For the landless agricultural labourers the new technology has been of little benefit with a decline in number of days of employment offsetting the increase in wages.

The rise of manufacturing has been a positive factor in enabling many agricultural labour and small cultivator households to survive, both directly by the employment it has provided and indirectly by inducing a rise in wages of agricultural labour.[2]

Some of these observations are very specific to Vadamalaipuram, but the role of resource power in directing the process of change benefiting from it has been common to Iruvelpattu also, and has been more pronounced there. In fact it is one of the major features of the post-Independence transformation of the Indian economy overall as we shall see from the rest of this chapter as well as from the chapters to follow.

There is another underlying feature of the transformation of the economy that the experience of the three villages bring out, viz., the role of the state. On this the Vadamalaipuram Resurvey Report goes on to say:

The ongoing process of modernisation assisted by state intervention has helped improve social structure, but here again the major beneficiaries have been the land owning strata.... Through all the changes that have occurred, the bigger land owners have kept their position intact and have enriched themselves. This should, of course, be hardly surprising since the changes have taken place within the context of a prior distribution of the ownership of means of production, and on the basis of the rules of the game that protect and reinforce the ownership-structure. State intervention too has scrupulously respected the rules of the game, and more often than not, actively intervened on behalf of the economically and socially dominant stratum.[3]

The role of differential resource power and the effort of the state to usher in economic changes without seriously altering the structure of resource power—these will be the two basic features that we shall have to pay attention to in trying to understand the working of the Indian economy since Independence. In the next section we shall try to see how the former defines and permeates a wide variety of interactions in the economy.

TRANSFORMATION IN TERMS OF ACTIVITY CHAINS

We shall, in the rest of this chapter, rely on the micro-global approach outlined in Chapter 7 to probe further into the post-Independence transformation. The basic elements of that approach are units and their links, or the activity chains. In Chapter 8 we traced how the traditional pre-capitalist units of the Indian economy and the activity chains associated with them underwent major changes with the introduction of capitalist units, and trade associated with capitalist economies elsewhere. That transformation was essentially a destructive one from the point of view of many of the pre-capitalist units which got delinked from their traditional activity chains, but were not incorporated into those that were being newly evolved. But our account of the three villages has shown many strong and positive elements of the more active capitalist transformation that has been going on since Independence arising from the fact that capitalist processes became much more internal to the country and had the backing of the state. There were some negative aspects as well. We shall postpone a full evaluation of the processes to Chapter 11. Here we shall concentrate on the processes themselves. These processes, as we noted in Chapter 7, will not be pure types of pre-capitalist or capitalist interactions, but various expressions of their inter-penetration.

Two examples may be mentioned. In pre-capitalist agriculture the relationship between those who own land and those who do not is essentially one of dominance and dependence of a fairly long duration which make the latter to become 'attached' to the former. A capitalist transformation must result in the emergence of 'free' labour, that is, workers who are free to sell their labour power to any employer of their choice, the price of the commodity offered for sale being the only consideration in that choice. In contemporary India we shall come across relationships which lie within a fairly broad spectrum within these two typical and pure cases. Or, to view it from the other side, a typical capitalist production unit is one where workers are hired for specific periods of time for stipulated wages and where all workers work in the same location, the factory. Such capitalist units were started in India even during the pre-Independence period and they have grown at a rapid rate since Independence. But in the Indian context there are other ways of achieving the capitalist objective of accumulating exchange value and one of them includes the preservation of and encouragement to pre-capitalist organisations of production. We shall examine some variants of this alternative that are prevalent in India today.

In this chapter we shall try to capture the nature of the variety of overlapping activity chains that have evolved as the economy experiences a capitalist transformation which, of necessity, has to interact with many pre-capitalist arrangements. For locating and understanding these activity chains we rely on specific instances. Again, the cases that we deal with cannot be claimed to be representative of what has been happening. They are essentially illustrative.

There are instances where the traditional and modern activity chains exist side by side without much interaction. Fishing in some parts of the country is an instance of this kind. Three distinctive activity chains—involving different kinds of production units, technology, marketing and user groups—have been identified, referred to as traditional, modern and ultra modern. The traditional sector's fishing activity is carried out by fisherfolk who have been in the trade for generations. They depend on technology which is completely non-mechanical consisting of locally made *kattamarams* and canoes with nets also locally manufactured and described as 'low in productivity, pollution and depletion'. The fishermen of this sector confine themselves near the sea shores and the fish they catch is meant mainly for the low-income consumers in the locality. The fish is carried to these customers as head loads or on bicycles. The modern sector is dominated by those who were initially associated with the fish industry either as big fishermen or as merchants. They use mechanised boats and improved varieties of nets. They try to cater to a more affluent constituency in the urban areas and hence go in for fish that suits their taste. The fish is transported by lorries or even vans fitted with freezer facilities and the distribution is through specially set-up outlets. The ultra-modern sector emerged in response to demand for shrimp and selected varieties of fish in foreign countries such as the U.S.A. and Japan and hence is taken up by some of the big business houses in the country who consider the export trade in fish a profitable area to enter into. Their production technology consists of trawlers, big boats, and gear of a different nature.[4]

The three sectors of the fish industry may thus be thought of as three distinctly different activity chains without any overlappings. At least this was the case in the early stages when the modern sector and the ultra modern sectors were just emerging. But the 'peaceful coexistence' did not last for long. The fishermen of the traditional sector found it to their advantage to go in for new kinds of nets that the modern sector had introduced. The modern sector started recruiting traditional fishermen as wage labourers in their production activities. The ultra modern sector whose fishing activities were to be in the deep seas, found it advantageous to poach into the territories of the traditional fisherfolk. And the catch did not always go out of the country, as a flourishing market for highly valued fish developed within the country itself. Thus the sectoral boundaries began to disappear.

In terms of the frame developed in Chapter 7, many of these transformations involve the h–2 units. When the pre-capitalist activity chains involving the h–2 units break down, the units may try to retain their characteristics and may grope for other forms of links. We may recall that unlike h–1 units, the h–2 units cannot exist without *some* links with other units. Whether they succeed or not does not depend on their will power alone, but essentially on whether they have enough resource power to continue as producers selling some goods. If they do not succeed they will become h–4 units directly selling their labour power. But selling their labour power may not be easy either, because the demand for labour power may be limited. Hence some *via media* may have to be found. And there are different kinds of organisational patterns that make this possible. This means that there can be temporal movements from h–2 to h–4 (and *vice versa*). Not only that, as mentioned in Chapter 7, the boundary between the units is not very clear cut and so it is more appropriate to think of an h–2 <——> h–4 spectrum with possibilities of overlapping making it difficult to say whether a unit is clearly of the h–2 type or the h–4 type. Neither is that the only possible spectrum. Other possibilities are h–2 <——> f, h–2 <——> h–3, h–2 <——> m. Each one of these can be thought of as different ways in which the differentiation of the units, the emergence of new activity chains and the transformation of the economy come about.

We shall consider some specific instances of this kind concentrating on the h–2 <——> h–4 spectrum.

The *bidi* industry

A clear case is the organization of the *bidi* industry in many parts of the country.[5] Bhandara district in the Vidarbha region of Maharashtra State and Sagar district (geographically close to it, but administratively belonging to Madhya Pradesh) were both originally parts of what was Central Province during the British days. They have been centres of the *bidi* industry from the beginning of the present century. The census of 1931 had stated: 'The bidi factories are the most important of the unregulated establishments of this province.... Approximately 866 of these establishments which manufacture a type of indigenous cigarettes, from Indian tobacco rolled up in tendu leaves, are scattered all over the province and provide employment to about 42,240 persons....' The workers included not only males and females, but also a large number of children. Between 1931 and 1951 there was phenomenal growth of the industry with close to 38 per cent of the workers in the two districts classified as being engaged in *bidi* making in 1951. But the majority of them were shown as 'independent workers' (h–2 units) in sharp contrast to workers in factory units (h–4 units). The main reason for this shift was that the Factory Act of 1929 brought establishments with 20 or more workers under its purview and the owners of factories did not want to come under the pressure of factory inspectors on the one hand and labour unions on the other. The 1981 census recognised 39,334 males and 50,333 females in Bhandara and 55,329 males and 49,004 females in Sagar as *bidi* workers in household industry. In recent decades the leading position that Bhandara has occupied has declined with Sagar showing a rapid increase mainly because *bidi* manufacturers prefer to operate in Sagar where the prescribed minimum wage for *bidi*-rolling is less than in Bhandara. As the figures given above show, the industry has also become female dominated. There is also a predominance of scheduled castes (Harijans) in the industry.

If we look at the *bidi* industry in terms of the finished product, it is one which consists of a few well known companies with whom and whose brand names the product gets identified. But if we view the industry in terms of the production process, it is seen as a highly decentralised industry because the production of *bidis* takes place in hundreds and thousands of households. The *bidi* production unit is, therefore, apparently of the h–2 type. The *bidi* production process is heavily labour intensive, a pair of scissors being the only instrument of production. The leading material inputs in *bidi* production are tobacco, tendu leaves and yarn. The organisation of *bidi* production is to see how these inputs are converted into *bidis* by the 'independent' household producers and then marketed by the big companies. Between these two there are factories which are responsible for collecting, sorting, grading, roasting, labelling and packing of the *bidis* produced, and contractors who mediate between the producers and the factories. There may also be other intermediaries, for instance those who collect the *bidis* and deliver them to the factories. The contractor, known as *sattedar* is the one in direct contact with the producers. He supplies the inputs to the workers and gathers the finished product from them and pays them a stipulated amount for the *bidis* produced, that is, it is a piece-rate arrangement.

The production process consists of cleaning and cutting the tendu leaves according to the required size, rolling the tobacco into the pieces of tendu leaves, turning in the edges of rolled *bidis* and then tying them with the yarn. The finished *bidis* must also be tied in bundles of the required number. All these are extremely labour intensive processes which also provide some scope for division of labour among the members of the family, men, women, and children. This may appear to be very simple and ideal for countries with abundance of unskilled labour power. The processes are, indeed, simple; but the relations or links are highly exploitative.

The pre-capitalist forms of exploitation are quite palpable. The *sattedar* wets the tobacco prior to distributing it to workers in order to make the tobacco heavier so that the actual quantity of tobacco that the workers get is less than what is required for the *bidis* they are expected to make. He distorts the proportion of tobacco and tendu leaves he gives to the workers so that they will run short of one of the crucial inputs and will turn to him to purchase it from him at prices he dictates. If they do not, then he makes a reduction in the payments to be made to them for shortage in the number of *bidis* delivered. He cheats on the number of *bidis* declared to be defective. And since *bidi* production is suspended during the monsoon and the workers have little other means of survival, they turn to him for consumption loans which he gives so as to have effective control over them subsequently. In many instances the *sattedar* is also the local grocer, the village landlord or has some other source of economic and social power.

The *sattedar*'s justification for these actions is usually that he, in turn, faces similar treatment from the company. He is only a commission agent of the company and his services can be terminated at any time. He has to arrange for the bulk purchase of the inputs and for transporting them to the village; he has to have them distributed; he has to take the risk that the products may not be delivered on time or that the quality may be poor. He has to deal with the *relaiwala* who transports the finished bidis to the collection centre and has to meet the expenses. He may have to bribe the counters and checkers to ensure that the quantum of rejection is kept low.

Whatever his position may be, the real squeeze is on the workers. The study we are relying on reports: 'An average household consisting of five members with 2.41 *bidi* workers earns only Rs. 4 per day from *bidi* work. This means the long hours put in to roll *bidis* earns a worker a shockingly low wage of Rs. 1.86 per day'. Some of the *bidi* worker families have other sources of income such as a little plot of land that they may cultivate. But for about one-fifth of the households engaged in *bidi* production it is the only source of livelihood. The government tries to intervene by prescribing minimum wages for *bidi* workers. Frequently these are not observed. Where they are, the consequence appears to be to make production clandestine, resulting in unbranded 'Number Two' *bidis* which make use of workers driven out of employment and the product sold at cheaper rates.

The responsibility of the companies that claim to be manufacturers of *bidis* is primarily to provide the brand name and organise the marketing operations; even the *bidis* that are rejected as poor quality are marketed under different brand names catering to a different clientele. Whatever may be the plight of the actual producers and of the intermediaries, for the companies the *bidi* industry is a very profitable one; some of the leading *bidi* manufacturing concerns are among the more flourishing business establishments in the country!

The general pattern

Similar activity chains linking producers, intermediaries, merchants, manufacturers and consumers of various sorts are seen in many other industries as well.[6] The handloom industry is another example which shows characteristics very similar to what has been described above. The pattern is also widely prevalent in the production and marketing of *zari, papads, masala, agarbatti,* locks, footwear and many other items that enter into daily use. Each one will have some specific aspect of its own. But there are also certain features which are common to all of them. We shall probe into these common features, while basing ourselves on the *bidi* industry.

We must view the phenomenon from below and above, that is, from the perspective of the producing household unit at the lower end and the selling company at the other. The intermediaries can be brought in subsequently. The *bidi* producing household is an h–2 unit whose main concern is the survival of its members. Its organising principle, therefore, is the generation of use value. In order to realise this objective, it must be able to make use of the labour power along with the non-labour resources at its disposal. The production process of *bidi* can be split up into a number of processes such as cutting of the tendu leaves, rolling the tobacco in the pieces, turning in the edges and tying the thread. These, therefore, permit a familial division of labour enabling the labour power of men, women and children, according to their different skills to be utilised in the production process. These arrangements are part of the internal structure of the unit. The unit's quest for use value, however, has to be mediated through exchange because it has to purchase the material inputs required for production—tendu leaves, tobacco and thread—and the *bidis* have to be sold, because the unit needs other goods—food, clothes etc.—from which it derives use value and these have to be purchased. So looking at the *bidi* industry from below, we have use value oriented production units which must, however, go through the exchange process.

Now, looking at the industry from above, we have an f-unit which has resources in the form of liquid capital and whose organising principle is the accumulation of exchange value. In order to accumulate exchange value, it must reach labour power which alone is capable of generating surplus, which must then be converted into surplus value through exchange. There are two options open to it.[7] The first is the 'typical' capitalist procedure of the direct purchase of labour power and material inputs and combining those under supervision in the production process. It involves incurring (at least) two more items of cost, the cost of the place (the factory) where the labour power engages in the production process and the cost of supervision. The second option is to hand over the material inputs to h–2 production units and get back the finished product from them, making a payment to them for the labour power they will expend in the production process. As a unit interested in getting the maximum profit through this process, which one of these two options will the f–unit exercise?

Let us make the reasonable assumption that irrespective of the option exercised, the *bidis* can be sold for a certain specified price. Hence the f unit must go in for the cheaper option where its costs for the entire process can be minimised. The second option of 'putting out' has two clear cost advantages as far as the f-unit is concerned; it can save on the cost of the factory as well as on the cost of supervision. The latter is achieved by entering into a 'piece rate' arrangement with the h–2 units. They will not be paid per unit of time (as is usually the case if they are brought in for work in a factory where wages are specified by the day, for instance) but of the product delivered*(let us say 1000 *bidis* of acceptable quality). There is a further advantage to the f unit via this option. A daily wage rate given in a factory is for a specified number of hours (at present eight hours in most cases), but through the piece rate system it is possible to get more hours of work done because the h–2 units do not usually have clearly specified hours of work. (We may recall the difficulty of defining 'work' in the context of household production units.) On the basis of these considerations we may infer that for the f unit the second option of 'putting out' is likely to be more advantageous.

How would the h–2 units view these two options of becoming h–4 units and working in a factory or of remaining h–2 units and working at home? The latter has certain advantages—one can set one's own pace of work, there is the opportunity of putting to use longer hours of labour power and the labour power of different members of the household. Of course, the incovenience of converting the household premises into a work place and of sacrificing leisure time for work must be set against these. But we must recall (from Chapter 2) that units with little non-labour resources and not much above the survivor limit are not likely to give very high preference to leisure because they cannot afford it. If so the h–2 units may also prefer the putting out option. There are other advantages also that the h–2 units can achieve through this option. They do not have to purchase the material inputs and do not have to bother about the sale of *bidis*; the latter, in particular, is likely to be a major consideration for h–2 units which are essentially production units, drawn into exchange and marketing only out of necessity.

In one sense, therefore, the rationale behind the arrangement in the *bidi* industry (and the other instances of a similar kind that we have examined) is that both the units at the bottom and the unit at the top find it advantageous from their own perspectives though the former view it essentially in terms of use values and the latter in terms of exchange values. A great advantage that exchange as a process has is that it can link up units with diverse perspectives.

But we must probe a little more into the *terms* of transactions of this kind which is an examination of the relative bargaining power of the parties concerned. Which of the two is likely to have more bargaining power? In Chapter 4 we saw that bargaining power depends crucially on the resource power of the two parties to an exchange, and from that point of view we can conclude, without much argument, that the f–unit will be in a position to impose the terms of the transaction. But let us look into the matter in some detail to bring out some of the factors which may not be so obvious. First, let us note that while there are several commodities involved in the transaction—tendu leaves, tobacco, thread, *bidis* and labour power—the basic issue is related to one of them, viz., labour power. We shall, therefore, concentrate on it, and bring in the transactions in the other commodities subsequently.

The fact that the basic transaction in this instance is of labour power must be obvious to the f–unit, but may not be so clear to the h–2 unit which may consider that the purchase of the material inputs and the sale of the finished product are the main concerns. However, these transactions are only a means for the disposition of the labour power of the h–2 unit. Unlike the material inputs that the h–2 units will have to purchase, for which, therefore, it will have to incur a cost, labour power is not something that it purchases, but possesses, and hence the unit may not be in a position to know its worth. On the other hand, the f–unit has a clearer notion of the worth of the labour power in the production of *bidis*. This asymmetry in the assessment of the worth of the good to be transacted put the h–2 unit in an initial disadvantage in the bargaining process. Where the (potential) seller of a good is in such a weak position and, consequently the (potential) buyer is in a relatively stronger position, there is said to be a 'buyers' market', that is, a market where the buyer is in a stronger position. This is reinforced by the fact that the good under consideration is also 'perishable'—labour power will not last long unless it is replenished by food, for instance. Both the potential seller and the potential buyer know this fact which, consequently, reduce the holding power of the seller.

Under the circumstances, the strategy of the f–unit is two fold: it must pretend that it has no interest in buying the good; it must also do whatever it can to prevent the seller from coming to have an appropriate assessment of the worth of the good. Going in for the first option of organising production on a factory basis has the great disadvantage of showing to the h–2 units the exchange value of labour power in the form of the wage rate that will have to be agreed upon and paid. On the other hand, the second option of the putting out arrangement enables the f–unit to conceal the exchange value of labour power and, indeed, to pretend that the exchange value of labour power is not being negotiated at all. At the same time through the terms simultaneously determined for the (sale of) material inputs and the (purchase of) finished good, the f–unit effectively decides on the exchange value of labour power which, normally, will be less than if an open exchange of labour power were to be done.

It can, of course be argued that if there is open bidding for labour power competitive bidding by potential sellers may bring the price down, and if the quantity desired to be sold is more than the quantity desired to be purchased, the exchange value of labour power must ultimately come down to zero. However, this technical 'solution' will have meaning only if workers (sellers of labour power) are willing to work for an employer (buyer) claiming nothing in return. Whatever may be the views of the workers in this regard, no f–unit can plan a production process counting on the free (that is costless) availability of labour power. Hence the preferred option for the f–unit will be to reduce the cost of labour power as low as possible by concealing the effective cost of labour power through a 'deal'. The fact that the effective cost of labour power (the earnings of the workers from the point of view of the h–2 units) in *bidi* manufacturing was brought down to as low as Rs 1.86 per day (of undefined duration) shows that the arrangements are indeed having the desired effect.

We must also look into the nature of the 'deal'. Its chief characteristics is the clubbing together of a number of transactions such that the terms of the individual transactions remain clouded and the 'deal' becomes a bilateral transaction between two parties. In the case of the *bidi* industry transactions brought together are those of the material inputs, the finished product and of labour power. Each one could be a separate transaction; there could be, and there are, separate markets for tobacco, tendu leaves, thread, *bidis*, and labour power. But the *bidi* making process becomes possible only when these are brought together, in which labour power is not an abstract and undifferentiated good, but the specific skill of the *bidi* workers. The deal is between the *bidi* workers and the *bidi* company where the company is in a position to use its resource power and lack of resource power of the workers to draw them into a clubbed transaction which is to its advantage. These conditions result in a 'buyers' market' for labour power and a 'sellers' market' for the material inputs which, together, reduce the bargaining power of the workers in the deal.

Once this basic principle is understood, it is not difficult to see that it can take different concrete forms under different specific circumstances. For instançe, most of the deals will have intermediaries, sometimes intermediaries at different levels. In the case of the *bidi* industry, the intermediary is the *sattedar*. The 'deal' can now be thought of as between the company and the *sattedar* on the one hand and the *sattedar* and the producer households on the other. The details of the deal need not be the same in the two cases; the tie-up may be looser in the former and stricter and broader in the latter. The *sattedar*, and the producers may have, as was noted, deals strictly speaking not related to *bidi* production, involving other 'markets' such as market for provisions and market for credit. This only means that the *sattedar* succeeds in drawing in the *bidi* workers into another deal which also has the same essential features as the previous one.

Further examples: the hosiery industry

The problem discussed above is not restricted to what may be considered traditional industries. Its essential features can be seen in the case of many 'modern' industries as well. The hosiery industry of Ludhiana in Punjab is a typical example.[8] Frame-knitting of hosiery started in the country late in the nineteenth century and fairly soon power-driven machines for cotton hosiery knitting were in use in different parts of the country. Since then the industry has experienced considerable technological transformation. Ludhiana specialises in woollen hosiery and nearly 90 per cent of the woollen hosiery production in the country is now concentrated in that city.

Knitting of socks was the only activity in the early part of the present century and the only equipment needed was a knitting frame which cost about Rs 115, but had to be imported from England. Since the workers in the industry could not afford to own frames, merchant-manufacturers introduced the standard 'putting-out' system advancing raw materials as well as renting out knitting frames to the workers who were also paid on piece rate basis for quantities delivered. During the First World War the demand for woollen goods increased and knitting frames came to be manufactured locally and so many households moved into the hosiery industry. After the war more advanced technology was imported from outside and the hosiery industry in the city came to have different segments, some consisting of household producers working with local frames, others large (employing up to 100 workers) and making use of imported machinery.

The industry continued to grow. A big boost came in the early 1960s when woollen hosiery goods started to be exported to the Soviet Union and East European countries. Within a decade the value of export rose from Rs 1.55 million to Rs 119.45 million. The Russian demand was for heavyweight items which could be knit only on manually operated knitting frames. Consequently the technological progress that the industry was making was reversed and the industry began to engage a large number of manual workers. The Russian export trade was given to 18 exporters, and although there was a tremendous increase in production and export no new exporters were recognised so that the original 18 came to have enormous control over the industry.

The growth of the industry has led also to the growth of manufacture of hosiery machines in Ludhiana, although some specialised machines are still imported. But the standard machine is the flat knitting frame and other common ones are power-winders, sewing machines, overlock machines, and dry cleaning machines. Most workers now own the 'flat' and the sewing machines required for their work. Exporters own specialised machines such as those for button-holding and button-stitching which are used in the final stages of manufacture.

In view of the essentially labour-intensive nature of the production processes, and in order to avoid the need to control and manage large numbers of workers, the exporters find it to their advantage to sublet the work to fabricators to whom they advance dyed wool and spell out the required specifications. The fabricators perform the liaison work between the exporting units and the workers. Like the *sattedars* in the *bidi* industry, the fabricators are the exporters' contractors. Many of them have risen from the ranks; they were initially workers, some with up to twenty years experience as flat workers. Most of them came up first by acquiring more flats, then by becoming petty employers and then selling off their flats to set themselves up as owners of independent workshops for performing job-work for the exporters. And on a day-to-day basis they work along with other workers so that they do not appear as employers, but more as supervisors. The employer-employee distinction is further blurred by the fact that most workers are employed on a piece-rate basis, so that in one sense, the whole manufacturing process can be thought of as a hierarchical chain of subletting and subcontracting. Under these institutional conditions the distinction between not only h–2 and h–4 units, but also between h–2 units and f–units as also between f and m units cannot be clearly maintained. However, the hierarchy has a clear bottom rung, the workers, mainly women, who cannot subcontract work to anyone else. Their earnings are about Rs 300 to Rs 325 a month. There is a pyramidal structure of earnings with the fabricators making about Rs 3000 a month, some of the owners of independent production units such as button-holing units and by claiming units earning slightly less or more and those who have ownership claims on the export companies being at the top. These earning differentials, to some extent, reflect differences in the kind of labour power contributed—physical and mental—by different persons but primarily they arise because of the differences in resource power and power over market processes.

Links between large and small units

On the basis of differences in resource power and the power over the market this kind of link between the small and the large where the large concentrate on marketing leaving production largely or entirely to small units is a fairly widespread phenomenon. Some of the well-known manufacturing concerns in the country (including companies with multinational connections) with well-known brand names in industries such as biscuits, footwear, sewing machines, electrical equipment, etc. are essentially marketing concerns depending on a large number of small units for the production of their products. Formally, such arrangements may appear to be deals between a large well-established company and an 'independent' production unit which can be treated as mutually beneficial; and so they are, up to a point. Through such arrangements the small producer is able to escape from most of the vagaries of the market. It is as though he is producing against orders with, in many cases, inputs and designs also supplied by the customer. In some instances, he may get credit and other facilities also from the customer. But in most such arrangements, the independence of the small producer is severely curbed. In the case of Bata, the well-known shoe company, an official enquiry found that the company's agreement with the small manufacturers included clauses which prevented them from selling their product to anyone other than the company; or if the company was not in a position to purchase, only to another party approved by the company and at prices also approved by the company.[9] The relationships are not 'open' market relationships but 'tied' transactions of various sorts by which, as in standard pre-capitalist arrangements, the relationship turns out to be not only between large and small, but also between units at different levels, one above and the other below. Indeed, such arrangements are meant not to ensure smooth horizontal transactions, but to make possible a vertical transfer of surplus generated in the process of production to those who exercise control over production through control over marketing. Decentralised production with centralised control is the basic principle in these cases.

Such arrangements are brought about in a variety of ways. A fairly typical pattern is seen from the electric fan industry in the country.[10] The production of a domestic fan, especially a ceiling fan, is basically a simple operation with some standard processes such as cutting the blades from readily available (aluminium) sheets, making the armature to house the electrical wiring, cutting the tie rod, making the regulator etc. But there can be differences in specific processes such as painting and finishing. Given the availability of bulk items and intermediate parts, fan manufacturing is essentially an assembling job which can be done by small and large units. Till the early 1970s both types of units were manufacturing the finished product and were competing in the market, the small units sellng fans without brand names at a somewhat cheaper rate than the bigger units which were marketing higher priced fans with brand names. According to one estimate, in 1972 the small units produced about one-third of the total production.

Since then, however, the pattern has changed and the big and small units have entered into a kind of complementary relationship. The big units have been encouraging the small ones to specialise in some of the processes in fan manufacturing—such as painting the fan blades—and to link themselves up with the big units. Once this is done, the operations which are mechanically carried out in the large units come to be sorted out into a series of processes—sanding the parts, applying paint primer, drying and painting—and most of them are manually done enabling the small units to take advantage of the cheap labour that is readily available. Large units encouraged this arrangement even when it was clear that the small units did not have any cost advantage in the processes they were handling and the quality of the product was suffering. But then why were the large units entering into this kind of arrangements with their erstwhile rivals?

A study which investigated this aspect found that the main reason was the fluctuation in the demand for fans (especially in the foreign markets) that the big concerns came to face in the 1970s.

The combination of large firms producing the basic bulk load of supply and supplementing it as and when necessary by putting out orders to small units works efficiently for the large firms because (i) it saves locking up capital in capacity likely to be under-utilised, (ii) it utilises marketing and sales overheads of large firms more efficiently, (iii) it overcomes the large mechanised units problems of matching the capacities of different machines meant for different stages of production of a given product, and (iv) it passes on the problems created by uncertainty of demand entirely to the small units. The latter provide the flexibility that the system needs for catering to a fluctuating demand. When orders expand, new small units come up or the existing units have extra workers. When orders are scarce, they dismiss workers or seek orders from other industries for similar processes (Banerjee, 1988: 190).

Because of this kind of link between the big and the small (clearly to the advantage of the former) small units as a species survive and play an important role in the market, even when individual units among them may frequently become 'sick' and the rate of mortality may also be high. Another industry in which the same tie-up relationship between the large and the small units is seen, and for the same reason, is the garment export industry where again large units specialising in marketing farm out work to small units when demand is favourable, making conditions very precarious for the small ones.[11] But why do the small units enter into such arrangements? The study on the fan industry gives the following answer: 'The standard small unit engaged in the fan industry is not a firm in the sense of an entrepreneur employing capital and labour in anticipation of demand. Rather, it is one version of the operation of an artisan who has developed some skills, has some conventional tools and is trying to make a living. He expects to get his payment mainly as a wage and also to collect whatever residual he can by keeping costs below the price set by the buyer in the contract'.

The phenomenon that we have been examining with different manifestations can thus be seen to be a standard pattern for capital to draw in more and more labour power under its effective domain so as to appropriate the surplus that it generates. From an organisational point of view it is the attempt to maximise profit by reducing labour cost as much as possible. Technology plays a role in it. It is the possibility of dividing production into different processes and differentiating them on the basis of the extent to which they need to be mechanised that facilitates the farming out of production to different groups. Consequently, one comes across a wide spectrum of technologies of different vintages and descriptions, from the most traditional to the most modern and from the most elementary to the most complex, coexisting in situations of this kind. But it is not merely a technological phenomenon; it cannot be. The coexistence of different kinds of technologies is possible because of the existence of production units with different kinds of cost calculations. The costs and prices of the material inputs in production (tendu leaves and tobacco in the case of *bidi*, blades, rods, and paints in the case of fans) themselves can differ from unit to unit. But the basic difference in cost calculations is related to the cost of labour power. To the f–units, labour power is also a purchased input and hence an item of cost that can be readily calculated. To the h–2 units, on the other hand, labour power is not a purchased item, but part of what it possesses; an asset with specific characteristics which is expected to earn a return for its own maintenance. The maintenance of that asset is a compulsion it must face, but on the returns that can be expected, it can have only vague notions. There is, therefore, a subjective element in the h–2 unit's calculations about the price and cost of labour power. The subjectivity arises from the fact that the extremely uneven distribution of non-labour resources makes it difficult for a large number of workers to survive without entering into exchange, but which simultaneously weakens their bargaining power when they do enter into it. It is this weakness and subjectivity which capital takes advantage of by providing a variety of package deals to workers making an assessment of each kind of situation and through appropriate organisational arrangements. It is capitalism's way of exercising domination over workers—without bringing them directly into capitalist methods of production or fully into capitalist relations of production—in which exchange and merchants' activities play a central role. While the organisational patterns differ—putting out, tied loans, sub-contracting of various sorts—they are all premised on the fact that at the bottom there are workers whose only effective way of bargaining is to tighten their belts—accepting *lower and lower* returns to their most important asset. This has been the essential feature of the on-going capitalist transformation of the Indian economy since Independence, rather than the emergence of capitalist units *per se*, although that has also been going on. It has a differential impact on those who are involved in it. Those at the bottom have a chance to make some earnings by exerting themselves to the maximum under very strenuous conditions—in 'sweat shops', in their own dwellings, or in some shed or factory. A hierarchy of intermediaries—the *sattedars*, the master weavers, the fabricators, the contractors, the merchants—find in the situation various ways of moving up. But the cream, of course, goes to the owners of big capital, the *bidi* companies, the export houses, those who can reap benefits on the basis of brand names and so on. The sharing of the benefits is more or less in proportion to the control that each category exercises on non-labour resources. That this phenomenon is an expression of the capitalist system can be seen from the fact that it has much wider application. The pattern is emerging conspicuously at the international sphere where big multinational corporations are applying the same principle to take advantage of differences in labour costs in different countries of the world. Minimising costs is one of the fundamental tenets of capitalism and the mobility of capital makes it possible to reach where costs are the lowest. On the other hand, labour power, the basic item of cost from the point of view of capital (but the source of earning from the point of view of the worker) tends to be specific and relatively immobile. Hence capitalism's tendency is to reach out to labour power where it can be obtained at the cheapest (within a country and across countries). Thus the Ford Escort automobile which comes out as a finished product in the United Kingdom and Germany has its parts produced in as many as 16 different countries of the world.[12] There are many other instances of this kind each one illustrating a variety of tie-ups, deals and collaborations. Whether within countries or across countries, the principle is the same both in terms of the organisation of production and the sharing of the benefits.

Returning to the Indian context, we may note that what is natural to capitalism has also been supported by some of the policy measures of the government. These measures can be grouped under three categories: factory and labour legislations, protective measures for small units and fiscal policies. Legislations defining the duration of the working day, physical conditions of the workplace and minimum wages have been part of the history of capitalist development throughout the world and are indicative of the social recognition that, left to itself, the capitalist thrust for accumulation will not exercise any restraints in the efforts to reduce labour cost. In most countries of the world such legislations have also been achieved through prolonged struggles of the workers. These measures, however, are confined to capitalist units of production: a factory, for instance, is defined as a place where a specified minimum number of hired workers work. Hours of work are indicated and conditions of work are defined in such a context. Where only a small fraction of the total workforce is brought under the direct domination of capital, many other avenues of work exist and it would be difficult, if not impossible, to implement these conditions in all such cases. Such measures, therefore, become an incentive for capital to reach out to where the bulk of the workers are. Sometimes legislative measures attempt to cover those areas also. In many states in the country now, minimum wages have been specified for *bidi* workers (that is, minimum to be paid for 1000 *bidis* rolled) but from an administrative point of view it is difficult to implement them. Where they are strictly implemented the industry either moves to a neighbourhood where it is not implemented, or the manufacture of 'No. 2' *bidis* readily comes up, in both cases the justification being the 'high' cost of labour resulting from minimum wage regulations.

Secondly, there are special legal provisions to protect 'small' producers. These include subsidised inputs and credit to them, reservation of the production of certain items exclusively to the small sector, provision of infrastructural facilities, preferential government purchases and so on. These are measures taken up recognising the special needs and handicaps of small producers, especially those engaged in traditional methods of production and the intention certainly is commendable. But such measures are also an invitation for large producers to gate-crash into the protective walls provided by the government to the small producers. One of the commonest ways by which this is done is for large producers to set up their own 'small units'—to take full advantage of the concessions and protection extended to the latter. A study which probed into this aspect came to the conclusion that 'the incentives, concessions and exemptions from administrative regulations available to the small scale sector could attract large houses to establish small scale units' and lists Tatas, Birlas, Bajaj, Mafatlal, Shaw Wallace, EID Parry, TVS, Simpson, Hindustan Lever, Godrej, and many other big concerns as among those that have their own 'small units'.[13] This was a common and recognised practice for many years. By the Industrial Policy Statement of 1980 the government excluded the subsidiaries of other concerns from the definition of the small scale sector, but through inter-corporate investment practices the large units are still able to exercise many forms of control over the small ones.

Thirdly, even standard fiscal measures can be made use of by larger units to forge links with the smaller ones. Excise duty, a tax on the volume or value of production, is one of the commonest fiscal instruments that most governments rely upon to raise revenue, and in India it is one of the largest sources of public revenue. One of the many concessions shown to small units is that many of them are exempted from excise duty on the ground that the volume of their production is limited. This serves as an incentive to large companies to leave production entirely or largely to small units and to convert themselves into marketing concerns lending their brand names to goods produced by hundreds of small units, thereby escaping excise duty.

All told, the tendency is that 'the larger companies would increasingly take up marketing of goods produced in the small scale sector in view of the associated multiple advantages. This saves them the labour problems, places them in a position to avoid excise duties, enables them to enter and expand in areas which have low priority, or are reserved for the small scale sector.' (Goyal *et al.*, 1984: 120).

As mentioned already, the advantages are not all one-sided going solely to large units. Small ones also benefit in some ways. But the central issue is one of increasing interdependence brought about by the capitalist system and associated exchange activities. Interdependence in itself is not a problem, and where the parties concerned are of fairly equal economic power, it can indeed be beneficial to all as it leads to an overall increase in economic activity; but where economic power is very unequally distributed, increase in interdependence has a built-in tendency to bring about, sustain and accentuate different forms of domination and dependence which enable the strong to take advantage of the weak.

In this sense exchange as an activity—or more accurately market as an institution—is not neutral. The market as the institutional arrangement that facilitates exchange as an activity is very much an ally of the strong because it is resource power that basically propels that activity, and in a capitalist set-up also provides signals for production through that activity. One of the major transformations that capitalism brings about, thus, is to exert control over production through the exchange activity and the market mechanism. It is this transformation of establishing new forms of domination and dependence through increasing market interdependence in the context of unequal distribution of economic power that we have featured in this section, and that is the essence of the transformation of the Indian economy since independence.

SOME ASPECTS OF THE TRANSFORMATION IN AGRICULTURE

As in the case of the colonial economy where imported capitalism had its impact more prominently in manufacture than in agriculture, the transformation caused by capitalism taking roots in the country since Independence too has been more visible in the non-agricultural sphere. The main reason for this is that agriculture (especially the production of food) tends to be more protected from exchange as productive activity and is meant largely for generating use value for the producers themselves. The transformation that a part of agriculture experienced during the colonial period, when there was a pronounced shift from agricultural production for use to agricultural production for exchange, was noted in the previous chapter. But even at the time of Independence Indian agriculture was dominated by the activity of h–2 units whose main intention was to produce foodgrains for their own consumption and who also depended on their own farms for most of the required inputs, primarily seeds and manure. In this sense agriculture was a substantially self-contained segment of the economy deriving its inputs from within and using its output also internally. The same could be said about a major component within agriculture, the peasants who owned their land, used family labour in productive activity, relied on their own resources as inputs in production and consumed the produce directly; they thus insulated themselves on the input side and the output side from interactions with others and consequently from interdependencies. Such units, therefore, could be thought of as being of the h–1 type. But it has been noted that there are varieties of inter-unit linkages in traditional agriculture—leasing in and out of land, periodic reliance on the labour services of other units; occasional borrowings and, of course, forms of

market transactions as well for purchase of clothing and other requirements and for the sale of excess produce. If these are also taken into
account, production units in agriculture, cultivators or farmers, would
have to be considered as h–2 units. Because the h–2 units in agriculture
are more isolated from exchange than h–2 units in fishing and manufacturing activities, they show greater resilience and tend to retain their
internal structure for long periods. For this reason agriculture is usually
thought of as a conservative sector in the economy.

If cultivators are considered generally as h–2 units, then (as seen in
Chapter 7) they still constitute the largest single occupational group in
the Indian economy claiming over 40 per cent of all workers. At the
time of Independence it was around 50 per cent, and thus there has been
some change in the unit structure within agriculture. It is worth considering
how this comes about.

A standard form of interaction among cultivators, arising substantially
from the technical conditions of production in agriculture, is the dependence on labour power from other units. Harvesting, for instance, has to
be completed within a few days after the crop (paddy, wheat etc.) is
ready to be harvested and the labour power of a single household may
not be adequate even in the case of small farms for this crash job.
Traditionally households with small farms manage this requirement on
the basis of mutual exchange of labour power. Households with larger
farms would normally have either tenants or labourers attached to their
farms to render such services. In the former case, part of the (informal)
tenancy contract would be some form of labour services apart from rent
to be paid in return for the use of land. In the latter case, especially
where traditionally attached labourers were also prevented (by social
regulations) from owning land, they would be more in the nature of h–4
units. That there were such units in the agricultural sector in the past
was noted in the previous chapter.

The essence of the social and economic transformation that takes
place in the sphere of agriculture is the differentiation of the h–2 households. On the one hand, some of them will emerge as those who come to
depend entirely on hired labour for all the work to be done on their
farms so that the units tend to emerge as typical capitalist units (f–units)
which own the means of production (land) and use the labour power
from h–4 units to carry out cultivation. At the other end, some of the
smaller h–2 units may be pushed into the h–4 category because of the
increase in their internal P/W ratio that makes it difficult for them to
continue as cultivators for want of adequate land; because of the difficulty
of obtaining land on tenancy; or because of the loss of land. The latter
two—the external conditions that cause a change in the status of h–2
units—are frequently caused by the emergence and acceleration of

capitalist tendencies in the system; particularly the manner in which exchange relationships in different spheres develop, generally referred to as the process of commercialisation of agriculture. The h–2 units that remain substantially as h–2 units will also experience many changes that come about in these spheres such as the manner in which they secure their inputs and dispose of their produce.

As was noted already, the process of commercialisation of agriculture started during the colonial period itself, the shift into crops being meant mainly for exchange rather than for direct consumption. But most other processes in agriculture continued to be along traditional lines up to Independence and even beyond. Changes involving other processes also were brought about by deliberate effort through the initiative of the state in the mid-1960s. The package of changes involving the adoption of high yielding variety of seeds, the use of commercial fertilisers and pesticides, the assured supply of water through modern methods of irrigation and the introduction of mechanical power has come to be known as the 'Green Revolution'.

The green revolution and new tie-ups

Many aspects of this technological transformation of agriculture initiated from above have been examined in the country.[14] The change in the input structure is reflected through the figures contained in Table 9.2. The pace of change is striking indeed and the momentum appears to be continuing. The figures themselves do not give any definite idea of the processes of change, especially the changes in the interdependence between agriculture and other sectors of the economy, not to speak of the inter-unit linkages which are our main concern. But it must be assumed that these too would have increased. We have some assessments of the former. The share in industrial inputs in agriculture increased from 1.41 in 1951–52 to 38.01 in 1979–80 at the all-India level. In Punjab where agriculture has undergone probably the greatest change, purchased inputs which were only 30 per cent of all inputs (the rest being farm-raised inputs) in 1960–61 shot up to 87 per cent in 1980–81 and must have increased even more in subsequent years.[15]

These figures give a clearer idea of the process of commercialisation taking place in agriculture. But what about the inter-unit linkages? Have they become fully mediated through the market? Or do they also show patterns similar to the ones discussed in the previous section? Surprisingly, though many of the technical and some of the institutional aspects pertaining to the technological transformation taking place in agriculture have received a great deal of attention, the pattern of inter-unit linkages has not been examined as carefully as it deserves.

Table 9.2 *Changes in Inputs in Indian Agriculture since Independence*

Year	Tractors (per lakh hectares of cropped area)	Electrically operated Pumpsets (per lakh hectares of cropped area)	Power (Kwh per thousand hectares of cropped area)	Fertilisers (Kg per thousand hectares of cropped area)
1951	7	16	1.5	600
1956	14	38	2.1	1,000
1961	20	131	5.5	2,200
1966	34	330	12.4	7,000
1970	61	834	23.3	13,600
1975	152	1,586	47.0	16,900
1980	279	2,331	79.5	31,500
1985	466	3,236	116.1	47,400
1986	503	3,440	131.0	49,400
1987	553	3,763	166.4	49,100
1988	605	4,082	196.7	60,600
1989	647	4,296	na	68,400

We shall, therefore, consider one of the rare case studies that addresses itself specifically to this issue, and which concludes that the rapid commercialisation taking place in agriculture leads to many tied transactions, similar to the ones seen in manufacture, and for the same reasons, viz., that interdependence is increasing in the context of unequal distribution of economic power and differential access of units to crucial inputs.

Agriculture has been noted for its traditional tied relationships as, for instance, where tenants (in particular crop-sharing tenants) are frequently forced to borrow from their landlord to meet pressing consumption requirements. The landlord-tenant relationships under such circumstances are mediated through transactions in land, in the products and through credit. If the tenant fails to repay the loan—not an unusual situation—he is left with little option except to pledge his labour services to the landlord. If so, the landlord-tenant relationship comes to be mediated through transactions in labour services as well. None of these transactions is independent. Because the tenant leases-in land, a part of his produce gets pledged to the landlord; because he takes a loan, he comes to pledge part of his labour service to the money-lender. Where the landlord and the money-lender happens to be the same person—a combination of landlord, merchant, money-lender and employer—all transactions become interlinked or tied. It is assumed that such tied transactions are the result or reflections of pre-capitalist relations which would disappear when technology changes raising productivity and market relationships replace traditional ones.[16] It is assumed too that as capitalism ushers in both technological progress and expansion of exchange, it would disentangle the interlinkages and establish independent markets for land transactions, produce, credit and labour services so that a person can lease-in land on the basis of terms most advantageous to him, sell his produce where it would fetch the highest price, take a loan from where the rate of interest is lowest and make his labour services available to the highest bidder.

The point that the case study we shall examine brings out is that whatever the prospects may be in the long run, it is not necessarily the case that improved technology and expanded markets *per se* get rid of the 'ties', but that new kinds of deals may emerge, that interlinkages can be an integral feature of a modern regime where there are no traditional tenancy relationships, where modern methods of irrigation have replaced traditional ones, where credit facilities have substantially increased and where the market for the produce is also fairly well established, but where other forms of disparities in economic power have emerged thanks to the changes that have been taking place.[17]

The study relates to the Sirunavalpattu village close to Kancheepuram town in the North Arcot District of Tamil Nadu. Agriculture has been the mainstay of the village for a long time and till the early 1960s was dependent mainly on tank irrigation. With the introduction of electricity in the late 1950s lift irrigation from private wells became a possibility and started picking up slowly. Concurrently, community efforts for the maintenance of the tanks began to decline and the tanks came to be neglected. The Green Revolution—introduction of high yielding varieties of paddy whose cultivation called for regular supply of water and the use of a fairly large dose of commercial fertiliser—was introduced in the village in the mid-1960s which gave a further incentive for well construction and lift irrigation with the help of electric pumpsets. When the study was conducted in 1982–83, wells accounted for over 80 per cent of the net area under irrigation in the village.

By that time practically all cultivators in the village had also become owner cultivators with tenancy accounting for only 10 per cent of the cultivated land. But there were considerable disparities in the distribution of land as well as in the ownership of wells. A little more than 31 per cent of the cultivator households had access to all the lift irrigation in the village, and among them the wells were more intensively concentrated in the larger holdings. In order to tap ground water the wells have to be fairly deep which meant that only cultivators with sufficient resource power could own and maintain wells and pumpsets. The average landholding of the cultivators who did not have wells was 1.5 acres while that of those with wells was as high as 7.4 acres. The average value of assets owned by the former group was Rs. 27,500 while for the latter group it was nine and a half times higher at Rs. 269,000. These figures give an idea of the differential resource power of the two groups.

Under such circumstances there is clearly a sellers' market for water because all cultivators need water, but few have access to it. Those who own and control water can not only sell water at exorbitant prices—one third of the gross output in kind being the prevailing rate—but are also in a position to exert other forms of pressure on the buyers, their bargaining power is considerably reduced, because on some pretext or the other (such as that the pumpset is not working) the seller can refuse to supply water when it is most crucially required and thus ruin the entire crop of the buyer. This power is put to good use by the water sellers to extract labour services of different kinds from the buyers in addition to the 'water rent' itself. Apart from this tie-up, the water sellers are able to strike a further deal with the buyers. Modern methods of cultivation have greatly increased the need for credit of all farmers, but more so of the larger farmers owning wells and pumpsets. The loans are not required for consumption and survival, but for production activitity itself. There are several sources of credit, both institutional and private, but traders in the neighbouring town are emerging as one of the main suppliers of credit. They make credit available to the farmers for the purchase of fertilisers and pesticides, new pumpsets and motor spares and to meet the costs of replacing motor coils. The traders are in a position to insist that farmers who borrow from them should also sell their entire produce to them. The big farmers who borrow from the traders are also required to direct those who purchase water from them also to sell their produce to the lending traders. Therefore, that also becomes part of the deal between the water seller and the water purchaser. The water purchaser who is greatly dependent on the water seller for an uninterrupted supply of water, has usually no option but to agree to the deal. The tie-up, therefore, is at two levels, directly between the water seller and water buyer as also between the trader-creditor and the water seller, and indirectly between the trader and the water buyer.

ACTIVITY CHAINS INVOLVING MAINLY H–4 UNITS

The presence of h–4 units in an economy is indicative of interdependence at the deepest level. They are units with nothing other than their labour power to offer in exchange for what they need. For sheer survival they must relate themselves to other units using their labour power for this purpose. The traditional pattern has been to attach themselves to units with more resources, especially land, than could be managed with their own labour power. The presence of such attached labour households during the colonial, and possibly even pre-colonial periods was noted in Chapter 8.

But their presence by itself does not say much about the nature of interrelationships they will have with other units because the relationships themselves can take different forms, ranging from near permanent attachment to complete freedom where the relationship is solely on the basis of employment with clearly defined terms about payment and duration. If the former is thought of as being typical of pre-capitalist relations and the latter of capitalist relations, in a transitional economy one should be able to come across cases of h–4 units at different points on the broad spectrum. Such indeed has been the case in the Indian economy since Independence. The transition from attachment to freedom may be referred to as the process of *casualisation* and that is what has been going on in recent decades.

Forms of 'attached' agricultural labour households can be seen all over the country. In many instances, particularly in isolated village situations where the waves of change have not reached, traditional forms of attachment including 'bondedness' still continue. Where changes do take place there is a certain helplessness that erstwhile attached labourers experience when they are released from the traditional set-up. The traditional pattern was one of unequal reciprocity with the weaker party having little power, other than widespread acceptance of tradition itself, to defend their rights. The stronger party usually has the power and the possibility to contract out of tradition when it is to their advantage to do so. And that is what usually happens in the process of transition. But the weaker party with no other alternatives may be forced to seek renewed forms of attachment. It may be recalled too that in the Indian context the economic subordination of the attached agricultural labourers is powerfully reinforced by the social subordination through the exercise of the caste hierarchy which makes them the lowest strata in society both in a relative and absolute sense.

Under such conditions consider a situation where all forms of traditional attachments are annulled, through economic processes and social pressures or through legislative interventions. The newly released labourers have nothing to fall back on. They need to live and for that they need to borrow. A natural tendency is for them to return to their former lords and plead for a loan. They offer their proven old time loyalties as collateral which, however, are not sufficient in the new situation. Consequently, they must place at the disposal of the lender the only thing they have, their labour power. It becomes both the collateral and the means of repayment of the loan. That process makes them once again 'attached' labourers, but with new conditions of attachment.

Attached and casual labourers

Attached agricultural labourers of this kind with different names—*hali* labourer in Gujarat, *siri* labourer in Punjab, *saldars* in Maharashtra, *mahindars* and *bagals* in West Bengal, *pannaiyals* in Tamil Nadu—are quite common even now. Except in the extreme case of bondedness where the period of attachment is indefinite, the standard pattern now appears to be an attachment for a period of one year at a time, but frequite common even now.[18] Except in the extreme case of boundedness and attached labourer is a multi-strand one. The duration of the working day is not defined and depending on the requirement it may start in the early hours of dawn and may go on late into the night with, perhaps, hours of free time in-between. An attached labourer is indeed an all purpose servant. He has to do a variety of specific jobs in the field relating to farming; he may have to look after domestic animals, drive carts, draw water, cut straw, run errands and so on. Usually, there are several components to his remuneration. One part of the wage is paid in terms of meals and, therefore, everyday. Another part is paid in cash and is usually reckoned for the whole year, although paid in a number of instalments. There are some standard periodic payments in kind as, for instance, some paddy and straw at the time of harvest. Often there are some fringe benefits also such as gifts from the landlord at the time of marriages and other ceremonies in the worker's family, or on other festival occasions.

Between attached labourers and casual labourers there is a broad category of semi-attached labourers of which the most common variant is 'beck and call' workers, bound by contract to work for employers as and when required by them, but free to seek work elsewhere at other times. Contractual arrangements are more formal in these instances where the worker is paid daily wages in cash when working for the employer. But the 'beck and call' worker may also be a tenant of the landlord and in that capacity may have less formal relationships. Semi-attachment of labour is an ideal arrangement for cultivators whose requirement of labour is quite important occasionally, but not so much as to make it paying to employ one or more persons as attached workers for the whole year.

Casual labourers are emerging as the largest category of h–4 units engaged in agriculture. They are employed for stipulated periods of time, usually for a day with the hours of work specified. Wages are in cash settled at the end of the day. An employer is free to engage anyone who is willing to offer his/her labour power to him, and the worker too is free to decide to whom he/she will offer the labour power. There are no other obligations on either side—at least in principle. But considering the fact that in our context there is generally a buyers' market for labour power, the seller may be at a disadvantage; there may not be enough buyers willing to buy his services, and hence he may have to accept reduction in wages directly, or indirectly by agreeing to work longer hours etc.

In many parts of the country forms of collective piece contracts or systems of contract gang labour are emerging whereby group of workers enter into contract with cultivators to carry out specific jobs on piece rates. Weeding and harvesting are the typical agricultural operations given out and taken up on this basis. In a sense it shows the foot-loose character of casual workers who are organised by contractors to move from place to place doing the same job. Not surprisingly the contractor emerges as an intermediary with the responsibility to supply and supervise the workers and getting a share out of the payment made to the workers. The arrangement is to the advantage of the farmers also. As a case study found: 'The time-bound nature of each agricultural operation makes it imperative to control the pace of work. At the same time work should not be speeded up so much as to affect the quality of work done. Cultivators thus seek to use forms of contract which, with the least supervision, allow them to control the pace of work, ensure its quality and yet peg the wage bill to the minimum' (Reddy, 1985:42–43).

In effect, therefore, the gang labour system in agriculture bears close resemblance to the subcontracting system in manufacturing and has its rationale as well.

Various combinations of these variety of forms are also possible and do exist. A 'beck and call' worker usually becomes a casual labourer when his services are not required by *his* employer. Even an attached worker may become a casual labourer for part of the year if the duration of attachment is less than a full year. He may then become an independent casual worker, or the member of a gang. Instances of marginal cultivators becoming casual labourers during certain parts of the year are also not uncommon. Each one of these shows a different kind of deal; the simplest in the case of the fully free casual labourer, but with variety of 'ties' in the other instances.

In the Indian context the majority of h–4 units is in agriculture. But they are found in other sectors of the economy also. In manufacturing the purest case is where capitalist units employ workers on the basis of well defined contracts. Factory workers are of this kind where their contracts are safeguarded by factory inspectors on the one hand and trade unions on the other. Elsewhere in the economy there are h–4 units whose members render labour services directly as porters, washer-workers, domestic servants and in many other ways.

But not all h–4 units may be able to sell their labour power directly. In urban areas they, therefore, seek other ways to make a living. Collecting of waste paper, rags and other forms of waste freely available and which can be converted into usable material in the production of other goods (dolls, packing cases etc.) is an important activity.[19] Soon there emerge collection depots, processing centres and the intermediaries that go with them. In turn, these provide the opportunity for 'tied' relationships also to appear: the owner of a collection depot may provide loans for his suppliers on condition that whatever the borrowers gather can only be sold to him. It may be noted also that there is an element of the transformation of units in instances like these where h–4 units have to resort to some form of trading activity in order to put their labour power into use. In the process they are turning out to be more like the m–units, initially without any stock of goods which merchants usually carry with them and without any of the skills of traders. But, of course, over time there is the possibility that they come to acquire these skills and also generate enough surplus to set themselves up at least as the owner of a collection depot. Once that threshold is crossed other possibilities may also open up. Not that the movement will always be upwards; there may be failures, bankruptcies and other routes downwards as well. Capitalist development is a story of successes and failures.

TRANSFORMATION SINCE INDEPENDENCE—A ROUND UP

After catching a glimpse of the complex process of economic transformation since independence through the experience of three villages, we have concentrated on the h–2 units to probe further into that process. We have left out many crucial aspects of the transformation—growth and diversification in particular which will be dealt with in the next chapter—and have concentrated on one aspect, the emergence of new kinds of activity chains, that is, relationships among units. For that the choice of the h–2 units has been deliberate. As they are the typical pre-capitalist units, they are the ones that experience the transformation that emerges drawing them into newer forms of interdependencies than they have been used to. During the period of transformation the h–2 units have a kind of amphibious existence, living both in an economy of use values and in an economy of exchange values, their internal structure still largely oriented to the former, but their links increasingly dominated by the latter. The exchange relationships that they are drawn into also undergo a qualitative change, from an accent on the exchange of the goods of their labour to their labour power itself. This transformation of exchange from a C–M–C process to an M–C–M process which presages the arrival of capitalism leads also to many changes in the organisation of production bringing production under the power of merchant capitalists.

Both during the transitional phase and during what may be described as the full capitalist organisation of production, the aim of those who own capital and use it for the further accumulation of capital through augmenting exchange value is to bring labour power under its domination, indirectly in the former phase and directly in the latter. The distinctive feature of economies like ours is the fact that these two phases, which in the natural evolution of capitalism appear sequentially, are present simultaneously.

It is important to note that in both these phases individual capitalists will try to gain as much control over the market processes as they can. If in the latter it is related to the 'realisation problem' in the former it is to reach out to the labour processes as much as possible. Where the two phases are simultaneously present, therefore, most markets will tend to be differentiated and segmented. The success of individual capitalists in this regard will depend very much on the extent of capital they are able to control. On this basis capitalism itself tends to get differentiated: there is tiny capitalism, small-scale capitalism, large-scale capitalism, mega capitalism. There is, certainly, a hierarchy here, but there can also be different forms of collaborations and interactions as the case studies referred to have indicated. In deciding on the mix of these types in any given situation state policies play a dominant role.

When capitalism begins to penetrate pre-capitalist orders, it is such a highly volatile economic environment that is generated and into which the h–2 units are drawn in. Most of them will be at a disadvantage because very quickly the economic environment that they were used to dominated by custom and consequently characterised by stability will be replaced by one that is propelled by resource power in which, therefore, control over resources come to be the dominating factor. That is the context in which the differentiation of the h–2 units takes place. Some will be sucked into the new processes at different levels; many will become rejects. But as the system itself gets transformed, survival will depend on the possibility to be drawn into its ambit, one way or the other. That will be the nature of the struggle of the h–2 units which provides capitalism many avenues to reach out to the labour power that they carry with them.

It is not claimed that the processes described in this chapter dominate the entire Indian economy. There is a segment of the Indian economy which displays the typical features of the full capitalist phase where capital exercises direct control over labour power, typically the f-units. This sector has come to be referred to as the 'organised' sector, and we shall make use of the term as also the corresponding term 'unorganised' for the rest of the economy.[20] But some clarifications are necessary. The first is that the tendency to refer to the former as capitalist and the latter as pre-capitalist with the implication that they operate on entirely different principles is not right. That the f–units have different kinds of links with the 'unorganised sector' has been noticed. The two sectors are also linked through the activities of traders and financial institutions. If capitalism does not respect national boundaries, it is too much to expect that within a country it will remain confined to one segment. As noted in Chapter 5, capitalism's built-in expansionary tendency takes it to wherever it can in search of its quest for accumulation. The unorganised sector offers it a potentially rich field for accumulation. It will certainly reach there, though its *modus operandi* may be different. The two sectors, are, therefore, only two different ways in which capitalism reaches out to labour power.

The term 'unorganised' should not be taken too literally either. The implication is not that it is so loosely organised that it tends to be chaotic. It may so appear to those who are familiar only with the organisational structure of the full capitalist phase and which is, therefore, considered to be the norm for economic organisation *per se*. Also, the variety of organisational patterns there may turn out to be too confusing to those who search for standardised and uniform relationships in the economic sphere. But beneath what is superficially confusing it is possible to find an underlying logic of capitalist penetration which we have tried to locate and analyse in this chapter.

One reason for concentrating on the unorganised sector in the treatment of the economy since independence is that the specific features of the transformation—the changing patterns of activity chains—are to be seen there. But there is another, and perhaps more important, reason. The h–2 units, as shown in Chapter 7, claim the vast majority of the workforce in the non-agricultural sector. If it is granted that in agriculture too, most of the production units are of the h–2 type and that the h–4 units in agriculture are closely connected with them, then from the point of view of the workforce, the unorganised sector covers the bulk of the economy, perhaps 85 to 90 per cent. So, the transformation we have examined is what has been affecting the lives of most of the people in the land.

DISTRIBUTION OF RESOURCES IN THE ECONOMY

Since the distribution of resources and differential resource power arising from it have been identified as the key factors in understanding the transformation, it may be useful to take a look at these aspects in a quantitative sense to wind up the chapter.

There are two major sources of information dealing with the distribution of resources in the Indian economy. The first is the All-India Debt and Investment Survey (AIDIS) brought out periodically by the Reserve Bank of India (RBI) which deals with the entire economy and all forms of resources. The second is the periodic reports of the National Sample Survey Organisation (NSSO) which concentrate on the distribution of land and consequently are related primarily to the rural areas. The data in the RBI's reports are also gathered by the NSSO. We shall rely on the *All-India Debt and Investment Survey 1981–82* (RBI, 1987) and the Report No. 330, *Report on Land Holdings* (NSSO, 1986) the latest available, although they give information on the distribution of resources in the economy in the early 1980s.

The units in both the sources are the households. However, each source has its own classification of households. The AIDIS divides households into rural and urban initially. The rural households are then divided into cultivator households and non-cultivator households, the latter consisting of agricultural labourers, artisans and other non-cultivator households. The urban households are divided into self-employed and non-self-employed.

The average value of total assets per household in 1981–82 according to AIDIS was Rs. 37,160 with the urban households being at a higher level of Rs. 40,573 compared to rural households whose average value of assets was Rs. 36,090. Within the rural households, the average value per rural cultivator household was Rs. 44,524, which was about five times that of non-cultivator household, Rs. 8,974. As for the urban households, the self-employed had a higher average at Rs. 55,320 while that of the non-self-employed households was Rs. 33,457.

Now, these figures refer to the 'stock' of resources as we used the term in Chapter 7. And considering the fact that they include all forms of assets—land and buildings, livestock, tools and machinery, and financial holdings, it can be seen how low is the asset position of an *average* household. But we know that the distribution of assets in the economy is far from equal and so the average does not give an adequate represent-ation of the real situation. In Table 9.3 we give a more revealing picture.

The first column of the Table gives the asset groups. The subsequent pairs of columns refer to particular households, the pair showing the percentage of households in that asset group (A) and percentage share of assets of that group (B) for each category of households. Thus columns 2 and 3 refer to all households, 4 and 5 to cultivator households in rural areas, 6 and 7 to non-cultivator households, 8 and 9 to self-employed households and 10 and 11 to the non-self-employed households. Looking at columns 1, 2 and 3, we can see that 7.8 per cent of all households in the economy have total assets valued at less than Rs. 1,000 and their share in total assets in the economy is 0.1. At the bottom of those

Table 9.3   A Profile of Asset Distribution in the Indian Economy

Asset Group (in rupees)	All households		Rural Households				Urban Households			
			Cultivation		Non-cultivation		Self-employed		Non-self-employed	
	A	B	A	B	A	B	A	B	A	B
1	2	3	4	5	6	7	8	9	10	11
Up to 1,000	7.8	0.1	1.6	—	19.2	1.0	9.9	0.1	16.7	0.2
1,000 – 5,000	18.0	1.4	11.3	0.8	40.3	11.9	15.3	0.7	18.6	1.5
5,000 – 10,000	14.2	2.8	13.4	2.2	18.3	14.4	11.1	1.5	13.7	3.0
10,000 – 20,000	17.9	7.0	20.7	6.8	12.1	18.6	14.9	4.0	15.8	6.8
20,000 – 50,000	22.6	19.4	28.8	20.8	7.5	24.7	21.1	12.5	17.7	17.0
50,000 – 1 lakh	11.1	20.9	14.0	21.9	1.8	13.4	13.6	17.3	10.1	21.2
1 lakh – 5 lakhs	7.9	39.5	9.7	39.8	0.8	14.7	12.9	46.0	7.1	39.7
5 lakhs and above	0.5	8.9	0.5	7.7	—	1.3	1.2	17.9	0.3	10.6
Total	100.0	100.0	100.0	100.0	100.0	100.0	100.0	100.0	100.0	100.0

A : Percentage of households in each asset group.
B : Percentage share of assets of each group.

columns (last but one row) it can be seen that 0.5 per cent of households
in the economy have assets of over Rs. 5 lakhs, but their share in assets is
8.9 per cent. The great disparities in asset distribution is seen from this
Table. The average asset value of Rs. 37,160 comes in the fifth row of
the Table (Rs. 20,000–50,000) which means that all households up to and
including the fourth row (57.9 per cent) are clearly *below* the average
and their share in assets is only 11.3 per cent. Actually, if the average
can be considered as slightly over the mid point of the fifth row, then
over 70 per cent of the households can be thought of as coming below
the average, with something like 17 per cent share in total assets. At the
other extreme, as has already been seen, 0.5 households at the top claim
close to 9 per cent of the total assets. The asset distribution within different categories of households can also be read similarly from the
Table. The household categories in the AIDIS are not similar to the
classification of units we have used, and yet the information contained
in Table 9.3 helps us to get a mental image of the distribution of resource
power in the economy.

It will be useful also to look at the type of assets. This is shown in
Table 9.4. It is not surprising that land accounts for over 50 per cent of
the value of all assets and buildings are the second highest, accounting
for about 25 per cent of all assets. The third position is claimed by
durable household assets such as furniture, precious metals etc. It may
be surprising that the fourth place goes to livestock and poultry and that
their value is more than double the value of all agricultural machinery.
Financial assets constitute 3.7 per cent of all assets, but shares among
them are only 0.2 per cent. Table 9.4, therefore, provides a profile of
the asset structure.

We shall now look into the National Sample Survey's account of the
distribution of land in the rural areas of the country in 1982. The average
area of land owned per household was 1.28 hectares, but this average
also hides the tremendous variation in ownership and hence more
detailed information is necessary which is given in Table 9.5. In the
Table households are classified according to the size of ownership
holdings (column 1). Columns 2 and 3 show cumulative percentage of
households and land owned respectively. The first row refers to landless
households and shows that 11.33 per cent of rural households are of that
kind. The second row gives information about households owning below
0.21 hectare: 39.93 per cent of households (*including* landless households, or 28.60 per cent of households owning land) have only such tiny
holdings and their share in land is only 0.9 per cent. Each successive row
gives information about the next size class and of all households that
own land below that size with the corresponding share of land. Thus row
4 shows that 66.64 per cent of all households, or 55.31 (66.64 minus 11.33)

Table 9.4 Percentage Distribution of Assets by Type of Households and Type of Assets

Type of household	Land	Building	Livestock and Poultry	Agricul- tural machinery	Non-farm equip- ment	Transport equip- ment	Durable household assets	Financial assets, shares	Other financial assets	Dues receivable	Total
1	2	3	4	5	6	7	8	9	10	11	12
All households	54.3	24.6	3.9	1.9	0.8	1.4	9.2	0.2	3.5	0.2	100.0
Rural-All Households	62.1	20.7	5.0	2.5	0.3	1.0	7.1	0.1	1.1	0.1	100.0
Rural-Cultivators	64.1	19.5	5.0	2.6	0.2	0.9	6.6	0.1	0.9	0.1	100.0
Rural-Non-cultivators	30.8	39.0	5.3	0.5	1.3	1.5	15.8	0.1	5.4	0.3	100.0
Urban-All Households	32.4	35.7	0.8	0.4	2.1	2.5	15.1	0.5	10.1	0.4	100.0
Urban-Self-employed	34.6	37.3	1.1	0.7	4.0	3.3	13.1	0.5	4.7	0.7	100.0
Urban-Non-self-employed	30.6	34.3	0.6	0.2	0.5	1.9	16.8	0.5	14.4	0.2	100.0

Table 9.5 *Distribution of Households and Area Owned over Size Class of Household Ownership Holdings, (Rural) 1982*

	Size class of household ownership holdings (hectares) 1	Cumulative percentage of households 2	Cumulative percentage of land owned 3
1.	0.00	11.33	—
2.	below 0.21	39.93	0.90
3.	" 0.41	48.21	2.75
4.	" 1.01	66.64	12.22
5.	" 2.03	81.34	28.71
6.	" 3.04	88.61	42.55
7.	" 4.05	92.12	52.09
8.	" 6.08	96.02	66.73
9.	" 8.10	97.66	75.55
10.	" 10.13	98.57	81.92
11.	" 12.15	99.01	85.73
12.	" 20.25	99.76	94.57
13.	All sizes	100.00	100.00

per cent of households owning land have less than 1.01 hectares with a share of 12.12 of land. From row 11, it can be figured that about 1 per cent of households (that is 100.00 minus 99.01) have over 12.15 hectares of land, but their share in land is about 15 per cent (that is, 100.00 minus 85.73). In other words, although individual ownerships of 12 or 20 hectares cannot be claimed to be too large, the top 1 per cent of land owners have a greater share of land than the bottom 66 per cent. In fact, from row 12 it can be read that 0.24 per cent of the very top owners account for over 5 per cent of the land, which also shows that as we move to the higher levels, the concentration of ownership becomes more pronounced. This can be brought out clearly by a regrouping of the size classes which is attempted in Table 9.6 and which is self-explanatory.

Both the AIDIS data on total assets and the NSS data on land bring out the generally low average level of resources as also the glaringly unequal distribution of assets among the households in the economy. Although the data on the distribution of resources have not been based on the kind of units designated in Chapter 7, it is possible to see from them that apart from the h–4 units, the other resource-poor units in the economy are the h–2 households, marginal farmers, artisans, petty manufacturers etc. They are the main constituents of the unorganised sector.

Table 9.6   *Distribution of Land by Major Size Classes, 1982*

Size class 1	Share of households 2	Share of land 3
Marginal (less than 1.01 ha)	66.64	12.22
Small (1.01—2.02 ha)	14.70	16.49
Semi-medium (2.03—4.04 ha)	10.78	23.38
Medium (4.05—10.12 ha)	6.45	29.83
Large (10.13 ha and above)	1.42	18.07

NOTES

1. The studies referred to are Guhan & Mencher, 1982; Athreya, 1984; and Guhan & Bharathan,1984.
2. Athreya, 1984, pp 117–18.
3. *Ibid*, pp 118–19.
4. Kurien, John, 1978.
5. Prasad & Prasad, 1985.
6. Patel, 1989.
7. Karl Marx in (Marx, 1976 Appendix, 'Results of the Immediate Process of Production') distinguishes between 'real' and 'formal' subsumption of labour under capital. The former is where labour is brought under specifically capitalist mode of production such as large-scale industry which changes the entire manner of work. On the other hand, 'formal' subsumption is where capital takes over an existing labour process, developed by pre-capitalist modes of production. In that sense instances such as these are cases of the formal subsumption of labour under capital.
8. Singh, 1990.
9. See Swaminathan, 1983.
10. Banerjee, 1988.
11. Kalpagam, 1981—Also, Bromley & Gerry, 1979.
12. The World Bank, 1987, Ch.3.
13. Goyal *et al.* 1984: 27.
14. See Frankel, 1971; Hanumantha Rao, 1975; Bhalla & Chadha, 1982; Athreya *et al.* 1990.
15. Bhalla *et al.* 1990: 24.
16. See Bhaduri, 1973; Balakrishnan, 1984; Nagaraj, 1981.
17. Janakarajan, S., 1986.
18. See Athreya *et al.* 1990, Ramachandran, 1990, Rudra, 1982, Nagaraj, 1981.
19. See Kalpagam, 1985. This sort of activity is simply an expression of what may be generally termed 'survival strategy' and it takes various forms. For a very incisive account of the variety of ways that the poor adopt for survival see Jansen, 1986. A more analytical account is given by Jaganathan, 1987.

20. The term 'informal sector' is also frequently used to refer to sectors of the economy which do not conform to certain standard which, however, are not adequately spelt out. It gained currency after the International Labour Organisation started using it in the early 1970s, see ILO, 1970, 1971 & 1976 and Joshi & Joshi 1976. The issue is not merely one of terminology. In many 'informal sector' studies there is the implication that it is a self-contained sector with an internal dynamics of its own. A critique of this view is provided by Breman, 1976.

Notes to Tables

Table 9.1 is taken from Athreya, 1984: 29.

Table 9.2 is compiled from data provided by Centre for monitoring the Indian Economy, *Basic Statistics Relating to the Indian Economy, 1990*, Vol I: All India.

Table 9.3 is based on Table 1A in Reserve Bank of India, *All India Debt and Investment Survey, 1981–82.*

Table 9.4 is from the same source, Table 2A.

The source of Tables 9.5 and 9.6 is *National Sample Survey* (37th Round) Report No. 330, Table IV.

10

Growth and Change: A Macro View

This chapter is complementary to the previous one and examines the transformation of the economy since independence from a macro perspective. Aggregating the labour force and the total output of the economy first overall, and then disaggregating them into the main 'sectors'—agriculture, manufacturing and services, or primary, secondary and tertiary—we take up issues relating to the economy's growth. 'Growth' here is primarily the increase in the total output of the economy converted into value terms, to represent 'national income' of the economy in successive years. The advantages and the major limitations of national income calculations are brought out indicating that because the conversion of physical output into value terms is done mainly in terms of market prices, the measurement of national income and of its growth over time is not socially neutral. It is, therefore, pointed out that the changes in the composition of national income are just as important in understanding the nature of the transformation of the economy as 'growth' itself.

In the preceding chapter we approached the transformation of the economy since independence from below or from within—in terms of its units and their interrelationships. Such an approach is necessary to enter into the working of the economy. But towards the end of the chapter many of the heterogeneous units were brought together into what was described as the 'unorganised sector'—shifting the emphasis from the units to a collection of units because that collection describes some characteristics of the economy which cannot be seen at the units level. That process is referred to as 'aggregation'. Aggregation and its complementary opposite disaggregation are procedures frequently resorted to for understanding complex entities such as the economy. We have already made use of them in our analysis when, for instance, we aggregated the establishments in the economy into household units, enterprises etc. and then disaggregated the household units into h–1, h–2, h–3 and h–4 types. Subsequently these disaggregated units along with some of the enterprises have been aggregated into the unorganised sector, thereby also disaggregating the economy into two segments or sectors, the unorganised and the organised sectors. The division of the economy into sectors of this kind could be in terms of persons or products. Another form of dis-aggregating the economy is with respect to activities. From this point of view the convention has been to divide the economy into three sectors, viz., agriculture, manufacturing and services, or into primary, secondary and tertiary sectors. It should be evident that each one of these sectors represents some aggregation. Agriculture itself is a variety of activities with the common feature that they are all basically land-related activities; manufacturing too consists of a wide range of simple and complex activities; the same can be said about services also which consist of different kinds of direct personal work such as administration, military and police, teaching and clerical work, medical and legal services, washing, tailoring and so on. When the sectors are designated primary, secondary and tertiary, there is more aggregation involved. Thus, the primary sector consists of not only agriculture, but other nature-based activities, in particular mining and quarrying. Similarly, the secondary sector includes manufacturing and construction. The tertiary sector more or less coincides with the service sector. But the problems are not over. It is necessary to indicate how the activities themselves are identified. In agriculture, for instance, the main issue is not to capture the sowing, reaping and threshing processes, though they may be important for certain types of analysis, but to say whether agricultural activities are viewed in terms of the workers involved or the output produced.

We shall soon be dealing with different kinds of aggregation and dis-aggregation and their justification and usefulness, but the important point is to note that because of the complexity of the economy a variety of approaches to it has to be resorted to in order to understand it and its functioning. Conventionally (as was seen in Chapter 3) the economy has been studied in terms of its units, or from a micro perspective and in terms of its aggregates referred to as macro analysis. The micro-global approach we have made use of in Chapters 7, 8 and 9 has been an attempt to understand the totality that is the economy in terms of inter-unit interactions, but in so doing it was not possible to pay attention to an important aspect of the economy—its performances in terms of output. That is the dimension of the economy we shall deal with in this chapter. It is a crucial one because as seen from the village studies referred to in Chapter 9, an increase in output has been a major feature of the trans-formation of the economy since independence. Reviewing the per-formance of the economy during the first three and a half decades after independence, the Sixth Five Year Plan document said: 'One of the most significant achievements of our development policy after indepen-dence has been the fact that the handicap of stagnation was overcome and the process of growth initiated'. That process of growth was maintained and accelerated during the Sixth and Seventh Plan periods as well.

However, before we turn to an assessment of the performance of the economy in terms of output we shall examine the changes that have been taking place in terms of population, labour force and its components, making use of the aggregation–disaggregation procedure.

POPULATION AND LABOUR FORCE

According to the 1951 Census the population of India was 361 million which moved up to almost 844 million in 1991. This has been a phenomenal increase of the kind that the country has never seen before. The magnitude of growth can be appraised in different ways. The population increase between 1951 and 1961 was 78 million; between 1961 and 1971, 109 million, between 1971 and 1981, 131 million and between 1981 and 1991 close to 160 million. By way of comparison it may be noted that as the population of the territory now constituting the Indian Union was around 235 million in 1901, the addition to the population during the five decades immediately prior to Independence was only about 120 million, less than the decadal increase in the 1970s and 1980s. The annual increase in population of around 15 million is larger than the total population of many countries in the world. An examination of the death and birth rates from the beginning of the century will show that the sharp increase in the population since the middle of the century has been the result of a drastic decrease in the former, while the latter has made only very modest decrease. The relevant figures are given in Table 10.1.

Table 10.1 **Death and Birth Rates (per 1000 population)**

Year	Death Rate	Birth Rate
1901	48.0	48.0
1911	43.0	49.0
1921	49.0	49.0
1931	37.0	47.0
1941	33.0	45.0
1951	31.0	43.0
1961	26.0	44.0
1971	20.0	42.0
1981	14.8	36.0

With the death rate and birth rate being fairly close in the early part of the century, total population remained stagnant and, indeed, there was a decrease in total population in the 1911–1921 decade which witnessed a widespread influenza epidemic that wiped out large numbers of people throughout the country. It also alerted the government about the need for public policy measures to improve health or at least to reduce deaths. And the death rate showed the first major decline in the subsequent decade with the birth rate still remaining almost as high as it was at the beginning of the century. The impact of public policy measures (essentially the eradication or control of some diseases like small pox, tuberculosis and malaria) has continued to be felt on the death rate bringing it down significantly to around ten by the end of the 1980s. Public policy measures have also been aimed at reducing the birth rate and in the decade of the fifties India became the first country in the world to have an *official* policy to curb the birth rate. However, unlike in the case of the death rate, public policy measures alone cannot have much of a bearing on the birth rate and it was only in the decade of the 1970s that the birth rate has shown any perceptible decline. It is too early to say whether that decline would establish a downward trend because children born in the earlier decades of population increase would be entering into the reproductive age in the decade of the 1980s and beyond. This is particularly so because the decline in the death rate is largely due to the reduction in infant mortality so that a larger proportion of children born will now be entering into the reproductive age. At the same time as a state like Kerala has shown, improvement in public health, increase in the literacy rate of women and the greater involvement of women in economic activities may reduce the birth rate also along with economic development itself and urbanisation.[1] But, of course, these factors operate rather slowly on the birth rate and with fairly long time lags and so the problem of growing numbers will continue to be a source of concern well into the next century.

'Workers'

Counting heads in a vast country like ours has its problems as every decennial census operation clearly shows. But these recede into the background in comparison with the problems of the classification of the population. One of our major interests is the P/W ratio, but the denominator in that ratio, 'workers' is not easy to determine. It is possible to make a purely demographic approach here by designating the age group of 15 to 59 as economically active population, the rough equivalent of workers. If this is done, the 1981 population of India can be divided into 54 per cent workers and 46 per cent non-workers.[2] But this is not very accurate because not all who are between the 15 to 59 age group are workers and some in the age group of below 15 and above 59 are workers. The real difficulty is arriving at a definition of 'work' which can be used to identify and count the number of 'workers'.

Where work is defined as paid jobs and if legal and institutional conditions specify the conditions of paid work, the identification of workers would be relatively easy. But there has been no economic system in the world so far that has succeeded in this task. We have seen (in Chapter 2) the difficulty of separating work or economic activity from other human activities in the rudimentary economy. The problem continues in the village economy too where the household remains the main economic unit also. It is often claimed that under capitalism a clear distinction can be drawn between 'work' and other forms of activity frequently identified as 'leisure', the former being activity undertaken for someone else for which one gets paid and the latter being activity that one does because one likes to do it. The claim seemed to have a semblance of validity when it was accompanied by another institutional condition, a sexual division of labour when 'work' became the responsibility of men and other activities, 'domestic chores', were considered to be the responsibility of women. But even that was not a tenable distinction apart from the question of its justification. The fact is that the definition of 'work' (and the consequent identification of 'worker') is not a limited economic question, but a broad and fundamental one of the social organisation of human beings which all forms of economic systems will have to deal with as best as they can.

We shall try to see how the matter has been handled in the Indian context. The Indian economy shares the problem faced by all national economies, irrespective of their specific economic systems, of how the distinction between work and other forms of activities is to be drawn within the household set-up. But the special problem in the Indian context arises because of the domination of h–2 units which combine the activities of households and enterprises. The two main sources estimating workers and the worker population ratios in the country,[3] the Census Reports and the Reports of the National Sample Survey Organisation, have made several attempts to deal with the problems of part-time work, seasonality of work and diversity of activities apart from that of the identification of enterprises as such arising from the widespread nature of h–2 units in the Indian economy. The technical aspects of these discussions are not important for us, but since the manner in which work and workers is defined will have a bearing on all subsequent classification of workers, we shall look into the major issues involved as the Census has grappled with them. The definition of work and of workers was seriously taken up in the 1961 Census. From then on till the 1981 Census 'work' has been defined as participation in 'any economically productive activity'. But since the term 'economically productive' has not been explained the definition by itself is not particularly enlightening. But the definition is used to classify the population into 'workers' and 'non-workers'. The latter category consists of: (i) All dependents such as infants and children not attending school or persons permanently disabled from work because of illness or old age; (ii) Students, that is, all those attending institutions of education; (iii) Beggars etc., that is, 'persons without indication of source of income and those with unspecified sources of subsistence who are not engaged in any economically productive work'; (iv) Inmates of institutions such as convicts in jails, those in mental or charitable institutions 'even if such persons are compelled to do some work such as carpentry, carpet weaving, vegetable growing etc. in such institutions'; (v) Retired persons not employed in some full-time or part-time work and rentiers living on rent, royalty or dividends and any other person of independent means for securing which he/she does not have to work; (vi) Those engaged in household duties, that is, all persons who are engaged in unpaid home duties and do not do other work; and (vii) other non-workers, primarily dependents who are looking for work. Of these seven groups of non-workers the first three and the last may be clear cases, but there is an element of ambiguity and arbitrariness about the others. The sixth, particularly, excludes the majority of women engaged in household activities from the category of workers. It is also clear that work tends to be identified with activities for which one gets paid.

The identification and classification of workers have not been without difficulties either, and it is on this aspect that the three censuses have differed. In the 1961 Census enumeration, a person was classified as worker if he/she had worked regularly during the season immediately preceding it or at least for a day in regular (non-seasonal) work during the preceding fortnight. At the 1971 Census a person was treated as a worker only if he/she spent his/her time mainly in work or if he/she worked at least for a day in regular (non-seasonal) work during the preceding week. It can be seen that the 1971 definition of worker was more restrictive than the 1961 definition and would exclude many, especially women, and those who worked occasionally as agricultural labourers, or in household industries etc. The 1981 Census tried to rectify this problem by dividing workers into 'main workers' and 'marginal workers'. Main workers were those who had worked for the major part of the year preceding the date of enumeration, that is, those who were engaged in any economically productive activity for 183 days (six months) or more during the year. Marginal workers were those who worked anytime at all in the year preceding the enumeration but did not work for a major part of the year, that is, those who worked for less than 183 days! The expectation was that the main workers of 1981 would corres-pond to the worker of 1971 and the main worker and marginal worker together of 1981 would correspond to the worker of 1961.[4] The verdict of the experts has been that as far as male workers are concerned the expectation has been fairly satisfactorily met, but in the case of females there are still problems in inter-temporal comparisons. The worker population ratios calculated from the three census reports are shown in Table 10.2 for males and females separately for rural and urban areas.

Table 10.2   Worker Population Ratios, 1961, 1971 & 1981

Year	Rural		Urban	
	Male	Female	Male	Female
1961	58.3	31.4	52.4	11.1
1971	53.6	13.4	48.8	6.6
1981 (Main workers)	52.6	16.0	48.5	7.3
1981 (Main and marginal workers)	53.8	23.2	49.1	8.3

Occupational patterns

Against this background we may examine the more important question of the changes in the occupational patterns of the labour force since Independence. Although the basis of the 1951 classification of the labour force was not the same as in the subsequent decades, for the sake of comparison over a longer period of time the 1951 figures are also usually taken into account and the same procedure is followed here also. Table 10.3 gives the relevant information dividing the occupations into nine major categories that the census uses.

Table 10.3   Occupational Classification of Workers: 1951 to 1981 (per cent)

Occupational Categories and Sectoral Groupings	1951	1961	1971	1981
1. Cultivators	50.0	52.8	43.4	41.6
2. Agricultural Labourers	19.7	16.7	26.3	24.9
3. Livestock, forestry, fishing, hunting, plantations, orchards etc.	2.4	2.3	2.4	2.3
A–Sector (1–3)	72.1	71.8	72.1	68.8
4. Mining and quarrying	0.6	0.5	0.5	0.6
5. Manufacturing	9.0	10.6	9.5	11.3
of which (i) Household Industry		6.4	3.5	3.5
(ii) Other than Household Industry	9.0	4.2	6.0	7.8
6. Construction	1.1	1.1	1.2	1.6
M–Sector (4–6)	10.7	12.2	11.2	13.5
7. Trade and Commerce	5.2	4.0	5.6	6.2
8. Transport, Storage & Communication	1.5	1.6	2.4	2.7
9. Other Services	10.5	10.4	8.7	8.8
S–Sector (7–9)	17.2	16.0	16.7	17.7
Total	100.0	100.0	100.0	100.0

Table 10.3 reveals many significant aspects about the occupational patterns of the labour force since Independence. The sectoral groupings

of the occupations shows stability during the 1951–71 period, and some variations in the decade of the 1970s. Although strictly comparable figures are not available for earlier periods it is generally accepted that there has been a stubborn stability of occupational patterns in the Indian economy throughout the present century with the variations noted in the 1970s being the first signs of change. It has been empirically established that as an economy develops there would be a shift of the labour force from the agricultural (A–sector) to the manufacturing (M–sector) and service sectors (S–sector).[5] Going by that criterion, therefore, the crowding of the labour force in the agricultural sector must be taken as an indication of the lack of development of the economy. However, at a more disaggregated level it would appear that the sense of stability is somewhat illusory. Within the A–Sector, for instance, there is a perceptible decline of the share of cultivators and a visible increase in the share of agricultural labourers (particularly during the 1960s) which amounts to a shift from h–2 to h–4 units. A similar change can also be seen within manufacturing where the decline in the share of the labour force in household industry and the increase in the share of 'other than household industry' is more prominent than the increase in the share of the sector itself. It may be noted too that in the 1981 census 'manufacturing' includes repairs also which may partly explain the increase in the share of that sector, especially in 'other than household industry'.

Information available from the National Sample Surveys also confirms the movement from h–2 to h–4 units. Rural labour households as a percentage of rural households increased from about 25 per cent in 1964–65 to 30 per cent in 1974–75 and 37 per cent in 1977–78. Similarly, those reporting their occupational status as 'employees' rose from 31 per cent in 1958–59 to 34 per cent in 1972–73 and to 35 per cent in 1977–78.[6] Further, within the class of wage labourers, the proportion reporting casual labour, as distinct from regular wage or salaried employment as means of livelihood has also risen. Among males, casual wage labourers accounted for 65 per cent of wage labourers in 1972–73 which went up to 72.7 per cent in 1983–84 while among females the proportion increased from 88.5 to 91.6 per cent during the same period.

Even within what is formally designated as 'cultivators' an increasing proportion must be finding it difficult to make a living solely on the basis of cultivation. In the previous chapter we saw that in terms of ownership of land close to two-thirds of rural households have less than 1.0 hectare of land. The share of operational holdings that are described as marginal (that is, farmers who operate less than 1.0 hectare whether they own the land or have leased in the land) has been increasing over time. Marginal holdings accounted for 50 per cent of all holdings in 1970–71, 54.5 per cent in 1976–77 and 56.5 per cent in 1980–81. To a certain extent this is the result of the decline in the land–man ratio as population increases, the partitioning of land (especially small ownership holdings) among members of the family and the distribution of small plots of land to the landless. But an analysis of the changes in operational holdings along with changes in the size of rural population has shown that these are not the only factors. A writer sums up the evidence thus:

A significant feature which is apparent...is the phenomenal increase in the number of marginal holdings from 36.02 million in 1970–71 to 50–52 million in 1980–87. Of course, distribution of ceiling surplus land to 3.24 million beneficiaries has to be accounted for in this figure. Even deducting the number of 3.24 million new beneficiary marginal holders the net figure would be 47.28 million—an increase of 11.08 million over 10 years. It means that on an average 1.1 million marginal holdings are coming into existence annually. The annual rate of marginalisation was 3.98 per cent or 4 per cent which was significantly higher than the 1.9 per cent annual rate of growth of rural population between 1971 and 1981. It, perhaps, indicates that marginalisation was more due to immiserisation rather than normal devolution of property (Bandyopadhyay, 1986).

A possibly related phenomenon has been an increase in the share of the labour force in non-agricultural activities in the rural areas. Table 10.3 has already shown the increase in the share of the labour force in non-agricultural activities in the country as a whole between 1971 and 1981. To some extent it is the reflection of the shift of the labour force from rural areas to urban areas where non-agricultural activities predominate. But a more detailed analysis of the census data shows that the shift out of agriculture and the diversification of occupations have been taking place in the rural areas also (as revealed also by the village studies referred to in Chapter 9). The data from the National Sample Surveys also confirm this.[7] However, how is this phenomenon to be interpreted? In particular, is this diversification an expression of increasing productivity and higher incomes in the rural areas or does it reflect that workers are being pushed out of agriculture and moving into anything else that becomes available? Both these are possibilities and, as in many other aspects, in this too there can be tremendous regional variations. A study which analysed the data at the level of the major states in the country comes to the following conclusion:[8]

1. The incidence of non-agricultural employment is seen to have a significant positive relation with crop output per head of agricultural population: that is, states with relatively prosperous agricultural

population tend to have a high proportion of rural workers in non-agricultural activity.

2. Higher inequality of operational holdings is seen to go with lower incidence of non-agricultural employment.

3. The percentage of area under non-food grain crops is positively related to non-agricultural employment.

4. There is a positive relationship between rural unemployment rate and the incidence of non-agricultural employment and this association is stronger than the others.

The evidence is inconclusive: the first and the third would seem to suggest that diversification is related to better performance, but the fourth appears to favour the opposite interpretation, that non-agricultural activities act to some extent as a residual factor absorbing labour which cannot find work in agriculture.

Apart from these factors there is another that explains the increase in non-agricultural activities in the rural areas, viz., the rapid expansion of public sector activities in rural areas, both in terms of administration and in terms of development projects. Expansion of the activities of the state in different ways has been a major factor in the increase of wage employment in the country and this must have been particularly so in the rural areas. There have been direct attempts by the governments, both central and states, to generate employment; extension of educational, public health, postal and other services also increase employment; the wide range of developmental programmes, including poverty eradication programmes too contribute to increase in employment directly and indirectly. Though all of these are wage employments in the strict sense of the term, a division of these into h–4 and h–3 categories will be useful for many analytical purposes. From the discussion in Chapter 7 it may be recalled that the distinction between the two is that the workers from h–4 units have no non-labour resources at all so that they must rely solely on the sale of their labour power to make a living whereas though workers from h–3 units also sell their labour power, they are backed by non-labour resources usually in the form of financial assets. It is difficult to draw a sharp empirical distinction between the two and what is usually referred to as the tertiary or service sector will consist of labour force from both types of units. However, since the bulk of the workers from h–4 units are in agriculture (agricultural labourers) and in manufacturing (wage workers in household industries, as also in the factory sector), it may be fair to say that the workers from the h–3 units are to be found mainly in the service sector. But the service sector itself is a very heterogeneous group consisting of trade, transport, communications, the wide range of 'professions', administrative and defence services etc. In all these categories workers from h–4 and h–3 units can be found. One area where the workers from the h–3 units are likely to dominate is the government sector consisting of administration and defence services. We shall have to come back subsequently to the role of the h–3 units in the Indian economy.

The major facts that emerge from the analysis of the changes in the labour force since Independence are that there has been a shift from self-employment to wage employment (from h–2 units to h–4 units and h–3 units); that within wage employment casual employment has been much more pronounced than regular employment and the tendency has been for casualisation to increase; that there has been some occupational diversification, particularly in the 1970s away from the traditional activities of agriculture and household industry into (modern) manufacturing industry and the services.

The unorganised sector

On the basis of the information available from the Census and other sources it is also possible to make a quantitative estimate of the unorganised sector both overall and within each of the major occupational categories. Table 10.4 provides the figures. It is seen that 90 per cent of the workers are in the unorganised sector. Not surprisingly all cultivators and agricultural labourers are in the unorganised sector. Other occupations where the unorganised sector dominates are trade and commerce (97 per cent) the residual sector within agriculture consisting of livestock, forestry, fishing, plantations etc. (74 per cent), manufacturing (73 per cent) and construction (67 per cent). Only in the case of mining and quarrying which accounts for less than 1 per cent of the total workforce is the share of the unorganised sector seen to be less than 50 per cent. These facts, therefore, bring out the all-pervasive nature of the unorganised sector in the Indian economy whose characteristics were examined in the preceding chapter.

GROWTH IN PRODUCTION

The village studies referred to in the previous chapter showed that in each one of these villages there has been a striking increase in production and productive activity since Independence. This has been the experience in most parts of the country and in respect of most sectors of the economy: there has been an increase in production; new goods have also become available. Even casual observation would substantiate these claims. And while there may be occasional scarcities for some specific good or the other, the upward trend in production would appear to be sustained.

Table 10.4 Workers in Organised and Unorganised Sectors, 1981

Occupational categories	Organised		Unorganised		Total		As p.c. of row totals		
	Lakhs	P.c.	Lakhs	P.c.	Lakhs	P.c.	Organised	Unorganised	Total
1. Cultivators	–	–	925	46.3	925	41.6	–	100	100
2. Agricultural Labourers	–	–	555	27.8	555	24.9	–	100	100
3. Livestock, Forestry, Fishing etc.	13	5.7	37	1.9	50	2.3	26	74	100
4. Mining and Quarrying	9	3.9	4	0.2	13	0.6	69	31	100
5. Manufacturing	68	29.7	183	9.2	251	11.3	27	73	100
6. Construction	12	5.3	24	1.2	36	1.6	33	67	100
7. Transport, Storage & Communications	28	12.2	33	1.6	61	2.7	46	54	100
8. Trade & Commerce	4	1.7	135	6.8	139	6.2	3	97	100
9. Other Services	95	41.5	100	5.0	195	8.8	49	51	100
Total	229	100.0	1,996	100.0	2,225	100.0	10	90	100

The Indian economy whose performance was rather lethargic during the colonial period has come to have a new dynamism since the middle of the present century.

Table 10.5 Increase in Production (Selected Items)

Items	Units	Period I (1950–51)	Period II (1988–89)	Entry in Period II as multiple of Entry in Period I
1. Foodgrains	mil. tonnes	55.0	170.2	3.09
2. Rice	"	20.6	70.7	3.43
3. Wheat	"	6.5	54.0	8.30
4. Oil Seeds	"	5.2	17.9	3.44
5. Pulses	"	8.4	13.7	1.63
6. Milk	"	17.0	51.5	3.02
7. Eggs	number(mil.)	1,000	19,500	19.50
8. Cotton	mil.bales	3.0	8.7	2.90
9. Fertilisers	1000 tonnes	92	8,964	97.43
10. Coal	mil. tonnes	32.8	200.8	6.12
11. Cement	"	2.7	45.4	16.81
12. Finished Steel	"	1.0	11.1	11.10
13. Electricity	mil. kwh	6,575	214,500	32.62
14. Cloth	mil. metres	3,401	13,282	3.90
15. Paper & Paper Board	lakh tonnes	1.3	21.8	16.76
16. Bicycles	number('000)	110	6,700	60.90
17. Motor Cycles, Scooters, mopeds	number('000)	19.4(1961)	1,674	86.28
18. Cars	number('000)	12.4	178	14.35
19. Domestic Refrigerator	number	600	991,400	1,652.30
20. Petroleum products	lakh tonnes	3.0	486.5	162.16

Table 10.5 which gives the production figures in different spheres of the economy in the early 1950s and the late 1980s captures something of that dynamism. It is seen that whether in terms of basic necessities of life like foodgrains and cloth, or comforts and conveniences like refrigerators and cars, or goods required for further production such as fertilisers and steel, there has been a noticeable increase in production, in some cases very striking indeed. In particular, the fact that foodgrains production showed a more than three-fold increase during this period, thus staying ahead of the population increase, and in contrast to the *decrease* in production during the first half of the century is quite commendable.[9]

National income and its valuation

The Indian economy, of course, produces many more goods (and services) and one of the questions to be considered is whether there is a way of aggregating all of these such that one can meaningfully talk about the 'production' of the economy or about its 'output'. Obviously, it is not permissible to add rice, cloth, electricity, cars etc. and to talk about total production in that sense. But as was seen in Chapter 4, exchange makes it possible for physical quantities of goods expressed in terms of their specific units to be converted into value categories so that heterogeneous goods can be expressed in terms of homogeneous exchange values which then can be added to provide an aggregate index of 'production'. Thus tonnes of rice, metres of cloth, kilo watt hours of electricity and numbers of cars, each yielding not readily comparable use values can be converted into their respective money values and the sum of these values can be termed the total production, (the total *value* of production to be accurate), of the Indian economy. If we are thinking of a 'closed economy', that is, a national economy without transactions with other national economies (via exports and imports, for instance) this value of production must also accrue as incomes to the members of the economy. On this basis the procedure of aggregating the value of output of an economy has come to be known as National Income Accounting.[10]

The detailed procedures of National Income Accounting are somewhat tedious,[11] but its basic principles can be easily comprehended. As noted above what is referred to as 'National Income' can be thought of either as the value of goods and services produced in the economy or as income accruing to the members of the economy over a standard period of time, generally one year. Since it is an attempt to measure the availability of goods and services (or the accrual of income) *over a period of time*, it is a *flow* concept unlike wealth which is the value of goods at *a given point of time* which, therefore, is a *stock* concept.[12] If the flow can be correctly estimated, it can be thought of as an indicator of the performance of the economy during that specified period and the indicator can then be used to make comparative evaluations. Thus, if national income can be estimated for two consecutive years which we shall designate as t1 and t2, it will be possible to find out whether it has increased or not; it will also be possible to calculate the magnitude of change. Following convention let us denote national income as Y with Y_{t1}, and Y_{t2} therefore representing national income in the two years. If Y_{t2} is greater (less) than Y_{t1}, we can say that national income has increased (decreased). It can also be stated ΔY which is $Y_{t2} - Y_{t1}$, is the change, i.e., growth (positive if $Y_{t2} > Y_{t1}$ and negative if $Y_{t1} > Y_{t2}$) in the national income and $\Delta Y/Y_{t1}$ expressed as a percentage is a measure of the *rate of change* or *growth rate* of national income. In making comparisons of national income over time, it is also important to consider whether the price level has changed in the meanwhile. National income expressed in terms of the prices prevalent at each period is referred to as national income *at current prices* and national income corrected for changes in the price level is referred to as national income at *constant prices*, or as *real* national income (as against *monetary* national income).

National income figures come in very handy to make numerical comparisons of the performance of the economy and we shall soon put these to use to gain an understanding of the economy somewhat different from what we have acquired so far. But before we do that, it is necessary to point out that beneath the numbers and the analysis of the economy in terms of commodity flows represented by them, there are certain crucial assumptions regarding the valuation procedure. It is not difficult to see that in converting physical quantities of production into value categories it is assumed that there is a valuation procedure that can be considered to be standard. If all goods that are produced are also exchanged, then they all come to have value assigned to them by the exchange process. Such an assumption would be valid in an economic system where what is produced is meant to be sold to someone else. In fact it is such an economic system that national income studies usually accept as the norm. The late Sir John Hicks of the United Kingdom who had contributed much both to the theory and measurement of national income expressed the rationale of that approach thus:

> People earn their living in all sorts of different ways—by manual work, by brain work, in factories, in offices, and on farms, in dull ways, in interesting ways — but the thing which is common to all ways of earning one's living is the doing of work for which one is paid, doing work and being paid for doing it.... It appears that the whole of the economic activity of humanity (that vast complex of activities which we call the Economic System) consists of nothing else but an immense cooperation of workers or producers to make things and do things which consumers want.... (Hicks, 1942: 11, 14).

From what we have already seen of the Indian economy it is not difficult to point out that the claim that 'economic activity everywhere (of all humanity) consists of work done for payment' is an overgeneralisation and hence a distortion. Such was not the case at all times; such is not the case in India and many other countries today. Statements of the kind that Hicks had made illustrate the all-pervasive tendency in economic analysis to assume that the institutional framework of the capitalist economy is universal. Even when Hicks and two Indian economists adapted the book to deal with India's national income, no difference was made in this basic assumption.[13]

Be that as it may, the issue to consider is how total production gets converted into value categories in economies such as ours where (as in the case of foodgrains) only part of the total output enters into exchange, the other part being consumed directly by the producers themselves. One possibility for valuation here is to use market prices to value both the marketed and non-marketed components of total production. The procedure could be justified if what is not marketed is only a negligible share of total output. But where this is not the case it would be incorrect to imagine that market price would remain unaffected if the entire produce were to be brought to the market, and so the use of the prevailing market price to value the total output is arbitrary and misleading. There is a further problem that while this procedure is resorted to in the case of goods produced, it is not generally followed in the case of services rendered, that is work done, which is not paid for. One of its consequences is that as services hitherto not paid for come to be paid when they become mediated through exchange, there will be an increase in income which is only illusory. When we turn to a detailed analysis of the Indian experience we shall have occasion to see the influence that the service sector has in the growth of national income.

There is a second problem of valuation closely associated with this. If the value of goods produced and services rendered is to be unambiguously arrived at, there must be a uniform price for every unit sold of each one of the goods and services. This too is usually taken for granted on the ground that as market transactions increase and markets become more and more competitive, price of every commodity will tend to be uniform throughout the system. We have seen that the generalisation of exchange can lead in that direction. But we have also seen that where the spread of exchange is mediated through profit maximising merchants, there is also the counter tendency towards differentiation and segmentation which prevents prices from turning out to be uniform. To the extent that the latter tendency has strength in the system, uniform valuation cannot be taken for granted.

Apart from these two considerations, which have significant bearing on the theoretical and practical aspects of valuation, there is a further and deeper social factor that influences the valuation of the total output. The problem of valuation is not something that emerges after production has been completed. On the contrary, production decisions themselves—what will be produced, how much will be produced, what processes will be used in production—are heavily influenced by value considerations. This can be seen readily with respect to the 'what will be produced' question, or the problem of the product mix. It is rather elusively maintained that in a capitalist system the decision on what will be produced is determined by the consumers for only production that is responsive to what the consumer wants will be profitable to the producers. However, it is not the consumers' preference that directs production, *but the purchasing power* of the consumers which is a derivative largely of their resource power. And the producer is not trying to meet the requirements of the consumers as such, but only of consumers who can back their requirements by the requisite resource power. Thus, housing is a requirement of all consumers, but only the housing requirements of a section of the consumers who can pay for what they want will be met. In a capitalist economy, therefore, each act of production is an expression of a valuation of what is important and valuable—but a valuation that reflects the distribution of purchasing power and of resources in the system. For, after all, production is a decision on how resources will be put to use, and in a capitalist economy, as we have already seen, that decision is made basically by those who own and control resources; although in any capitalist country some production priorities and decisions are made by the state on considerations other than resource power. All subsequent valuations are derived from this underlying valuation process. To put it differently, in a capitalist system the prevailing distribution of resource power (rather than the preferences of consumers or the needs of the members of the society) determines what will be produced and how each good that is produced will be valued when it becomes commoditised. Hence national income is as much a reflection of the prevailing distribution of resource power in the economy as it is a measure of the volume of goods produced in it.

These considerations show that the numbers that national income calculations throw up cannot be thought of as socially neutral. This is not surprising because, after all, valuation is a social process. Apart from this general problem, there are special problems in the calculations of national income in the Indian context.[14] However, used with caution national income figures can provide an understanding of the economy to supplement what we have seen so far.

Growth and change in national income

At 1980–81 price level, the national income of India increased from Rs 40,454 crores in 1950–51 to Rs. 166,593 crores in 1988–89.[15] If the 1950–51 figure is taken as 100.0, the 1988–89 index corresponding to it becomes 411.8 which makes it easier to assess the magnitude of change over this period. The average annual compound rate of growth of national income (the annual growth rate) that is derived from these figures is 3.8 per cent. Dividing the national income by the population, the per capita national income can also be calculated which was Rs 1126.9 in 1950–51 and Rs 2082.4 in 1988–89. When indexed with 1950–51 as the base the latter figure becomes 184.8. The annual growth rate of per capita income is 1.6 per cent.

These figures will make sense only when they are compared with some other figures of a similar nature. One possibility is to compare them with corresponding figures relating to the first half of the century. For the period from 1900–1901 to 1944–45 it has been estimated that the annual growth rate of the Indian economy was 1.2 per cent and per capita growth rate was 0.2 per cent. The comparison, therefore, substantiates the claim made about the post-Independence dynamism of the economy.

A further possibility is to compare the experience of the Indian economy with those of other countries. According to one calculation covering the period from 1950 to 1983 the growth rate of the Indian economy was 3.6 per cent, of Sri Lanka 4.4 per cent, Pakistan 4.8 per cent, Indonesia 5.5 per cent, Philippines 5.7 per cent, Thailand 6.8 per cent and South Korea 7.2 per cent.[16] Inter country comparisons of growth rates have several problems, but the difference between India and these other Asian countries is so pronounced that one does not have to entertain any doubt that the performance of the Indian economy was one of the poorest in the region in the second half of this century.

We shall continue to concentrate on the performance of the Indian economy and shall try to gain further insights into it by examining the contribution of the major sectors to the overall growth performance. As in the case of the allocation of the labour force among the major sectors, so in the case of national income the expectation is that as an economy grows, the share of the agricultural sector will get reduced and that of manufacturing and services sectors will increase. Panel A of Table 10.6 shows that this has been the Indian experience also. The share of the A–sector in national income is reduced substantially from 57.2 per cent in 1950–51 to 34.9 per cent in 1988–89 and a steadily declining trend is noticed over the period. The share of the M–sector has gone up from 16.2 per cent to 26.8 per cent during the same period and the upward movement has been maintained throughout. The S–sector too has shown an increase, from 26.6 per cent in 1950–51 to 38.3 per cent in 1988–89. That the S–sector has played a dominating role in the growth process is seen from Panel B of Table 10.6 where the contributions of the three sectors to the increase in national income have been assessed. Taking the period as a whole, the contribution of the S–sector to the increase in national income (that is, $\Delta S/\Delta Y$) is as high as 42.0 per cent, much higher than either of the other two sectors. The contribution of the S–sector to the growth of national income was rising during the 1950s, 1960s and 1970s, with its contribution being above 50 per cent in the 1970s, though in the 1980s it has come down to 43.0 per cent. There

Table 10.6   *Analysis of the Growth of the Indian Economy: 1950–51 to 1988–89*

	1950–51	1960–61	1970–71	1980–81	1988–89
A. *Share of Major Sectors in National Income* (Y)					
Agriculture (A)	57.2	52.6	46.5	39.8	34.9
Mining & Manufacture (M)	16.2	19.6	22.4	24.3	26.8
Services (S)	26.6	27.8	31.1	38.9	38.3
	1950–51 to 1960–61	1960–61 to 1970–71	1970–71 to 1980–81	1980–81 to 1988–89	1950–51 to 1988–89
B. *Contribution of Major Sectors to Growth in National Income*					
$\dfrac{\Delta A}{\Delta Y}$	42.6	31.6	19.3	25.6	27.9
$\dfrac{\Delta M}{\Delta Y}$	26.7	29.6	30.2	31.4	30.1
$\dfrac{\Delta S}{\Delta Y}$	30.7	38.8	50.4	43.0	42.0

has been no major change in the contribution of the M–sector to growth over this period except that it increased from 26.7 per cent in 1950s to 29.5 in the 1960s after which the variations have been marginal. The contribution of the A–sector has varied quite significantly. It came down from 42.6 per cent in the 1950s to less than 20 per cent in the 1970s after which there was a recovery to 25.6 per cent in the 1980s, which, in a sense, was the result of the very good performance in 1988–89 when there was a substantial recovery in the performance of the sector compared with the very poor performance during most of the decade. A more detailed examination of the data shows that the performance of the A–Sector has been very erratic with the annual growth rate being negative or zero in 15 out of the 38 years and high recovery rates such as in 1988–89 being achieved from time to time. As the M–Sector's contribution to growth has not varied much, the increasing contribution of the S–Sector has been compensating for the not so impressive performance of the A–Sector to maintain a steady increase in national income.

Two observations are in order on the basis of the sectoral performance seen above. The first is to note that while the Indian experience of shifts in the sectoral composition of national income conforms to what has been happening in most parts of the world, there is a major difference too. Generally, the decrease in the share of the A–sector in national income is also accompanied by a decrease in the share of the labour force in that sector. In what are considered to be advanced countries, the decrease in the A–Sector's share in national income is associated with an even more pronounced decrease in the labour force in that sector indicating an increase in relative labour productivity in the sector. On the other hand, the fact that a sharp fall in the share of the A–Sector in the national income in India is accompanied by a fairly stable proportion of the labour force in that sector shows that there has been a relative decline in productivity there. Taking the changing share in national income and labour force of the A–Sector in the Indian economy, therefore, one must conclude that the evidence suggests the poor performance of the A–Sector rather than the healthy performance of the economy as a whole.

The second observation is related. There has been no major shift of the labour force into the S–Sector as Table 10.3 has shown, but there has been a substantial increase in the sector's share in national income. Can this be thought of as showing an increase in labour productivity in that sector? In a formal sense such is the case. But what exactly is the meaning of 'productivity' in this instance? There is no easy way of measuring productivity of labour in the service sector (unlike in the goods producing sectors) and what is considered productivity is nothing other than the earnings of the workers employed. If, therefore, payments to those employed in the service sector increase, national income will also correspondingly increase. This may come about in two ways. In the first place as more and more services that were not being paid for come to be mediated through the exchange process (the growing commoditisation of labour power) there will be an increase in the volume of payments in the service sector. Secondly, an increase in wage rates in the sector will also have the same result. The service sector in the Indian economy, as we have noted already, consists of both h–3 and h–4 households. While it is not easy to say which of these two has been increasing in the service sector, there is reason to think that there has been a growth in the h–3 units in the economy and their earnings have, on the whole, been increasing. It is, therefore, quite likely that what is seen as the growing share of the S–Sector in the national income is mainly a reflection of the increase in the number of h–3 units and their increasing earnings, or the phenomenon of the emergence of an affluent salaried class in government service, and in the private sector.

The growth of the Indian economy's national income thus shows the poor performance of the goods producing sector (particularly agriculture) and the swelling of the goods demanding sector indicating some serious distortions a consequence of which is to keep up the inflationary pressures in the economy.

Changes in sectoral composition

A further division of the national income that is of interest is as between the organised and unorganised sectors and between the public sector (or the state sector) and the private sector within the former. The division of the national income into the organised and unorganised sectors is available in national accounts statistics for the period from 1960–61 to 1984–85. Table 10.7 gives the figures for selected years. Although column 5 of the Table indicates a drop in the share of the unorganised sector over time from roughly three fourths in the early 1960s to a little less than two thirds in the mid-1980s, it also brings out the continuing significance of the sector. It is equally important to note that the corresponding growth of the organised sector is achieved solely as a result of the increase in the share of the public sector, (column 2) the share of the organised private sector (column 3) having registered a marginal decline.

The growth in the share of the public sector indicating the increasing role of the state in economic activity is quite impressive. It was of the order of 5 to 6 per cent in the early 1950s, but started moving up quickly with the active participation of the state in economic activities through the programme of planned development. From then on it has been steadily going up claiming (or accounting for) about a quarter of the national income by the mid-1980s.

Table 10.7 *Changes in the Sectoral Composition of National Income (per cent)*

Year	Public Sector	Private Sector	Organised Sector	Unorganised Sector
1	2	3	4 (2+3)	5
1960–6¹	10.6	14.9	25.5	74.5
1965–66	13.2	16.0	29.2	70.8
1970–71	14.5	13.0	27.5	72.5
1975–76	18.3	12.4	30.7	69.3
1980–81	20.4	12.9	33.3	66.7
1984–85	24.5	13.2	37.7	62.3

Because of the dominance of the agricultural sector in the Indian economy and the absence of direct state participation in that sector, the figure of 25 per cent as the share of the state in national income may not quite convey the role that the state has in economic activity for in some branches of the economy the share of the state is 100 per cent. Table 10.8, therefore, gives a more detailed account of the state's share in the value of output of the major branches of the economy during the middle of the 1980s.

SAVINGS AND INVESTMENT

We had denoted national income by Y and its growth by $\triangle Y$. Income

Table 10.8   *Share of the State in the Value of Output in Different Sectors, 1984–85*

Sector	Percentage share of the state
1. Agriculture	1.8
2. Forestry	39.6
3. Mining & Quarrying	94.3
4. Manufacturing	20.2
5. Construction	17.1
6. Electricity, gas and water supply	92.0
7. Transport, Storage & Communication	47.6
a) Railways	100.0
b) Transport, by other means & storage	23.9
c) Communication	100.0
8. Trade, hotels and restaurants	4.7
9. Banking & Insurance	80.0
10. Public administration & defence	100.0
11. Other services	44.2

(Y) is the value of goods produced during one year. Some of the goods produced are used up (consumed) during the year, but part will be accumulated (or saved) for the future. The value of goods consumed during the year may be represented as C (for consumption) and the value of goods saved for the future as S (for savings) so that income may also be split up into C and S whereby $Y = C + S$. However, goods (such as machines and factories) meant to produce other goods subsequently (next year) are referred to also as investment goods and their value is usually designated as I. Hence we may also say that $Y = C + I$. Since $Y = C + S$ and $C + I$, it follows that $S = I$ (that is, S and I are identical). In terms of national income accounting it means that the volume of savings made in the economy (by those who dispose of their income as consumption and savings) must correspond to the value of investment goods produced (by those who produce goods). The meaning of this relationship is self evident in the case of a rudimentary economy where what is set aside for the future ('saved') can only be in the form of goods produced for use in the future ('invested'). But in an economy with many units whose specialised activities are mediated through exchange and money, it is possible for those who wish to save to hold their savings in monetary or financial forms and for those who are producing goods to produce some that are not meant for immediate consumption. In an economy that consists of h–3 units and f–units, savings can become the function of the former (held in the form of claims or financial assets including money) and investment to become the responsibility of the f–units who may borrow the savings generated by the h–3 units by promising to pay them later. Such an economy may also come to have financial intermediation with specialised units (b–units) receiving the savings of the h–3 units and lending to the f–units.

To some extent the financial interme iation function may be done by the state too.

These relationships and mediations exist in the Indian economy. But the Indian economy has h–2 units also which may produce both consumption goods and investment goods that they require. A farmer, for instance, may produce grain that he uses up during the year, but may also dig a well to improve cultivation in the future. What he 'saves', therefore, is in the form of physical (and not financial) assets.

We shall look into the macro picture that corresponds to these different methods of providing for the future in the Indian economy based primarily on an official study that was done in the middle of the 1980s.[17]

In the early 1950s the savings rate of the Indian economy was very low, just about 10 per cent. This was taken to be a reflection of the general low performance of the system and of the inability of a poor economy to set aside resources for future growth. Hence it was assumed also that raising the rate of savings would be a very difficult task, and so it appeared till about the end of the 1960s when the rate was still below 15 per cent. But for reasons which have not been adequately explained so far, the savings rate started rising rapidly in the 1970s reaching an all time high of 24.7 per cent in 1978–79 which was one of the highest rates among capitalist countries at that time. From then the rate started coming down and was just a little over 21 per cent in the late 1980s. This means that starting from setting aside a tenth of its gross output for the future in the early 1950s, the Indian economy was able to spare almost one fourth of its gross output for the future by the late 1970s, and the figure has come down to a little over one fifth in more recent years which is still quite a creditable performance. How an economy with low levels of production and productivity is able to achieve such high rates of savings is something that needs to be explained.

Another noteworthy aspect of the savings of the Indian economy is its sectoral composition. For this purpose the standard procedure has been to divide the economy into three sectors, the public sector, the private corporate sector and the household sector. The first two correspond to the public sector and private sector as shown in Table 10.7 and hence the third residual sector, 'households' corresponds roughly to the unorganised sector in that Table.

Pattern of savings of the household sector

One of the significant aspects of the Indian economy is that the bulk of the savings is done by the household sector whose share in total savings was almost 75 per cent in the early 1950s with the public sector accounting for about 17 per cent and the private corporate sector the rest, 8 to 9 per cent.

It was expected that as the economy grew the share of savings of the corporate sector would increase (as has happened in other capitalist countries) and that the share of the household sector would get correspondingly reduced. For a while it appeared that this was happening. By the early 1960s, the corporate sector's share in savings had gone up to 13.4 per cent and the share of the public sector to 20.6 per cent with that of the household sector getting reduced to 66.0 per cent. Since then, however, the trends have been reversed in favour of the household sector whose share went up, once again, to close to 75 per cent in 1985–86 with that of the public sector getting reduced to 15.6 per cent and of the corporate sector coming down to less than 10 per cent. In fact, in 1988–89 the share of the household sector moved up further to 83.6 per cent; of the public sector the share came down drastically to 7.7 per cent; of the corporate sector the share moved down to 8.7 per cent. The household sector, therefore, continues to dominate the generation of savings in the Indian economy.

The household sector is an heterogeneous group consisting of h–2, h–3, and h–4 types. It will be reasonable to assume that h–4 units do not (are not able to) save. In the case of the h–2 units (consisting of household production units and all unincorporated enterprises such as partnerships) savings are likely to assume physical form. Official statistics relating to savings do not distinguish between h–2 and h–3 households, but provide separate figures for physical and financial savings. As may be expected, physical assets constituted the major share of the savings of the household sector in the early period after independence, close to two-thirds in the first half of the 1950s. Since then this share has been coming down and the share of the financial assets has been correspondingly going up—with the two getting equalised in 1980–81 and the share of the financial assets exceeding that of physical assets from then on till the mid-1980s. After that, once again, there has been a reversal with physical assets claiming 55 per cent of the total household savings in 1988–89. The increase in the volume and share of the financial assets (consisting of currency, bank deposits, shares and debentures, life insurance, provident and pension funds etc.) from the early 1950s to the late 1980s may be interpreted as the growing significance of the h–3 units in the economy. At the same time the stubborn persistence of the physical assets shows that financial intermediation is still not adequately developed in the Indian economy.

But there is substantial intermediation which makes it possible for the savings and investment decisions to be separated. While the household sector accounts for the major share of the savings in the economy, investment is done primarily by the other two sectors. In the early years since Independence the household sector accounted for the major share of investment or capital formation in the economy, around 58 per cent. Capital formation in the public sector was then 23 per cent and the rest, 19 per cent in the private corporate sector. From the period of the Second Five Year Plan onwards, the share of capital formation by the public sector began to increase, generally reducing the shares of both the corporate and household sectors. In the mid-sixties, for instance, the share of the public sector accounted for 50 per cent, of the corporate sector 15.7 per cent and of the household sector 34.2 per cent. During the second half of the sixties and throughout the seventies the share of the public sector was lower than the peak figures reached in 1965–66 and at the beginning of the 1980s it was slightly less than 45 per cent. Since then it picked up once again to 48.7 per cent in 1986–87. The household sector's share came down to about 42 per cent by the beginning of the 1980s and touched the low figure of 25 per cent in 1982–83, but moved up to 36 per cent in 1986–87. The share of the private corporate sector has also fluctuated going down to less than 10 per cent in 1978–79, but recovering subsequently to 24.5 per cent in 1985–86, but coming down to 15.2 per cent in 1986–87. The trend that is discernible since Independence is for the state to emerge as the leading sector as far as capital formation is concerned accounting for a little less than half of the total in recent years. The household sector's share has certainly come down, but in spite of the sharp increase in public sector activity and the substantial growth of the private sector, the household sector still accounts for well over a third of the capital formation in the economy. It is the performance of the private corporate sector that is different from what might have been expected.

Resources from outside

Because of the flow of resources into the economy from the rest of the world, investment or capital formation in the Indian economy has been more than what would have been possible in terms of domestic savings. During the years immediately following the Second World War when the problem of the 'underdeveloped' countries started receiving international attention, it was generally believed that because of their poor economic conditions they would not be able to generate growth on their own and that therefore foreign aid would have to be a major component in their development programmes. The 1960s, therefore, became the United Nations' Development Decade with an accent on the need for the richer countries of the world to aid the development of the poorer ones. India was one of the major recipients of the global aid programme and hence, not surprisingly, net inflow of aid constituted almost 4 per cent of India's national income and 44 per cent of capital formation in the mid-sixties. But the big inflow did not last long. By the end of the decade it was only about 1 per cent of national income and less than 10 per cent of capital formation. Both because of the growth of the economy and because of the drying up of aid, foreign assistance in the 1980s has only been in the neighbourhood of 0.5 per cent of national income and around 5 per cent of capital formation. It may be noted that much of aid is in the form of loans although the terms of these loans may be more favourable than commercial borrowings which the country has been resorting to in more recent years. The outstanding external debt of the economy from all sources in 1989–90 was of the order of over Rs 80,000 crores.

Direct investment by foreign concerns has also increased substantially of late, especially in the 1980s. Private foreign investment in the Indian economy was very negligible in the 1950s, 1960s and 1970s. Even in 1980 it amounted to less than Rs 10 crores. But from then on it began to accelerate rapidly crossing Rs 100 crores in 1984, but continuing more or less at that level till 1987. In 1988 it shot up to Rs 240 crores and in 1989 further to Rs 315 crores indicating the impact of the 'opening up' of the economy during the Seventh Plan period.

Through an analysis of the changing patterns of the labour force, the growth and composition of national income and savings and capital formation we have tried to capture some aspects of the changes taking place in the Indian economy since Independence to supplement the insights gained through the accounts given in the preceding chapter. In the next chapter we shall try to see what impact these changes have had on the different sections of people that constitute the Indian economy and society.

NOTES

1. On Kerala's experience see United Nations, 1975 and Bhat & Rajan, 1990 and other studies referred to in them.
2. Those below 15 years constitute around 40 per cent of the total population.
3. The worker population ratio that the Census refers to is the reciprocal of our P/W ratio.
4. See Krishnamurthy, 1984.
5. The outstanding empirical work on this aspect has been done by the American economist, Simon Kuznets. See Kuznets, 1966.
6. See Vaidyanathan, 1986.
7. See Vaidyanathan, 1986 and Basant and Kumar, 1988.
8. Vaidyanathan, 1986.
9. The figures in the last column of Table 10.5 must be properly interpreted. The magnitude of increase from period I to period II depends a great deal on the base figures

themselves. Thus, foodgrains production was already 55 million tonnes in 1950–51 and increased over three times by period II. On the other hand, the production of refrigerators in 1950–51 was as low as 600 and so it could register a 1652 times increase by 1988–89. Obviously, the multiple of three in the case of foodgrains and of 1652 in the case of refrigerators cannot be compared directly.

10. National income of 'open economies' (that is, national economies that have transactions with other economies) can also be calculated making appropriate provision for exports and imports.

11. Most textbooks on economics, especially macro economics provide details of how national income estimates are made.

12. In order to understand the distinction between 'flow' and 'stock' a comparison may be made to a water tank into which a specified quantity of water comes in every hour (flow) and which will have a certain quantity if measured at any given time (stock). If water has been flowing into the tank for a while the stock may be larger than the flow.

13. Hicks et al., 1984.

14. These have been dealt with in Rao, 1983.

15. The figures quoted are from Government of India, Economic Survey, 1989–90.

16. These figures are taken from Sundrum, 1987, Table 2.6. The book also has a detailed analysis of India's national income from 1950–51 to the early 1980s.

17. The reference is to the Reserve Bank of India's Report of the Committee to Review the Working of the Monetary System (1985) which is commonly referred to as the Chakravarty Committee Report as (the late) Sukhamoy Chakravarty was the Chairman of the Committee.

Notes to Tables:
The information in Table 10.1 has been gathered from official sources.

Table 10.2 is based on different Census Reports.

The source of Table 10.3 is Centre for Monitoring the Indian Economy (CMIE), Basic Statistics Relating to the Indian Economy 1990, Vol I: All India, from Table 9–1–B.

Table 10.4 is also based on the same source as Table 10.3.

Table 10.5 has been compiled from different official sources.

Table 10.6 has been calculated from information provided by CMIE, op. cit., Table 8.5.

Table 10.7 and 10.8 are based on official National Income Statistics.

11

Poverty and Affluence

What has been the impact of the transformation of the economy on different sections of the population? This is the question examined in this chapter. A review of the kind of transformation of the economy envisaged during the Freedom Movement and what has been actually happening since Independence, including under the regime of national planning, shows that the radical changes postulated earlier have not materialised and a choice has been made in favour of a gradual and orderly transformation guided by a democratic state. Many policy measures were attempted to bring about some structural transformation of the economy, but most of these had to be given up because of opposition by interested groups. Hence more recently the attempt has been to let the pattern of production be determined by the natural propensities of the emerging capitalist order with state power being used to keep them under control as well as to ensure that there is some redistribution of benefits in favour of the weaker sections. The achievements and limitations of this strategy are examined, leading on to an assessment of the major crisis that the economy confronts at the beginning of the 1990s.

The division of society into the many who are poor and the few who are affluent has been a very visible aspect of our country from time immemorial. It was so during the pre-colonial period. Colonial rule accentuated the distinction. And in spite of all the resolve and effort since Independence to remove social evils, mass poverty is still with us and the affluent few are becoming still more affluent. We shall examine this phenomenon in greater detail in this chapter.

INEQUALITY AND POVERTY

The coexistence of poverty and affluence may be analysed from two different but related angles. In the first place it denotes inequality in the distribution of resources—of income and wealth. The glaring disparities in the distribution of wealth has been noted already in Chapter 9. Even casual observation will confirm that the same must be true with respect to incomes as well. Statistics relating to the distribution of income are less readily available than to the distribution of wealth, but according to a frequently referred private estimate, the bottom 40 per cent of households in the country claim about 16.3 per cent of the income while the top 5 per cent claim 22.4 per cent with the top 1 per cent alone having 7.7 per cent.[1]

But inequalities of this kind are not unique to India; indeed, a case can be made out that from the point of view of inequality of incomes in other countries, the Indian situation is not too unsatisfactory. There is, however, another way of looking at the problem of the coexistence of poverty and affluence, and that is to decide on some *absolute* level to designate either poverty or affluence, or both, and to see the numbers and proportion of the population below the poverty level and/or above the affluence level. The procedure that has been followed in India and many other countries of the world in recent years is of this kind. The standard practice now is to set some absolute and empirically verifiable norm for identifying poverty, use it to draw a 'poverty line' and then find out the proportion of the population below that line.[2] Such measures can then be used to make intertemporal comparisons to find out whether the level of poverty is decreasing or not over time. They can also be used to probe into the causal factors responsible for the persistence or changes in the level of poverty. Studies of this kind are quite common in India, particularly since the early 1970s.[3]

The 'poverty line'

The norm that is officially recognised in India for identifying poverty is what an Expert Committee set up by the Government of India in 1962 described as 'desirable minimum level of consumer expenditure'. The Committee arrived at a figure of Rs. 20 per head per month at 1960–61 prices as the cut-off line. It is not clear exactly how this figure was arrived at, but later exercises have shown that perhaps it was related to nutritional requirements, that is, the calories considered necessary for an average human being. In any case it was evident from the very outset that the norm suggested was very low, hardly sufficient to meet the expenses of essential consumption, therefore, primarily food, and excluding expenditure on health and education both of which, it was assumed, would be provided by the State. One of the very first official documents that made use of the norm to assess the extent of poverty in the country indicated how low the accepted norm was. It said:

The per capita annual income in 1960–61 was approximately Rs. 330. The average expenditure on consumption is about Rs 300 per head per year or Rs 25 per head per month. *This is too meagre to sustain a level of living which could be considered tolerable in the modern context.* The situation is actually far more distressing because the condition of large proportion of the people is much worse than the average would suggest. It is a measure of extreme poverty of the great mass of our eople that more than 60 per cent of them have a level of consumption lower than Rs 25 per capita per month and about 30 per cent less than Rs 15 per capita per month.... Judged against the standard of consumption expenditure of Rs 20 per month per capita, considered generally to be the bare minimum, it is obvious that half of the people live in abject poverty (Srinivasan & Bardhan, 1974: 12–13).

So what the norm accepted in 1962 (and remained unchanged since then), identified was not poverty in India, but *abject poverty*. How abject it is can be seen from a recent study which recorded every day, for a period of six months, the consumption level and the living standard of those who were below the poverty line in one Indian state. (Bhattacharya *et al.*, 1991). Since rice is the staple diet in the state, the authors regarded *variations* in the consumption of rice as a better indicator of poverty than its average level. They found that for a third of the households surveyed the gap between the maximum and minimum per capita consumption of rice during the six month period was over 500 gms, compared with the overall average of 387 gms, showing that there must have been days when the consumption level must have been extremely low. The study found also that half the female adults did not have even two sarees, that 90 per cent of the households did not have any bedding whatsoever and that 70 per cent of the households did not have any vessels made of brass, steel or glass for cooking, serving or eating food. There is no reason to think that the findings of the study are exceptional. The fact is that the officially recognised poverty line is, indeed, a rock bottom level.

The Expert Committee that laid down the poverty norm had suggested that the aim of planning in the country should be to ensure that every household in the country should be brought above the national minimum within a period of 15 years, that is by 1975–76. Official plan documents had also suggested from time to time target dates for the eradication of poverty. In the early 1970s *garibi hatao* (abolition of poverty) had become a political creed and the Fifth Five Year Plan was meant specifically to initiate the process and to take up the task as a crash programme. Now we know that nothing of the kind has happened. According to official statistics there has been a slow reduction of the percentage of population below the poverty line, but at the end of the 1980s, it was still close to 30 per cent although an exercise conducted by the World Bank put it at 40 per cent, that is, a total of close to 325 million people.

Why mass poverty continues

It is not worth arguing whether the correct figure is 30 per cent or 40 per cent.

What needs to be examined is why mass poverty continues in the country in spite of the many attempts to eradicate it. There is a related question too. Why is it that in the midst of such acute and widespread poverty the living standards of a few—perhaps the top 10 per cent of the population—are going up fairly rapidly and quite visibly? There is no 'affluence line' corresponding to the 'poverty line' and hence it is not easy to specify what percentage of the population can be considered as affluent and no precise manner as to measure how their affluence is increasing. We must resort to an indirect way of dealing with this issue. In Table 10.5 we have seen that among the goods whose production has shown substantial increase since Independence, the most prominent have been a set of items that go to meet the needs of those whose incomes are steadily rising—refrigerators, cars, scooters etc. We know also of goods not included in the Table—T.V. sets, air conditioners, kitchen gadgets of various sorts, to name but a few—which have become widely available in recent years. Hence it can be safely inferred that the living standards of a section in society must be going up, and hence the incomes of that section must also be increasing. The puzzle—if there is puzzle—is how and why the economy is able to cater to the needs of a small section almost without limit, when even the basic requirements of the many are not being met. It is necessary to consider these two together to understand the socio-economic phenomenon that is commonly described as mass poverty. In other words, it is the twin phenomena of the continuing poverty of the masses *and* the growing affluence of the few that needs to be explained.

It may be helpful to clarify, also, that the problem being investigated is the *social* phenomenon of mass poverty and not the poverty (or affluence) of specific individuals. At the individual level the explanation of poverty will have to be sought in a wide range of specific issues such as ability and inclination to work, spending habits, and personal characteristics of various sorts. Similarly affluence of particular individuals (or more likely particular households) may also have many explanatory factors. But our quest will be to come to grips with the general problems of poverty and of affluence as we confront these in the Indian economy and society. The attempt will be to examine how these general problems are related to the nature of our economic system and whether and to what extent they are influenced by the policies of the state.

POVERTY AND POLICY

The poverty of India was one of the keenly discussed and contested issues during the colonial period. Indian opinion, expressed by leaders like Dadabhai Navroji and Rammohan Roy, shared also by some European writers, was that the economic drain caused by the colonial administration was the main reason for the worsening conditions of the people of the country.[4] The argument played a crucial role in the Freedom Movement and provided the rationale for mobilising the people against the Raj. Consequently a decisive transformation of the economy constituted a major item on the agenda suggested for the post-Independence period, particularly after *Poorna Swaraj* (full Independence of the country, rather than constitutional reforms within the British rule) was accepted as the political creed of the Freedom Movement.

Two alternatives

Two distinctly different alternatives for the reorganisation of the economy were considered by the leaders of the Movement which were labelled as the 'Gandhian alternative' and the 'Socialist alternative', the latter sometimes also closely identified with the views of Nehru. Gandhi was a great admirer of what he considered to be the traditional set-up of the economy and of administration in India—the village republics. Substantial village level autonomy, participatory form of administration and economic self-sufficiency were the principles that he considered to be cardinal for the future reorganisation of the polity and the economy. On the economic front he would have liked to see each household becoming as self-sufficient as possible in the production of the basic necessities, food and clothing, limiting these needs to essentials. Gandhi attached great importance to manual labour and at one stage held the view that modern industrial civilisation was responsible for the economic and moral problems of societies, although at a later stage he clarified that he was not against machinery as such, but would welcome any machine that would reduce the drudgery of work without displacing labour from productive work. He was also against all forms of exploitation of the human being and considered the employer–employee relationship to be inherently exploitative. On this basis he was an ardent supporter of self-employment. Since he knew that individual self-sufficiency was impossible and because he attached importance to human interactions, he preferred small human communities—the household and the village—which would give full scope for the development of individual personalities and harmonious interrelationships. Taking all these factors into account, it would be right to say that the ideal economic set up from his point of view would have been a village economy of h–2 units linked together through limited forms of horizontal transactions. He was honest enough to admit that he had not given the time and thought to work out the details of such an economic set-up, especially how to move from the existing unequal and unjust economic order to the ideal set-up. He would not accept the collective ownership of land and other resources because he was of the opinion that collective ownership would result in a totalitarian state which would hinder the development of individual personality, even if it might bring about some economic advancement. He would, instead, exert moral pressure on the owners of resources to treat property as being held by them as a trust, to be used for the welfare of society as a whole. Although many aspects of the Gandhian alternative remained vague, Gandhi's standing in the National Movement, and the fact that some elements of his alternative (such as the emphasis on handspun yarn and hand woven cloth, had become symbols of the freedom struggle) gave the hope in certain quarters that once the country became free there would be a reorganisation of the economy along the lines suggested by him.

However, this was something of a minority view. A more influential section under the leadership of Nehru was of the opinion that the post-Independence reorganisation of the economy must be along socialist lines. Nehru himself was an admirer of British Fabian socialist thinking and of the socialist experiment in the Soviet Union which he had an opportunity to observe in 1927. The resolution of the All India Congress Committee in 1929 said: 'In the opinion of this Committee, the great poverty and misery of the Indian people are due, not only to foreign exploitation in India but also to the economic structure of society, which the alien rulers support so that their exploitation may continue. In order, therefore, to remove this poverty and misery and to ameliorate the condition of the masses, it is essential to make revolutionary changes in the present economic and social structure of society and to remove the gross inequalities.' The Congress session in 1931 reiterated it; 'In order to end the exploitation of the masses, political freedom must include real economic freedom'. But there was no indication as to how the revolutionary changes were to be brought about.

Indeed, the specific steps suggested on economic matters were: living wages for industrial workers, reduction of agricultural rent, imposition of a progressive income tax on agricultural incomes, protection of indigenous cloth, control by the state of key industries and ownership of mineral resources. Not much later, it became necessary to point out that the reference to 'revolutionary changes' should not be carried too far. The Working Committee of the Congress in 1934 stated:

Whilst the Working Committee welcomes the formation of groups representing different schools of thought, it is necessary, in view of loose talk about confiscation of private property and necessity of class war, to remind Congressmen...that confiscation and class war are contrary to the Congress creed of non-violence. At the same time the Working Committee is of the opinion that the Congress does contemplate wiser and juster use of private property so as to prevent the exploitation of the landless poor, and also contemplates a healthier relationship between capital and labour.

With the setting up of the National Planning Committee in 1938 under the Chairmanship of Nehru, the socialist goals were reaffirmed. Its Sub–Committee on Land Policy had recommended and the NPC had accepted that 'agricultural land, mines, quarries, rivers and forests are forms of natural wealth, ownership of which must vest absolutely in the people of India collectively'. Also, 'the cooperative principle should be applied to the exploitation of land by developing collective and cooperative farms in order that agriculture may be conducted more scientifically and efficiently, waste avoided, and production increased, and at the same time the habit of mutual cooperation for the benefit of the community developed in place of the individual profit motive'. At a subsequent session of the NPC Nehru reported that as laid down by the Congress in 1931, 'the principle of State ownership or control of key industries and services, mineral resources, railways, waterways, shipping and other means of public transport has been accepted' and that further, 'it has been decided that Defence industries should be owned and controlled by the State; that public utilities and all key industries should be owned or controlled by the State; and that the principle of State ownership or control legitimately applies to other large-scale industries or enterprises which are likely to be monopolistic in character, or even to other large-scale enterprises'.

From radicalism to pragmatism

These pronouncements gave the impression that independent India's economic set up would show radical departures from the past. In retrospect it is clear that nothing of that kind has happened either when Independence came or any time thereafter. The British administration in India had no direct interest to see a quick or thorough capitalist transformation of the Indian economy. But it provided some of the prerequisites for such transformation—the legal structure for a regime of private property, the opening up of the country and the developing of a communication network, and substantial increase in commercialisation. In effect, post-Independence economic policies have followed the capitalist path with an attempt to use state power to moderate the capitalist propensities and, if possible, to provide some socialist appearances. The constitution of the new Republic which came into effect in 1950 stated in Article 38: 'The State shall strive to promote as effectively as it may a social order in which justice, social, economic and political, shall inform all the institutions of the national life'. On the economic order, Article 39 imposed on the state the obligation to ensure that 'the ownership and control of the material resources of the community are so distributed as best to subserve the common good' and that 'the operation of the economic system does not result in the concentration of wealth and means of production to the common detriment'. These are rather vague statements compared with the very specific recommendations of the National Planning Committee, and to that extent showed a retreat from any radical restructuring of the economy if ever such a commitment was seriously made.

It is possible to argue that the decision to continue along the capitalist path after Independence was taken more by default than by design. There was always a pragmatic compulsion to ensure that there was an uninterrupted increase in production to meet the needs of a large population that was at very low levels of living and increasing at an alarming rate. One of the subsequent Five Year Plan documents provided the following account of the conditions that prevailed at the time of Independence:

When Independence came, India had a slender industrial base. Millions of her rural people suffered under the weight of a traditional agrarian structure. A long period of economic stagnation, against the background of increasing pressure of population followed by the burdens of the Second World War, had weakened the Indian economy. There was widespread poverty and want. The partition of the country had uprooted millions of people and dislocated economic life. Productivity in agriculture and industry stood at low level. In relation to needs the available domestic savings were altogether meagre. The promise of freedom could only be redeemed if the economic foundations were greatly strengthened.... It was essential to rebuild the rural economy, to lay the foundation of industrial and scientific progress, and to expand education and other social services.... Planned development was the means of securing with utmost speed possible, a high rate of growth, reconstructing the institutions of economic and social life and harnessing the energies of the people to the tasks of national development.[5]

The description of the conditions at the time of Independence was quite fair. One could also add the unsettled social and political conditions that resulted from the partition of the country. The crucial question was whether such were the proper circumstances to attempt a radical transformation of the economy. There were many voices that lent support to initiating such a process but a powerful section in society was opposed to any moves in that direction and the political leadership, now under Nehru's prime ministership, decided against any major break with the past preferring a gradual and orderly transformation of the society and the economy.

The choice of a gradual transformation was based on two considerations. The first was the perceived possibilities of using political power through democratic processes based on universal adult franchise; and with all the power of the state to aid it to bring about fairly rapid and far-reaching changes in the economic structure. Such was the thinking reflected in the First Five Year Plan. A process of 'all-round and orderly development' was the task that the First Plan document envisaged to 'raise living standards and to open out to the people new opportunities for a richer and more varied life'. On how these were to be achieved, the document stated:

> The question of the techniques to be adopted for planning is linked up with the basic approach that a community decides to adopt for the realisation of its objectives. It is possible to have a plan based on regimentation and on immediate measures for levelling down in the hope ultimately of being able to level up. It is possible to take the view that mass enthusiasm cannot be created except on the basis of reprisals against those classes which have come to be associated in the public mind with the inequities and deficiencies of the old order. But the basic premise of democratic planning is that society can develop as an integral whole and that the position which particular classes occupy at any given time...can be altered without reliance on class hatreds or the use of violence. The need is to secure that the change is effected quickly and it is the positive duty of the State to promote this through all the measures at its command. The success of such planning no doubt depends on the classes in positions of power and privilege respecting the democratic system and appreciating the rapid changes it calls for.[6]

If a political transfer of power from the alien rulers to the people of the land could be brought about through orderly processes, it should be possible for the majority of the people to have their economic rights also recognised through similar processes especially since the state was on their side in the new set up, was the basis of the argument.

This political argument was supplemented by an equally persuasive economic argument. The basis of poverty, it was noted, was the inadequacy of goods to meet the requirements of a large and growing population. And hence increasing production was to be the primary task in the battle against poverty. And if production would increase, it would reach everyone—'trickle down'—thus ensuring a richer and more varied life to all in due course. The history of the advanced countries seemed to supply the empirical evidence for this logic. And capitalism had a clear track record of increasing output whatever might have been its record in terms of distributive justice.

The Indian strategy to fight poverty, therefore, has been one of relying on capitalist processes to increase production and on democratic processes to bring about the desired distributive pattern. The Industrial Policy Resolution of 1948 said: 'A dynamic national policy must therefore be directed to a continuous increase in production measures to secure its equitable distribution'. Over the past four decades there has been no change in the strategy, but from time to time it has appeared in different forms. In what follows we shall critically review the elements of the strategy and examine how they have affected poverty and affluence.

ATTEMPTS AT STRUCTURAL CHANGES

To say that post-Independence economic policies have followed the capitalist path does not mean that there have been no structural changes at all. There have been and many of them have resulted from deliberate policy decisions. First and foremost, the capitalist processes in India were not to be left to their own devices; they were to be under the direction and control of a state which derived its power from the majority of the people. A planned economy has been an attempt to bring the capitalist processes under overall social direction via the instrumentalities of the state. The state would not only legislate on matters economic, but would enter directly into economic activities by becoming a major producer, a major purchaser and seller, a leading employer, a supplier of critical services and the hub of the economy's monetary, credit and banking systems. The purpose has been to permeate the economy and to ensure that its working is constantly kept within the broad social objectives—the eradication of poverty being one of the most important among them. The state was to get hold of the 'commanding heights' of the economy and to set the pace and pattern of its functioning without necessarily bringing all resources under its direct control and by providing a legitimate role for the private sector. Specifically, the public sector was to take up production and investment exclusively in certain sectors of the economy and was to accept primary responsibility for these in some other sectors. It was to have an impact on production and investment in most other sectors of the economy by becoming the sole supplier of some of the crucial inputs such as electricity, by exerting influence on prices and by regulating the credit operations. It was to prevent the concentration of economic power in private hands; it was to enhance the rate of savings in the economy; and it was to play a leading role in stepping up the export performance of the economy.

As was seen in the last chapter, there has been substantial increase in the share of the state in economic activity since Independence. But it is very doubtful whether even with such expansion, the activities of the state and of the public sector have been able to alter the basic structure of the economy or to influence significantly its sense of direction. It is vain to speculate what the pattern of development of the economy would have been if the state were not to play a major role in it. And the argument sometimes put forward both by the supporters and the opponents of socialism that a dominant role by the state by itself makes an economy socialist is clearly wrong (as Chapter 6 has shown). What needs to be examined is the kind of impact the operations of the state have been able to exert on the system. We shall probe into this issue via the activity chains involving the state.

Role of the state

With minor modifications in the early 1980s, the role of the state in the Indian economy has been governed substantially by the Industrial Policy Resolution of 1956 which concentrated on specifying the roles of the public and private sectors in the industrial sphere, as agriculture is almost entirely in the private sector. According to the 1956 Resolution, industries exclusively reserved for the public sector were arms and ammunitions, atomic energy, iron and steel, heavy machine-building, power generation and distribution, railways, shipbuilding, telephone and telegraph apparatus, civil aviation and some minerals. Machine tools, fertilisers, road and sea transport, and intermediate chemicals were to come increasingly within the state sector. Hence the public sector industries are essentially those that supply overhead facilities for the economy as a whole and provide it some of the crucial inputs and amenities. Most of these are also production areas into which the private sector would be slow to enter because of the heavy investment and high risks. Thus an important function of the public sector has been to provide the private sector with goods and sevices it requires, but would not find attractive to produce—clearly the third duty that Adam Smith had assigned to the state in a capitalist economy.[7] To that extent, therefore, the role of the state in the Indian economy has not been to alter its basic structure but to reinforce it.

Within the private sector itself, the natural clientele of the public sector has been the organised sector, and more particularly the larger ones among them. This was documented by one of the earliest official enquiries into the operations of the public sector. With special reference to the public and quasi-public enterprises dealing in finance and credit, the finding of that enquiry was that 'the growth of the private sector in industry and especially of the big companies has been facilitated by the financial assistance rendered by public institutions like the Industrial Finance Corporation (IFC), the National Industrial Development Corporation (NIDC) etc'. On that basis the government set up yet another committee specifically to enquire 'whether policies pursued by specialised financial institutions in advancing loans to industries have resulted in any undue preference being given to larger industrial houses' and the committee came to the conclusion after examining the evidence that 'in the whole system of financial assistance for the private sector, there is built-in mechanism which favours the large industrial sector'. Subsequent studies have shown that agencies such as the Life Insurance Corporation of India, Unit Trust of India, and publicly owned banks also have been biased in favour of the larger units in their financial policies.[8]

It is therefore, possible to show that a major activity chain in the Indian economy involving the state is one that links it physically (in terms of the goods produced in the public sector) and financially with the major components in the private organised sector. Another component of this chain is the h–3 units in the system, households that supply their labour power to the public sector units and the units in the private organised sector and who are linked with the banking and financial units via their financial assets. A distinguishing feature of this chain linking the units of the state, of the private organised sector, of the banking system and of the h–3 units is that in terms of income flows as well as asset position it constitutes the top layer of the Indian economy. We shall refer to it as the *top circuit*. It represents the affluent section of the economy encompassing possibly 10 per cent of the total population. As can be seen, it has been in formation from the very early days; it has come to play a more decisive role in the functioning of the economy in recent years, a theme that we shall come back to later in the chapter.

It would be wrong to infer from the above discussion that the state has identified itself completely with the top circuit or any one of its components. In fact through a variety of instruments, particularly the licensing system, the power of the state was used to some extent to curb the power and influence of the private organised sector.

And there are other activity chains of which the state forms a part. Of these one of the most widely publicised is the chain that links the state and the traditional industries, sometimes also referred to as cottage industries, village industries etc. This is a chain involving the state and a segment of the h–2 units as well as some parts of the banking units. Apart from providing financial assistance to the h–2 units, the state through these links has attempted to break their built-in isolation; and to draw them more and more into the national economy by enlarging their markets, including opening up of foreign markets to them, protecting them from the fierce competitions of the modern sector, and raising their productivity through technological upgradation. In this case the activity chain has tried to intervene in the normal working of the system; and although it has afforded some protection to those at the bottom, it has not succeeded in insulating them from the aggressive onslaughts of the more powerful forces as was seen in Chapter 9.

Attempts at land reform

Another area where structural changes were contemplated and attempted was in relation to the ownership of land.[9] That during the colonial period effective control over land in many parts of the country was exercised by a class of intermediaries (particularly zamindars) while the ownership issue remained ill-defined was brought out in Chapter 8. The abolition of zamindari rights was one of the major land reform measures taken up and effectively completed during the first decade after Independence. Legally, at least, it changed the predominantly feudal character of land relationship in the rural areas and some 20 million tenants were brought into direct contact with the state. To this extent the abolition of intermediaries changed the structural pattern of the economy. But its potential impact was limited in many ways. In the first place, the abolition of intermediaries was basically a reform of revenue administration rather than a measure of land redistribution. Hence its impact was primarily legal, only secondarily economic. In fact there was not much of a reduction in the economic power of zamindars because with one or two exceptions, in all states even this legal measure was achieved by paying handsome compensation to those who claimed the traditional right of ownership. Thus, there could not have been any real change in the ownership of *property* as a result of the abolition of intermediaries, but only a change in the composition of the property of the erstwhile 'owners' making them more liquid, thereby conferring upon them more effective potential control over resources in general. Also because the provisions pertaining to retention of land for 'personal cultivation' were liberal and vague, in many states land has continued to be effectively under the control of the former intermediaries. A combination of all these factors led to the emergence, in many parts of the country, of a new class of rich peasants with control over land, links with industries, power over poor peasants and agricultural labourers alike and with enormous possibilities to extend their sway into the political realm as well. Soon they became an important part of the top circuit.

In terms of ownership and control of land another attempt that was made was to launch a massive campaign for cooperative farming.[10] It was thought of as a *via media* between private individual ownership on the one hand and socialised state ownership on the other retaining the advantages of former and incorporating the potential benefit of large-scale operations of the latter. Nehru was one of the staunch protagonists of the idea. 'I am convinced it is essential for us to have cooperative farming', he wrote to the Chief Ministers in 1956 elaborating the advantages he perceived from it: economies of large-scale production; possibilities of increasing productivity and the incomes of the rural masses; an expansion of the internal market linking agriculture and industry.

From then on he made use of the Planning Commission, the National Development Council and the many deliberative and decision-making bodies of the Congress Party to canvass actively for cooperative farming. The Nagpur session of the Congress in 1959 unanimously approved a comprehensive resolution on agricultural reorganisation that called for the immediate transformation of the agrarian structure including the completion of all land reforms already suggested, particularly ceiling on land ownership, and the formation of cooperative farms. On cooperative farming the Nagpur resolution stated: 'The future agrarian pattern should be that of cooperative joint farming, in which the land will be pooled for joint cultivation, the farmers continuing to retain their property rights, and getting a share from the net produce in proportion to their land. Further, those who actually work in the land, whether they own the land or not, will get a share in proportion to the work put in by them on the joint farm'. The resolution also recommended that land that would become surplus on the basis of the implementation of the ceiling legislations should vest in the village panchayats rather than with individuals and be managed through cooperatives of landless labourers. A further recommendation was the introduction of state trading in foodgrains assuring minimum floor prices at which crops might be sold directly to the government.

Although each one of these specific steps had been incorporated in earlier public documents, such as the Second Five Year Plan Document and the draft of the Third Five Year Plan, the bringing together and the eagerness that Nehru showed in pushing them by setting specific dates for implementation led to the galvanising of the conservative elements in the Congress Party and outside—especially the landlords and the traders—to work against the resolution becoming a reality. Cooperative farming was signalled as a prelude to collectivisation and that, in turn, as the beginning of totalitarianism. With the support of senior leaders like Rajagopalachari, the opposition to the cooperative farming proposal began to gather momentum, and step by step Nehru and the government were forced to retreat. In particular when the 1961 Census revealed that the annual rate of growth of population was closer to 2.3 per cent than the 1.5 per cent assumed in the earlier plan exercises, it appeared logical to say that the national priority should be to increase production and not to attempt major structural changes. Thus was a major proposal for the alteration of the structure of the economy given a quiet burial.

However, in order to give the impression that structural transformation was not totally abandoned, attention was turned from cooperative farming to land ceiling legislations. Although the central government had provided the guidelines in this regard the legislations were to be enacted by the state governments. Under the pressure of the landed interests, the state governments were not particularly enthusiastic about imposing ceilings, though some of them did enact legislation that, on paper, appeared to be very radical, bringing the ceiling to between 10 and 15 hectares in most cases. But the record is summarised by a commentator thus: 'The principle of imposing ceilings on land holdings was first announced in 1953; detailed recommendations for legislation were not made until 1956; and most states did not actually pass enabling legislation until 1960 or 1961. The landowners, therefore, had a period of seven or eight years to arrange partitions and transfers of holdings to escape the impact of the new laws' (Frankel, 1978: 192–93). Not only that, the legislations were so full of loopholes that another commentator was led to say that an elephant could easily walk through them. Almost two decades later, the Sixth Five Year Plan 1980–85 admitted: 'The progress of taking over and distribution of ceiling surplus land has been tardy. Out of about 15.74 lakh hectares declared surplus in different states, as in March 1980 only about 9.56 lakh hectares have been taken possession of by the states and about 6.79 lakh hectares distributed' (Sixth Plan: 114–15). That document then recommended that the programme of taking possession and distribution of ceiling–surplus lands should be completed by 1982–83. That too has remained little more than a pious resolution!

These accounts go to show that except for the growth of the share of the state in economic activities no major or radical change in the basic structure of the Indian economy has come about or been brought about since Independence, especially towards any form of 'socialisation'. On the contrary, the reform measures that have been taken up—abolition of intermediaries, land ceiling legislations and the steps taken to protect the rights of tenants—have generally reinforced the tendency to make private ownership of land more explicit and exclusive. Other changes in the system have further strengthened these tendencies. Agricultural implements of various kinds and a wide array of consumer durables have become symbols of private ownership, as also of social position. The growth of the banking system in the rural areas and the increased supply of credit also emphasize the exclusive ownership of assets, as frequently title deeds that affirm exclusive ownership are required and used as collateral for loans.

The Indian economy since Independence has been essentially one of private ownership of resources with those resources very unequally distributed. Strategies adopted to reduce and eradicate poverty must be assessed against that structural pattern of the economy.

POVERTY ERADICATION STRATEGIES

It is not surprising that the initial response to the question of how mass poverty should be eradicated is to say that production and productivity must increase. It appears to be the obvious solution: vast millions do not have enough food, so more food must be produced; do not have shelter, hence more houses have to be constructed; and so on. One of the early plan documents that addressed itself to poverty eradication and declared clearly that 'the central concern of our planning has to be the removal of poverty as early as possible' went on to say, 'to raise the standard of living of the vast masses of people, output therefore would have to be increased very considerably'.[11] It pointed out also that in countries at very different levels of development and with varying socio-political environments, the distribution of incomes followed a remarkably similar pattern, especially in respect of the proportion of incomes earned by the lowest three or four deciles of the population. On this basis it was hypothesised that the income of the poorest segments as a result of spontaneous economic development may be expected to increase in more or less the same proportion as total income in any country. The document, therefore, came to the policy conclusion that 'the attainment of specified level of minimum income within a given period then becomes purely a function of the rate of development'. Thus 'growth' was considered to be the strategy for the eradication of poverty.

Growth as a poverty eradication measure
Since this argument is put forward in a variety of forms—'the cake has to grow in size so that everyone can have more' being its oft repeated

popular version—it is worth pointing out its validity as well as its inadequacy.[12] Since a major attribute of poverty is material deprivation, it stands to reason that in goods, especially goods needed by the poor, must increase as a necessary condition for poverty eradication. Similarly, it can also be conceded that a redistribution of a low level of income cannot be a solution to the problem of poverty, particularly for that solution to be sustained over time. Further, it is quite reasonable to maintain that within an economic system which has been performing at a fairly low level, stimulus to productive activity at any point will have some sort of percolating or 'trickle down' effect, thereby activating productive effort elsewhere also. On all these grounds the recommendation of growth as an antidote to poverty can be validated.

But it does not follow that growth by itself will suffice to remove poverty, especially growth as an abstract concept or as an aggregated figure. For instance, the increase in the production of armaments or luxury apartments, or motor cars will all have their positive impact on 'growth' but it is doubtful whether such growth will lead to much reduction of poverty. If so, it can be argued also that certain kinds of growth may *increase*, rather than reduce poverty. In any case, a *goods-specific* growth is a minimum condition for poverty eradication. Even a goods-specific growth may still fail to make a positive contribution to poverty eradication, for while it will ensure that goods needed by the poor became *available*, it does not ensure that these goods become *accessible* to the poor. For instance, if an increase in the availability of food is achieved by large scale mechanisation of agricultural processes leading to the displacement of labourers, that increase may not contribute to poverty eradication. Thus, certain kinds of productive activities and certain kinds of production may lead to the reduction of poverty; certain other kinds of activities and goods may not have such an effect. Growth expressed as the increase in the value of goods produced fails to reflect these features and hence reliance on growth alone cannot be adequate to deal with mass poverty. Whether goods and processes conducive for poverty eradication will come about in an economy is not determined by the mechanics of growth, but by the broader socio-economic factors of which growth and poverty are but reflections. One of its consequences is that under most conditions a quantum of growth cannot have uniform impact on different sections of society: some will certainly benefit by it, but others may be adversely affected. 'Growth', thus, is not a socially neutral quantity, but the reflection of a variety of processes with differential impacts on different sections of the population.

Such indeed, turned out to be the Indian experience similar to the experience at the global level as seen at the end of the United Nations first Decade of Development, the 1960s. In India, as has been noted already, pragmatic considerations themselves indicated high priority to a production oriented strategy, particularly in relation to agriculture and foodgrains. The main thrust of the First Five Year Plan (1951–56) was on irrigation, to bring more land under cultivation, and foodgrains production which had shown very poor performance throughout the first part of the century and did, in fact, achieve a major boost. Foodgrains production shot up from 55.0 million tonnes in 1950–51 to 69.3 million tonnes in 1955–56 and 82.3 million tonnes in 1960–61. But with the possibilities of area expansion slowing down, foodgrains production began to stagnate again and by the mid-sixties the country was facing a food crisis of major dimensions. The response to the situation was partly to import foodgrains, especially under the USA's P.L 480 programme, but partly also to change the strategy of growth to a 'selective and intensive' one. A few selected areas in the country well endowed in terms of terrain and availability of water were selected for concentrated effort to increase food production. Well endowed farmers were also selected who were subsidised to sink wells of their own, including tube wells to tap ground water, fertilisers were provided on subsidised rates, high-yielding seeds were supplied and credit on fairly liberal rates was made available to purchase agricultural machinery and to finance agricultural operations in general. This seeds–water–fertiliser–credit package, which came to be celebrated as The Green Revolution, certainly succeeded in increasing foodgrains production which, from a low level of 74.2 million tonnes in 1966–67 shot up to 99.5 million tonnes in 1969–70 and 108.4 million tonnes in 1970–71 and with occasional dips initially and major fluctuations subsequently has kept up the upward movement.

Growth and poverty—the empirical evidence

Against this background several attempts were made to examine the relationship between growth and poverty. In view of the inadequacy of statistical data, differences in the choice of initial and terminal periods for comparison and a variety of methodological problems, arriving at a definitive conclusion about that relationship has not been easy; and in the late sixties and the early seventies the problem of the measurement of poverty and the impact of growth on poverty provided the basis for many heated debates in the country.[13] We shall not enter into the technical aspects of these debates and controversies. But two major conclusions have come to have a substantial measure of professional agreement. The first is that when foodgrains production increases, particularly when the per capita availability of foodgrains increases, the percentage of population below the poverty line shows a decline. This finding is not a matter of surprise because, after all, poverty is identified in terms of the level of per capita consumption; and since foodgrains account for a very high proportion of total consumption at low levels of consumption, it means that when foodgrains availability increases, the level of consumption of foodgrains also increases. The second conclusion has been that so far no definite and clear relationship has been established between *upward* trends in the production of foodgrains and *downward* trends in the extent of poverty. A clear negative relationship between these two trends would have given strength to the argument that growth tends to eliminate poverty.[14] But in the Indian context so far such relationship has not been unambiguously established.

While these discussions were going on in India, a major study comparing the experience of the developing countries of the world after the first Development Decade of the United Nations also threw some doubts about the efficacy of growth as a poverty eradication measure. Its major finding was: 'It is now clear that more than a decade of rapid growth in underdeveloped countries has been of little or no benefit to perhaps a third of their population. Although the average per capita income of the Third World has increased by 50 per cent since 1960, this growth has been unequally distributed among countries and socio-economic groups.' (Chenery, 1974: xiii).

In any case the finding that four Five Year Plans, each dedicated to improve the conditions of living of the people, had made very little dent on the problem of poverty and that in the early seventies almost half the total population was still below the low level of consumption indicated by the official poverty line, led to a political turmoil in the country. Indira Gandhi, who was then Prime Minister, called for general election to Parliament with *garibi hatao* (eradication of poverty) as the slogan and promise of her party, and won a massive mandate. From the Fifth Five Year Plan onwards the reduction, if not elimination of poverty has become an explicit objective in each Five Year Plan and specific strategies beyond general growth have been worked out from time to time. We shall refer to these as the 'growth plus' strategies.

'Growth plus' strategies for poverty eradication
The change in strategy was heralded by one of the preparatory documents of the Fifth Plan:

There would seem to be a conspicuous element of historic inevitability in a direct approach to reducing poverty becoming the main thrust of the Fifth Five Year Plan. The Plan is being formulated by a government that has massive mandate from the people, both in the Parliamentary elections of 1971 and the state elections of 1972, on the basis of a programme whose centre piece is *garibi hatao*.... This should enable bold and imaginative proposals being put through on the basis of an enlightened national consensus.

The enormous political backing arising from a substantial majority in Parliament, and governance by the Congress Party, or parties friendly towards it in all the major states, was going to be used to bring about a major change in economic policies and planned development to favour the weaker sections in society. The emphasis on growth was not going to be given up. On the contrary, it was noted that a frontal attack on poverty called for simultaneous attention being paid to growth and reduction in inequalities. Hence the Plan targeted an annual growth rate of 5.5 per cent, much higher than was achieved till then. The 'bold and imaginative' step suggested by another of the preparatory documents was to reduce the *consumption* of the top 30 per cent of the population and divert the resources that would become available to increase the *income* and *consumption* of the bottom 30 per cent. In other words, accelerated growth would raise the income of the top 30 per cent; but planned redistributive measures would prevent their consumption from going up and augment the consumption of the bottom 30 per cent. When some exercises showed that the reduction of consumption by the top 30 per cent would also reduce the import requirements of the economy, the strategy was considered to be the most appropriate one to achieve the twin objectives of growth with distributive justice and self-reliance.[15]

The target group approach

In retrospect it can be seen that the Fifth Plan did not achieve any of its major objectives—its targeted growth rate, its projected poverty reduction or its attempted self-reliance. Consequently, the strategy had to be modified again especially as far as poverty eradication was concerned. As the Fifth Plan's macro strategy of transfer of resources from the rich to the poor had not materialised, the Sixth Plan suggested a micro strategy of reaching out to the poorer sections. The modified strategy was spelt out thus:

The poorest sections belong to the families of landless labour, small and marginal farmers, rural artisans, scheduled castes, scheduled tribes and socially and economically backward classes. The household will remain the basic unit of poverty eradication in target group oriented programmes. Families differ in such vital respects as dependency ratios, asset holding, skills and even the ability to perform manual labour on public works. Hence each household below the poverty line will have to be assisted through an appropriate package of technologies, services and asset transfer programmes.

The diagnosis underlying this 'target group' strategy to eradicate poverty is certainly valid.[16] For, poverty is not deprivation in the abstract. It is a malady that takes specific forms in the case of particular households and individuals and no matter what the nature of an anti-poverty strategy is, it will begin to yield results only when and to the extent that its operations reach out to each one of the deprived individuals and groups. Hence a micro strategy with specific targets has a better chance of yielding results than a macro strategy with unspecified operational methods. During the Sixth Five Year Plan and the Seventh Five Year Plan (the decade of the 1980s) the target group approach has been the official anti-poverty strategy in the country. A variety of programmes aimed at different groups that come below the poverty line have been designed and are being implemented by the Centre and State governments. These have been of three or four major kinds. There are many schemes that provide employment to those who need it to earn a living; there are programmes of asset transfers to those who would be able to put them to use to supplement their earnings—milch animals to agricultural labourers, sewing machines to young women and widows and carts or tri-cycle carriers to vendors being the best examples; there are training programmes and other forms of assistance to those who wish to enter into self-employment; and there are many schemes of loans and financial assistance through different agencies to those in need. There has also been an integrated rural development programme (IRDP) which provides a package of these deals in selected rural areas.

Apart from its economic content the target group approach has also become popular as a political programme of the leading political parties. The public visibility of these schemes and their ability to reach out to specific groups and individuals has become of great significance in a parliamentary democratic system based on adult franchise and where the majority of the voters are poor people. Parties are coming to be assessed in terms of the 'beneficiary programmes' they offer.

Change in the pattern of growth
The decade of the 1980s has also seen another new thrust in the development strategy, that is, measures to favour the more affluent sections of the population by changing the pattern of growth. For the sake of further analysis it will be useful to attempt a more precise identification of what has been referred to as the affluent sections. One way to ascertain

who constitutes the affluent section is to seek what percentage of the households' in the country accounts for the total household sector savings. This, as has been noted already, has been and continues to be the largest component of total savings of the economy. There are no official estimates in this regard. But the findings of a national survey conducted in the mid-seventies by the National Council for Applied Economic Research, one of the leading private research organisations in the country, showed that out of the total savings of the household sector, the share of the bottom 70 per cent was only over 6 per cent, while that of the top 10 per cent was about 68 per cent and of the top 5 per cent alone around 50 per cent. On that basis what we have already designated as the 'top layer' of the Indian economy must be deemed to consist of about 10 per cent of the households and thus, also of the total population. If the top 10 per cent of households account for such a large share of the savings of the economy they should also be presumed to be the major beneficiaries of the economic growth of the past four decades or so. There is no rigid iron barrier separating this section from the rest and, certainly, many below that level must have also received some benefits including households in the lower half. Hence it would be more appropriate to say that the cream of the benefit would have gone to the top layer with a rather thin spread for those below.

The strategies of the past were not overtly meant for enriching further the richer section of the economy; the emphasis of the plans were always explicitly on the small man. Occasionally, as in the strategy of the Fifth Plan, it was even suggested that there should be curbs on the richer section, at least as far as consumption was concerned. A distinct reversal came in the 1980s when it was recognised that the economy would not grow unless the better off sections were permitted and encouraged to consume more. The support for the new strategy was provided both from the supply side and from the demand side.[17] From the supply side it was argued that the wide range of controls and regulations on production, especially in the industrial sphere, which were probably necessary during the early phase of development had outlived them and were now acting as a drag on better performance and further growth. On this basis a strong case was made for the liberalisation of the economy both internally and in terms of greater openness to foreign investments so that a new era of rapid industrialisation could be inaugurated. The argument from the demand side was that something like the top 10 per cent of the population (amounting to around 75 million people) backed by the affluence they had acquired over the years constituted a very attractive domestic market for a wide range of goods. The calculation was that removing the breaks on the economy and energising the potential domestic market would stimulate a new era of rapid industrial growth which, in turn, would activate the entire economy. It was argued also that the opening up of the economy would enable the economy to export more and to be better integrated with the global economy. These inter-connected ingredients constituted what soon came to be known as the New Economic Policy. The overall strategy launched in the early eighties via the Sixth Plan and intensified from the mid-eighties through the Seventh Plan has been to stimulate growth and to set aside a part of it to provide relief measures to the weaker sections; an attempt to cater deliberately to the growing affluence of the few and the more rapid eradication of the poverty of the many.

The new economic policy

In this strategy the state has come to play a more active role which is clearly reflected in the activities of the Central Government.[18] The total expenditure of the Central Government was about Rs 17,800 crores in 1979–80 which moved to Rs 22,000 crores in 1980–81 and to a massive Rs 82,000 crores by 1989–90. This increase in total expenditure resulted partly from an increase in public administration and defence and other services; this expenditure also came to be the direct contribution of the Government to national income and consequently to the growth in national income of this period. The increase in expenditure of the Government was not met by a corresponding increase in taxes, particularly direct taxes which fall on the more affluent sections. On the contrary, in 1985 the rates of personal income tax and of the corporate income tax were drastically reduced. Simultaneously, the Government also decided to go in for large-scale borrowing offering very liberal tax concessions to those who were willing to hold their savings in the form of financial instruments offered by the Government, that is, to those who were willing to lend to the Government.[19] Even with such large scale borrowing, it was not possible to meet the growing expenditure of the Government and hence the gap or deficit between receipts (including tax and non-tax revenues *and* borrowing) came to be met by borrowing from the Reserve Bank of India and by printing more currency notes. This 'deficit financing' by the Government, therefore, amounts to the Government spending more than what it takes away from the system and thus results in pumping more money and purchasing power into the economy than would have otherwise been the case. It also reflects the power of the Government to confer purchasing power on itself. During the second half of the 1970s internal borrowings and deficits constituted 19.2 per cent and 7.5 per cent respectively of the total budget of the Central Government. In the first half of the 1980s these had moved up to 27.9 per cent and 8.2 per cent respectively. Subsequently the share of borrowings came down somewhat, but the deficit increased to an average of 10.6 per cent in the 1985–86 to 1989–90 period and to 13.4 per cent in 1989–90. One of the consequences of enhanced borrowings over this period is that interest payments alone came to occupy about 22 per cent of the Central Government's expenses, thereby generating something of a vicious circle of more borrowings or deficits becoming necessary in an attempt to pay interests on past borrowings.

What has been the rationale behind this change in fiscal policy and of the so-called 'resource crunch' that became the central point of fiscal discussions in the 1980s? It must be noted that in terms of the performance of the economy, as seen from the national income figures, the decade of the 1980s has been the best period since Independence with an annual growth rate of 5.5 per cent from 1980–81 to 1988–89. Hence, for the economy as a whole, there was no resource crunch. The problem, therefore, has been that the Government failed to mobilise sufficient resources to meet its requirement. The crisis, if any, has been about *resource mobilisation*, not of resources as such. The issue to be considered is whether it reflects the inability or the unwillingness of the Government to resort to a more adequate mobilisation programme.

In the context of the new economic policy that was launched in the early 1980s and pursued with vigour in the second half of the decade, the new fiscal policy must also be viewed as part of the overall design. It was part of the attempt to allow the affluent section to exercise its purchasing power freely to produce the kind of goods it required so that a stimulus was provided to the performance of the economy. It has been a strategy of demand-led growth. One of the sectors that has grown most rapidly in the decade is the consumer durables sector—producing such goods as motor cars and host of luxury motor cars, television sets and VCRs, air-conditioners and vacuum cleaners, cooking ranges and microwave ovens, and so on. This is proof enough to substantiate this claim. These goods exhibited on an average 'an uninterrupted high annual growth, ranging from 8 per cent to 22 per cent' during the first 8 years of the decade as an official report indicated.[20] Thus the fiscal strategy has been part of the overall effort to induce growth by and for the affluent in the hope that its spin-off effects will confer some benefits to others and that more amounts could be utilised for the direct anti-poverty programmes. Several official assessments have claimed that the strategy has been successful in what it proposed to achieve.

One of the boldest claims was by the *Economic Survey 1986–87* which said: 'There is strong evidence that the Indian economy is now on a new growth path.... In the eighties, the average annual rate of growth has been 5 per cent which is much higher than the historical trend rate of growth. The industrial growth rate is increasing and, despite three successive weak monsoons the food situation remains comfortable.... These are substantial achievements, made possible by a sound and responsive macro-economic policy environment'. While achieving high rates of growth, figures seemed to suggest that there was a perceptible fall in the percentage of population below the poverty line too. It would appear that a strategy of overall improvement, benefiting the rich and supporting the poor has finally been evolved. Whether it is indeed so must be critically evaluated.

STRUCTURE AND STRATEGIES: AN ASSESSMENT

It has been noted that the deliberate attempts to alter the structure of the economy have not been particularly successful. And yet from the colonial period at least there has been a slow but sustained structural transformation that has been going on, from pre-capitalist to a capitalist order. Strengthening of the private ownership of resources, especially land, has been one aspect of that transformation; growing monetisation and marketisation has been another; technological progress has been a third; diversification of output a fourth; increase in production and changes in the organisation of production have been another; augmentation of the surplus and the manner in which it is appropriated and utilised have also been manifestations of that transformation. Above all, the ways in which labour is used in production and claims are settled, have also been undergoing change. It is the complex interaction of all these changes that somewhat conveniently, but also quite misleadingly, summed up as growth. It is because of the vast range and diversity of processes that lie hidden beneath growth that it is not, and can seldom be, socially neutral. Strategies, or policy interventions, take place in the context of, rather right in the midst of, these ongoing processes. Their effect, therefore, will depend not mainly on what they profess to be or intend to achieve, but crucially on how they impinge on the many strands of the structure. The outcome will reflect the dynamic engagements between the internal dynamics of the ongoing structural transformation and an intervention into it. The intervention may strengthen the dynamics of the system, may neutralise it, may hold it in abeyance—or have a bearing in other ways. It is very difficult to predict a priori how these will turn out. But once again it is reasonable to say that if structural transformation itself is not socially neutral, the interaction of structure and strategy is also not likely to be so. At the same time, it will be misleading also to argue that it will necessarily polarise society (a growing cleavage between the poor and the affluent, that is) or work in the opposite direction.

While prediction is made difficult, there is another task that remains to be done, and that is to look into the record of the interaction of structure and strategy of the past in order to gain a better understanding of the dynamics itself. That is what we shall attempt to do.

Interaction of structure and strategy

That increase in production, particularly in the production of foodgrains, had to have top priority immediately after Independence has already been noted. The slack that existed in the old order in the form of unutilised land, and readily available labour power had to be energised for this purpose which could be achieved only by making water available. The availability of water is, to a large extent, a geographical determinant and hence stimulating productive activity turned out to be region specific. To make what is produced in specific areas available elsewhere, both trade and transport facilities became necessary. The opening up of the territory provided a further stimulus to trade and to the marketisation process which, in turn, stimulated other forms of economic activities too. It also provided new opportunities to a large number of people—cultivators, labourers, merchants, contractors, construction workers, financial intermediaries and so on.

Stimulating economic activities and increasing production must have been beneficial to many. But these may have adversely affected others. If production was beginning to be based more and more on commercial calculations, some traditional sharing must have been abandoned, depriving some of what they were used to. Settlement of wages may have changed from payment in kind to payments in cash and, if the prices of wage goods had tended to go up, wage earners would have been adversely affected. Even among those who became beneficiaries, there would have been a differential impact. Those with control over substantial resources and access to information would have been in a position to take better advantage of the changes than others. Thus, even the most elementary changes would have had vastly different impacts on different sections. Some would have certainly become better off; others could have been adversely affected. The dynamics, therefore, is one that simultaneously generates affluence and poverty.

Irrigation as an example

More complex changes too must be analysed in a similar manner. A change that had very diverse impact in many parts of the country was in the irrigation pattern.[21] Viewed as an attempt to increase the availability of water, the pattern of irrigation may appear to be of little consequence. But from a societal perspective each form of irrigation has a different kind of impact. Indigenous irrigation systems were substantially community oriented, especially where the source was a canal or tank (rather than a well). There were community regulated arrangements both for the use of water and the maintenance of the system. But in an effort to increase the production of foodgrains, especially in the second half of the sixties and the early part of the seventies, there was a shift in many parts of the country towards tapping of ground water via tube wells. Since the tube wells were sunk on privately owned land, they also brought about a shift from community regulated irrigation to privately regulated irrigation. When private owners of land came to have privately owned sources of water also, there was a substantial augmentation of their resource power. In most instances sinking of tube wells was parti-ally subsidised by the state, and although the subsidy was not meant exclusively or specifically for the larger farmers, only those who had the means to meet the rest of the rather high cost of the tube well could have effective access to the subsidy. Thus the subsidy programme had a built-in bias in favour of the richer farmers. With the availability of water under their control they were also in a position to change their cropping pattern in favour of the more profitable crops, such as from millet to paddy or from paddy to sugar-cane, thus augmenting their resource power further. And as was noted in Chapter 9, they could also supply water to their neighbours using their bargaining power to determine the terms of the transaction. Hence for one section, the change in the irriga-tion pattern would open up an upward cumulative process.

In the meanwhile, the private availability of water frequently induces them to withdraw from the traditional irrigation arrangements which, therefore, come to suffer by neglect. Its consequence will be borne by the smaller farmers who face water shortage and may also become sub-servient to the new waterlords. With land becoming a profitable asset, traditional tenancy patterns may change and erstwhile tenant farmers may become casual labourers either in the rural areas or in urban centres. Further, what were once common property lands to which most people had access—to graze their cattle, for instance—may also tend to get privatised.[22] This may result in agricultural labourers, who used to hire themselves out along with their bullocks, not being able to do so if they have no alternate ways of maintaining their animals. Corresponding to the cumulative upward processes for those who were well endowed, there may, therefore, be a cumulative downward process for those who were initially poorly endowed. Even so, the net impact need not neces-sarily be 'to make the rich richer and the poor poorer' as is frequently claimed. For new opportunities are being created also. The growth of trade and markets could enable some who are displaced from land to move into commerce. Similarly, the introduction of pumps for lifting water would provide opportunities for maintenance and repair works, into which persons displaced from traditional crafts could enter. The net impact, therefore, would depend on a wide range of specific circumstantial factors which would have to be empirically evaluated.

However, two general conclusions may be drawn. The first is that apart from the many processes that emerge, each with its own pattern of impact on different sections, there is no determinate relationship between growth and poverty. Growth is not an orderly macro process converting investment into output; it is a convulsive micro-global process involving the variety of units in the system and having different kinds of impact on them. It will lead to the differentiation of the h–2 units, changing some into h–3 and many into h–4, converting some into f and others into m. It will present different opportunities to all these and will differentially affect their resource power and possibilities of performance. It will influence inter-unit and intra-unit settlement of claims. A detailed assessment of all these aspects will be required to find out what impact any initial process of change, a policy intervention, for instance, will have on different units or sections in the economy. In the eagerness to establish direct and simple quantitative relationships between growth and poverty, it is all too easy to overlook this essential processual nature of growth, and that has been responsible for many of the fertile controversies about the relationship between the two.

The second general conclusion that can be drawn is that in an economy undergoing a transformation into capitalism, most processes of change confer positive differential advantage to those who already have the advantage of resource power. This is because, as we have already seen, a capitalist system, is basically one in which resource power is used to gain further resource power. Hence if a capitalist process is initiated against the background of differential economic power, those with more would tend to attract more.

Market and resource power

In this process the market becomes the natural ally of the rich. It is not difficult to see why. There is the dialectical relationship between exchange value and resource power which was noted in Chapters 4 and 5. In a capitalist system only those things on which exchange affixes a positive price become resources, and the propeller that moves exchange is resource power. In the transition into capitalism this dialectical relationship unfolds itself in different ways. When traditional transfers are converted into exchange relationships, those with traditional resource power are at an advantage because in most instances they will be able to determine the *rates* of exchange because of their higher bargaining power. This is most clearly seen when labour power is converted into a commodity. It happens in the context of a prevailing regime of reciprocal obligations of an unequal nature where those who have traditional resource power are already the dominant party. As capitalist tendencies emerge they are the ones who will decide which of the traditional relationships will continue and which will be transformed into exchange relationships. A traditional relationship where the landlord had the obligation to provide the basic necessities of life to all workers attached to his land could easily be converted into payment for work done, with the landlord also having the power to decide when and how long work will be available. And the payment too will depend on the profitability calculations of the landlord and not on any assessment of the needs and requirements of the workers. Similarly, it will be the landlord who will decide, on the basis of his calculations, whether payment will be made in kind or in cash.

In other spheres such as manufacture, there are organisational arrangements (such as the putting out system) which provide considerable flexibility for those who come to have command over labour power to push down payment for work done and to segment the market to their advantage. This systemic feature of the 'labour market'—or more explicitly, the economic dominance of resource power over labour power—tends to seep into other exchange relationships also, into the goods market, land market, and credit market, for instance, in all of which the general tendency will be for those with adequate resource power to come to have dominance over the market. - The rates of exchange that result through these processes, the prevailing market prices are, therefore, the expression of that dominance. And as more and more transactions come to be mediated through markets, the hold of the powerful over the system becomes more entrenched. It is on such a structure that growth promoting strategies impinge. Since these strategies themselves are largely matters of transfer of resources from the state to other economic units in the system via subsidies, credit operations etc., it is not surprising that resource power attracts and absorbs resources, as a magnet attracts and attaches metals. Under the circumstances, then, there need be little doubt that the better off sections are the direct and natural beneficiaries of 'growth'.

But some of the benefits percolate also down as the growth process stimulates economic activities of various sorts involving different sections of the population. The general finding, however, in the context of mass poverty of the kind that India and many Third World countries have, is that such trickling down is too inadequate and too slow to make any dent on poverty, and certainly to remove the conditions that continue to generate poverty. That finding provided the rationale for the 'growth plus' strategy.

Interventionist strategies

The growth plus strategy, in essence, is to make a direct intervention on the distributive aspects of the system leaving its basic structure intact. It is the response of the political recognition that without some form of *redistributive* measures, the distributive mechanism of the system that rests on resource power will exclude vast sections of the population who are without adequate resource power, and that such a situation is politically untenable. And the attempt is to influence the pattern of distribution through administrative measures, (essentially through some fiscal devices) without intervening in the production operations of the system. It is, therefore, an effort to modify some of the structural consequences without altering the structural characteristics. Hence it must be evident, *a priori*, that it cannot go far enough to eradicate mass poverty which is basically a manifestation of the structural characteristics of the system.

But how far can it go and what can it do? Interventionist strategies of this kind have a number of built-in drawbacks.[23] The first arises from the fact that it is an administrative operation. Budgetary allocations for its many programmes can be decided upon without much difficulty, because that is essentially a macro decision; but the implementation of the programmes calls for a great deal of effort: identification of the target groups, selection of those within the groups who are to become beneficiaries at any given period, ensuring that those who are not potential beneficiaries do not gate-crash into the programmes and the like. These involve very specific micro decisions and actions. The implementation of the strategy has come under criticism on all these accounts. A second type of problem has been that since the major component of the strategy is a transfer of financial resources, it has a tendency to generate methods of cornering the funds by those who are directly and indirectly involved in its administration. This is particularly so when the beneficiaries are poor people who do not have the expertise or experience in dealing with official agencies. Instances where the granting of loans has involved corruption, where touts have misled and cheated the beneficiaries and where rural landlords and moneylenders have succeeded in using beneficiaries to divert the funds to them have also been quite common. A third set of problems have been even more serious. Some of the beneficiaries have been ruined by participating in the programme. A typical example has been an agricultural labourer getting a buffalo under the IRDP scheme of asset transfer. Usually a part of the cost of the animal is a loan given to the recipient which he is expected to repay in instalments as he sells the milk. But if he finds it difficult to meet the cost of feeding the animal, the milk supply may go down and he may not be able to repay the loan unless he borrows to do so. Cases of participants in such programmes ending up in debt traps have been reported.

Many of these are avoidable and some have indeed been avoided as the implementation of the programmes has improved over time. The most serious limitation of the strategy is that it aims at providing relief to the poor and not at poverty eradication. This is particularly true of the programmes providing employment. A casual worker may find employment for a few months under one of the many government sponsored employment programmes and while he is on the programme may figure as being above the poverty line. After the programme is over, he will again become an unemployed casual worker below the poverty line. The asset transfer schemes have a more permanent impact on the poverty situation, but they too can only be transient and marginal as long as the major asset in the economy, land, remains concentrated in the hands of a few.

Notwithstanding these limitations, the target group strategy has had some impact on the poverty situation in the country. Hence the claims made that during the eighties there has been some reduction in the percentage of population below the poverty line may be conceded, even when there are some doubts about the quantitative significance of the reduction. It can also be granted that a part of this reduction resulted from the higher rate of growth, especially the increase in the production of foodgrains, and another part was the result of the new target group oriented poverty eradication strategies. What is not quite clear is how lasting these effects will be. Only the future course of events can provide a definite answer. But there are reasons to think that during the decade itself some changes in the opposite direction may have been taking place.

Demand-led growth—possibilities and limitations

The target group strategy may have been meant to give relief to the poor. But in retrospect it can be seen that it could also be seen as a necessary prelude to let the natural propensities of the system take their own course as far as productive activity and growth are concerned. This has been the thrust of the new industrial policy initiated in the early eighties, along with the target group strategy, and pursued with greater vigour in the second half of the decade, during the Seventh Plan period. As noted already, it was a demand-led growth strategy which, in a reversal of what was postulated in the Fifth Plan, came to depend on the increased consumption of the affluent sections to stimulate and sustain industrial growth. A major component of the new demand that came into play, according to an official spokesman, was 'the revisions in the wage structures of government employees and others and the bulk payment of arrears'.[24] On the basis of this additional demand and changes in other policy measures, the rate of growth of the industrial sector during the 1980s had gone up to 8.4 per cent per annum compared with 4.4 per cent per annum during the 1970s. Along with good performance in the agricultural sector, this also resulted in a higher growth rate for the economy as a whole, as already noted.

But towards the end of the decade the efficacy of the strategy has come into question for a variety of reasons. In the first place, doubts have arisen about the sustainability of this pattern of industrial growth. During the last year of the decade (1989–90) there was a perceptible change in the pattern of growth. An official survey said:

> The pattern of industrial growth during 1989–90 was significantly different from that in the previous year, or generally, from the previous eight years (1980–81 to 1988–89) when the tempo of industrial growth witnessed a distinct acceleration over the growth rate in the decade of the 1970s.... First, the consumer durable goods industries, which exhibited on an average an uninterrupted high annual growth ranging from 8 to 22 per cent for the past eight years, faced a precipitate fall in their growth rate to 1.9 per cent during 1989–90 due to constraints in consumer demand.... Secondly, substantial deceleration occurred in 1989–90 as compared with the preceding year as well as with the performance in the previous eight-year period, in basic industries and intermediate goods industries...[In the manufacturing sector] of the 17 major industrial groups, as many as eleven...experienced either a visible deceleration or decline.... The performance of infrastructure industries during 1989–90 generally reflected slow down in industrial growth.[25]

Constraints in consumer demand alone was not the cause for this general deceleration, and it is quite possible that it is a temporary phenomenon. And yet the symptoms are disturbing and pose questions about how tenable the strategy can be.

The employment situation
But in another sphere the desirability of the strategy has been more clearly questioned. The period of rapid industrial growth has also been one of sluggish growth in employment. Total employment in the organised private sector was 72.27 lakhs in 1980. It reached 75.52 lakhs in 1983 and thereafter it has consistently remained below that level. The fall in employment in the organised manufacturing sector has been much more conspicuous. From a peak of 46.61 lakhs in 1982, it fell to 42.83 lakhs in 1988 showing an absolute fall of nearly 6 per cent over a period of six years.[26] Rapid growth with declining employment could have been beneficial only to a select few.

The overall employment pattern of the 1980s has been a matter of serious concern. In practically all major sectors of the economy the rate of growth of employment in the decade of high growth has been lower than in the previous decade, as can be seen from Table 11.1. The rate of growth of employment in the economy as a whole declined from 2.82 per cent in the 1972–73 to 1977–78 period to 2.22 per cent in the 1977–78 to 1983 period and to 1.55 per cent in the 1983 to 1987–88 period. Even in the agricultural sector which also witnessed significant increase in output, growth rate of employment declined from 2.32 per cent in the first period to 1.20 per cent in the second period and to a miserably low level of 0.65 per cent in the third period. Only mining and construction showed higher growth rates in employment in the third period compared to the preceding two. The Seventh Plan document had estimated that the labour force would be increasing at an annual rate of 2.56 per cent during 1985–90 and at 2.24 per cent during 1990–2000. If the growth rate in employment during part of the Plan period was only around 1.55 per cent as against the growth rate of labour force of 2.56 per cent, there can be no doubt that the decade of high growth rate would end up with an unemployment problem of very serious magnitude..

Table 11.1 *Growth Rate of Employment by Major Sectors 1973–88*

Sector	1972–73 to 1977–78	1977–78 to 1983	1983–84 to 1987–88	1972–73 to 1987–88
1. Agriculture	2.32	1.20	0.65	1.37
2. Mining	4.68	5.85	6.16	5.47
3. Manufacturing	5.10	3.75	2.10	3.61
4. Construction	1.59	7.45	13.69	7.23
5. Electricity, Gas & Water supply	12.23	5.07	4.64	7.06
6. Transport, Storage & Communication	4.85	6.35	2.67	4.65
7. Services	3.67	4.69	2.50	3.05
Total	2.82	2.22	1.55	2.17

A further disconcerting feature of the decade of high growth rate has been the strain it has exerted on the balance of payments. The acceleration in the industrial growth was made possible by a liberal regime of imports. Imports increased almost three-fold during the decade, going up from Rs 12,500 crores in 1980–81 to Rs 35,400 crores in 1989–90. Exports also showed a very impressive increase from Rs 6,700 crores in 1980–81 to Rs. 27,700 crores in 1989–90. But the excess of imports over exports increased from Rs 5,800 crores to Rs 7,700 crores. Recurring trade and payments deficits had to be met by borrowings which has led to a phenomenal increase in the foreign debt of the country and a steady decline in the value of the rupee in relation to leading foreign currencies. As the decade ended the country was faced with a severe balance of payments crisis. Future industrial growth may get reduced on account of it.

We must conclude, therefore, that the strategy of growth by and for the affluent section has generated a glitter of growth but it has also brought in serious economic and social problems. It is also doubtful whether the boost to growth can be sustained for long.

Inflation

For tracing the interactions between structure and strategy there is one more aspect that calls for comment. This is inflation. Inflation, or the rise in prices, has been a fairly constant feature of the Indian economy since Independence. The index of wholesale prices, one of the indications used to assess the change in price level, moved up from 46.5 in 1950 to 465.0 in 1989 (taking the prices in 1970–71 as 100). There have been a few years when the price level declined in comparison with the year preceding (1951 to 1952, 1953 to 1954, 1954 to 1955, 1975 to 1976) but otherwise the price level has been rising. There have been only a few instances of 'double digit inflation' where the annual increase in prices was 10 per cent or more (the major instances being 1972 to 1973, 16.5 per cent; 1973 to 1974, 28.6 per cent; 1979 to 1980, 20.2 per cent; 1990–91, 13 per cent) and so the Indian experience has been one of 'creeping inflation'. The reasons for the price increase are complex— increase in general economic activities, especially stepping up of investment which generates incomes to spend without immediate increase in goods; increase in money supply; fiscal measures of the Government particularly deficit financing; performance of different sectors of the economy, especially agriculture etc.[27] The more important question is the impact of inflation on different sections in society. Like growth, inflation also is not socially neutral. For instance, it is harmful to those with fixed incomes, because with increase in prices their purchasing power will go down; and is generally beneficial to those whose earnings (by way of profits, for instance) go up along with rise in prices. Wage earners, specially, tend to suffer on account of inflation because wage rates fixed in money terms tend to become sticky. Salary earners usually have some built-in mechanism to protect themselves against inflation such as dearness allowance and periodic revision of salary scales. The beneficiaries of inflation usually are business people, and traders. A creeping inflation of around 7 per cent per year of the kind that we have been experiencing in recent years, would amount to a doubling of prices in a decade because of compound growth; and hence a rule of thumb is that all those whose money incomes do not double in a decade can be considered to be victims of inflation. On this reckoning, it is reasonable to conclude that post-Independence inflation, whether caused by structural factors or resulting from policy measures or a combination of both, must have adversely affected the poorer sections in the country and thus become a cause for continuing mass poverty.[28]

The general price level, however, is an averge of changes in the prices of different goods. In order to assess the impact of inflation on different sections, therefore, it is necessary to take into account movements in prices of specific goods. For instance, an increase in the price of foodgrains is likely to affect the poorer sections more than others, because foodgrains will constitute a much larger proportion of their total expenses than those of other sections of the population. In evaluating the consequences of inflation it is, therefore, necessary to deal with consumer price indices (rather than wholesale price index) and such indices are available for different sections such as agricultural labourers, industrial workers, and urban non-manual employees.

Black money

There is a phenomenon closely associated with inflation, both as a cause and a consequence, viz., 'black money'. Black money is not a different form of money or currency, but essentially incomes which accrue through illegal measures and which, therefore, are kept out of accounts and escape taxation. One of the commonest ways of generating such incomes is the under-reporting of the value of property when it is bought and sold. To the person who buys property, under-reporting of the value makes it possible to reduce the cost of registrations which is a percentage of the reported value. It is advantageous to the seller because it will show a reduced capital appreciation and thus help to reduce or escape capital gains tax. The difference between the actual amount received and the reported value accrues as black money to the seller which he is in a position to use as he likes. Under-reporting of income to evade income tax (mainly because the rate of income tax goes up for higher levels of income) also generates black money for those who do it. Manufacturing concerns under-report the extent of production to escape excise duty and thus generate unaccounted incomes for themselves. All forms of bribes become unaccounted income for those who receive it. In all these ways the generation of unaccounted earnings or of black money is a widely prevalent practice in the economy. It provides additional purchasing power to those to whom it accrues and thus adds to the inflationary pressures. However, those who have fixed incomes can argue that when prices are rising they are not able to make both ends meet unless they have additional incomes, and to that extent black money may be thought of as a consequence of inflation also.

Once unaccounted incomes are generated they tend to enter into the overall working of the economy in many different ways. There will be greater inducement to spend unaccounted earnings. Usually the spending will be on durables whose values are likely to appreciate because of the rise in prices, particularly precious metals and real estate. And because unaccounted earnings are generated through such transactions a vicious circle soon sets in, as can be seen in the manner in which urban property values have been shooting up in recent years. But unaccounted incomes can be spent on just about anything, purchase of consumer durables, entertaining, giving 'gifts', financing crime and elections. In view of this easy access to the normal economy, it will not be correct to say that what unaccounted money does is to create a parallel economy or underground economy, distinctly separated from the actual economy. The relationship between the two is rather like milk and water in one container. It may be possible to say that the stuff in the container is a mixture of two different liquids, but the two do not remain horizontally or vertically separated.

Because of the very nature of the generation of unaccounted incomes and of their utilisation it is not easy to make any precise estimate of their magnitude. But there have been many attempts to arrive at some order of magnitude. A quasi-official estimate for 1989–90 showed that the quantum of black money was probably Rs 3 lakh crores, corresponding to around 75 to 80 per cent of the national income of that year with an annual accretion of at least Rs 50,000 crores.[29] Hence it is impossible to overlook its impact on the economic processes in the system. As black money is largely generated by, and accrues to those who are direct tax payers and those involved in transactions of high magnitude, it must be taken to belong to the top layer of the economy, considerably enhancing their affluence and the power they exercise over the system.

POVERTY AND AFFLUENCE: A SUMMING UP

In order to understand the functioning of the Indian economy and how it affects different sections of the populations we concentrated on the processual aspects in Chapters 8 and 9, and on aggregate quantitative aspects in Chapter 10. Together those chapters give an account of the evolution of the capitalist order and its confrontation with the traditional village economy first under colonial rule and then in Independent India. In the present chapter we have examined the role of the state in the unfolding capitalist process; particularly to stimulate and sustain growth and to ensure that the benefits of growth become available to as large a section of the population as possible—especially to that big but heterogeneous segment commonly referred to as the 'weaker sections'.

The production processes and patterns in the Indian economy are based on the pronounced unequal distributions of the privately owned non-labour resources, the state assisting private efforts in many ways and moderately regulating them to ensure that in the context of a democratic polity, economic operations do not turn out to be detrimental to the vast majority of the people. And yet it is private resource power that largely propels the system. Consequently the major beneficiaries of the quickened pace of growth since Independence have been the owners of such resources whose effective domination over the system has certainly increased, especially during the demand-led pattern of growth of the 1980s. While in the 1950s and 1960s the state made an attempt to set the pattern and pace of production, through direct participation in and physical regulation of the economy, in the 1980s through a process of fiscal and financial liberalisation the role of the state turned out to be to aid and assist the private sector to determine the path of growth. In quantitative terms the performance of the economy improved, but the access to the increase that resulted was more than before confined to the top layer.

The increase in production that has taken place since Independence has made it possible to sustain a rapidly growing population. It may have even brought down the percentage of population below the very low poverty line accepted in the early 1960s. The diversification of economic activities that accompanies growth has also provided opportunities for more people to eke out a living. But the proportion of people having a precarious and insecure livelihood has certainly increased— the small and marginal farmer, the agricultural and non-agricultural labourers in the rural areas and the majority of the workers in urban areas who are all becoming increasingly casualised; those dependent on traditional crafts who are being rapidly displaced or brought under the control of those who benefit by their labour; the multitudes who are engaged in petty trade; together constituting well above 50 per cent of the workforce and of the population.

The Indian experience has been that capitalist growth benefits first and foremost a very small minority at the top; perhaps, the top 10 per cent, and percolates down in trickles to a further 30 or 40 per cent, but fizzles out thereafter. The benefits of the system accrue primarily in proportion to the ownership of non-labour resources, partly because control over such resources effectively regulates production and partly because productive activity augments property incomes and, unlike labour income, property incomes grow cumulatively simply by the efflux of time. Even the special efforts to bring about a more extended redistribution of the benefits of growth have been only marginally successful. In particular the high growth decade of the 1980s even while accompanied by a wide range of official schemes to increase employment and support the weaker sections through asset transfers, led to a major *reduction* in the rate of growth of employment bringing it far below the rate of growth of the labour force, thus clearly demonstrating the systemic exclusive feature of capitalism.

Both the analysis of the aggregate data and the case studies we have noted in Chapter 9 indicate that those whom the capitalist processes benefit are those with resource power, who come to have more and more control over the system via their increasing resource power itself and through the domination that they gain over the market operations. Similarly, those who are excluded by the capitalist process, and exploited when included, are those with little or no resource power, once again demonstrating a clear systemic feature of capitalism.

It is seen also that the attempt to tame capitalism and to make it responsive to the needs of the people at large through the use of the power of the state has been only of limited success, and so far economic power has had the upper hand. This too has been a systemic feature of capitalism; its tendency to let economic power exert decisive domination over all of society, unlike other economic systems that have functioned within effective social control.

NOTES

1. Sundrum, 1987: 38–39. Statistics on distribution of income are more difficult to come by because income is a flow concept and the flows over a period such as one year may consist of many sources, some regular and some irregular; some in kind and some in cash etc. Because of this it is now common to use consumer expenditure as a proxy for income in studies relating to poverty. This does not overcome all difficulties and poses some new ones, but it is assumed that expenditure on consumption is more easy to obtain than income. The distribution of income usually refers to distribution at the national level and must, therefore, be aggregated from incomes accruing to different persons.
2. For a recent simple exposition of the concept of 'poverty line' see The World Bank, 1990. Kurien, 1978 discusses how the poverty line has been arrived at in India.
3. The early studies were Dandekar & Rath, 1971; Minhas, 1974; Srinivasan & Bardhan, 1974. For more recent work see Ahluwalia, 1978 and 1986. Naidu, 1987 and Tendulkar, 1988 provide reviews of studies.
4. See Ganguli, 1977, especially Chapter 6 for a discussion of the 'drain theory'.
5. Government of India, *Third Five Year Plan*, p. 6.
6. Government of India, *First Five Year Plan*, p. 31.

7. This was anticipated by and was acceptable to the private sector which had, even before Independence, asked for a major role for the state in the future development of the economy in a document which has come to be known as the 'Bombay Plan', 1944.

8. See Chaudhuri, 1975.

9. For a brief review of attempts at land reform see Parthasarathy, 1988.

10. See Frankel, 1978, Ch. 5 for a detailed account.

11. Perspective of Development, 1961–76: "Implications of Planning for a Minimum Level of Living" reproduced in Srinivasan and Bardhan, 1974.

12. See Kurien, 1978 for a critical evaluation.

13. See studies referred to in Note 3 above.

14. Ahluwalia, 1986.

15. 'A Technical Note on the Approach to the Fifth Five Year Plan of India, 1974–75 to 1978–79'.

16. For a discussion of the target group strategy see Kurien, 1986, Kohli, 1987, and Parthasarathy, 1991 and references in them.

17. See Jha, 1980.

18. See Kurien, 1987a.

19. The tax concessions given to those who hold National Saving Certificates (NSC) and deposit in National Saving Scheme (NSS) are of this kind.

20. Reserve Bank of India, *Annual Report 1989–90*, p. 20. But the boom came to an end soon when they 'faced a precipitate fall in their growth rate to 1.9 per cent in 1989–90 due to constraints of consumer demand'.

21. For a case study see Kurien, 1981a, Chapter 6.

22. See Jodha, 1990 and references given there.

23. One of the earliest studies to identify these drawbacks was MIDS 1980. Since then there have been many other studies dealing with similar issues. See Rath, 1985 and references in it.

24. The Deputy Governor of the Reserve Bank of India in *Reserve Bank of India Bulletin*, May 1990: 363.

25. Reserve Bank of India *Annual Report 1989–90*: 20, 22 & 23.

26. *Ibid.*: 28–29.

27. The two digit inflations of 1972–74 and 1978–80 were associated with droughts and the consequent poor performance of agriculture, foodgrains production in particular. However the two digit inflation of 1990–91 did not have such an excuse. In fact, the year saw a record foodgrain production. It is, therefore, likely that the part played by nature in earlier high price rises is now taken by economic policies. The tremendous increase in purchasing power pumped into the economy from 1985 onwards through government deficits appears to be the main factor underlying the 1990–91 inflation.

28. In a striking passage Max Weber said: 'Money prices are the product of conflicts of interest and of compromises: they thus result from power constellations. Money is not a mere "voucher for unspecified utilities" which could be altered at will without any fundamental effect on the character of the price system as a struggle of man against man. "Money" is, rather, primarily a weapon of this struggle, and prices are expressions of the struggle; they are the instruments of calculation only as estimated quantifications of relative chances in this struggle of interests'. Weber, 1978; I: 108.

29. This estimate has been reportedly made by the Planning Commission, see, *Economic Times*, March 11, 1991.

Notes to Tables

The source of Table 11.1 is Planning Commission, 1990, *Employment—Past Trends and Prospects for 1990s*, Table 2.

Many aspects discussed in this chapter are dealt with in greater detail in Kurien, 1992.

12

Shaping the Economy

As the economy is always under human deliberations and control, even when it appears to be governed solely by its own internal laws, shaping the economy is a distinct possibility. The question to consider is whether its internal structure can be altered so as to direct it towards some specified goals. This chapter sets up four such goals in the Indian context, the chief among them being meeting the basic material conditions of life of *all* members. Whether a reformed capitalist system can attain these goals is then examined. Capitalism can accommodate certain kinds of reforms and in some parts of the world it has succeeded in meeting desired social goals. But its primary objective of enabling those who have resource power to accumulate more resources sets serious limitations in directing it to meet the needs of those who do not control non-human resources. The feasibility of shaping the Indian economy as a post-capitalist system is then considered. It is shown that while from an economic point of view it can be done, the existing power structure in Indian society is very unlikely to permit it. Some measures to alter the balance of power in favour of the vast majority of the people necessary to facilitate a post-capitalist transformation are indicated.

Is it possible and desirable to shape the economy? There are different responses to this question. A very widely held and actively canvassed view envisages the economy as something like an automatic watch that has a momentum built into it and performs best when it is left to its internal movements and without external interventions. No questions are asked as to how the watch came to be made. That it is there is accepted as a matter of fact and the effort is to see that it is left to its own devices. 'Leave it to the market' is the popular expression of this view. Occasionally attempts are made to look into the mechanism and to indicate how it functions. Two leading economists of our time who have carefully studied the internal arrangements of the instrument say: 'There is now a long and fairly imposing line of economists from Adam Smith to the present who have sought to show that a decentralised economy motivated by self-interest and guided by price signals would be compatible with a coherent disposition of economic resources that could be regarded, in a well-defined sense, as superior to a large class of possible dispositions. Moreover, the price signals would operate in a way to establish this degree of coherence ' (Arrow & Hahn, 1971: vi). Individual self-interest as the invisible mainspring and prices as the visible signals are the main components of the economy, according to this view, and the corollary, it is said, is to leave it to function as it stands. In spite of the warnings by those who have looked into the internal structure carefully, that it is a highly conditional statement which is not applicable in many crucial aspects of economic decision-making,[1] it is repeated in a parrot-like fashion by business people, politicians and by many who claim to be students of economics.

Our explorations into the economy have shown that the nature of the economy is very different. Even when self-interest becomes a major factor in the functioning of the economy and markets play a decisive role in its operations, many more constituent parts of the economy must be recognised if its working is to be properly understood. Institutional arrangements for the ownership and control over resources constitute a major plank of the economy; the state is one of its unavoidable components; many other social forces influence its working. The economy is not a set machine. It undergoes major changes as a result of its own working. And there have been instances where social forces, not immediately arising from it, have significantly altered it. In the light of these findings from the preceding chapters, the answer we can give to the question posed at the beginning of this chapter can only be yes, the economy can be shaped, and is constantly being shaped. It cannot be otherwise if it is accepted that the economy is not an autonomous entity, but is society's arrangement to provision the material needs of its members.

THE ECONOMY AS A STRUCTURE OF SOCIAL RELATIONSHIPS

In order to gain a better understanding of this aspect of the economy let us look a little deeper into our depiction of it as a structure of social relationships. What is the nature of human relationships that characterises society? Is it basically one of good-will and harmony or of conflict and antagonism? The honest answer will have to be that it is a curious and somewhat confused mixture of the two, because we experience both in real life situations. As our main concern is with a national economy, and the nation in that sense becomes the society and community within which the economy is embedded, the specific question to consider is what constitutes the nation as a community. The answer is not easy. There are many things that unite the nation and hold it together. At one level we can identify the memories of the past, many shared experiences and various other 'vague' elements. On the other, there are very specific things like a written constitution, defined conditions of citizenship, laws that govern all members of the nation, the authority of the state and the power of the armed forces. The forces that divide the nation are more easy to identify—languages, religion, ethnicity and the like. Are the forces that unite the nation strong enough to hold it together against those that divide it? This is not too remote an issue from our perspective. For, if a national economy is to be consciously shaped, it will have to be done by the nation which constitutes the community behind it. It is not surprising that when conscious restructuring of economies is the specific agenda, the 'nationality question' surfaces suddenly—as is most clearly and painfully visible in the Soviet Union and in Yugoslavia at present. The connection between economy and community is so intimate that it is difficult to deal with the one without also dealing with the other. Any attempt to shape the economy is also an attempt to shape the community of which it is a part.

Harmony or conflict?

We must, however, go more directly into the economy. If the economy is mentally carved out from society, the essential characteristics of society can be seen in the economy too, elements that hold it together and those that tend to divide it. Since the economy is, at the most elementary level, society's arrangement to meet the material needs for the sustenance of life, the instinctive interest to survive is the basic factor that holds it together. As we have already noted, survival strategies of various kinds constitute a major share of economic activities in countries like ours where most members cannot afford to take survival for granted. Some of these strategies and activities may not pass the test of 'economic rationality' as it has come to be understood. An example may make it clear. Economic rationality would indicate that in the production process inputs should be economised and that, therefore, a production process that makes use of more of *all* inputs required for a particular product is inefficient compared to another which uses less of at least one of the inputs in the production of the same product. Thus a weaving process that uses more of both labour time and capital in the production of a defined unit of cloth, must be considered inefficient in comparison with another which uses less of at least one of them. Studies on traditional production processes in areas like weaving, oil pressing etc.[2] have found that many of them are inefficient in this sense. But then why do they continue? Why are they not competed out by the efficient production processes? The answer can only be that for the producers concerned there may be no other alternative to eke out a living. In other words, there is a sense in which the struggle for survival is the supreme economic rationality and all other considerations are subservient to it. If most contemporary economic discourses and theories do not pay attention to this basic issue it is only because they emanate from situations where survival can be taken for granted.[3] The reason why in economies like ours, household production units (h–2 units) continue to play a crucial role is because the family as a social unit is still the best (and only) 'insurance policy' for many.

The economy also has its basic elements of conflict, and writers on the economy from the early times have taken note of them as *classes*. Adam Smith and Ricardo recognised three classes—'the proprietor of the land, the owner of the stock or capital necessary for its cultivation, and the labourers by whose industry it is cultivated' and whose shares in the produce were noted as rent, profit and wages. They recognised these classes more than as categories for economic analysis: to them the classes constituted the actual and visible divisions in society. each with its many distinguishing social characteristics.[4] And yet their specific economic features were also clear. They differed in their ownership patterns and in their claims and Ricardo, particularly, held that the interests of landlords was opposed to those of the rest of society. This element of class antagonism became more pronounced in the writings of Marx. Concentrating on industrial capitalism, Marx recognised two basic classes, the owners of the means of production and workers selling their labour power to them. As we saw in Chapter 5, Marx used this presentation of class not merely to identify two groups, but to bring out the underlying conflict of interest in the capitalist system between its two components. That representation of the capitalist economy is possibly the clearest exposition of the element of conflict in the economy. Marx himself did not insist that the element of conflict would be equally pronounced in other forms of economies also (pre-capitalist economies) or that capitalist economies have only two classes.[5] The important point to note is that as in society at large so in the economy too there are basic elements of conflict and that for analytical purposes it will be helpful to relate these conflicts to classes identified with reference to the economic categories of ownership, role in production and share in the produce.

In theoretical representations of the economy the tendency has been to concentrate either on the element of harmony or of conflict. In what has come to be known as the neo-classical tradition in economics the emphasis is on harmony. The scholars referred to at the beginning of this chapter spell it out. After referring to the claim that the price signals, if adhered to, establish a degree of coherence, they go on to say:

It is important to understand how surprising this claim must be to anyone not exposed to this tradition. The immediate "commonsense" answer to the question "what will an economy motivated by individual greed and controlled by a very large number of different agents look like?" is probably: There will be chaos. That quite a different answer has long been claimed to be true and permeated the economic thinking of a large number of people who are in no way economists is itself sufficient ground for investigating it seriously (Arrow & Hahn, 1971: vii).

What that serious investigation brings out is that harmony and coherence can be shown as the outcome of economic processes, not because those processes are motivated by self-interest, but because the very large number of different agents are all considered to be similar in terms of their resource endowments—one theoretical version, in fact, suggesting that all the agents should be thought of as basically self-sufficient peasants who enter into exchange on the basis of their surplus production. It has also been demonstrated that if the initial endowment conditions are different, the nice conclusions of coherence do not emerge.[6]

On the contrary, the Marxist tradition tends to put the emphasis on the element of conflict in depicting the economy. Which of these two is more relevant in any given situation—in the case of any particular national economy—is a theoretical, and more so, an empirical question, relating to the realities of the situation, that is. An important derivative of the conflict-oriented representations is that what are frequently posed as problems of a national economy must be examined and understood from different class perspectives. In the preceding chapter we have seen that problems relating to the growth of national income are perceived differently by different groups in the economy: for some it implies availability of greater variety of goods; for others it means loss of jobs. Inflation, or rising prices, may be welcomed by some groups who find in it opportunities for higher profits and earnings; for most others it may indicate loss of purchasing power.[7]

Whatever may be the nature of theoretical representations, these and similar instances show that conflict of interests must be accepted as an important factor in dealing with real life economic situations. They, certainly, will have an important bearing on how the economy is shaped. In that connection it is important to consider also whether such conflicts inherent in an economy are held under control, and if so, how. The survival instinct itself tones down the element of conflict by making those at the verge of survival basically subordinate to those whose economic interests are very different as the analysis of Chapter 9 has shown.

The state as a social institution

There is also the state as an institution whose responsibility very often is to contain and control conflicts. We have already examined the role of the state as a unit in the economy. Even as an economic unit, the state is a distinct entity. But, like the household, the state is more than an economic institution; they are two of the social institutions from which the economy is carved out. The state, in a sense, is the epitome of society and hence will reflect both the elements of harmony and conflict in it. Hence in the context of the economy it will be wrong to portray it either as an external umpire, judiciously and impartially supervising the operations, or as the executive wing of the major class always eager to protect and promote its interest over the rest of the economy and society. True, in a society dominated by one of the classes, the state will come to reflect that domination, but it also has autonomy of its own, particularly where, as often is the case, class interests are not sharply distinguished. The significant feature of the state is that it is a locus of power in the social system, which too gets reflected in its role as a constituent of the economy, where this aspect is manifested in its role as the authority that sanctions the economic order in many different ways. It is the authority that defines the nature of ownership of resources, provides the legal requirements of production organisations and the backing for legal tender, adjudicates over contractual obligations, performing all these functions apart from any role it may have as a unit in the economy, owning resources, becoming a producer, seller, purchaser etc.[8]

When exchange spreads as an economic activity and market emerges as a specific economic institution, the state comes to play a special role in the economy. In the first place, it becomes the authority that sanctions and validates the appropriations made through the exercise of economic power. We saw in Chapter 4 that exchange is appropriation by exercising economic (purchasing) power and what is thus appropriated becomes the possession of the person who has exercised that power. The purchaser does not have to defend that possession any more because the state performs that function on his behalf. If somebody else tries to grab that possession (by exercising physical power, for instance) the legal owner can seek and obtain the power of the state. Market operation, therefore, is a form of exercise of power which derives its validity from the power of the state.

Secondly, again, as was noted in Chapter 4, every society must determine what will be and what will not be subjected to the jurisdiction of the market. Social customs, however undefined they may be, are mainly responsible for drawing and maintaining that distinction, but increasingly the power of the state has to be brought into play to decide what will *not* be marketised. Thus, if in the former case the state is seen as the defender of an economic institution, here it becomes society's representative *against* the economy.

The role of the state in the economy and its relationship to classes do not remain static. There is a constant ongoing interaction between state, classes and markets.[9] Crucial to the understanding of this interaction is the manner in which control is exercised over resources where *de jure* and *de facto* considerations may not get synchronised. An extreme case may be where by a decree of the state all resources are socialised, but effective control remains with those who had it prior to the decree. Other, and more day to day, examples can also be thought of. If different classes in society accumulate, but if the rate of accumulation is not uniform, the relative economic power of the classes may change which may have a bearing on the state. Both state and market may have been responsible for the differential accumulation as well. Class interests too do not remain invariant over time for they are based not only on what a particular agent (or a class of agents) has, but also on what other agents have. Hence class interests must be thought of essentially as relative comparative advantage, and not posited in isolation from specific conjectures. If so, the same objective conditions can be given different subjective interpretations by different agents or groups in the economy. Strategies of action always arise from subjective appraisals of objective conditions. These considerations imply that if classes exercise their influence over the state, the state can, through a variety of options open to it, in particular through its power to alter conditions of control over resources and through the power it can exert on markets, also influence classes.

The economy, then, is a network of .these changing relationships which are always shaping and reshaping it. The pertinent question, therefore, is not whether it is possible to shape the economy, but whether the ongoing processes can be directed in some desired manner and whether that decision should be made by just a few in society or by the informed participation of all its members.

DIRECTIONS OF CHANGE

The directions for change cannot be derived from the economic processes themselves: they are not internal to the economy. This is not surprising because if the economy is society's arrangement for a purpose, that purpose can only be a social decision, reflecting social values and commitments. In that sense, and with the Indian situation specifically in mind, let us first indicate what the goals of economic changes should be.

1. Basic necessities of life for all

If the economy is society's arrangement to provision the material needs of its members, the first criterion in deciding on the directions of change must be that the basic necessities of life of *all* members should be met.

2. Increase in productivity

An increase in productivity is required in the Indian context to reduce the drudgery of work of vast millions who now toil incessantly simply to make a living, and also to ensure that more than the elementary requirements of life become available to all members.

3. Concern for future generations

If an increase in the availability of goods and services is to continue beyond the present generation, productive capacity itself must increase, but it will have to be done in such a way that the balance of nature is not disrupted.

4. Maintaining inequalities within tolerable limits

Recognising that beyond the basic necessities of life it will be virtually impossible to ensure that the claims on goods and services are equal, partly because innate human capacities differ, partly because preferences also differ, a major consideration will have to be to strive to maintain inequalities within tolerable limits. The goal must be to reduce as far as possible, inequalities in opportunities.

As these goals, or societal criteria, for shaping the economy are likely to be generally acceptable we shall not try to probe into the rationale that lies behind them except to point out that they are expressions of social values. The more important issue is how they are to be actualised, brought into the economy and to become incorporated in its working arrangements. That is the operational meaning of the expression, 'shaping the economy'. Let us consider some selected aspects relating to it.

Nature of social decision-making

Many people, especially those who envisage society simply as the sum of the individuals who constitute it, feel uneasy about *social* decisions. They think of decision-making as a personal and individual act and find it difficult to see how something as abstract and impersonal as society can make decisions. In the economic context where all decisions are supposed to be based on personal preferences made known through the market via its price signals, the question boils down to the feasibility of non-market decisions. There can be no doubt that decision-making is a human activity. But, certainly, not all decisions are individual decisions. There are many instances of group or collective decisions although there are problems associated with the processes and procedures associated with them.[10] Within the sphere of the economy too there are both individual and group decisions. While market decisions may appear to be according to personal preferences (but can the social factors shaping personal or individual preferences be completely overlooked?) non-market decisions relating to the economy are essentially group decisions, formal or informal. The clearest example in modern societies and economies is the decision regarding defence expenditure. What priority national defence should have and how much of a nation's resources should be devoted for that purpose are matters decided by 'society at large', and not on the basis of individual preferences even in the most individualistic of societies and the most marketised economies. These are not once and for all decisions either; they are made year after year. It may be that there are some members of the nation who are totally opposed to the use of resources in this manner and many may have disagreements with the extent of resources used. And yet a social decision binding on all members is arrived at. Defence, however, is not the only area about which a decision of this kind is taken. In most societies education and health are areas where social decisions about the use of resources is quite pronounced. Most countries also have social decisions about the preservation of national monuments, the maintenance of parks etc. There are also, increasingly, decisions regarding the protection of nature and wild life, all taken outside of market considerations, and frequently going against market calculations. In fact, even within what is usually considered as the private sector, many major decisions are taken not in response to individual preferences revealed through the operations of the market. There are few instances where the decision to produce a new good (particularly a new brand of a good in regular use) is made in response to price signals and indicated personal preferences. When such decisions are made, they are taken by some group or the other. The institutional arrangements for arriving at these 'social' decisions differ greatly from country to country and society to society, but they are taken, and they are very much part of social and economic processes. And they are all answers to the rhetorical question usually posed: 'But how does society make decisions?' If it is reasonable and usual for most societies to decide how much of resources should be devoted for national defence, is there anything peculiar if some societies make a collective decision that the first charge on their resources will be to ensure that *all* their members have the basic necessities of life?

Social decisions do not have to be directly about the use of resources. They are the basis by which norms of economic activity are arrived at. In the early days of factory production there were no norms about the length of the working day, but something like an 'eight-hour working day' has come to have fairly universal acceptance now wherever factory forms of production is practised. The orgainsed effort of workers, the support they received from the enlightened public and legislation by the state were instrumental in arriving at such a norm. In many parts of the world now there are attempts to change that norm to have shorter working days. At one stage lower payment for women workers was a widely prevalent norm; now the trend is to accept equal pay for equal work as the norm. In all these instances too decision-making has been a social process involving diverse methods and many groups of people.

In the Indian context the wide acceptance that the 1962 'poverty line' has come to have is another good example of how social decisions are made and social norms are evolved. It had the views of some experts as the basis, but there were also arbitrary elements in arriving at the final figure, and yet it is now generally accepted and treated as 'official'.[11]

That will also answer the criticism sometimes made that concepts such as 'basic minimum ncessities of life' are subjective, depending on a variety of considerations such as custom, climate, as well as the level of economic development itself. It does not take much effort to show that it is true. What the basic necessities of life are will depend on the conditions of the person concerned—age, sex and occupation; on the society of which he or she is a member—the physical conditions in which it exists and its culture; and what is necessary will change as time goes on and economic conditions change. That is why the concept of basic necessities of life is not a physical one, but a social one. There is nothing strange about this. Market price or exchange value too is a social concept, not a physical entity. The economy, in fact, can be thought of as a procedure for converting physical entities into social categories. All the four goals we have identified are societal categories in this sense. Consequently, decisions regarding them are social decisions. That does not mean that they are more arbitrary than private or individual decisions, or that they are less liable for quantitative specification.

It may be noted too that when a set of social goals (of the kind we have indicated) are taken together, there may be some incompatibilities or tensions. At low levels of economic performance there is likely to be understandable emphasis on meeting current needs—high priority for the production of food, for instance—which may come in conflict with the needs for the future. Clearing forests may bring more land under cultivation now, but it may cause soil erosion and/or reduce rainfall in the future. Or, an irrigation project may lead to increase in food production in the future, but it may displace many people and deprive them of the means to make a livelihood at the present time. Such conflicts cannot be avoided. A major aspect of social decision-making is to see that the trade-off in instances like these are clearly evaluated and the tensions resolved as effectively as possible.

In shaping the Indian economy according to the criteria specified above, social decision-making as such, therefore, is not likely to present any insurmountable problem. What needs to be examined in greater detail is how exactly the goals are to be translated into the institutional structure of the economy.

REFORMED CAPITALISM?

Since the Indian economy is at present undergoing a capitalist transformation, we may first examine whether the institutional framework of the capitalist economy can be reformed to accommodate the goals indicated. The experience of a century or more of capitalist development in the country dealt with in Chapters 8 to 11 does not provide any evidence that the economy is moving in the direction that, from the perspective of its goals, can be described as desirable. On the contrary, what we have seen is that in spite of the backing professedly provided by the state and the political processes based on adult franchise and parliamentary democracy, the economy is not turning out as it was anticipated. But is it because the effort has not been adequate or because the time has not been long enough? These questions must be given due consideration because in some other parts of the world, in Western Europe, North America, Japan and Australia in particular, capitalist economies seem to have succeeded in assuring its members the basic necessities of life, and a steadily rising level of living. They also appear to have reduced inequalities of opportunities and to have become alert in dealing with the relatively new problems of ecological balance.

We shall not take up each one of these cases to see how capitalist economies succeeded in achieving the designated goals. Instead, we shall identify some conditions under which capitalist economies have reached these goals.

Welfare possibilities under capitalism

The early classical writers on capitalism, especially Adam Smith, were mainly concerned with the wealth that capitalist processes would bring to the *nation*; how it would be shared among different sections within the nation was only a secondary matter. It may be useful to point out that Adam Smith was convinced that 'servants, labourers and workmen of different kinds' who made up 'the greater part of every great political society' must get a proper reward: The argument was: 'what improves the circumstances of the greater part can never be regarded as an inconveniency to the whole. No society can surely be flourishing and happy, of which the far greater part of the members are poor and miserable. It is but equity besides, that they who feed, clothe, and lodge the whole body of people, should have such a share of the produce of their own labour as to be themselves tolerably well-fed, clothed and lodged' (Smith, 1966: I, 70).

For that, he staunchly advocated increased production of food and productivity of agriculture. He also canvassed that workers should be educated at public cost. But beneath all this was the notion that 'the labouring poor', or 'the inferior ranks of people' as he referred to them, would continue as a socially distinct group and in their appointed lot. There was anticipation, however, that the wealth of the nation would ultimately raise their standard of living too, but perhaps indirectly. 'The houses, the furniture, the clothing of the rich in a little time, become useful to the inferior and middling ranks of people. They are able to purchase them when their superiors grow weary of them, and the general accommodation of the whole people is thus gradually improved, when this mode of expenses becomes universal among men of fortune' (Smith, 1966: I, 310–11). This statement indicates one of the conditions for capitalist economies benefiting all members of society: it will be a gradual long-term process where the initial affluence of the few will ultimately percolate down to all, provided the accumulation of capital goes on satisfactorily. When the economic conditions are fairly satisfied, political processes can be activated to convert capitalist countries into 'welfare states'.[12] This is how it happened in the United Kingdom, the Scandinavian countries and other West European Nations. And it is the same pattern that many now advocate in countries like ours also, asking the poor to wait and promising them on the strength of historical evidence that some day they too will have their turn.

A second condition under which a capitalist economy can attain a form of general welfare may be referred to as the 'new country' pattern, that of North America and Australia where the initial condition was abundant availability of physical resources, especially land, to all, such that the provision of the basic necessities to everyone did not become a matter of economic and social constraint. If the basic necessities of life of all are relatively easily taken care of, productivity can increase rapidly and opportunities for higher levels of living can also become readily available if other social factors (such as discrimination against the blacks in the U.S.A. for a long period of that country's history) do not block them. Capitalist development incorporating most members of society was made possible in Japan immediately after the Second World War and in South Korea through major land reform measures which provided mimimum resource base to the bulk of the population enabling them to become active participants in the capitalist process.[13]

There is a third condition which most early capitalist countries had and which many advanced capitalist countries still make use of—their easy access to physical resources and labour power of other countries of the world. European capitalist countries had their colonies and all leading capitalist countries have their capital all over the world reaching out to physical resources and appropriating surplus value throughout the globe. It will be interesting to speculate what will happen to capitalist countries such as the U.S.A., Germany and Japan if international law were to insist that countries may invest their capital only within their own geographical territories.

Capitalist options for India

Now, if India is to follow the capitalist path which of these options is available to her? Indian capitalism is too weak to make its presence felt in other parts of the world although Indian business concerns are already active in some foreign countries.[14] It is very doubtful if a capitalist land reform measure of the kind that was done in Japan or South Korea will take place in our country. And so the only option that the capitalist path offers India is the one of gradualism. But historically the social backing for capitalist gradualism was the view widely shared a century or two ago that the 'servants, labourers and workmen of different kinds' constituted an inferior group in society whose aspirations would be low and who, in any case, could be and should be made to wait till capitalism's 'trickling down' would bring drizzles of blessings on them. That social philosophy is not totally obsolete even today, but it cannot be as crudely and vehemently articulated now as it used to be because of the change in social consciousness globally and our own political commitment about the equality of all citizens of the country.

Gradualism, however, finds new support today from a totally different perspective which can only be described as pseudo-internationalism. The proposition is that if capitalism within countries like India is weak, global capitalism is stronger than ever (especially after the collapse of many socialist regimes) and that linking domestic capitalism to international capitalism can lead to quick economic results internally through capital, technology and management techniques all of which will flow in liberally if only a political decision favouring such a path is taken. Since the path involves greater global connections, it is sometimes referred to as *outward orientation*; also as *liberalisation* because one of its objectives is to liberate the economy from what are considered to be unnecessary and excessive social control so that it will follow the rational principles of its own self-regulation.

This option has been under political consideration in India from the early 1980s and the first steps in that direction were taken during the decade, especially its second half, as noted in the previous chapter. By mid-1991 the indications are that there will be a fuller and more rapid acceptance of that line.

Trans-national corporations

To evaluate this option an understanding of the nature of international capitalism at the present stage is necessary. As was seen in Chapter 5, capitalism has always had an innate tendency to transcend national boundaries and to become global. But till recently the national identities of capitals—as British capital, French capital, American capital, Japanese capital etc.—were preserved and consequently global capitalism remained to a large extent under the overall political supervision and control of national governments. International trade was the flow of goods (and services) from production units within national economies to economic units within other national economies.

A new phenomenon of global capitalism of the past two or three decades has been the rapid growth of trans-national corporations (TNCs) which could make their global economic decisions comparing labour costs, government subsidies and taxes, exchange rates and political conditions in different parts of the world.[15] They can locate their production operations in one or many countries taking these factors into account and also pull out their operations to suit their calculations. They can enter into various kinds of collaborative arrangements with units in a host country or with its government if so desired. They can have the parts of their product (like the Escort automobile referred to in Chapter 9) manufactured in different countries of the world, thus making the whole world their workshop. They can sell the goods in the country (or countries) in which they are produced or export them to other countries. These possibilities enable them to internalise not only production decisions but also decisions regarding the movement and distribution of goods, thus providing them the power to supersede market transactions which are inter-unit activities. TNCs are of different sizes and activities, but some of the largest among them have sales which exceed the total gross domestic product of most Third World countries. In many major industries, such as oil refining, aluminium, vehicles and tobacco, a substantial proportion of the capitalist world's production is accounted for by a handful of TNCs. An estimate by the United Nations showed that some 350 TNCs controlling 25,000 subsidiaries all over the world accounted for close to 30 per cent of the gross domestic product of the entire capitalist world in 1980.[16] The share must have gone up further since then.

Two features of the TNCs are worth noting. The first is that they represent enormous economic power in private hands with the tendency to augment capitalism's innate propensity to move to more and more concentration. The second is that this power is used to have prices fixed largely on the basis of their internal calculations. Their oligopolistic power is exercised not only over products and prices, but also over technology. Global technology (and a great deal of research relating to it) in many spheres of production are under their control. In view of all these, global capitalism now has come to be described as 'techno-industrial, transnational oligopolistic capitalism'.

It is to such concentrated power of global capitalism that weak national capitalisms are being exhorted to link themselves with the promise that global resources and technology will be put under their disposal for a gradual but thorough transformation of their economies. Many small countries and some large countries like Brazil and Mexico have already accepted this path of 'development'. It has a fairly standard progression too. The beginning is usually a critical balance of payments position which is interpreted as paucity of resources for economic growth. Ostensibly to tide over the situation, the external value of the national currency is brought down so as to make exports from the country more attractive to outsiders. It is followed by a sudden increase in the flow of capital from interested TNCs to the host country made possible by the tremendous increase in the international mobility of money capital in recent years. Internal producers become collaborators with (effectively subsidiaries to) the TNCs. New technologies and management methods are introduced; new goods are produced and widely advertised, all of which give the appearance of growth and prosperity. But the oligopolistic element is transmitted from the global level to the national level and hence instead of greater competition greater concentration becomes the pronounced characteristic internally with prices determined on the basis of what the market will bear. Since these processes generate some incomes which too become heavily concentrated, these goods, which come to be known as prestige goods, are purchased by a small segment of the population who, however, praise their finish, variety and ready availability that the country has been able to produce thanks to the new arrangements. A second round of economic activity, employment and incomes is also generated in the form of production of a few ancillaries, repair shops, retail trade etc. Statistics begin to show that the 'national economy' is picking up and prospering, but the fact will remain that the prosperity is confined to a very small segment of the population—the upper crust—with the rest having no access at all to the goods except when and to the extent that 'the superiors grow weary of them'. Soon the new prosperity will give place to a new crisis because imports would have increased, exports would not have been adequate to pay for them, and the TNCs may be ready to move to a new host country.

Whatever may be the external manifestations, the basic logic of capitalism remains: it is an economic order at the disposal of those who have control over resources to come to have more resources through the accumulation of exchange value. Everything else is peripheral. The peripherals will be tolerated, even encouraged, as long as they do not interfere with what is central. Consequently, there are severe limits to the extent to which capitalism can be reformed or modified. In a poor country where many have no control over physical resources, capitalism cannot be moulded to provide them the basic necessities of life. A capitalist economy has no such mission; its role is to augment the resources of those who have it and in that process service those who can afford it. Others who have no resource power to enter its orbit are excluded. At this point even political power has its limitations as the Indian experience so far has shown. Capitalism is like a magnet, someone has said. It will attract and attach metal pieces but it can only pass over sawdust.

IS A POST-CAPITALIST ALTERNATIVE FEASIBLE?

Unlike a capitalist economy, a post-capitalist economy is not an economic system with its own internal propelling power and dynamics. It is the social framework of a modern economy relying on technological progress and exchange, that permits use value to become its organising principle. Its specific features are to be determined by society itself. It is, therefore, hospitable to social decisions and requires social direction for its functioning.

Its generic features have been discussed in Chapter 6. To recall, it is an inclusive economy accepting the provisioning of the basic necessities of life for all its members as its primary task. It is one where production responds to needs of the present and of the future as indicated by society. Its organisation of production respects the producers' attachments to the tools and instruments that they generate and with which they work. It leaves major decisions about production to workers and substantially eliminates exploitation as a means for private enrichment. By reducing the role of property as a means to generate private income it aims to bring down inequalities of income, wealth and opportunities and relates the accrual of income to abilities and skills in work. It has a micro-global coordinating procedure in which exchange as an activity plays a major role. It designs a variety of institutions to ensure wide participation in social decision-making.

Actualising social decisions

The first step required to establish a post-capitalist economy of this kind is to give the control over resources to those who work. In a *de jure* sense this is achieved by declaring that all resources belong to society collectively, and in a *de facto* sense it is operationalised by designing appropriate organisations of production and terms of contract for leasing resources from society by those who make use of them in production.

Here the discussion must become more specific taking into account the Indian situation. A *de jure* declaration to bring all land and other productive forces under social ownership is assumed as the first step and it is examined in some detail subsequently. Since the vast majority of the labour force is still confined to agriculture we shall start there. Those who are directly involved in cultivation are basically the agricultural labourers (h–4 units) and the smaller ones among the cultivators (h–2 units) together constituting close to 50 per cent of the labour force in the country as shown in Chapter 7. Land for the former must be made available for team cultivation with the team deciding on the allocation of work and the arrangements for settling claims, essentially on the 'to each according to his work' principle. The h–2 units that now cultivate land (either as owner cultivators or as tenant cultivators) should be allowed to continue as independent cultivators using family labour or be encouraged to form cooperatives. In the case of all these three categories (teams, household farms and cooperative farms) a local authority familiar with actual · field practices and including representatives from the producer groups should decide on the share of the produce to be handed over to society in return for society's land (and other resources such as farm equipment). In arriving at this share, the local authority must take into account a locally acceptable minimum quantity that the producers must be allowed to keep for their own needs. Producers must be encouraged and enabled to increase production and productivity over time. A decision should also be made as to whether the 'social rent' that the local authority collects will be used locally to meet the needs of non-agricultural producers in the locality itself, or be passsed on to a central pool.

As for cultivators now cultivating land with hired labour, the options should be to convert their farms into team cultivation in which the erstwhile owners become equal members of the team along with their former employees or to leave land and cultivation (especially if they have been absentee landowners) to take up work elsewhere. Large estates, particularly those that produce commercial crops should initially become state enterprises with the option given to the workers to convert them into cooperatives. The over-riding considerations in agriculture (as well as in other sectors of the economy) will have to be to bring about three different kinds of production organisations as indicated in Chapter 6, household production units using only family labour (self-employment), cooperative production units and state enterprises.

We shall use these changes in agriculture to see how they help in the actualisation of the four-fold social goals. The pattern suggested shows how the social responsibility to ensure the basic necessities of life is to be achieved. We shall, for the moment, take food as the representative of the basket of goods constituting basic necessities, recognising that the basket must have other goods also and that agricultural production is not confined to foodgrains. One of the commonest misconceptions about ensuring minimum needs is that it involves the state accepting responsibility for distributing (heavily subsidised and where required freely also) food to everyone. Such a procedure becomes necessary in a capitalist country because productive activity is substantially privately organised without social considerations becoming a direct responsibility of the producers. Social considerations, then, can be fulfilled only by the state accepting responsibility for redistribution of what is produced, as the normal distribution of the produce will also go by private consider-ations. In a post-capitalist economy, on the other hand, basic needs of all are met by society making use of its control over productive forces to direct production on the basis of social criteria, so that redistribution for social purposes after production takes place is not necessary. There is a related second aspect too. Ensuring basic requirements of everybody is not a responsibility relegated to a remote state; it becomes the respons-ibility of *all* members. What the state, as the representative of society, does is to provide everyone the opportunity to actualise a social goal. In other words, the responsibility to satisfy social goals goes with the responsibility to *work* towards it. Social goals will come to have meaning only to the extent that members of society internalise them as their own responsibility.

The same is also true about increasing productivity. To the extent that producers realise that increasing productivity is in their own interest, so that they can have more and that the drudgery of their work can be reduced, they are certain to put in the effort. Effort alone is not enough to increase productivity. Knowledge and expertise that they do not possess may have to be made available. Also since increase in producti-vity must get translated into availability of goods that they themselves do not produce, coordinated decisions relating to other sectors of the economy will have to be made. There is also the question of taking into account ecological factors in the production process. In the case of agriculture many of these have a direct bearing on the operations and may even be well known to those who are familiar with land, nature and farming. Once again, the main consideration is that those directly involved must internalise what may, from another perspective, appear to be external and remote.

Changes in the pattern of ownership and use of resources and in the organisation of production also lead to considerable reductions in inequalities; because glaring inequalities wherever they exist are almost invariably linked to the skewed distribution of resources other than those directly resulting from the exercise of one's own labour power, physical and mental. By socialising the ownership of non-human resources and by providing equal opportunities to use them in the exercise of labour power, a post-capitalist economy undermines the basis of unfair inequalities in income and wealth. Here again, the procedure is distinctly different from the attempts in capitalist societies where after permitting and encouraging inequalities based on the private ownership of property and the accrual of property income, some efforts are made through fiscal operations to reduce inequalities. It may be noted too that while a post-capitalist economy has built-in measures to keep inequalities under control, it does not aim, even in principle, to bring about perfect equality which is neither feasible nor even desirable from a social point of view.

Coordinating decisions

We shall now turn to other sectors of the economy without going into all the details, but concentrating on two main issues, viz., how to ensure that the basic requirements of all members are met and how different economic activities are to be coordinated to achieve this and other goals.

From the point of view of the basic necessities of life a section of the labour force that requires special attention is the group of artisans, craftspeople, and those engaged in 'traditional industries'. They are, in a way h–2 units, but because of their unavoidable links with the rest of the system (for securing their inputs and disposing their outputs) they come to be drawn into many forms of exploitative arrangements in the context of the acceleration of the capitalist expansion as seen in Chapter 9. Their basic problem is that their productivity is extremely low because they work with primitive technologies and low levels of productive forces. In the Indian context they constitute what may be considered the residual sector of the economy—they are where they are mainly because they have no other alternatives. A post-capitalist order must have a two-fold strategy to deal with them. As long as they have no other alternatives, they must be enabled to continue with what they are doing which may involve some transfer of resources to them (in the form of subsidised inputs for their production requirements, supply of basic necessities of life to them at subsidised rates etc.). But the long-term strategy must be to draw them out of the occupations to which they tenaciously hold and move them to more productive avenues.[17]

Since links with the rest of the system is one of their characteristics, we may turn now to the broader aspects of the place of exchange in a post-capitalist economy. Exchange as an activity, we have seen, is virtually unavoidable as long as every production unit does not become self-sufficient and autarchic. Whatever may be the virtue of such an arrangement, within the context of a national economy it is impossible to function without exchange. It is possible and necessary to take a more positive view of exchange as an activity and the market as an institution. They are among the major and most beneficial of social arrangements that humanity has, and it is a pity that attempts have been made to reject them in the name of some theories or ideologies—strangely enough in the quest for greater socialisation. A post-capitalist economy has no reason to jettison them; on the contrary, it must make effective use of them.

Under certain circumstances, of course, exchange and markets have become distorted, especially under certain forms of capitalism. As exchange and markets are propelled by resource power they get distorted, when by the exercise of resource power they can be turned to the private advantage of a few. To put it differently, the problem with the market is that it can be captured by 'the same power that propels it, and that, therefore, it becomes subservient to those with excessive resource power when resource power is unequally distributed. Because of this, the distortion of the market is built into capitalist economies as they lead to concentration of resource power through their normal operations.

Exchange as a social activity

A post-capitalist economy has an advantage here because keeping in-equalities of economic power under control is one of its objectives and it also has the possibility to achieve it.[18] Hence a post-capitalist economy can make use of exchange as a social activity and market as a social institution without fear of these getting distorted. Further, we have seen in Chapter 6 that exchange can be effectively socialised by keeping it properly linked to production, by making an objectively determined and fully publicised cost of production as the basis of the rate of exchange between commodities.

In an economy such as ours, dominated by small producers who are dependent on the market for the purchase of their inputs and the sale of their produce, market operations will have to be carefully supervised to ensure that control over markets does not lead to control over production and producers which is the perennial problem of small producers under capitalism, especially in the early phases of capitalism as was seen in Chapter 9. A post-capitalist reordering of the economy must guard against this danger by entrusting exchange and trade to socially informed and socially responsible agencies who will sustain the objective basis of exchange and use it as a channel of information about production. This does not mean that trade as an activity will be completely 'taken over'. Retail trade is a way of making a livelihood for a significant proportion of the labour force and there is no reason why that arrangement cannot continue. Appropriate mark-up over cost of production will make it possible for those who take up retail trade to make a living, their social obligation being fulfilled by legally requiring that the prices of all goods they sell must be prominently advertised. The new decision in a post-capitalist economy will have to be about wholesale trade which must be entrusted to an agency consisting of representatives of producers, retail traders, the Bureau of Costs and Prices etc. In a way, there is no novelty in the suggestion that wholesale trade should be brought under an agency that will coordinate it. That is how wholesale trade takes place even in most capitalist economies. The difference is that in a post-capitalist economy it will form part of a larger effort to bring all economic activities under social supervision.

Apart from trade, there will be other forms of transfers also mainly from the state to those who are unable to work and from the state or production units directly to those who have retired from work etc., details of all of which also have to be worked out. Similarly, arrangements for banking and provision of credit will have to be attended to. Macro planning of the kind indicated in Chapter 6 also must be carefully organised. In that respect the task in a post-capitalist economy is not likely to be more difficult than what we have become familiar with in the country during the past four decades.

If the economy comes to be shaped along post-capitalist lines, it will not have to close its borders to international trade or even foreign investments. But both these will have to be done on a selective basis, such that they will uphold social priorities and effectively assist the patterns of production, income distribution and consumption as internally determined.

Consumption in a post-capitalist set-up

A word may be added about consumption. If production comes to be organised according to social priorities, the pattern of consumption too will change. Similarly, reduction in inequalities of wealth and income will also get reflected on the patterns of consumption. There will be a tendency (at least initially) for consumption to get more standardised.

The waste that results from the proliferation of different brands of the same good certainly will be eliminated. Quantity restrictions may have to be imposed in some instances and queuing introduced in others. In selected spheres such as transportation, greater reliance may have to be placed on public agencies; housing may have to be brought considerably under social regulation; the import of consumer goods also will have to be carefully restricted. But none of these is totally absent in other kinds of economies, including capitalist economies. For instance, many people may not know that social conditions attached to the construction and upkeep of private residences in urban and suburban areas in an advanced capitalist economy like the United States are more stringent than the corresponding ones in practice in our country, and more strictly enforced by public authority.

A post-capitalist economy does not solve all problems of economic organisation and it is certainly not the kind of utopia that some 'scientific' socialists dream about, wherein economic problems themselves cease to exist. It is only a set-up which permits society to specify concretely what its economic problems are and how they are to be dealt with. Neither is it an economic system where most economic decisions are handed over to the bureaucracy. A post-capitalist economy, on the other hand, is a collection of heterogeneous economic units—subeconomies—with a multilevel structure of decision-making where the lowest level makes many of the crucial decisions and the higher level concentrates on decisions regarding overall social policies and of coordination of decisions and actions. It must be recognised too that the working of a post-capitalist economy will generate problems of its own. One of the basic ones of this kind is that because production will be increasing over time and economic inequalities exist, accumulated wealth will find expression in different forms which may change set patterns of production and the distribution of the produce. If this problem is not recognised and effectively dealt with from time to time, a post-capitalist economy can easily slide back into the capitalist order. Questions such as the extent to which inter-generational transfer of accumulated private wealth may be permitted; how private wealth can be prevented from exerting undue influence on production processes; and how the flow of information is to be steadily maintained on different aspects of economic operations will all be required to be carefully examined, and institutional procedures to tackle them will have to be evolved.

Will a post-capitalist transformation come about?

If such is the nature of a post-capitalist economy, it is certainly not beyond the realms of possibility, and a post-capitalist reorganisation of the Indian economy too is a feasible proposition. In fact, in view of the many participatory arrangements in the political sphere and the dominating position that the h–2 units and the state has in the economic sphere, Indian society can be thought of as a suitable candidate for a post-capitalist transformation.

But that does not mean that it will take place, in the immediate future at any rate. And the reason is not far to seek either. The basic premise of a post-capitalist transformation of the economy is the socialisation of resources, especially those that are in the existing set-up treated as private property. The excessive concentration of land and other forms of resources in the hands of a small segment of the population has resulted in a tremendous concentration of economic power which, in many ways, also seeps into the political realm. The short-term and long-term socio-economic objectives of the different classes that constitute this group may differ considerably, but they will unite to prevent any form of effective social control over resources. They will be given support by all who, in the emerging capitalist ethos, perceive their own opportunities for private acquisitions. Such support will come from different sections of the Indian economy and society, either because they too expect benefits from the existing order in the not too distant future, or because of their diffidence about major socio-economic changes. Many who are likely to benefit by a post-capitalist transformation—those from the h–2 and h–4 units—may also join hands to defend the existing order for the same reasons. Even in the political sphere the forces committed to a radical socio-economic transformation are rather weak.

In terms of the shaping of the economy, therefore, the chances are that the Indian economy will continue along the capitalist path that it has entered upon and has been pursuing with restraint at first, but boldly, almost defiantly in recent years. The economic conditions of a few will definitely improve which may also have some limited percolation effect. The 'national economy's' performance may appear to be improving too, although there will be severe strains of various sorts from time to time. But the vast majority of the people will have little to look forward to except the occasional crumbs that fall from the tables of 'the men of fortune'.

ECONOMY, POLITY AND SOCIETY

That would have been the bottom line but for the fact that the interactions between economy and polity are far too complex to be clearly enunciated. One of the most important lessons brought home by the collapse of socialist regimes in Eastern Europe in 1989 and 1990 is that in the final analysis the power of the people asserts itself and that there are ways of mobilising it even under the most difficult circumstances. The progress of the social sciences during the past century has yielded many clues about the nature of social processes, but the excessive specialisation of the different disciplines within the social sciences has also led each one of them to lose the capacity to perceive social processes in their totality. By relegating some aspects of society to the realm of the economy and some to the realm of the polity, for instance, and each one evolving its procedures of analysis independently of the other, the two disciplines, economics and politics, seem to have lost touch with the ground realities of social dynamics that result from constant interactions of what are attempted to be put into water-tight compartments.

Understanding social dynamics

In economics this tendency has become more prominent. Classical writers on the economy invariably had the analysis of some real life problem as their main task. Even when they differed considerably in their perceptions of the problem, as did Adam Smith and Karl Marx, on how to expound and interpret the emerging capitalist economic order, there was no doubt as to the central issue they were dealing with. Each one relied on his procedure of abstraction to carve out 'the economy' from the totality of social processes they were dealing with; but they never allowed that procedure to overlook the fact that as a social organisation the economy was constantly influenced by other forces in society, particularly those emanating from the realm of the polity and directed through the state.

This classical tradition of viewing the economy as part of an ongoing totality of social processes gradually disappears as economics as a separate area of study began to gather momentum.[19] One by one the social context of the economy was jettisoned in an attempt to establish the internal coherence of the economy—thus converting it into a 'physico-mathematical science'. The search became to establish that the economy had a unifying principle of its own, like gravity in Newtonian physics. In that process it was arbitrarily, but via the procedure of accepting assumptions to facilitate analysis, delinked from social classes, from the activities of merchants and of the state and from anything that stood in the way of 'clear' analysis. Naturally, the emphasis shifted from substance to form. A writer on the subject has said, 'modern economists, like modern artists and poets seem all too often to feel quite at home in a world where the form is reality, of which the substantial is only a shadow' (Meek, 1972: 96).

A major consequence of this change was that the internal interconnections of the economy in terms of its mechanical analogue came to occupy the central stage in the study of economics to the total exclusion of its interconnections with the rest of the society and of historical processes in general. Another critical writer has observed: 'Mechanics knows only locomotion and locomotion is both reversible and qualityless. The same drawback was built into modern economics by its founders.... And these architects succeeded so well with their grand plan that the conception of economic process as a mechanical analogue has ever since dominated economic thought completely. In this representation the economic process neither induces any qualitative change nor is affected by the qualitative change of the environment in which it is anchored. It is an isolated, self-contained and ahistorical process' (Georgescu-Roegen, 1971: 2). To bring out the untenability of such an approach to the economy has been one of the major objectives of the present study. The academic discipline of political science too may have fallen into similar traps as economics has got into.

What is to be done?

For an examination of the relationship between economy and polity—parts of the same social reality, but mentally carved out as two distinct spheres of activity—to come to know the possibilities of social change, therefore, we may have to go much more into their real-life manifestations in the specific Indian context. Social changes are brought about by people's active involvement in social processes.[20] We shall identify three major avenues of empowering people to gain clarity about social goals and to shape the economy to achieve those goals.

The first, obviously, is the electoral process. Elections based on adult franchise and the institutions of parliamentary democracy cannot find solutions to all social problems, especially economic problems. But their potential for shaping and mobilising public opinion should not be underestimated. Also, in one sense, political parties play a tremendous role in articulating economic issues and designing specific measures to deal with them. Election manifestos, in particular, make many promises about economic matters. People at large should be encouraged to take political parties and their programmes seriously not only at the time of elections, but on a day-to-day basis. Since all political parties owe allegiance to the Constitution, they should be pressurised to take the provisions about the economy and the guarantees given to the citizens, especially in the section on Directive Principles of State Policy, seriously and to commit themselves to implementing them. Not that these will be done immediately or wholeheartedly. But as a prelude to bringing state power effectively under popular control, it is necessary to establish people's power over political parties. Parties should also be pressurised to implement existing legislative measures such as those relating to minimum wages and land reform. Once political parties are made to be responsive to popular will, it will be easier to get each one of them to accept certain basic economic measures as part of their platform. The end of single party domination in the country is an indication of the common people becoming more sensitive to the political processes and more discriminating in the expression of their support to parties. It has brought an element of instability to the polity, but there can be no doubt that it has also led parties to be more responsive to the public at large. This situation should be fully made use of in order to get parties to pay greater attention to the genuine needs of the people instead of moving away from them by concentrating on issues of short-term emotional appeal. Differences of opinion will continue and may even become more pronounced as to what are or ought to be the genuine needs of the people, and as to which sections of the population are to be given special consideration, but open discussions about them involving larger partici-pation can help to clarify issues and consolidate the social processes.

As was noted earlier, the shaping of the economy is not a limited economic agenda to be dealt with and decided by experts alone, although in this, as in other matters of social policy, expertise has its role to play. But a fundamental restructuring of the economy is essentially a political and social task. A major instrument in that process will be the state. Hence attempts to bring the political processes and the state under the true sovereignty of the people at large is a pre-condition to the transfor-mation of the economy.

Secondly, within the existing political and administrative set-up an effort must be made to make the exercise of state power substantially decentralised. This is necessary to make the administration respond to the day-to-day problems of the people. Also at lower levels, like the districts and the panchayats, the artificial distinction between economic and political matters will largely disappear. There society presents itself as it is, and will also have to be dealt with as it is. Decentralised decision-making and implementation of policies are extremely important to perceive social realities in their totality. Above all, effective decentrali-sation of administration is a vital step in actualising the sovereignty of the people as has been amply demonstrated in states like West Bengal and Karnataka where it has been tried out.[21]

Thirdly, people should be encouraged to participate in well-defined and properly organised popular movements. These could be where they formulate and put forward their own problems and fight for their own rights. They could also be issues relating to the rights of others with full awareness that involvement in them will not advance one's own claims, but may, in fact, lead to curtailment of one's rights and privileges. They could also be matters of common concern for society as a whole such as the protection of the environment. These are ways in which individuals can internalise social values, discover themselves as participants in the social purposes and come to have commitments to fellow human beings and common causes.

Through such efforts a sense of community should be evolved with members becoming aware of their rights and consciously defining their material needs. They must also develop a wholesome respect for nature and be informed by a sense of justice to their neighbours of the present and future generations. A post-capitalist economic order will be a concrete manifestation of such a community. It is a distinct possibility for Indian society and for all humanity. But it can become a reality only if there is a determined effort to establish it.

NOTES

1. Fred Hirsch lists the following external conditions for the system to function: informal social controls in the form of socialised norms of behaviour, including what will be brought and sold in the market, and what will not be; controls needed to make the market process efficient in its own terms such as central control over money supply; fiscal and administrative regulation of many kinds; and distributional correctives. See Hirsch, 1977: 120–21. See also Sen, 1984, Chapter 3, and Hahn, 1981.

2. See Kurien, 1989b and case studies in Kanesalingam, 1989.

3. 'Apt though we are to lose sight of the fact, the primary objective of economic activity is the self-preservation of the human species.... The almost fabulous comfort, let alone the extravagant luxury, attained by many past and present societies has caused us to forget, however, the most elementary fact of life, namely, that of all necessaries for life only the purely biological ones are absolutely indispensable for survival. The poor have had no reason to forget it'. Georgescu-Roegen, 1967: 93.

4. In fact, according to Adam Smith, classes were 'the three great, original, and constituent orders of every civilised society'.

5. In the logical analysis of the capitalist mode of production Marx works with just two classes, but in *Theories of Surplus Value* (Marx, 1975) which was meant to be Volume IV of *Capital*, Marx makes it explicit that real societies by no means consist of only the class of workers and the class of industrial capitalists (Ch. 17, sec. 6). Marx also points out that Ricardo forgets to emphasise 'the continual increase in the number of the middle classes....situated midway between the workers on the one side and capitalists and landowners on the other.' (Ch. 18, B1 d). And in his classic work *The Eighteenth Brumaire of Louis Bonaparte* (Marx, 1967) he shows how different classes in a given specific situation interact with one another.

6. See Kurien, 1970.

7. Hence inflation will be to the advantage of the class whose income is derived primarily from profits while the class of people who rely on wage income will find it oppressive. Mitra, shows that even within a sector of the economy such as agriculture, price variations have very different impacts on different groups such as big landowners, small peasants and agricultural labourers. (Mitra, 1977)

8. On the role of the state in the economy see Poulantzas, 1978; Urry, 1981; Jessop, 1982; Wells, 1973.
9. See Kurien, 1987b.
10. Arrow, 1951; Olson, 1965; and Mueller, 1979.
11. A reference has already been made in Chapter 11 about the Indian poverty line. While there is now a generally recognised poverty line, it has had a controversial history which is dealt with in Rudra, 1974. After noting that for India what is considered as a minimum level of living would have to be an absolute minimum such that anything less is incompatible with the maintenance of physical well being, Rudra indicates the steps required to arrive at such a figure. In the first place, experts on nutrition would have to work out normative diets for different sections of the population taking into account age, sex, size of body and working conditions. The dietary norms (let us say in calories per day) will have to be converted into appropriate baskets of food items where wide variety is possible. Then the basket of goods must be converted into value categories taking into account prices. Differences of opinion among experts can come up in each one of these stages and hence Rudra refers to the figure of Rs 20 per capita per month at 1960–61 prices accepted for drawing the poverty line as a 'magic number'.
12. For a brief account of the growth of welfare states in Europe and their present position see IDPAD, 1983.
13. After the Second World War was over and the Japanese surrendered to the Allied forces, General MacArthur brought about a major land reform partly to crush the political power of the rural landlords and partly to increase agricultural production by encouraging cultivation by owner cultivators. In 1952 a 3 hectare limit was set on farm sizes and all land thus acquired was sold within two years to the occupying tenant farmers. In South Korea, too, land reforms were brought about when it was under US military occupation. In 1945 the US Military Government limited rents to a maximum of one-third of crop production and prohibited unilateral cancellation of tenancy contracts. Many landowners, anticipating further land reforms sold their farmland to their tenants which brought about an increase in owner cultivators. In 1950 a ceiling of 3 hectares was imposed on farm ownership and the surplus land obtained was distributed to about one million farming families. For an account of these reforms see King, 1977, Chapters 8 & 10 and Inayatulla ed., 1980, Chapter 9.
14. See Indian Investment Centre, 1983.
15. There is a vast and controversial body of literature on Transnational Corporations. A critical review of the literature along with an extensive bibliography can be seen in Jenkins, 1987. On the nature of foreign collaborations in India, see Reserve Bank of India, 1985.
16. Jenkins, 1987: 8.
17. For a discussion of this issue see Kurien, 1989a.
18. In one of the early discussions on the economics of socialism, the Polish economist, Oskar Lange claimed that markets can work as they are supposed to only under socialism, as socialism removes economic disparities and permits markets to reflect the preferences of participants. See Lange, 1964.
19. For a brief exposition of this theme see Kurien·1981b. See also Oommen ed. 1987. More detailed treatments are available in Georgescu-Roegen, 1967, Part I. The three volumes by Levine have a comprehensive critique of economics from this perspective. See Levine, 1977, especially Vol. I.
20. This does not mean that any desired social change can be readily brought about. The problem was described by Marx thus: 'Men make their own history, but they do not make it just as they please; they do not make it under circumstances chosen by themselves, but under circumstances directly encountered, given and transmitted

from the past.' (Marx, 1967: 10). There is also the problem that there will be disagreements on what is desirable. Those who work for social change immediately discover that those who benefit from a prevailing situation will defend it and oppose attempts at change. The discussion in the last chapter on the attempts to bring about cooperative farming is one of the clearest example from our own recent history.

21. For a discussion of the decentralisation experience in West Bengal see Kohli, 1987, Chapter 3 and in Karnataka, Krishnaswamy, 1991.

Bibliography

The bibliography lists only books, journal articles and other publications referred to in the text. Where further references may be useful, attention has been drawn in the Notes to the Chapters to bibliographies in the sources cited. Official publications such as the Census Reports, the Five Year Plan documents, National Income Statistics, National Sample Survey Reports etc. referred to in the text and in the notes have not been included in the bibliography.

The year used to identify the source is the year of publication of the volume (or article) actually referred to. But in the case of some of the classical writings the year of the original publication is given in brackets. Thus Smith, Adam, 1966 (1776) indicates that the edition referred to is the 1966 one, although the book was published in 1776. In the text references given are to the author, year of publication of the book and page number as, Godelier, 1986: 13.

Those who are not trained in economics and related subjects will not find it easy to follow the writings of professionals who use special terminologies of their own. Most of the items listed in the bibliography are of that kind. Sources using simple language have been identified by an asterisk (*) mark.

Adiseshiah, Malcolm S. (ed.) 1987. *Economics of Environment* (New Delhi, Lancer International)

Ahluwalia, Montek S. 1978. 'Rural Poverty in India, 1956–57 to 1973–74' in *India: Occasional Papers* (World Bank Staff Working Paper No. 279)

——————. 1986. 'Rural Poverty, Agricultural Production and Prices' in Mellor, John W., and Desai, Gunwant M., eds., *Agricultural Change and Rural Poverty* (Delhi, Oxford University Press)

*Ambirajan, S. 1978. *Classical Political Economy and British Policy in India* (New Delhi, Vikas Publishing House)

*Anderson, Perry. 1978. *Passages from Antiquity to Feudalism* (London, Verso)

Arrow, Kenneth J. 1951. *Social Choice and Individual Values* (New Haven, Yale University Press)

Arrow, Kenneth J. and Hahn, F.H. 1971. *General Competitive Analysis* (Amsterdam, North-Holland Publishing Company)

Ashton, Basil. *et al.*, 1984. 'Famines in China, 1958–1961', *Population and Development Review*, December

*Athreya, V.B. 1984. *Vadamalaipuram-Resurvey* (Madras, Madras Institute of Development Studies, Working Paper No. 50)

——————. *et al.*, 1990. *Barriers Broken-Production Relation and Agrarian Changes in Tamilnadu* (New Delhi, Sage Publications)

*Baden-Powell, B.H. 1977. *Indian Village Community* (Delhi, Cosmos Publications)

Bagchi, A.K. 1972. *Private Investment in India, 1900–1939* (Cambridge, Cambridge University Press)

Bahro, Rudolph. 1978. *The Alternative in Eastern Europe* (Oxford, NLB)

Baker, Christopher John. 1984. *An Indian Rural Economy, 1880–1955* (Cambridge, Cambridge University Press)

Balakrishnan, P. 1984. 'On the Significance of Inter-linked Factor Markets in Agrarian Economies', *The Indian Economic Journal*, 4

Bandyopadhyay, D. 1986. 'Land Reforms in India: An Analysis', *Economic and Political Weekly*, Review of Agriculture, June 21–28

*Banerjee, Nirmala. 1988. 'Small and Large Units: Symbiosis or Matsyaanyaya?' in Suri, K.B., (ed.) *Small Scale Enterprises in Industrial Development* (New Delhi, Sage Publications)

*Baran, Paul A. and Sweezy, Paul M. 1966. *Monopoly Capital* (New York, Modern Reader Paperbacks)

Basant, Rakesh and Kumar, B.L. 1988. *Rural Non-agricultural Activities in India: A Review of Available Evidence* (Ahmedabad, The Gujarat Institute of Area Planning, Working Paper No. 20)

Bhaduri, A. 1973. 'A Study in Agricultural Backwardness Under Semi-Feudalism', *Economic Journal*, March

Bhalla, G.S. and Chadha, G.K. 1982. 'Green Revolution and Small Peasant: A Study of Income Distribution in Punjab', *Economic and Political Weekly*, May 15 & 22

Bhalla, G.S. et al., 1990. *Agricultural Growth and Structural Changes in the Punjab Economy* (Washington D.C., International Food Policy Research Institute, Research Report 82)

Bhat, Mari and Irudaya Rajan S. 1990. 'Demographic Transition in Kerala Revisited', *Economic and Political Weekly*, Sep 1–8

*Bhattacharya, Nikhilesh. et al, 1991. 'How do the Poor Survive?' *Economic and Political Weekly*, Feb. 16

*Bloch, Marc. 1965. *Feudal Society* (London, Routledge & Kegan Paul) Vol.I & Vol.II

*Braverman, Harry. 1974. *Labour and Monopoly Capital* (New York, Monthly Review Press)

Breman, Jan. 1976. 'A Dualistic Labour Supply? A Critique of the Informal Sector Concept', *Economic and Political Weekly*, 48–50.

Bromley, Ray and Gerry, Chris. ed., 1979. *Casual Work and Poverty in Third World Cities* (Chichester, John Wiley and Sons)

*Buchanan, D.H. 1966 (1934). *The Development of Capitalist Enterprise in India* (London, Frank Cass & Co.,)

Cambridge Economic History of India (CEHI) 1984. Vol. I., ed. by Tapan Raychaudhuri & Irfan Habib, Vol. II., ed. by Dharma Kumar (Delhi, Orient Longman in association with Cambridge University Press)

*Carr, E.H. 1964. *What is History?* (Harmondsworth, Penguin Books)

Centre for Science and Environment, 1982. *The State of India's Environment*, First Citizens' Report (New Delhi)

Chaudhuri, Assim. 1975. *Private Economic Power in India* (Delhi, People's Publishing House)

Chayanov, A.V. 1966. (1925) *The Theory of the Peasant Economy*. Edited by Daniel Thorner et al.(Homewood, Richard D. Irwin)

Chenery, Hollis. et al., 1974. *Redistribution with Growth* (London, Oxford University Press)

*Critchley, John. 1978. *Feudalism* (London, George Allen & Unwin)

Dandekar, V.M. and Rath, N. 1971. *Poverty in India* (Poona, Indian School of Political Economy)

Das Gupta, K.K. 1989. *Marxism and the Political Economy of Socialism* (New Delhi, Sterling Publishers) .

Davey, Brian. 1975. *The Economic Development of India—A Marxist Analysis* (Nottingham, Spokesman Books)

*Dobb, Maurice. 1963 (1947). *Studies in the Development of Capitalism* (London, Routledge & Kegan Paul)

—————. 1966. *Soviet Economic Development since 1917* (London, Routledge & Kegan Paul, Sixth Revised Edition)

Dorfman, Robert. 1964. *The Price System* (Englewood Cliffs, Prentice-Hall)

Dorfman, Robert. et al., 1958. *Linear Programming and Economic Analysis* (New York, McGraw-Hill)

*Dutt, Palme R. 1947. *India Today* (Calcutta, Manisha)

*Dutt, Romesh. 1960 (1901). *The Economic History of India* Vol. I, *Under Early British Rule, 1757–1837* (Government of India, Publications Division)

Elson, Diane. 1988. 'Market Socialism or Socialization of the Market?' *New Left Review*, Nov-Dec.

Frankel, Francine. 1971. *India's Green Revolution* (Princeton, Princeton University Press)

*—————. 1978. *India's Political Economy, 1947–77* (Princeton, Princeton University Press)

*Gadgil, D.R. 1971 (1924). *The Industrial Evolution of India in Recent Times, 1860–1939*, (Delhi, Oxford University Press, Fifth Edition)

Galbraith, John Kenneth. 1967. *The New Industrial State* (New York, Signet Books)

*—————. 1979 (1958). *The Affluent Society* (Harmondsworth, Penguin Books)

*Ganguli, B.N. 1977. *Indian Economic Thought—Nineteenth Century Perspectives* (New Delhi, Tata McGraw-Hill)

Georgescu-Roegen, N. 1967. *Analytical Economics: Issues and Patterns* (Cambridge, Harvard University Press)

—————. 1971. *The Entropy Law and the Economic Process* (Cambridge, Harvard University Press)

Godelier, Maurice. 1986. *The Mental and the Material—Thought Economy and Society* (Norfolk, Verso)

Goyal S.K. et al., 1984. *Small Scale Sector and Big Business* (New Delhi, The Indian Institute of Public Administration, The Corporate Study Groups: Studies in National Development No. 2)

*Guhan, S. and Mencher, Joan P. 1982. *Iruvelpattu Revisited* (Madras, Madras Institute of Development Studies, Working Paper No. 28)

*Guhan, S. and Bharathan K. 1984. *Dusi: A Resurvey* (Madras, Madras Institute of Development Studies, Working Paper No. 52)

Hahn, Frank. 1981. 'General Equilibrium Theory' in Bell, Daniel and Kristol, Irving ed., *The Crisis in Economic Theory* (New York, Basic Books)

Hanumantha Rao, C.H. 1975. *Technological Change and Distribution Gains in Indian Agriculture* (New Delhi, Macmillan)

Hasbulatov, Ruslan. 1989. *Perestroika as seen by an Economist* (Moscow, Nov osti Press Agency Publishing House)

Hayami, Yujiro and Kikuchi, Masao. 1981. *Asian Village Economy at Cross Roads* (Tokyo, University of Tokyo Press)

Heilborner, Robert L. 1962. *The Making of Economic Society* (Englewood Cliffs, Prentice-Hall)

—————. 1980 (1953). *The Worldly Philosophers* (New York, Simon and Schuster, Fifth Revised Edition)

—————. 1985. *Nature and Logic of Capitalism* (New York, W.W. Norton & Co.)

—————. 1988. *Behind the Veil of Economics* (New York W.W. Norton & Co.)

Hicks, J.R. 1942. *Social Framework: An Introduction to Economics* (Oxford, Clarendon Press)

Hicks, John. 1969. *A Theory of Economic History* (Oxford, Oxford University Press)

Hicks, J.R. et al., 1984. *Framework of the Indian Economy: An Introduction to Economics* (Delhi, Oxford University Press)

Higgins, Benjamin. 1959. *Economic Development-Principles, Problems and Policies* (New York, W.W. Norton & Co.)

*Hill, Christopher. 1969. *Economic History of Britain: Reformation to Industrial Revolution* (Harmondsworth, Penguin Books)

Hirsch, Fred. 1977. *Social Limits to Growth* (London, Routledge & Kegan Paul)

Holland, Stuart. 1987. *The Market Economy-From Micro to Mesoeconomics* (London, Weidenfeld and Nicolson)

Holton, R.J. 1985. *The Transition from Feudalism to Capitalism* (London, Macmillan)

Howe, Irving. ed., 1986. *Essential Works of Socialism* (New Haven, Yale University Press, Third Edition)

*Huberman, Leo and Sweezy, Paul M. 1968. *Introduction to Socialism* (New York, Monthly Review Press)

Husain, Zakir. 1967. *Capitalism—Essays in Understanding* (Bombay, Asia Publishing House)

Inayatulla. ed., 1980. *Land Reform: Some Asian Experiences*, Vol. IV (Kuala Lumpur, Asian and Pacific Development Administration Centre)

Indian Investment Centre, 1983. *Indian Joint Ventures Abroad—An Appraisal*, (New Delhi)

Indo-Dutch Programme on Alternatives in Development (IDPAD), 1983. *The Welfare State in Europe* (Proceedings of the IDPAD Seminar, The Hague)

International Labour Office (ILO) 1970. *Towards Full Employment: A Programme for Columbia* (Geneva)

———— (ILO) 1971. *Matching Employment Opportunity and Expectations: A Programme of Action for Ceylon* (Geneva)

———— (ILO) 1976. *World Employment Programme: Research in Retrospect and Prospect* (Geneva)

Jaganathan, Vijay N. 1987. *Informal Markets in Developing Countries* (New York, Oxford University Press)

*Jale'e Pierre. 1977. *How Capitalism Works* (New York, Monthly Review Press)

Janakarajan, S. 1986. *Aspects of Market Inter-Relations in a Changing Agrarian Economy* (Unpublished Ph.D Thesis, Madras Institute of Development Studies and University of Madras)

Jansen, Eirik, G. 1986. *Rural Bangladesh: Competition for Scarce Resources* (Oxford, Oxford University Press)

Jenkins, Rhys. 1987. *Transnational Corporations and Uneven Development* (London, Methuen)

Jessop, Bob. 1982. *The Capitalist State* (Oxford, Martin Robertson)

Jha, L.K. 1980. *Economic Strategy for the 80s* (New Delhi, Allied Publishers)

Jodha, N.S. 1990. 'Rural Common Property Resources—Contribution and Crisis', *Economic and Political Weekly*, June 30

Joshi, H. and Joshi V. 1976. *Surplus Labour and the City: A Study of Bombay* (Delhi, Oxford University Press)

*Kalpagam, U. 1985. 'Coping with Urban Poverty in India', *Bulletin of Concerned Asian Scholars*, 1

Kalpagam, U. et al., 1981. *Female Labour in Small Industry—The Case of Export Garments* (Madras, Madras Institute of Development Studies, Working Paper No. 18). Also *Economic and Political Weekly*, Nov. 28

Kanesalingam. V. 1989. *Appropriate Technology for Rural Development—The Case of South Asia* (New Delhi, Tata McGraw-Hill)

Keynes, J.M. 1936. *The General Theory of Employment, Interest and Money* (New York, Harcourt, Brace and Co.)

King, Russel. 1977. *Land Reform—A World Survey* (London, G. Bell & Sons)

*****Kohli Atul.** 1987. *The State and Poverty in India—The Politics of Reform* (Cambridge, Cambridge University Press)

Koopmans, Tjalling C. 1957. *Three Essays on the State of Economic Science* (New York, McGraw-Hill)

Kornai, Janos. 1980. *Economics of Shortage* Vol. I & Vol. II, (Amsterdam, North-Holland Publishing Company)

Krishnaswamy, K.S. 1991. 'Decentralisation and Planning', in Kurien C.T. *et al.*, ed. *Economy, Society and Development* (New Delhi, Sage Publications)

Krishnamurty, J. 1984. 'Changes in the Indian Workforce', *Economic and Political Weekly*, Dec 15

Kumar, Dharma. 1965. *Land and Caste in South India* (Cambridge, Cambridge University Press)

Kurien C.T. 1970. *A Theoretical Approach to the Indian Economy* (Bombay, Asia Publishing House)

*—————. 1978. *Poverty, Planning and Social Transformation* (New Delhi, Allied Publishers)

—————. 1981a. *Dynamics of Rural Transformation: A Study of Tamil Nadu, 1950–1975* (Madras, Orient Longman)

—————. 1981b. 'Social Problems and Social Sciences' in Institute of Economic Growth, *Relevance in Social Science Research* (New Delhi, Vikas Publishing House)

*—————. 1986. 'Reconciling Growth and Social Justice: Strategies Versus Structure' in Dantwala M.L., *et al.*, eds., *Asian Seminar on Rural Development—The Indian Experience* (New Delhi, Oxford & IBH Publishing Co.)

—————. 1987a. '1987–88 Budget and the New Fiscal Strategy', *Economic and Political Weekly*, April 11

—————. 1987b. 'State and Market in Economic Processes—Some Basic Issues', *Economic and Political Weekly*, Annual Number

*—————. 1989a. *The Future of Village Industries*. Prof. N.G. Ranga Endowment Lecture, Andhra University

—————. 1989b. 'Overview' in Kanesalingam V., ed., *Appropriate Technology for Rural Industries* (New Delhi, Tata McGraw-Hill)

—————. 1992. *Growth and Justice—Aspects of India's Development Experience* (Madras, Oxford University Press)

Kurien C.T. and James Josef. 1979. *Economic Change in Tamil Nadu* (Delhi, Allied Publishers)

Kurien G.T. *et al.*, (eds.) 1991. *Economy, Society and Development* (New Delhi, Sage Publications)

*****Kurien, John.** 1978. *Towards an Understanding of the Fish Economy of Kerala* (Trivandrum, Centre for Development Studies, Working Paper No. 68)

Kuznets, Simon. 1966. *Modern Economic Growth: Rate, Structure and Spread* (New Haven, Yale University Press)

Lange, Oskar. 1964 (1938). 'On the Economic Theory of Socialism' in Lippincott, Benjamin E. ed., *On the Economic Theory of Socialism* (New York, McGraw-Hill)

Lenin, V.I. 1964 (1908). *The Development of Capitalism in Russia* (Moscow Progress Publishers)

Levine, David P. 1977. *Economic Studies: Contribution to the Critique of Economic Theory* (London, Routledge & Kegan Paul)

Levkovsky, Alexei. 1987. *The Developing Countries' Social Structure* (Moscow, Progress Publishers)

Lewis, Arthur W. 1954. 'Economic Development with Unlimited Supplies of Labour', *The Manchester School of Economic and Social Studies*, May

Luxemburgh Rosa. 1968. *The Accumulation of Capital* (New York, Monthly Review Press)

Macpherson, C.B. 1977. *The Life and Times of Liberal Democracy* (Oxford, Oxford University Press)

Madras Institute of Development Studies, 1980. *Structure and Intervention: An Evaluation of DPAD, IRDP and Related Programmes* (Madras)

Marshall, Alfred. 1961 (1890). *Principles of Economics* (London, Macmillan)

Marx, Karl. 1952. *Wage Labour and Capital* (Moscow, Progress Publishers)

————. 1967 (1869). *The Eighteenth Brumaire of Louis Bonaparte* (Moscow, Progress Publishers)

————. 1971. *Capital* I (1867), II (1885) III (1894) (Moscow, Progress Publishers)

————. 1972. *Pre-Capitalist Economic Formations*. Edited with introduction by E.J. Hobsbaum (New York, International Publishers)

————. 1973. *Grundrisse* (Harmondsworth, Penguin Books)

————. 1975. *Theories of Surplus Value* (Moscow, Progress Publishers)

————. 1976. *Capital*, Vol. I, Introduced by Ernest Mandel (Harmondsworth, Penguin Books)

Marx, Karl and Engels, Frederick. 1971 (1848). *The Manifesto of the Communist Party* (Moscow, Progress Publishers)

————. 1976. *The German Ideology* (Moscow, Progress Publishers)

Meek, Ronald. 1972. 'The Marginal Revolution and its Aftermath' in Hunt, E.K. and Schwarts, Jesse G., ed., *A Critique of Economic Theory* (Harmondsworth, Penguin Books)

Minhas, B.S. 1974. *Planning and the Poor* (New Delhi, S. Chand)

Mitra, Ashok. 1977. *Terms of Trade and Class Relations: An Essay on Political Economy* (London, Frank Cass)

Mueller, Dennis C. 1979. *Public Choice* (Cambridge, Cambridge University Press)

Musgrave, Richard A. and Musgrave, Peggy B. 1973. *Public Finance in Theory and Practice* (Tokyo, McGraw-Hill Kogakusha)

Nadkarni, M.V. 1991. 'Economics and Ecological Concern' in Kurien C.T., *et al.*, ed., *Economy, Society and Development* (New Delhi, Sage Publications)

Nagaraj, K. 1981. *Structure of Inter-Relations of the Land, Labour, Credit and Product Markets of South Kanara* (Unpublished Ph.D. Thesis, Indian Statistical Institute)

*Naidu, Chandrasekara V.** 1987. *The Impact of Agricultural Growth on Poverty—A Review of Literature* (Madras, Madras Institute of Development Studies, Digest Series, No. 5)

Neale, Walter C. 1962. *Economic Change in Rural India in Uttar Pradesh, 1800–1955* (New Haven, Yale University Press)

Nove, Alec. 1969. *An Economic History of the USSR* (London, The Penguin Press)

Olson, Mancur. 1965. *The Logic of Collective Actions—Public Goods and the Theory of Groups* (Cambridge, Harvard University Press)

Oommen, M.A. (ed.) 1987. *Issues in Teaching of Economics in Indian Universities* (New Delhi, Oxford & IBH Publishing Co.)

Pandian, M.S.S. 1990. *The Political Economy of Agrarian Change* (New Delhi, Sage Publications)

*Parthasarathy, G.** 1988. 'Land Reform and the Changing Agrarian Structure' in Uma Kapila ed., *Indian Economy since Independence* (Delhi, Synapse)

————. 1991. 'Rural Development—Growing Relevance of Macro Issues' in Kurien C.T., *et al.*, *Economy, Society and Development* (New Delhi, Sage Publications)

Patel, B.B. ed., 1989. *Problems of Homebased Workers in India* (New Delhi, Oxford and IBH Publishing Co.)

*Pavlov, V.I. 1979. *Historical Premises for India's Transition to Capitalism* (Moscow, Nauka Publishing House)

*Polanyi, Karl. 1957. *The Great Transformation* (New York, Reinhott and Co.)

*Postan, M.M. 1972. *The Medieval Economy and Society* (Harmondsworth, Penguin Books)

Poulantzas, Nicos. 1978. *Political Power and Social Classes* (London, Verso)

Prasad, Eswara K.V. and Prasad Anuradha. 1985. *Bidi Workers of Central India—A Study of Production Processes and Working Conditions* (New Delhi, National Labour Institute)

Ramachandran, V.K. 1990. *Wage Labour and Unfreedom in Agriculture—An Indian Case Study* (Oxford, Clarendon Press)

Rao, V.K.R.V. 1983. *India's National Income, 1950–1980* (New Delhi, Sage Publications)

Rath, N. 1985. 'Garibi Hatao: Can IRDP do it?' *Economic and Political Weekly*, Feb 9

Reddy, Rammohan. 1985. *Rural Labour Movement in Varnad* (Geneva, International Labour Office, World Employment Programme Research, Working Paper)

Reddy, William M. 1984. *The Rise of Market Culture* (Cambridge, Cambridge University Press)

Renner, Karl. 1949. *The Institutions of Private Law and their Social Functions* (London, Routledge & Kegan Paul)

Riskin, Carl. 1987. *China's Political Economy* (Oxford, Oxford University Press)

Rosen, George. 1975. *Peasant Society in a Changing Economy* (Urbana, University of Illinois Press)

Rudra, Ashok. 1974. 'Minimum Level of Living—A Statistical Examination' in Srinivasan T.N., and Bardhan P.K., eds., *Poverty and Income Distribution in India* (Calcutta, Statistical Publishing Society)

—————. 1982. *Indian Agricultural Economics—Myths and Realities* (New Delhi, Allied Publications)

Sahlins, Marshall. 1974. *Stone Age Economics* (London, Tavistock Publications)

Samuelson, Paul A. 1954. 'The Pure Theory of Public Expenditure', *The Review of Economics and Statistics*, Nov.

—————. 1955. 'Diagrammatic Exposition of a Theory of Public Expenditure', *The Review of Economics and Statistics*, Nov.

Schumpeter, Joseph A. 1954. *History of Economic Analysis* (New York, Oxford University Press)

*—————. 1974 (1943). *Capitalism, Socialism and Democracy* (London, Unwin University Press)

Scot, James C. 1976. *The Moral Economy of the Peasant* (New Haven, Yale University Press)

Seddon, David. ed., 1978. *Relations of Production: Marxist Approach to Economic Anthropology* (London, Frank Cass & Co.)

Sen, Amartya K. 1984. *Resources, Values and Development* (Delhi, Oxford University Press)

*Shelvankar, K.S. 1940. *The Problem of India* (Harmondsworth, Penguin Books)

Singh, Manjit. 1990. *The Political Economy of Unorganised Industry* (New Delhi, Sage Publications)

Singh, Narinder. 1978. *Economics and the Crisis of Ecology* (Delhi, Oxford University Press, Second Edition)

*Slater, Gilbert. ed., 1918. *Some South Indian Villages* (London, Oxford University Press)

Smith, Adam. 1966 (1776). *The Wealth of Nations*. Two Volumes divided into V Books (London, Everyman's Library)

Srinivasan, T.N. and Bardhan, P.K. (ed.) 1974. *Poverty and Income Distribution* (Calcutta, Statistical Publishing Company)

Stinchcombe, Arthur L. 1983. *Economic Sociology* (Orlando, Academic Press)

Sundrum, R.M. 1987. *Growth and Income Distribution in India* (New Delhi, Sage Publications)

Swaminathan, Padmini. 1983. *Concentration in Productive Capacity* (Madras, Madras Institute of Development Studies, Working Paper No. 45)

Sweezy, Paul. *et al.*, 1978. *The Transition from Feudalism to Capitalism* (London, Verso)

Tawney, R.H. 1972 (1922). *Religion and the Rise of Capitalism* (Harmondsworth, Penguin Books)

*――――. 1982 (1921). *The Acquisitive Society* (Norfolk, The Thetford Press)

*Tendulkar, S.D. 1988. 'Economic Inequalities and Poverty in India: An Interpretative Overview' in Uma Kapila ed., *Indian Economy since Independence* (Delhi, Synapse)

Thorner, Daniel and Alice. 1962. *Land and Labour in India* (Bombay, Asia Publishing House)

United Nations, 1975. *Poverty, Unemployment and Development Policy* (New York, United Nations Publications)

Urry, John. 1981. *Anatomy of Capitalist Societies—The Economy, Civil Society and the State* (London, The Macmillan Press)

Vaidyanathan, A. 1986. 'Labour Use in Rural India—A Study of Spatial and Temporal Variations', *Economic and Political Weekly*, Dec. 27

Vajda, Mihaly. 1981. *The State and Socialism* (London, Allison & Busby)

Vanek, Jaroslav. 1971. *Participatory Economy* (Ithaca, Cornell University Press)

Wallerstein, Immanuel. 1983. *Historical Capitalism* (London, Verso)

Walras, Leon. 1954 (1874). *Elements of Pure Economics* (Tr. by William Jaffe, Homewood, Richard D. Irwin)

Washbrook, D.A. 1976. *The Emergence of Provincial Politics: The Madras Presidency, 1870–1920* (Cambridge, Cambridge University Press)

Weber, Max. 1976 (1930). *The Protestant Ethic and the Spirit of Capitalism* (London, George Allen & Unwin)

――――. 1978. *Economy and Society, Vol.I & Vol. II* (Berkeley, University of California Press)

Wells, David. 1987. *Marxism and the Modern State* (New Delhi, Selectbook Service Syndicate)

World Bank, The, 1987. *World Development Report 1987* (New York, Oxford University Press)

――――. 1990. *World Development Report 1990* (New York, Oxford University Press)

Youngson, A.J. ed., 1972. *Economic Development in the Long Run* (London, George Allen & Unwin)

Index

abject poverty, 352
absolute prices, 90
abstraction, 17, 22–24
abundance, 35–36
accumulation of exchange value, 26, 27
acquisitive society, 154–56
activity, 29, 30
activity chains, 215, 226–29; transformation in, 287–304
adimai, 254
Adiseshiah, M., 110n
adult franchise, 152, 153
advanced countries, 359
advertisements(ing), 87, 89, 142
affluence, 35, 351, 353
aggregation, 37, 323, 324
Agra, 255
agricultural labourers, 237–38, 241, 254, 282, 328, 405
agriculture, 48, 284, 285, 324, 330, 341–43, 406; commercialisation of, 265–67, 306, 307; prices, 183; production, 174; shift from, 282; transformation in, 304–9
Ahluwalia, M., 387n, 388n
'all exchange' economy, 117, 122, 123, 146, 153
All India Congress Committee, 355
All-India Debt and Investment Survey (AIDS), 316, 318
allocation, of resources, 115
Ambirajan, S., 270, 276n
analysis, and description, 24
analytical frame, features of, 232–35
Anderson, Perry, 69
anti-poverty programmes, 92
appropriation, 97, 394
Arrow, Kenneth J., 156n, 390, 393
Ashton, B., 206n
Asiatic societies, 247
Assam, 268
asset(s), distribution, of rural and urban households, 316–21; transfer schemes, 380
Associated Labour, 178

Athreya, V.B., 321n
attached labour, 254, 287, 305, 309–10; and casual labour, 310–12
auction, 88, 89
Aurangzeb, 251
Australia, 399, 400
authority, 66–67, 100, 103, 107, 146, 151, 152
autonomy, 43

Baden-Powell, B.H., 45, 49
Bagchi, A.K., 276n
Bajaj, 303
Baker, C.J., 276n
Balakrishna, P., 321n
balance of payments, 382
Bandyopadhyay, D., 331
Banerjee, N., 300
bank(s), 135, 136; deposits, 136
banking system, 275, 365
Baran, P.A., 157n
Bardhan, P.K., 352, 387n, 388n
bargaining power, 77, 87–89; and resource power, 89–90
barter, 75–78, 84
Basant, R., 348n
basic amenities, 33, 34
basic necessities, 166, 395
Basic Organ of Associate Labour (BOAL), 178
Bata, 298
'beck and call' workers, 311, 312
Bellary, 266
Bengal, 259, 260, 268
Bentham, 153
Berlin Wall, 184
Bhaduri, A., 321n
Bhalla, G.S., 321n
Bhandara, 289, 290
Bharathan, K., 321n
Bhat, M., 348n
Bhattacharya, N., 352
Bhuvaneshwar, 255
bidding power, 90

bidi(s), 232; industry, 289–92; workers, 302
Birlas, 303
birth rate, 325, 326
black money, 384–85
Bloch, M., 45, 52, 55, 65, 73
Bombay, 268, 271
Bombay Plan, 388*n*
Bombay Presidency, 264
'bondedness', 310, 311
bonds, 136
borrowings, 372–73
Brahmins, 284
Braverman, H., 157*n*
Brazil, 403
'breaking-up' of lands, of feudal re-
    tainers, 118
Breman, J., 322*n*
Britain, 172, 400; administration of, 273;
    administration, impact of, 269–72;
    economy of, 259; land system in, 263;
    markets. 259
British interests, 271
Buchanan, D.H., 268
budgets, deficit, 150
Bureau of Costs and Pricing (BCP), 200,
    205, 409
Bureau of Research and Development
    (BRD), 200, 205
bureaucratic system, 187
buyer and seller, 80
'buyers' market', 294, 295

Calcutta, 271
Cambridge Economic History of India, 249
capital, 119, 152; accumulation, 128, 132,
    135, 145, 154; formation, 347; money,
    134; movement of, 139; physical, 134
capitalism, 26, 68, 71, 108, 359, 399–404;
    as economy of owners, 118–19; draw-
    backs of, 160; workers and capitalists
    under. 125–27
capitalist economy, 15, 22,84, 111*ff*,212,
    392; development of, 132–45
Carr, E.H., 27*n*
caste system, 57, 62, 257
casual labourers, attached and, 310–12
casualisation process, 310
C-C form of exchange, 78–79, 81–83;
    and C-M-C, 80
central authority, 67–68
Central Provinces, 265, 289
centralisation, 132, 185–87

centralised command model, 175
Census, 244*n*; of 1931, 269, 289; of 1941,
    269; of 1951, 325; of 1961, 327, 328,
    364; of 1971, 328; of 1981, 236, 237,
    290, 327, 328, 330; Report, 238,
    239, 327
Centre for Science and Environment, 110*n*
Chadha, G.K., 321*n*
Chakravarty, Sukhamoy, 349*n*
Chamberlin, E.H., 244*n*
Chaudhuri, A., 388*n*
Chayanov, A.V., 44*n*, 244*n*
cheap labour, 299
Chenery, H., 368
cheri, 279
Chiang Kaishek, 179
Civil War, in America, 265
claims, 38, 197; settlement of, 171, 203–5
classes, 392, 411
C-M-C type of exchange, 80, 81, 83, 85,
    222, 313
Cold War, 179
collaboration, 402
collective farms, 175, 177
collectives, 180, 182, 183
colonial economy, 304
colonial impact, 258
colonial period, 27, 247
colonisation, 51
command economy, 39
command mobilisation, 185; system,
    186–88
commanding heights, 197, 359
commerce, 255
commercial crops, 255, 266, 271
commercialisation, 273–75; of agriculture,
    265–67; private property and, 267–68
commission agent, 291
commoditisation, 78, 84, 102, 104, 105,
    170, 224, 342
communism, 173, 174, 179
Communist Party, 179, 182, 187
communitarian elements, 252
community, 28, 161–62, 279, 390, 391
competition, 129–30, 132, 199–200
competitive economy, 113
Complex Organisation of Associated
    Labour (COAL), 178
compulsory labour, 67
conflict, 392, 393, 398
Congress Party, 355, 356, 363, 369

conquest, 51
Constitution, 357, 413
constraints, 36, 38, 69
consumer durables, 373, 381, 410
consumer price index, 384
consumers, 114, 115, 117; sovereignty, 115–18, 202
consumption, 64, 221, 344, 369; expenditure, 351–52; loans, 291; nature of, 169–72; in post-capitalist set-up, 409–10
contract gang labour, 312
contractor, 312
contracts, 96, 97, 100, 196
Cookson, H.C., 276n
cooperative(s), 174, 175; enterprise, 196, 201, 203; farming, 175, 180, 363, 364; principle, 356; society, 280
corporate tax, 372
cost(s), 199; calculations, and cost of labour, 300; plus mark up, 199; prices and, 92, 94
cottage industry, 362
cotton, export of, 262–65; industry, 262–63; trade in, 275
Council of Economic Affairs, 204–5
creative destruction, 130
credit, 98, 367; destruction, 130; facilities, 308, 309; for consumption, 143; institutions, 275; role of, 135–37
creeping inflation, 383
Critchley, John, 69
crop-sharing tenants, 307
Crown, 265
cultivators, 237, 241, 305, 308, 312, 330, 405
customs, 39, 61, 72, 255, 394
Cuba, 158, 159, 169
Cultural Revolution, 182
Czechoslovakia, uprising of 1968 in, 189

Dandekar, V.M., 387n
Dasgupta, K.K., 206n
Davey, B., 276n
deals, 188, 295, 296
death rates, 325, 326
debt-bondage, 282
Debreu, G., 156n
Deccan, 253, 265
decentralisation, 177, 181, 185, 414
decision-making, 28, 39, 45, 72, 162
deficit financing, 372
Defoe, Daniel, 27n

demand(s), 141–43, 202; constraints, 34, 37; deficiencies, 142,150; -led growth, 373, 380–81
democratic planning, 358
demographic features, 70
Deng Xiaoping, 182
depression, 143
developing countries, 127, 154, 213
dictatorship, 152
differential accumulation, 395
differential bargaining power, 88–89
differentiation, 338; and segmentation, 223–25
direct taxes, 372
Directive Principles of State Policy, 413
disaggregation, 323, 324
disparities, 258
distribution, 17, 22, 201- 4
districts, 414
division of labour, 29, 131, 161, 211, 252, 290
Dobb, M., 73n, 110n, 133, 134, 135, 156n, 163, 206n
domestic work, 30, 327
domination, 40, 56, 64, 72, 303, 304
Dorfman, R., 156n
double coincidence of needs, 76
double digit inflation, 383
The Drain Theory, 272
dual economy, 65, 226
Dusi village, 283–85
Dutt, R., 260
Dutt, R.C., 276n
dynamic macro-global analysis, 217
dynamics, of the system, 231–32

East Germany, 184, 189
East India Company, 246, 258–61, 268, 270, 271, 273
Eastern Europe, 158, 159, 167, 297, 411
economic activities, 49, 50, 240, 407
Economic Census, 239–41, 245n
economic change, goals of, 395
economic coordination, 198
economic models, 23
economic organisations, 49
economic relationship, 17
economic system, 337
Economic Survey 1986–87, 373
economy, definition of, 20; described, 20–22; polity and society, 411–14; as relationship, 16–17; and social relationship, 390–95; and state, 152

education, 167–68, 397
egalitarian society, 170
EID Parry, 303
electoral process, 413
electric fan industry, 299
Elson, D., 207n
employees, 330
employment, 58, 177, 242, 255, 269, 370, 380–83
enclosure movement, 118
endowment, initial, 117
Engels, 44n, 131, 163, 164, 165
England, 130, 147, 246, 262, 265, see also, Great Britain
English, 163
enterprise, 176, 239, see also, firms
environment, community and, 32
equality, 151, 153
Escorts automobile, 402
establishment, 218, 239
Europe, 124, 125, 130, 155, 178, 213, 258, 400, 401
European colonialists, 274
European markets, 259
European socialist countries, 188
evaluation, of Indian economy, 246ff
exchange, 26, 45, 61–62, 69, 74ff, 91, 113, 127, 186, 203, 221, 225, 394; and bargaining, generalised, 85–87; emergence of, 46–48; and markets, 100–8; impact on production, 92–94; and ownership, 96–98; and production, 122, 127; relationships, 77; settlement of claims, 94–96; as a social activity, 408–9; socialisation of, 198–201; and traders, 98–100; transformation of, 78–85; value, 25–26, 78, 82, 91, 122–23, 292
excise duty, 303
exclusive economic system, 124
exclusive owners' club, 124
exploitation, 66, 121, 160, 177, 179, 193, 204, 272, 354
Expert Committee, 351, 352
exports, 403; of cotton, 262, 265; of hosiery goods, 297
external authority, 66
external shocks, 216
externalities, 103

Fabian socialists, 355
fabricators, 297
Factory Act 1929, 290

factory production, 268–69
feudal economy, 15
feudal Europe, 56
feudal system, 107
feudalism, 45, 54, 62, 68, 71, 118
finance capitalism, 137
financial assets, 346
financial intermediation, 195, 222, 344–46
financial policies, 361
firms, 222, 225, 230, 231, 234–36, 294, 295, 297, 314, 315
Fiscal Commission, 272
fishing industry, 288
'five guarantees', 184
Five Year Plans, (India) first, 358, 367; second, 347, 363; third, 363; fifth, 352, 368, 369, 371; sixth, 324, 369, 370, 372; seventh, 348, 370, 372, 380, 382
Five Year Plan (Russian), 175
fixed capital, 138
foodgrains production, 335, 367, 368
food productive economy, 48
footwear industry, 232
Forbes, James, 276n
Ford Escort automobiles, 302
foreign investments, 348, 371
foreign markets, 299, 362
forests, 30, 52
Fourier, Charles, 206n
France, 172
Frankel, F., 321n, 364
free labourers, 118, 120, 287
free markets, 74, 182
free ride, 38, 181
free trade, 271
Freedom Movement, 350, 354

Gadgil, D.R., 266
Galbraith, John Kenneth, 44n, 157n
Gandhi, Indira, 368
Gandhi, M.K., 354, 355
Gandhian alternative, 354, 355
Ganguli, B.N., 276n, 387n
garibi hatao, 352, 368, 369
garment export industry, 300
general equilibrium, 108
generalised exchange economy, 114
geo-physical factors, 248–49
Georgescu-Roegen, N., 413, 415n
Germany, 172, 173, 401, see also, East Germany
global aid programme, 347

global economy, 213
global technology, 403
goals, 389
Godelier, M., 27n, 40
Godrej, 303
goods-sharing, 30
goods-specific growth, 366
Gorbachev, M., 176
Government expenditure, 372, 373
Goyal, S.K., 303
Great Britain, 112, 118, 119
Green Revolution, 306–9, 367
group decisions, 397
growth, 374; and change, 323ff; 'plus' strategies, 368–69; and poverty eradication, 365–67
Guhan, S., 321n
Gujarat, 311

Habib, Irfan, 276n
Hahn, F.H., 390, 393
handloom industry, 292
handloom weaving, 232
hardboiled solution, 37
Harijans, 279, 290
harmony, 392
Hasbulatov, R., 176
Hastings, Warren, 259
Hayami, Y., 73n
health, 166–68, 397
Heilbroner, R.L., 44n, 130, 138, 144, 151
hereditary tenants, 118
Hicks, J.R., 44n
Hicks, John, 337
Higgins, B., 244n
high yielding variety, seeds, 308, 367
Hill, C., 109n
Hindus, 250, 278
Hindustan Lever, 303
hired workers, 219, 239, 241, 243, 302, 305
Hirsch, Fred, 415n
historical socialism, 27, 158; crisis of, 184–90
history, 24
Holton, R.J., 73n
Hong Kong, 179
horizontal interactions, 220
horizontal transfers, 60, 63
hosiery industry, 296–98
household(s), h-1 unit, 218, 233, 304, 323; h-2 unit, 219, 226, 228–29, 232–37, 239–41, 243, 289, 293, 294, 297, 301, 304, 305, 313, 314, 323, 346, 392; h-3 unit, 230, 231, 233, 323, 346, 361; h-4 unit, 230–32, 241, 243, 289, 293, 297, 309–13, 323, 346; household(s), economy, 15, 16, 18, 19, 21; with financial resource and labour (h-3), 222; industry, 238; with only labour (h-4), 222, 227; production units, 43, 196; sector savings, 345–47, 371
Household Responsibility System, 182
Howe, I., 207n
Huberman, L., 167
Hungary, 167, 184
human relationship, 20–21

ideal type, 163
'imperial preference', 272
implicit price, 90
imports, 382
inamdars, 250
incentives, 182, 303; clauses, 60
inclusive economy, 171
income, distribution, 350
income tax, 372
indebtedness, 262
Independence, of India, 246, 325, 333, 346, 347, 356, 357, 373
India, 112, 169, 325; economy of, 15, 22, 24, 27, 211ff, 277ff; economy, structure and functioning of, 225–35; economy, evaluation of, 246ff
Indian Standards Institution (ISI), 104
Indonesia, 340
Industrial Commission, 272
Industrial Finance Corporation (IFC), 360
Industrial Policy Resolution, of 1948, 359; of 1956, 360
Industrial Policy Statement, of 1980, 303
Industrial Revolution, 246, 259, 273
industrialisation, 272, 371
industries, growth of, 102, 381; inputs to agriculture, 306; production in, 268; workers in, 269
inequalities, 170, 183, 396, 409; and poverty, 350–53
inflation, 100, 143, 178, 183, 383–84
informal sector, 322n
information, asymmetries, 200; inadequacies of, 81, 86
innovations, 130, 131
input-output links, 198, 199
institutional mould, 24

institutions, 21, 100, 101; structures, 189, 214–15
integrating principle, 41
Integrated Rural Development Programme, 370, 379
interest, 136
inter-enterprise (unit) transfers, 26, 45, 61, 62, 71, 198, 199, 215
inter-sectoral balance, 198
inter-unit division of labour, 61
intermediaries, 67, 135, 188, 291, 292, 296, 301, 312, 362; abolition of, 364
intermediation, 227
internal dynamics, 216
international economy, 15
International Labour Organisation, 322n
international trade, 273, 402
intervention strategies, 379–80
investment, goods, 344; opportunities, 144–45
invisible hand, 115
irrigation, 308, 370
Iruvelpattu village, 278–81, 286

Jagannathan, V.N., 321n
jajmani system, 252
Jalée, P., 111
Janakarajan, S., 321n
Japan, 112, 125, 179, 288, 399–401
Jenkins, R., 416n
Jessop, B., 416n
Jha, L.K., 388n
Jodha, N.S., 388n
joint stock companies, 147
Joshi, H., 322n
Joshi, V., 322n
jute industry, 268

Kalpagam, U., 321n
Kancheepuram, 255, 283, 285, 308
Kanesalingam, 415n
Karnataka, 414
Kerala, 326
Keynes, I.M., 116, 142, 144, 149, 150
Keynesian revolution, 116
Kholi, A., 388n
Kipling, 261
Kikuchi, M., 73n
King, R., 416n
kinship relationship, 50
Kornai, James, 207n
Koshak, Erazim V., 207n

Kozhikode, 255
Krishnamurthy, J., 348n, 417n
Kudimaramat system, 279
Kumar, B.C., 348n
Kumar, D., 276n
Kurien, C.T., 157n, 388n, 415n, 416n
Kurien, John, 321n
Kuznets, Simon, 348n

labour, 98, 281, 282; commoditisation of, 120, 377; constraints, 36, 37, 55, 56; cost, 144–45, 295, 300, 301; force, population and, 325–33; force, profile of, 236–44; households, 56–59; mobilisation of, 171; power, 27, 95, 118–22, 124, 199, 203–4, 243, 294, 300; process, as basis of economy; productivity, 262; and resources, 191–93; use, 20, 22, 62, 42
Lahore, 255
laissez-faire, 178, 270
land, as asset, 318; ceiling on, 280, 363, 364; holdings, 283, 284; and labour, 58–60, 101–2; reforms, 362–65; revenue, 263, 264; rights on, 250–52; sale of, 62; settlement pattern, 263–65; system, 251
Land Decree, 173
landless labourers, 363
landlords, 69, 267, 280–82, 286, 379, 392; households, 56–59; -labour relationship, 311; -tenant relationship, 307; -man ratio, 330; revenue, 263, 264
Lange, Oskar, 416n
large-scale capitalism, 314
large and small units, 298–304
laws, of the market, 105
leasing, of land, 58, 59, 196, 220
legal tender, 98
legislation(s), 147; factory and labour, 302
Legislative Assembly, 280
Lenin, V.I., 132, 164, 165, 173, 174, 175
levies, 203
Levine, D.P., 416n
Levkovsky, A., 244n
Lewis, A.W., 244n
liberal democracy, 152, 153
liberalisation, 386, 401
licensing system, 361
life boat principle, 38
Life Insurance of India, 360
liquidity, 136

literacy rate, 166
livelihood, 30
loans, 348, 365
losses, 141
lower limit, to productive activity, 36, 37
Ludhiana, 296, 297
Luxemburgh, Rosa, 157n

MacArthur, General, 416n
machines, 128, 129
Macpherson, C.B., 153
Macpherson, W.I., 276n
macro planning, 409
macro view, 46
Madhya Pradesh, 289
Madras, 271, 278
Madras Institute of Development Studies, 278
Madras Residency, 264, 266
Madurai, 255
Mafatlal, 303
Maharashtra, 289, 311
'making money', 155
manufacturing, 286, 324, 330
Manchester, 273; manual labour, 354
Mao Zedong, 179, 180; reforms after, 182–84
marginal holdings, 330, 331
marginal workers, 328
market (s), 113, 198, 274,390, 394, 408; biddings, 103; decisions, 396–97; dominance, 116; economy, 101, 113, 152, 153; exchange, 100–8; forces, 104; ideology, 101, 106–8; laws, 151; pricing, 149, 338; regulations, 102; and resource power, 377–78; role of, 69; segmentation, 224; socialism, 177–79; surplus, 175
'marketised' economy, fully, 106
Marshall, A., 27n, 278
Marx, Karl, 27n, 44n, 75, 80, 84, 112, 119, 139, 142, 144, 156n, 163, 164, 165, 247, 321n, 392, 412, 415n, 417n
Marxist tradition, 393
mass poverty, 350, 353, 384
material(s), 128; balance, 197; goods, 35, 37, 39, 160; needs, 18–20
M-C-M form of exchange, 82–85, 146, 222, 313
means of production, 191–93
mechanisation, 183
medium of exchange, 79
Meek, R., 412
mega capitalism, 314

Mencher, J.P., 321n
mercantilism, ideology of, 107
merchants, 81, 82, 106–7, 119, 222, 227, 228, 230, 255; capitalism, 137, 275
Meillassoux, Claude, 44n
Mexico, 403
micro-global approach, 287
micro-global profile, 22–31, 227, 216–25, 235
micro view, 46
migration, 37, 177, 284
military expenditure, 143
Mill, James Stuart, 144, 270
Minhas, B.S., 387n
minimum needs, 406, 407
minimum wages, 126, 302
mining, 324
mirasdars, 250
Mitra, A., 415n
mixed economy, 213
mixed type, of link, 220
mobility, 243
model, 23
modernisation, 286
modern sector, 238
monarchy, 152
money, 79, 82, 136, 198; substitute, 136; use value of, 83
money-lender, 307, 379
monopoly, 87–88
monopsony, 87–88
Morris, D., 276n
Moscow, 133
Mueller, D., 416n
Mughal(s), 270, 274; conquerors, 250, 251; period, 251–52, 255, 258, 265
Mulchulacks, 260
multilateralism, 85
multinational corporation, 301
multiple activity chains, 224
multi-structural economies, 226
Munro, Thomas, 261
Musgrave, P.B., 109n
Musgrave, R.A., 109n
Muslims, 250

Nadkarni, M.V., 110n
nadu, 249
Nagaraj, K., 321n
Naicker, 283, 285
Naidu, C., 387n
nation, 161, 390; -state, 19, 102, 107, 147

National Council for Applied Economic Research, 371
national defence, 397
National Development Council, 363
national economy, 16, 19, 21, 43, 46, 66, 213–17, 403, 411
national income, 323, 335 –39; at constant prices, 337; at current prices, 337; growth and changes in, 339–42
National Income Accounting, 336
National Industrial Development Corporation (NIDC), 360
National Movement, 355
National Planning Committee, 356
National Sample Survey, 316, 318, 320, 330, 331; Reports, 327
National Savings Schemes, 388n
nationalisation, 187, 191
Native States, 262
nature, 30–32
Navroji, Dadabhai, 272, 354
Neale, W.C., 250
needs, 33, 35, 42
Nehru, Jawaharlal, 262, 354, 355, 356, 358, 363, 364
neo-classical tradition, 392
New Economic Policy, 174, 372–74
new industrial policy, 380
non-agricultural employment, 331, 332
non-labour resources, 120, 123
non-market principle, 106
non-workers, 32, 326–28
North America, 213, 399, 400
North Arcot District, 308
North Korea, 158, 159, 180, 189
Nove, A., 206n
n-units, 297

occupational pattern, 248, 249, 282, 284, 329–33
Olson, M., 416n
Oommen, M.A., 416n
open economy, 73
operational holdings, 330, 332
opportunity cost, 58, 70
organisation, of production, 27, 42, 137, 193–96, 301
organised sector, 277, 314, 334, 343, 381
organising principle, 24–25
outward orientation, 401
Owen, Robert, 206n
own-account units, 239, 243

'owners only', capitalism and, 117
ownership, aspects of, 53; concept of, 26, 211, 274; emergence of, 45–48; exchange and, 96–98; rights and, 51–54, 121–122, 192; and scarcity, 46–47

package deals, 301
Pakistan, 340
panchayats, 414
Parliamentary democracy, 152
Parliamentary elections, 368
Parthasarthy, G., 388n
participatory ownership, 52, 53
Patel, B.B., 321n
patron-client relationship, 56, 57
Pavlov, V.I., 251
peasant (s), 252; agitation, 71
people's communes, 180–82
People's Liberation Army, 179
People's Republic of China, 158, 159, 165, 169, 172, 179–85, 189
per capita income, 351, 368
perestroika, 176
Permanent Settlement, 263, 264
Philippines, 340
physical resources, 18, 346
piece rate system, 293
P L 480 programme, 367
planned economy, 359
planning, 171, 178, 197
Planning Commission, 363
Planning Committee, 357
plantation, 268
Poland, 167, 184, 189
Polanyi, K., 96, 102, 156n
policy intervention, 374, 377
political parties, 413–14
Poorna Swaraj, 354
population, of India, 236, 269; increase in, 266–67; and labour force, 325–33
Portuguese, 258
Postan, M.M., 15
post-capitalist economy, 158ff, 404
Poulantzas, N., 416n
poverty, 15, 27, 278; and affluence, 350ff; eradication programme, 332, 365–74; and policy, 353–59
poverty line, 34, 351–52, 367, 370, 380, 386, 398
Prasad, A., 321n
Prasad, E.K.V., 321n
pre-capitalist economies, 137

pre-colonial period, Indian economy in, 247–58
prestige goods, 403
prices, 113, 141, 171; capitalism as a system of, 114–15; and costs, 91–92; rate, 293; regulations, 202; role of, 116; signals, 114–17
primary sector, 324
primitive economy, 28
private property, 166, 170; commercialisation of, 267–68; right to, 151
private sector, 343, 361; corporate, 345–47
produce, claims on, 53, 54; distribution of, 59–68
production, 73, 221; in capitalist economy, 112, 121–23, 127–32; and consumption, 33–35; decisions, 95, 117; growth in, 333, 335–43; and exchange, 92–94, 130, 133; physical features of, 54–56; process, 19–20, 65, 386; relations, 50, 54–59; under socialism, 167–68; units, 134, 197–98, 227, 228, 404, 406, 407
productive activity, 30–37, 42, 74, 98, 127, 192–94, 196, 227, 251
productive capitalism, 137
productivity, 183, 201, 342, 357, 396, 406, 407
profit, 115, 129, 138, 149, 300
proletariat, 118, 164; revolution, 164
promissory notes, 97
property, 152; acquisition of, 148; rights, 59, 60, 64, 70, 147, 192
pseudo-internationalism, 401
public policy, 326
public sector, 343, 345–47, 359, 360, 361
public works, 149–51
Punjab, 296, 306, 307, 311
purchasing power, 90, 117, 339
'putting out' system, 137, 293

qualitative attributes, of goods, 86–87
quantity adjustment, 171
quarrying, 324

rainfall, 279, 281, 284
Raja, 250
Rajagopalachari, C., 364
Rajan, I., 348n
Ramachandran, V.K., 321n
Rao, Hanumantha, 321n
Rao, V.K.R.V., 349n
Rath, N., 387n, 388n

Reagan, Ronald, 157n
real cost, of labour, 58
real national income, 337
reciprocity in unequal obligations, 51
redistributary system, 38
Reddy, R., 312
Reddy, William M., 110n
Reformation, 155
relaiwala, 291
relative price, 90
Renaissance, 155
Renner, K., 157n
rent, 58, 63
rentier class, 53, 54, 72
representation, forms of, 23–24
research and development, 200
Reserve Bank of India, 275, 316
resource, constraint, 36, 37, 55; control, 20, 22, 30–37, 53, 59, 64; crunch, 373; distribution, 315–21; -labour ratio, 70, 71; mobilisation, 171, 373; ownership, 27, 100; power, 117, 286, 339; use, 17, 20, 22, 31–33, 113
retail trade, 409
Ricardo, David, 27n, 112, 270, 392, 415n
Robinson Crusoe, 20
Romania, 184
Roosevelt, 150
Rosen, G., 73n
Roy, Rammohan, 354
rudimentary economy, 28ff, 211
Rudra, A., 321n
rural economy, 66
rural labour households, 330
rural-urban divide, 66
Russian Revolution (1917), 158, 163, 172, 175, see also Soviet Union
ryots, 266
ryotwari settlement, 264

Sahlins, M., 44n
Sagar, 289, 290
Samuelson, P.A., 109n, 244n
Sattedar, 290, 291, 296
Sattur, 282
savings, 135, 146, 344, 371; and investments, 343–48
Scandinavian countries, 400
scarcity, 33–36, 46–47
scheduled castes, 290
Schumpeter, Joseph, 130, 131, 144, 156n
secondary sector, 324

Scot, J.C., 73n
sectoral composition, changes in, 343
Seddon, D., 44n
segmentation, ⌐ ¦223 –26, 338
sellers' market, 295
Sen, A.K., 415n
service sector; 324, 330, 332, 340, 342
sexual division, of labour, 29, 30, 61
share-cropping, 57, 284
shared ownership, 52
shares, 136
Shaw Wallace, 303
Shelvankar, K.S., 259
silk weaving, 285
Simon, Saint, 206n
Simpson, 303
Singh, M., 321n
Singh, N., 110n
Sirunavalpattu village, 308
scissors crisis, 188
Sivakasi, 281
Sixth Five Year Plan 1980–85, 364
skilled labour, 143
slack, 34–35
Slater, Gilbert, 278
Slater villages, 278
slaves, 77, 254
small producers, 302, 303
small-scale sector, 303
Smith, Adam, 27n, 107, 110n, 112, 116,
    131, 144, 147–51, 156n, 270, 360, 389,
    392, 400, 412, 415n
social control, over resources, 166–67
social decisions, 396–99, 405
social division, of labour, 257
social framework, 24–25
social institutions, 24, 25, 40, 41
social ownership, 177, 212
social relationship, 17–18, 99
social sciences, 412
socialisation, 167, 168, 191, 195, 364,
    408, 411
socialism, 158
socialist economy, 15, 22, 159, 163–72
socialist regimes, failure of, 27
solidarity, 189, 281
South Arcot, 278
South Korea, 340, 400, 401
Sovereign, duties of, 148–51
Soviet Union, 159, 164, 185, 297, 391;
    1965–66 reforms in, 188; political

system in, 165; socialist economy
    in, 172–76
Sri Lanka, 340
Srinivasan, T.N., 352, 387n, 388n
Stalin, J., 175
State, 97, 222; in capitalist economy,
    145–47; duties of, 147–48; enterprises,
    197; functions of, 150–51; ownership,
    177, 195; role of, 360–62; as a social
    institution, 393–95
State Trading Corporation, 203
Stein, Burton, 276
Stinchcombe, 44n
structure, of relationship, 21, 22, 214; and
    strategy, 374–85
sub-economies, 43, 45, 54, 66, 203,
    216, 410
subordination, 56, 72
subsidy, 376, 416
subsistence, 33–34, 63, 154
Sundaram, R.M., 349n, 387n
Swaminathan, P., 321n
surplus, 63–65; appropriation, 64–66, 74,
    119–21, 123, 126, 152, 258; generation,
    64, 65, 120
'survival kit', 32
'survival limit', 31
'sweat shops', 301
Sweezy, P., 73n, 157n, 167

Taiwan, 179
Taj Mahal, 23
talukdar, 250
Tamil Nadu, 278, 308, 311
target groups, 369–70, 379, 380
Tatas, 271, 303
taxes, 67, 78, 103, 251, 256, 384
Tawney, R.H., 154, 157n
technical information, 200, 201
technology, 48, 69, 130–32, 300; in agri-
    culture, 285, 306; changes in, 144–45;
    progress in, 126, 145
tenancy, 57, 305
Tendulkar, S.D., 387n
tertiary sector, 324
Thailand, 340
Third World, 184, 368, 378, 402
Thorner, Daniel, 44n, 234, 247, 264, 267
tiny capitalism, 314
Tirupati, 255
top circuit, 361
trade, 70, 102, 243, 274, 275

trade unions, 126
traders, 81–82, 99; exchange and, 98–100
traditional agriculture, 265
traditional industries, 407
traditional production process, 391
traditional sector, 226, 238
training, 201
transaction, 47, 78, 79, 135, 294
transfers, horizontal and vertical, 60–63
transformation, 26, 234, 258–76
transitional mixed system, 174
transnational corporation, 402–4
'trickle down', 359, 366, 401
tribal economy, 26, 29, 32, 42
tribe, 28, 50
trusts, 174

unaccounted income, 385
unemployment, 124, 143, 177, 178, 183;
  rural, 332
underdeveloped countries, 347
United Nations, 402
United Nations Development Decade, 347
United Nations First Decade of Development, 366, 368
unorganised sector, 277, 314, 315, 320, 323, 333, 334, 343
Unit Trust of India, 361
United States, 112, 124, 125, 143, 273, 288, 401, 410
universal adult franchise, 232, 358
universal equivalent, 79
unskilled labour, 290
urban economy, 15, 65–66, 255–56
urbanisation, 326
Urry, J., 416n
use value, 25–26, 91, 96, 129, 161
Utopian socialism, 163
utilitarianism, 153

Vadamalaipuram, 281–83, 285–86
Vaidyanathan, A., 348n
Vajda, M., 207n
Vanek, J., 206n
Vanniars, 279, 285
Varanasi, 255
Vasco Da Gama, 258
vertical transfer, 62, 63, 251, 298
Vidarbha, 289
Vietnam, 158, 159
village, community, 50, 247–49. 251;

economy, 15, 45ff, 211, 217; economy, as historical entity, 48, 49; economy, transformation of, 68–71; industries. 362; transformation at, 277–86
Village Panchayats, 280
Villupuram, 278
Virudhunagar village, 282

wage(s), 283; employment, 333; –goods, 62; income, 126; labour, 119, 120, 138, 330
Wallerstein, I., 132
Walras, Leon, 108, 110n, 116
War Communism, 173, 186
Washbook, D.A., 276n
wastelands, 52
water, availability, 375, 376; facilities, 280; sellers, 309
wealth, 128
weavers, 261
weaving, 284, 285
Weber, M., 157n, 388n
welfare, 399–401; states, 400
Wells, D., 416n
West Bengal, 311, 414
West Germany, 189
West Indies, 268
wholesale price index, 383
women, in household activities, 328; work, 30; see also, domestic work
woollen hosiery, 296
worldly philosophers, 39
work, 194, 236; definition of, 326–27; -point, 180–82; ratio, 29; in rudimentary economy, 29
workers, 29, 32, 119, 326–29; capitalist and, under capitalism, 125–27; classification of, 237; main, 236, 237; marginal, 236, 237; non-, 236, 237; 'other', 237, 238
World Bank, 352
World War, First, 172, 269, 272, 296; Second, 159, 165, 179, 347, 357, 400

Youngson, A.J., 276n
Yugoslavia, 172, 185, 391; market socialism in, 177–79

zamindari, rights, abolition of, 362; system, 263
zamindars, 250, 264, 362

DATE DUE